RAINBOW LIBERTY

This volume uses classical liberal thought to present new theoretical and empirical perspectives on freedom of lesbian, gay, bisexual, transgender, and queer (LGBTQ) individuals and communities.

Rainbow Liberty emphasizes the institutions that sustain tolerance, pluralism, and freedom of association, which empower marginalized communities to build civil associations in the face of social and political pressures. Classical liberal methodological and normative studies on LGBTQ life have been conspicuously absent in scholarly literature but are applied in this volume to explore the circumstances and implications of queer agency and freedom. The ideas of Adam Smith, F. A. Hayek, James M. Buchanan, and Vincent and Elinor Ostrom, among other thinkers in the classical liberal tradition, give a unique and underappreciated perspective on LGBTQ issues.

This volume is an invaluable resource for scholars exploring sexuality and gender from a variety of disciplines, including economics, political science, philosophy, sociology, and related fields. *Rainbow Liberty* appeals more broadly to anyone interested in how queer freedoms have shaped, and continue to shape, our world.

Nathan P. Goodman is a Senior Fellow with the F. A. Hayek Program for Advanced Study in Philosophy, Politics, and Economics at the Mercatus Center at George Mason University.

Jordan K. Lofthouse is a Senior Fellow with the F. A. Hayek Program for Advanced Study in Philosophy, Politics, and Economics at the Mercatus Center at George Mason University.

Mikayla Novak is a Senior Fellow with the F. A. Hayek Program for Advanced Study in Philosophy, Politics, and Economics at the Mercatus Center at George Mason University.

"*Rainbow Liberty* is a deeply personal and deeply analytical, bold, and timely contribution that brings the insights of classical liberalism and mainline political economy to the study of LGBTQ freedom. True radical liberalism is a political philosophical doctrine grounded in the recognition that we are one another's dignified equals. It is about respect of humanity in its great diversity, and it trusts ordinary individuals with freedom – freedom of choice in all endeavors, including bodily autonomy and intimate relationships with others. Freedom of thought, freedom of association; toleration and experiments in living. In short, anything that is peaceful. But this is not just a set of normative commitments, but follows from the persistent and consistent application of the economic way of thinking to all human affairs including who we are, who we love, and who we associate with. There are choices and consequences; there is productive specialization, entrepreneurial discovery, and social cooperation. Nathan Goodman, Jordan Lofthouse, and Mikayla Novak have assembled an outstanding group of scholars who demonstrate how the core ideas of the liberal tradition—individual liberty, voluntary association, entrepreneurship, and polycentric governance—help illuminate the processes through which marginalized communities secure dignity, opportunity, and flourishing. The essays in this volume show that the tools of Austrian, Virginia, and Bloomington political economy offer powerful ways to understand how social cooperation emerges from below, often in ways that challenge prejudice and expand the scope of human freedom. By opening a productive dialogue between queer studies and classical liberal thought, *Rainbow Liberty* significantly enriches both conversations. This book is creative, courageous, and intellectually exciting—an important step forward in the study of freedom in a diverse and evolving society."

Peter Boettke, *Distinguished University Professor of Economics, Department of Economics, George Mason University*

"The deepest test of any liberal order is whether it makes room for the people that power has most relentlessly tried to exclude. *Rainbow Liberty* meets that test with rigor, originality, and moral seriousness. Goodman, Lofthouse, Novak, and their contributors demonstrate that the mainline tradition of political economy, from Adam Smith through Hayek, Buchanan, and the Ostroms, has always contained the resources for a genuinely radical liberalism—one that takes queer freedom not as an afterthought but as a test case for the tradition's deepest commitments. This is the book that classical liberals should have written decades ago, and it was worth the wait."

Matt Zwolinski, *Professor of Philosophy, Director, Center for Ethics, Economics, and Public Policy, University of San Diego*

"*Rainbow Liberty* is an important and remarkable book. A great deal of queer theory presumes that liberation needs control of state policy and the abolition of capitalism. This collection written by fresh and emerging scholars argues compellingly that the institutions of the free society, namely markets, private property, and voluntary association, offer much surer protections for sexual and gender minority rights. These institutions allow queer communities to experiment and grow spontaneously. The individual chapters are rich with historical and conceptual evidence, along with careful and nuanced recounting of intersectional experiences. A truly unique work that challenges existing assumptions."

Nick Cowen, *Associate Professor in Criminology, School of Social and Political Sciences, College of Arts Social Sciences and Humanities, University of Lincoln, UK*

"*Rainbow Liberty* is a welcome and overdue contribution, showing how the classical liberal perspective on liberty, toleration, and pluralism can deepen our understanding of gender and sexuality in fresh and compelling ways. Rich in applications and interdisciplinary reach, this volume brings classical liberal tools into fruitful dialogue with gender and sexuality studies for perhaps the first time at this scale. Rainbow Liberty offers a powerful reminder that classical liberalism remains an indispensable framework for thinking about difference, dignity, and freedom."

Alexander W. Schaefer, *Assistant Professor, Department of Philosophy, State University of New York at Buffalo*

"Gender and sexual minorities are often entrepreneurs, not only in the economic arena but in having to daily negotiate socio-cultural norms that marginalise and isolate them. It is a tragedy, therefore, that the tradition which has done so much to understand the role of entrepreneurship and the threats to it has paid little attention to the experiences of LGBT people. This superb collection fills that gap with considerable aplomb."

Mark Pennington, *Director, Centre for the Study of Governance and Society, Department of Political Economy, King's College, University of London*

"*Rainbow Liberty* is an important and overdue contribution to classical liberal thought, showing that the liberal tradition is not only a defense against coercion but a framework through which emancipatory change can take root. Contributors explore how the norms and institutions of a free society—constitutional restraint, market dynamism, and civil society—create room for experimentation, association, and lives lived in dignity on one's own terms. By bringing mainline political economy into conversation with queer studies, the contributors illuminate how free and open societies learn, adapt, and over time, tend to become more fully liberal. The result is a timely and constructive book that expands the reach of classical liberal scholarship while deepening our understanding of freedom as a social achievement."

Emily Chamlee-Wright, *President & CEO, The Institute for Humane Studies*

"Classical liberals are not conservatives, the state is not your lover, and the market is radically queer. This pioneering volume gets the news out. Liberty is liberty, love is love, who you are who you are, says the market."

Deirdre Nansen McCloskey, *Distinguished Senior Scholar, Isaiah Berlin Chair in Liberal Thought, Cato Institute, Distinguished Professor Emerita of Economics and of History, Professor Emerita of English, and of Communication, University of Illinois at Chicago*

RAINBOW LIBERTY

Liberal Political Economy and Queer Freedom

Edited by Nathan P. Goodman, Jordan K. Lofthouse, and Mikayla Novak

Routledge
Taylor & Francis Group
LONDON AND NEW YORK

Designed cover image: Getty Images/Credit: Glowimages

First published 2027
by Routledge
4 Park Square, Milton Park, Abingdon, Oxon OX14 4RN

and by Routledge
605 Third Avenue, New York, NY 10158

Routledge is an imprint of the Taylor & Francis Group, an informa business

British Library Cataloguing-in-Publication Data
A catalogue record for this book is available from the British Library

ISBN: 978-1-041-01644-1 (hbk)
ISBN: 978-1-041-01643-4 (pbk)
ISBN: 978-1-003-61578-1 (ebk)

DOI: 10.4324/9781003615781

Typeset in Times New Roman
by KnowledgeWorks Global Ltd.

CONTENTS

LIST OF FIGURES

LIST OF TABLES

ABOUT THE EDITORS

Nathan P. Goodman is a Senior Fellow with the F. A. Hayek Program for Advanced Study in Philosophy, Politics, and Economics at the Mercatus Center at George Mason University. He earned his Ph.D. in economics at George Mason University and worked as a postdoctoral fellow at New York University. His research focuses on border militarization, defense and peace economics, public choice, and self-governance.

Jordan K. Lofthouse is a Senior Fellow with the F. A. Hayek Program for Advanced Study in Philosophy, Politics, and Economics at the Mercatus Center at George Mason University. He received a Ph.D. in economics from George Mason University. His research explores the intersection of the Austrian, Virginia, and Bloomington schools of political economy. Some of his research topics include environmental economics, Native American economic development, entrepreneurship, and disaster recovery.

Mikayla Novak is a Senior Fellow with the F. A. Hayek Program for Advanced Study in Philosophy, Politics, and Economics at the Mercatus Center at George Mason University. She received a Ph.D. in economics from RMIT University (Melbourne, Australia), and a Ph.D. in sociology from The Australian National University (Canberra, Australia). Her key research interests include Austrian and evolutionary economics, economic sociology, institutional economics, public choice, and social theory and philosophy.

LIST OF CONTRIBUTORS

S. Elliot Bowers is an Educator in the fine arts program at College of DuPage, Chicago. He is a doctoral candidate in visual arts (philosophy, aesthetics, and art theory) at the Institute for Doctoral Studies in the Visual Arts (IDSVA). His research interests include social classification and gender studies, and advocates for interdisciplinary study at the intersection of philosophy, visual culture, and socio-political analysis.

Byron Carson, "Trey", is an Associate Professor of Economics and Business at Hampden-Sydney College, in Hampden-Sydney, Virginia. He teaches courses on introductory economics, money and banking, development economics, health economics, and urban economics. He earned a Ph.D. in Economics in 2017 from George Mason University and a B.A. in Economics from Rhodes College in 2011. His research interests include economic epidemiology, public choice, and Austrian economics.

Bryan Cheang is the Director of the Hayek Program and Research Fellow at the London School of Economics. He is also a Senior Fellow at the Centre for the Study of Governance and Society at King's College London, where he received his Ph.D. in Political Economy. His research interests are on the efficacy of state-led industrial planning, the philosophy of development, and liberalism in non-Western cultures.

Carolina Dalla Chiesa is a Cultural Economist and Cultural Anthropologist. She is an Assistant Professor of Arts and Culture Studies at Erasmus University Rotterdam, The Netherlands, where she researches and teaches on cultural economics, cultural organizations, and economic sociology applied to culture.

Alexander W. Craig is an Assistant Professor of Economics at Saint Mary's College in Notre Dame, Indiana. Before coming to Saint Mary's, he was a Postdoctoral Fellow in the Department of Economics at New York University and earned his Ph.D. at George Mason University, where he was a Hayek Fellow in the F. A. Hayek Program for Advanced Study in Philosophy, Politics, and Economics. His research focuses on the social and cultural elements of economic development, disaster recovery, and progress.

Malia Dalesandry is an Independent Scholar living in the Appalachian region of the United States. She has a BFA from Ohio University, an MPP from George Washington University, and a Ph.D. from George Mason University. Dalesandry examines how persistent criminalization has become a protracted crisis for sex workers, as well as how sex workers individually and communally overcome stigma and pursue decriminalization while coping and even thriving.

Zane Austin Willard is a Doctoral Candidate in the Department of Communication at the University of South Florida. His scholarship is grounded in a critical cultural tradition with a focus on media, rhetoric, and surveillance, and draws on critical race and queer studies to ask questions about who belongs within the nation-state, who is excluded, and how privilege and marginalization persist.

Yana Zaharieva has a bachelor's degree in the Arts and Culture Studies from Erasmus University Rotterdam. They work as a festival producer and freelance writer in Rotterdam, The Netherlands. They are pursuing further education in cultural, media, and audience studies.

ACKNOWLEDGEMENTS

I have been interested in LGBTQ rights since I was quite young. In middle school, I argued with my peers about these issues. I also argued about these topics on internet forums and even recorded YouTube vlogs about my views on LGBTQ rights. My commitment to queer and trans freedom deepened as I read thoughtful defenses of freedom, whether from classical liberals like John Stuart Mill, anarchists like Emma Goldman, or libertarians like Wendy McElroy.

In high school, I moved to Salt Lake City, Utah. I came out as bisexual. I experimented with various forms of gender expression. But more importantly, I got involved in the local queer and trans community. At the Utah Pride Center, I met people who found support, love, care, and solidarity among other queer and trans people. I met teenagers who had been kicked out by their parents simply for their sexual orientation or gender identity. I saw the power of voluntary association, civil society, and emancipatory social movements for queer and trans freedom.

My involvement in local LGBTQ politics and civil society continued when I went to college at the University of Utah, where I studied mathematics. In my spare time, I gave speeches on the intersection of LGBTQ rights, criminal justice, and state violence. I continued attending local events that offered mutual support and affirming social space to queer and trans people. I wrote articles for the Center for a Stateless Society (C4SS) that highlighted state violence against queer and trans people. I also wrote on these topics at various other small libertarian blogs. Throughout this period, I engaged in a mix of activism and writing at the intersection of queer and trans liberation, state violence, criminal justice, and civil liberties. This led me to read more deeply about the possibilities of self-governance and the incentives that drive state violence. This led me to the work of George Mason University (GMU) economist Peter Boettke and his students. I found this research inspiring. I realized that I could use social science to better understand the issues that I was passionate about.

As a result, I concluded that I might want to pursue a Ph.D. in economics at GMU. I started taking economics classes, and eventually I applied to GMU. I was accepted and received a generous fellowship from the Mercatus Center. At GMU, I learned about mainline economics. I conducted research applying mainline economics to topics such as militarism, policing, border security, civil society, and social movements. All of this deepened my appreciation for the ways that mainline political economy can enhance our understanding of queer and trans freedom.

I was therefore delighted when my colleague Mikayla Novak asked me to co-edit this volume on the intersection of mainline political economy, classical liberalism, and LGBTQ freedom. I was also grateful that she asked Jordan Lofthouse as well. Jordan and Mikayla are both outstanding scholars, and their insights, hard work, and dedication made this volume possible. I thank them for their outstanding work on this project, as well as for all they've taught me over the years.

I also extend my thanks to all my colleagues at the Mercatus Center, who have been incredibly supportive of my research. Every day that I come into the office, I get the chance to learn from some of the finest minds in philosophy, politics, and economics. There is no better place to study classical liberal thought and mainline political economy.

In addition, I am grateful to everyone at the Center for a Stateless Society for supporting me as I first developed my voice as a writer. I also thank everyone who I met in social movements over the years, who helped me appreciate the various that we can struggle for a better world. I thank my parents and sister, who have always been supportive.

Finally, I thank my partner and spouse Andie Schwanz. Andie brings me joy, passionately debates ideas with me, supports me, helps me learn and grow, and encourages me to live a life that matches my values and aspirations.

Nathan P. Goodman

This volume reflects my intellectual and personal journey. I'm a relative latecomer to both classical liberalism and mainline political economy. As an undergraduate geography major, I had little exposure to economics or liberal political thought. A pivotal episode in my life occurred in 2013 when I interned in the US House of Representatives. I didn't have a well-formed political ideology yet, but I wanted to simply observe policymaking up close.

What I found left me disillusioned. The staffers I worked with were intelligent and decent people. Yet witnessing the realities of lobbying and political bargaining eroded my faith in what political institutions can accomplish.

During my internship, I made a friend named Nick Hilton, who introduced me to the work of James M. Buchanan and the field of public choice economics. Reading Buchanan's essay "Politics without Romance" for the first time was a lightbulb moment for me. Buchanan's insights helped explain what I had seen during my internship.

I began to learn more about public choice economics, and from there, I became more interested in mainline political economy and classical liberalism. Ultimately, my path led me to pursue a Ph.D. in economics at George Mason University.

As I was discovering these ideas, I was also navigating the journey of coming out as a gay man. I grew up in a small, highly religious community in Idaho and remained closeted until age twenty-four. The first person I came out to was Nick – the same friend who had introduced me to Buchanan's ideas.

This volume reflects the convergence of two important aspects of my life: my academic study of liberal political economy and my identity as a gay man. I know the joys and sorrows of living as a queer person. I have concluded that a classical liberal social order offers the broadest possibilities for the flourishing of queer people. If readers of this volume care about the dignity and well-being of the queer community, I hope they will seriously engage the arguments here.

I am grateful for the insights and influence of all my colleagues at the Mercatus Center at George Mason University, especially my co-editors on this volume, Nathan Goodman and Mikayla Novak. I am eternally grateful to my husband, Troy Olsen, who has supported and encouraged me in everything that I do.

Jordan K. Lofthouse

This project is, for me, the culmination of a decade of contemplation and effort in applying classical liberal theory and mainline political economy to the conditions experienced by LGBTQ individuals and communities.

During the mid-2010s, I started writing newspaper editorial columns about how classical liberal and libertarian commitments provide an uplifting, emancipatory vision for gender and sexual minorities. At about that time, I wrote a short piece for the Cato Institute about trans liberalism, coupled with a monograph on the same topic for the Center for a Stateless Society (C4SS). I moderated a short-lived blogsite, labeled "LGBTQI Freedom," which featured pieces by the famed transgender economist Deirdre McCloskey and Tim Wilson, now a prominent Australian politician. Other writings may have been produced, such as guest posts for another short-lived blog (called "Can't Steer Queer"), but throughout this earlier period I wanted to contribute something deeper, something more profound concerning what I believe to be the strong complementarities between liberalism and queer freedom.

I trust that this current effort, coedited with my friends and colleagues Nathan Goodman and Jordan Lofthouse, has finally met these earlier aspirations. I sincerely thank Nathan and Jordan for their willingness to collaborate on this project, and for sharing their deep insights as well as time in making this volume a reality.

I wish to thank the team at Routledge for publishing this book. Andy Humphries played an important part in guiding us every step of the way from project proposal to the product now in your hands (or on your screen). I would also like to thank the Mercatus Center at George Mason University for providing the wonderfully unique and supportive intellectual space to allow my colleagues and I to co-edit this volume. There is nowhere else on the face of this earth that allows scholars to delve into such an expansive arena of inquiries in Austrian, Bloomington, and Virginia political economy, and so I thank my colleagues at the Center for their camaraderie and sound advice.

Last, but not least, I thank my spouse Deanna Trainham for her unwavering encouragement and support, and for helping me fulfill my intellectual ambitions and bearing the sacrifices necessary to bring such ambitions to life.

Mikayla Novak

1

INTRODUCTION

Queer Classical Liberalism – An Outline

Nathan P. Goodman, Jordan K. Lofthouse, and Mikayla Novak

A remarkable feature of the modern world is the relative improvement in the economic, political, and social conditions of lesbian, gay, bisexual, transgender, and queer (LGBTQ) individuals.[1] Over recent decades, queer[2] people have increasingly attained access to economic opportunities. The LGBTQ community, especially in Western countries, has gained important civil, legal, and political rights with respect to such issues as employment, health care, recognition of self-identification, and same-sex marriages. Social norms have transformed, and queer people now enjoy a more prominent role in socio-cultural life. Opinion polling indicates a sense of growing comfort with public expressions of, and associations with, diverse gender and sexual norms.[3]

The pace of these changes has been astounding from a historical perspective. Scholars and activists have many explanations for these general improvements. One explanation is that LGBTQ individuals have strategically destigmatized themselves by promoting visibility and normalization through "coming out" (Jay and Young 1972; Saguy 2022). Increasing contact between queer and non-queer individuals has led to further destigmatization (Herek and Capitanio 1996; Tadlock et al. 2017; c.f., Skipworth et al. 2010).

Another explanation is that the economic cost of discriminating against LGBTQ people may have increased (as hypothesized by Becker 1971). Additionally, the broader acceptance of "emancipative" values, and their translation in fields such as law and politics, may have improved living conditions for LGBTQ people (Welzel 2013). In practical terms, all these elements, and perhaps more, have contributed to wealthier, healthier, safer, and democratically engaged queer lives.

Despite much progress, previous generations of queer communities faced difficult oppression and repression. Many LGBTQ individuals remained "closeted" for fear of intense ostracism or being denied resources. The past was no idyll for

DOI: 10.4324/9781003615781-1

LGBTQ communities because of persecution (including criminalization) and mistreatment (including on medical grounds) by law enforcement personnel, healthcare professionals, and public officials.

Queer acceptance and liberation have not been comprehensively or perfectly achieved, even in developed and liberal-democratic regions of the world. LGBTQ people have enjoyed great strides in terms of their liberties and rights, but challenges remain, such as ongoing battles over "conversion therapy," child adoption by same-sex couples, and backsliding over transgender rights (e.g., Shaw 2023; Brechenmacher 2025). In many areas of the Global South persistent cultural and political restrictions hamper queer individuals' freedoms.

Certainly, there is more to do in respect of improving queer life. But still, the trajectory of emancipation seen across the West and gradually elsewhere is historically exceptional. Social science can help us comprehend and scrutinize how legal and socio-cultural progress occurs for queer people. However, the scholarly understanding of these processes may be limited when certain conceptual or normative insights epistemically dominate others.

Queer emancipation is a laudable development of modern liberty. It is striking, and somewhat ironic, that classical liberal treatments of LGBTQ progress have tended to be underrepresented in scholarly literature.[4] The classical liberal project fundamentally concerns itself with the freedoms of all people, and especially members of oppressed minorities. However, despite the emancipatory implications of classical liberalism, scholarship on queer issues currently overrepresents analytical frameworks that are skeptical of markets, limited government, and cosmopolitanism.

This book aims to connect classical liberal thought to queer studies and to counter the perception that classical liberal thinkers have neglected queer issues. The contributors of this book articulate theory, analysis, and empirical cases through a framework we label "*queer classical liberalism*" (QCL). QCL examines queer issues through the conceptual and normative insights of classical liberal philosophy and the theoretic architecture of "mainline political economy" (MPE). In contrast with the "mainstream" of the economic profession, MPE draws on a set of core insights that have constituted the "mainline" of economic scholarship since the days of Adam Smith. Smith and other scholars in the mainline emphasized that social order can arise from the bottom-up, leading to undesigned social order that appears as if were constructed by an "invisible hand." Yet this type of order is not inevitable. Instead, it arises under particular systems of rules, or *institutional frameworks*. MPE scholars study bottom-up social cooperation *via* institutional analysis. Today, MPE is a combination of the Austrian, Bloomington, and Virginia schools of political economy, which are three distinct but compatible approaches that emerged from the classical liberal tradition (Boettke 2012; Boettke and Snow 2014; Boettke et al. 2016).

This book's contributors are experts from several social-scientific disciplines who illustrate the theoretical, analytical, and empirical capabilities of QCL. The chapters provide an intellectual vision for queer studies that is generally receptive toward economic exchanges through markets as a means of LGBTQ empowerment. The book emphasizes effective social exchange (including "direct action" possibilities) throughout civil society to amass LGBTQ community resources, including shared senses of pride and solidarity. Governments can also play their part toward the improved status of LGBTQ individuals and communities, but the role of the state as codifier and guarantor of queer rights is a more qualified one vis-à-vis narratives presented by non-liberal queer scholars. All in all, the QCL approach stresses the significance of polycentric environments to sustain freedom of association, tolerance, and pluralism for queer people.

This book does not present a comprehensive scope of research possibilities under QCL. Although the contributors strategically engage with queer and other theories (e.g., feminism, critical studies, etc.), this book is conceptually restricted to a blending of classical liberal philosophy with MPE insights. The applications of QCL raised in the book are largely restricted to the Global North (for discussions about LGBTQ issues in the Global South, see, e.g., Brown et al. 2010; Mason 2018; Rao 2020). And, unless otherwise stated, the chapters will restrict discussions of gender identity and sexual orientation to lesbian, gay, bisexual, and transgender communities.

This volume's chapters pursue novel approaches to the relationship between LGBTQ issues and classical liberal thought. The contributors present new theoretical and empirical perspectives concerning the freedom of queer people to express their gender identities and sexual orientations. The broader exercise is to reveal how diverse forms of queer expression can flourish in a liberal society in which heterogeneous cultures, beliefs, and lifestyles can coexist peacefully. This book's unique contribution is that it uses the QCL framework to examine the complex process of queer liberation as well as exploring ongoing opportunities and challenges facing queer communities.

The structure of this introduction is as follows. The next section profiles core aspects of queer theory in shaping our understanding of the intricacies and nuances of LGBTQ existence and discusses tensions between queer and major related theories. This is followed by an explication of QCL. The introduction then proceeds with a selective account of classical liberal (and libertarian) contributions to queer thought and the examination of LGBTQ issues. Finally, we outline the structure of the book.

A profile of queer theory: Contributions and tensions

Summarizing the modern evolution of queer theory

Over the past several decades, the social sciences have experienced immense change, including the proliferation of disciplines. One of the newer approaches to the study of the human condition has been Gender and Sexuality Studies, and more recently, Queer Theory. Gender and Sexuality Studies developed during the

1960s and 1970s, with an interest in the lived experiences of women (including lesbian and bisexual women) and gay men. Queer Theory began to mature decades later, emerging onto the intellectual scene to elevate postmodern (as well as post-structuralist) inquiries that challenge the essentialism (or normalization) of heterosexuality and cisgender identities. Key queer theorists have included historians, sociologists, philosophers, and political theorists such as Michel Foucault, Adrienne Rich, Judith Butler, Gayle Rubin, Eve Sedgwick, John D'Emilio, Dennis Altman, Susan Stryker, and the queer economist M. V. Lee Badgett.

"Queer studies" has been growing as a scholarly field, especially since the late 1980s (Renn 2010; An and Batra 2022; Thelwall et al. 2023; Yeo et al. 2024). However, queer studies is not a monolithic intellectual enterprise, and scholars have used numerous frameworks to study LGBTQ issues. For instance, a loose set of "queer socialism" doctrines has challenged capitalist economic hegemony as a factor in the exploitation of LGBTQ people (Floyd 2009; Lewis 2016; Hennessy 2017; Gleeson and O'Rourke 2021). Queer socialists further targeted their critiques at dominant, heteronormative cultures – including those that elevate the economic unit of the family as a site of reproducing future workers – that have been seen as repressing the fullest expression of queer sensibilities. Marxian and other socialistic themes have occupied a niche within queer activism in North America, Europe, and other advanced countries over the past few decades (e.g., Downs 2016; McCann and Monaghan 2020; Cloud 2022).

Queer socialism has not gone unchallenged by theorists. The charge of "over-materialistic" accounts in Marxism and other strains of socialism have loomed large among the critiques, as well as questions surrounding the vexed record of existing socialistic regimes when it comes to protecting LGBTQ minorities (Adam 1987; Tschantret 2020; Alexander 2023). One of the many alternatives to socialist-theoretic accounts of queer life was, again, a constellation of loose and fluid ideas known as "queer postmodernism." Postmodern ideas suggest that gender identity and sexual orientation are not "natural" or "essential" facets of the human condition. Rather, postmodernists see gender and sexuality as socio-cultural constructs which are actively negotiated and developed collectively (Simon 1996; Baber 2009). Postmodern thinking leads to an understanding that identities that constitute queer selves are contingent and subject to change.

One of the founding figures of queer postmodern thinking was French philosopher Michel Foucault. In his volume *The History of Sexuality*, Foucault (1978) proffered the thesis that homosexuality was a socially constructed identity that emerged from the late nineteenth century, and which corresponded with developments in science (especially psychiatry), law, and technologies of surveillance. The social construction of homosexuality according to Foucault was tainted with the stigma of antipathy and prejudice vis-à-vis heterosexuality.[5] The emergence of discourses[6] which produced (and then, reproduced) social knowledge about the relative status positions of heterosexuality and homosexuality was reinforced by legal pathologization of gay men and the rise in scientific investigations into gay identity (and, later, lesbianism and transgenderism). These historical developments had an obviously profound effect upon the lived experiences of LGBTQ people, especially regarding their marginalization from the mainstream of societal affairs.

Another key influence in the early development of queer postmodernism was Judith Butler, whose major work is entitled *Gender Trouble: Feminism and the Subversion of Identity*. Butler emphasized the notion that the social construction of gender embodies *performative* qualities. Conceptions of "male" and "female" in modern Western societies are performed through acts, arrangements, and routines that include gendered dress codes, gendered behavioral expectations, gendered discourses and language, and the use of materialities (such as commodities produced by markets) to signify gender classifications to others.

Butler's (1990) theory of gender performativity implies the de-naturalization of the gender binaries of male and female (or man and woman), for it is possible for individuals and groups to modify taken-for-granted gender norms and stereotypes and, thus, transforming gender constructs into something new. *Gender Trouble* and subsequent works by Butler have elicited debates among queer theorists concerning the place of transgender, non-binary, and other gender nonconforming identities within social constructionist accounts of gender (e.g., Butler 2024; Schiapponi 2024).

Queer theory in tension with adjacent concepts: Feminism and postcolonialism

Some of the myriad applications of queer theory have arisen from the negotiation of intellectual tensions with similar, and perhaps rival, conceptualizations of queer existence within social science. Two examples are feminism and postcolonial studies.

Since its inception, feminism has challenged patriarchal systems, in which men dominate over women culturally, economically, and politically. Queer theorists largely see their normative enterprise as overlapping, if not building upon, feminist challenges to the appropriateness of heteronormative claims and arrangements – or, as Adrienne Rich (1980) put it, the system of "compulsory heterosexuality."[7]

Feminism and queer theory do not necessarily align perfectly. Engagements between queer theorists and feminists have contributed to robust debates about the degree of subjectivity inherent in gender identity *versus* the influence of genetic and other biological factors. Some feminist scholars influenced by second-wave radical feminism have opposed the recognition and inclusion of transgender, non-binary, and other gender non-conforming people (Raymond 1980; Jeffreys 1997, 2014; Stock 2021). However, this view is far from hegemonic among feminists. Even some prominent second-wave radical feminists advocate inclusion and liberation for transgender women, non-binary people, and gender non-conforming individuals (e.g., Dworkin 1974; MacKinnon et al. 2024). Outside of the second-wave radical feminist milieu, large swathes of feminist theory strongly support transgender, non-binary, and gender non-conforming people. For instance, a growing literature on "transfeminism" advances feminist theory with a particular focus on trans liberation (Carrera-Fernández and DePalma 2020; Koyama 2021).

Intellectual entanglements between queer theory and studies of postcolonialism have also generated new insights and puzzles. Over recent decades, scholars have analyzed the effects of imperialism and colonial settlement on indigenous communities. Diverse configurations of non-Western meanings and practices surrounding gender and sexuality were often erased by settler-colonial law enforcement (e.g., Morgensen 2012; Han and O'Mahoney 2018). Therefore, modern researchers have sought to recover (or "decolonize") a diverse range of indigenous (and minority subaltern) gendered and sexualized discourses and histories.

Some scholars question whether queer theory is sufficiently anti-colonial. The broadly intersectional turn within queer theory (Crenshaw 1989; Rahman 2010; Olive 2015) conceptually, epistemically, and methodologically invites new and diverse perspectives. Some researchers now question the extent to which queer theory is itself "colonial," and in response they attempt to amplify perspectives from queer thinkers throughout the Global South (e.g., Rao 2015a).

Queer theory's critique of liberalism

Scholars using queer theory have had varying degrees of hostility toward classical liberalism. One rationale for this proposition may be that it serves as a focal point for queer-theoretical boundary keeping.[8] Queer theorists' objections to liberalism fall mainly in three interwoven theses: (1) "*ontological inadequacy*"; (2) "*market corruptibility*"; and (3) "*impoverishing reform*."

The ontological inadequacy thesis assumes that the individual in a classical liberal framing is an autonomous person capable of liberatory self-mastery. The individual can remove external obstacles that may frustrate their ability to realize their full potential. Queer theorists see this ontological conception as problematic because it seemingly neglects human relationships. Majoritarian beliefs, laws, norms, and practices of cisgender identity and heterosexuality have a profound effect in imposing severe restrictions upon LGBTQ individuals to undertake actions, express themselves, and uphold their own preferences. In effect, queer theorists see liberal approaches as neglecting societal power effects that subjugate diverse gender identities and sexualities.

Although some of liberalism's queer critics may concede that the preceding depictions of liberal ontology are "too strong," they might object to the abstract qualities of the liberal individual as being unrepresentative of the queer experience. Not only is an LGBTQ individual embedded within an intricate web of societal relations and power dynamics, as Foucault would suggest, but crucial aspects of gender identity and sexual orientation are unstable under circumstances of time and place (Samuels 1999). In other words, queer ontology stands as a refutation of liberal ontological conceptions of stable, and perhaps universalized, abstract selves.

Queer theory and liberalism also disagree on the effects of markets upon LGBTQ individuals and community relations. The "market corruptibility" view is a Marxian-inspired idea that the scale and scope of markets diminish the capacity of queer communities to meet the intimate and social needs of their members. This view suggests that the commercialization of products catering to LGBTQ people (and, similarly, the provision of goods and services by "queer-friendly" providers) diminishes the relative importance of queer materialistic self-reliance and small-scale communal bonding necessary to sustain LGBTQ enclaves.

Queer theorists have also criticized the growth of mainstreamed "pink markets" that target LGBTQ consumers and mass-produce queer aesthetics for non-LGBTQ market segment. These developments are supposed to devalue LGBTQ identities, in turn compromising the richness of the queer "lifeworld" more generally. Authors such as Chasin (2000), Whitney (2006), and Drucker (2011) claim that market actors tend to privilege, as well as cater to, a stereotypical vision of a queer person to the exclusion of the intersectional complexities of color, gender, race, and other factors informing diverse LGBTQ identities. In a global context, Rao (2015b: 47) castigates the emergence of "homocapitalism" that "builds on concepts like homonormativity and homonationalism to signify the selective incorporation of some race-, class-, and gender-sanitized queers into capitalism and the disavowal of others through a liberal politics of recognition that obviates the need for redistribution."

The "impoverishing reform" critique is that enhanced freedoms and rights for LGBTQ individuals within liberal institutions limit the full scope of emancipative opportunities that could be achieved. A "thin," legalistic account of emancipation can only go so far in addressing broader aspects of cultural, economic, and social life for queer community members, such as dignity, recognition, and respect. In other words, liberal legal reform is incapable of engendering the necessary transformations of norms and values to allow queer people to flourish.

Another potential objection is that liberal legal reform could at best neutralize, or at worst undermine, novel adaptations in response to repressive environments. Some gays and lesbians were critical of the impetus toward same-sex marriage laws because they effectively co-opted queer individuals into the "bland" legal conventions of marriage that were previously the preserve of heterosexual couples. Consistent with this, alternative forms of relationships, such as polyamory, were excluded from legal reform considerations. Critics also argued that same-sex marriage would largely benefit those who already had resources to share with their partners, but that the most vulnerable and marginalized would be left out (Spade 2015). Another example is allowing transgender individuals to change their gender markers on official documentation, but which potentially leaves the status of non-binary genderqueer and similar people remaining in doubt.

Queer critics argue that liberalism merely permits reform within the context of formally "equal" protections or rights, but that formal rights focus on what the law *says* while ignoring what the law *does*. The rules on paper may appear equal but be enforced unequally in practice. Even in a best-case scenario where formal equality is implemented effectively, queer theorists might be suspicious about the extent or permanence of such liberal legal changes. Contemporary reforms cannot evade the broader critiques surrounding the historical, and still contemporary, ill treatment of queer communities by the state. Reforms may not be robust to adverse changes in public sentiment toward LGBTQ people, which might then be conducive to the upscaling of homophobic or transphobic politics within democratic systems.

Classical liberal ideas have been given short shrift by queer theorists, and there are plentiful opportunities for more constructive intellectual exchanges between liberalism and queer theory (not to mention analysis and practice).

Queer classical liberalism: Understanding queer life using classical liberalism and mainline political economy insights

Classical liberalism gives QCL its philosophic and normative foundations

Classical liberalism is a set of doctrines that prioritizes and normatively values individual freedom. It emerged from the struggles with political absolutism and religious intolerance in Europe from the sixteenth to the eighteenth centuries. The broader classical liberal tradition has internal nuances and contested perspectives, with numerous sub-strands. Prior to the nineteenth century, leading figures included Thomas Hobbes, John Locke, the English Levellers, Montesquieu, Voltaire, Adam Smith, David Hume, Benjamin Constant, Thomas Jefferson, and James Madison. Classical liberal thinkers and activists of the nineteenth century included Jean-Baptiste Say, Frederic Bastiat, Richard Cobden, John Bright, Herbert Spencer, Jeremy Bentham, John Stuart Mill, Josiah Tucker, William Graham Sumner, and many more.

During the twentieth century, notable classical liberals led the charge against communism and fascism, paving the way for the revival of liberal doctrines. These figures included Ludwig von Mises, Friedrich Hayek, Frank Knight, James Buchanan, Robert Nozick, and Milton Friedman. The twenty-first century has a growing list of active contributors to classical liberal thought.

Far from there being a uniform liberal "thought collective" as suggested by some critics (e.g., Mirowski and Plehwe 2015), liberalism's complexities can be put on a broad spectrum. At one end are an array of "anarcho-capitalist" and "market anarchist" views that emphasize the potential of private governance arrangements to enable a flourishing, free society without the state (Friedman 1973; Rothbard 1973; Benson 1990; Chartier 2012).[9] At the other end is a "limited government" view in which the state protects life and property, finances and provides certain public goods and social services, and engages in some constrained welfare redistribution (Gaus 1983).

Modern classical liberalism is often seen, including in a critical light, as synonymous with Western thought and traditions. However, the core tenets of liberalism is discernible through many non-Western modes of thought and practice (as outlined, e.g., in Boaz 1997).

Classical liberalism contains several core commitments and principles:

- *Freedom of the individual*: Individuals possess the right to undertake their preferred courses of action in the absence of impediments (including coercive force) by other individuals. Thinkers such as Locke insist that individuals have natural rights to exercise their autonomy to act and choose, while utilitarians (e.g., Bentham, Mill) indicate that individual freedom is correlative with social welfare. Liberals conceive of individual freedom extensively, including self-sovereignty over the use of one's body and labor, the management of justly acquired properties, and instigating voluntary contractual arrangements.
- *Free market economy*: Free markets are the preferred means of economic production, distribution, and exchange. Within a system of property rights and the rule of law, entrepreneurs discover value-added exchange opportunities. Producers have the freedom to enter, and exit from, markets. Consumers can enjoy the relatively unrestrained ability to engage in trades and choose their preferred goods and services from (domestic or international) suppliers.
- *Civil society and freedom of association*: Voluntary forms of civic association more effectively cater to the intimate and social needs of individuals than other types of collectives (especially governments). Robust civil societies consist of numerous forms of human association, mutuality, and solidarity – such as families, clubs, charitable organizations, religious orders, interest groups, and other voluntaristic forms of collective activity. Civil societies are important sites through which freedom of assembly, expression, and conscience are exercised, as well as the performance of social acts such as caring, education, love, socialization, and support.
- *Personal and civic freedoms*: Individuals are free to make decisions, and to express their preferences and values, without undue interference from other individuals and by public authorities. Such freedoms are typically coupled with a range of civil liberties – for example, freedom of speech, press, assembly, and religion, and legal rights against arbitrary detention, searches, and seizures by other citizens and law enforcement.
- *Limited government*: The powers of government, and the scale and scope of public sector activities, are restricted by constitutional provisions, laws, and legislative statutes. Coercive governmental power is divided by the separation of functions across executive, judicial, and legislative branches, and among levels of government. A government's proper role is to finance and provide essential public goods that cannot be feasibly provided by commercial or civic entities.
- *Rule of law*: Public laws should be abstract in their specification and generically applied to avoid discriminatory legal treatments. Laws should also be impartially enforced by law enforcement personnel and an independent judiciary.

- *Toleration and peace*: A tolerant society permits a wide array of beliefs and practices, even if they incur a certain degree of moral disapproval. The exercise of governmental coercion can only be justified in clear instances of harm, as opposed to mere disapprobation. Toleration enables numerous "experiments in living" that are conducive to social learning and human progress. A tolerant society is conducive to peaceful (rather than violent) interactions between heterogeneous individuals.

Classical liberalism is a dynamic system of ideas that are relevant to a variety of situations. According to Macedo (1991: 9),

> [l]iberalism embraces individuality, religious and social diversity, and commercial energy, by enshrining toleration and personal liberty as core political values. It protects personal liberties by imposing procedural and substantive limits on the ways that persons or governments can interfere in the lives of others.

Liberalism is an innately radical posture. Principles such as freedom, equality, and justice are powerful indictments of domination and privilege throughout economic, political, as well as social spheres. Novak (2025) argues that emancipative values have been at the forefront of liberal radicalism that have, in turn, been implicated in sweeping historical trends as: industrialization and the expansion of the global economy; political democratization and the development of constitutional government; and extensive social inclusion associated with the norms and practices of tolerance and peace. These radically liberalizing trends have largely been beneficial to LGBTQ individuals and the flourishing of queer life.

Mainline political economy brings conceptual, analytical, and empirical scaffoldings to QCL

Classical liberalism is the philosophical foundation of QCL, and MPE is the analytical structure to operationalize QCL. MPE is a strand of heterodox political economy relative to the "mainstream" of the contemporary economics profession. It emphasizes epistemic diversity, emergent social coordination, and the use of institutions to guide human activities.

The mainline tradition takes its core assumptions and theories from foundational thinkers in classical liberalism, namely Adam Smith (1723–1790) and Carl Menger (1840–1921). Both scholars studied the underlying characteristics of human action (and interaction) that gave rise to the achievements of productive economic and social coordination. As Boettke et al. (2016: 4) argue, the most notable implications of Smithian-Mengerian scholarship are that

> (1) there are limits to the benevolence that individuals can rely on and therefore they face cognitive and epistemic limits as they negotiate the social world, but

(2) formal and informal institutions guide and direct human activity, and, so (3) social cooperation is possible without central direction.

MPE uses methodological individualism, meaning that the individual is the fundamental unit of analysis. Collective outcomes arise from the interactions of individuals. Individuals act purposefully (though imperfectly) and in response to incentives. Human interactions fundamentally entail processes of exchange in the ongoing pursuit of gains. Methodological individualism is not atomistic or otherwise reductive. MPE scholarship emphasizes a dialectical relation between structure and agency. People are unquestionably influenced by worldly structures as they decide and act, but they are not inert or passive in the face of informal and formal institutions, such as culture and laws. Therefore, people use their idiosyncratic knowledge together with the capacity to act entrepreneurially to seek advantages with others through economic, political, and social domains.

MPE contrasts the neoclassical mainstream approach, which MPE (and other heterodox political economy) scholars see as being typified by representative agents, equilibrium theorizing, and exogenously imposed social coordination by planners (Boettke 1997). The neoclassical representation of a robotically responsive economy as one that is amenable to exogenous stimulus has incurred the sharp intellectual rebuke of numerous MPE scholars, including Hayek in his 1974 Nobel Prize lecture (Hayek 1989).

The insights of the Austrian school (e.g., Mises, Hayek), Bloomington school (Elinor and Vincent Ostrom), and the Virginia school (e.g., Buchanan, Gordon Tullock) are the interconnected components of the MPE research agenda. Table 1.1 provides a summary of the core principles of Austrian, Bloomington, and Virginia approaches that comprise MPE.

The *Austrian school* is grounded in methodological individualism and subjectivism of preferences, expectations, and values. This approach stresses that the market is a perpetually dynamic process that generates and communicates knowledge about value-added means of production and exchange (Hayek 1945). Under considerable (if not radical) uncertainty, entrepreneurs are pivotal in discovering creative and profitable ways to better serve customers, and to correct economic errors over time. Decentralized coordination within the market stands in contrast to the gross inefficiencies of centralized economic planning (Mises [1920] 1935). Key figures in the Austrian tradition include Menger, Eugen Böhm-Bawerk, Mises, Hayek, Joseph Schumpeter, Ludwig Lachmann, Murray Rothbard, Israel Kirzner, and Don Lavoie.

The *Bloomington school* emphasizes polycentric orders of governing economic, social, political, and other human orders of interaction. A polycentric order consists of multiple, and potentially nested, sites of relatively autonomous decision-making through which various individual and collective elements (or units) both compete against, and cooperate with, each other (Ostrom et al. 1961; Ostrom 2005). The

TABLE 1.1 Mainline political economy concepts and application to queer studies

Conceptual orientation	*Key representatives*	*Fundamental postulates*	*Applicability to queer studies*
Austrian school	• Carl Menger • Eugen von Böhm-Bawerk • Ludwig von Mises • Friedrich Hayek • Israel Kirzner • Ludwig Lachmann • Don Lavoie	• Methodological individualism. • Subjectivism in values, preferences, knowledge, and expectations. • Heterogeneity and multi-specificity of capital, and situating capital with a broader production structure. • The market as a process. • Entrepreneurship. • Spontaneous and emergent orders. • Economic calculation.	• Acknowledging diverse and fluid identities, expressions, and choices. • Highlighting various dimensions and motivations of entrepreneurship in economic, political, and social contexts. • Appreciating societal transformations through decentralized actions beyond the decision-making remit of any given individual.
Bloomington school	• Elinor Ostrom • Vincent Ostrom • Michael McGinnis • Paul Dragos Aligica • Vlad Tarko	• Non-market and non-state collective decision-making. • Polycentric governance, institutions, and organizational arrangements. • Voluntary and self-governance capabilities.	• Recognizing properties of collective action alternatives beyond markets and states. • Awareness of minority groupings within polycentric arenas of action and conduct. • Building self-governance capacities among minority groups, including through democratic deliberation and agreement-making.
Virginia school	• James M. Buchanan • Gordon Tullock • Mancur Olson • Robert Tollison • Richard E. Wagner	• Behavioral symmetry between decision-making in private and public sector environments. • Collective action theory. • Rules of public governance, political conduct, and organizations.	• Illuminating strategies and techniques of collective action, including by minorities pressing for rights claims and overcoming repressive policies. • Appreciating instrumental and expressive political motives and political choices by individuals and groups. • Emphasizes constitutional constraints and political non-discrimination (including generality and rule-of-law principles).

Source: Novak (2021) and authors' illustration.

polycentric vision of order contrasts with hierarchical, monolithic view. Normatively, polycentricity is valuable because it empowers people with diverse backgrounds and interests to discover and implement their own solutions to social dilemmas (Ostrom 1990, 1998). Important figures in the Bloomington school tradition include Elinor Ostrom, Vincent Ostrom, Michael McGinnis, Roberta Herzberg, and Paul Dragos Aligica.

The *Virginia school* is grounded in the "economic analysis of politics," studying the behavior of voters, legislators, bureaucrats, and members of the judiciary. Political actors are assumed to further their self-interest (Brennan and Buchanan 1988). To prevent the exercise of political self-interest translating into public maladies such as rent seeking, policy discrimination, and political predation, constitutional constraints and other institutional rules can channel self-interested behavior in socially productive ways (Buchanan 1987). Its main figureheads include Buchanan, Tullock, Mancur Olson, Randall Holcombe, and Richard Wagner.

The combination of the Austrian, Bloomington, and Virginia approaches can bring fresh lessons about the world by showing that the market is a dynamic process, which is shaped by institutional and cultural context, and those institutions are the product of exchange (Boettke 2012; Boettke and Snow 2014).

What is queer about queer classical liberalism?

QCL integrates the philosophical and normative foundations of classical liberalism with the conceptual, analytical, and empirical tools of MPE to study LGBTQ experiences. Figure 1.1 illustrates how classical liberalism and MPE fit within the broader framework of QCL.

A QCL perspective can respond to the three core arguments of (non-liberal) queer theory: ontological inadequacy; market corruptibility; and impoverished legal reform. We post three counter-theses using QCL: "*ontological adequacy*"; "*market virtuosity*"; and "*enriching reform*."

First, the "*ontological adequacy*" thesis highlights that a liberal ontology can accommodate both the non-atomistic and fluid nature of gender and sexual expressions. Second, the "*market virtuosity*" thesis indicates markets can support entrepreneurial activities and provide material and non-material resources that are conducive to queer flourishing. Third, the "*enriching reform*" thesis specifies that the open-endedness of liberal-democratic politics and associational life provides abundant opportunities for LGBTQ individuals and community to press for both legal reforms and social change.

A liberal ontology includes non-atomistic, relational beings who cooperate with one another, and love and support each other, in a variety of ways. Adam Smith ([1759] 2002) devoted a book-length treatment discussing how human emotions and judgments are shaped by the perceptions of (and perceived responses to individual actions by) others. Since that time, liberals have focused on extending cultural, economic, political, and social analyses beyond the *über*-individual

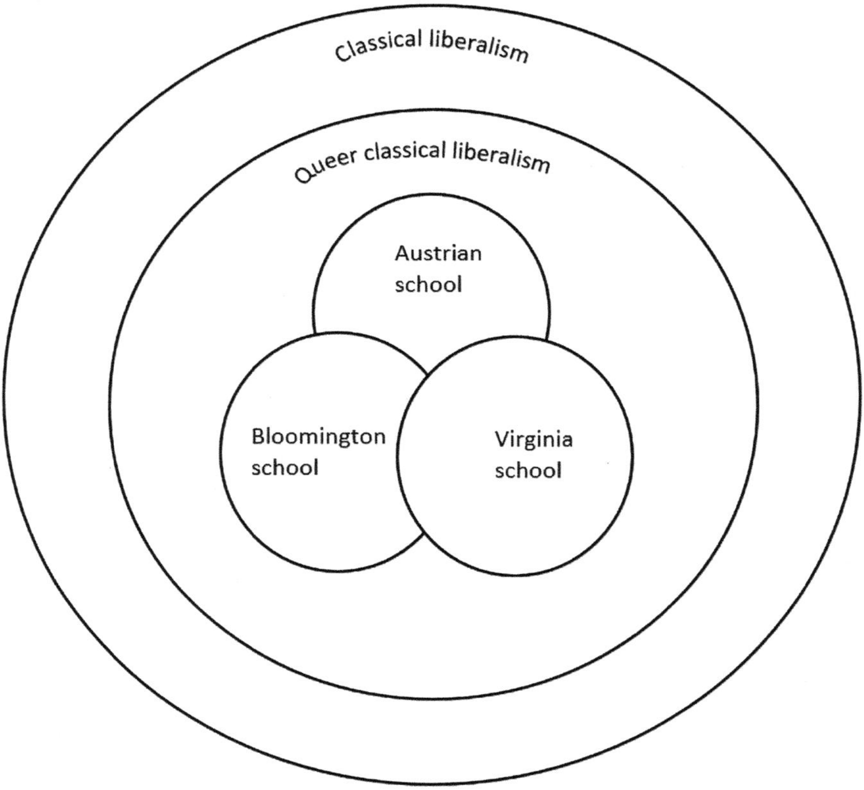

FIGURE 1.1 Theoretical system of queer classical liberalism

Source: Authors' illustration.

caricature of Robinson Crusoe. An important implication of such studies is that "when many Crusoes interact, patterns emerge *that would never have occurred through isolated individual action*" (Wagner 2010: 14; emphasis added). Liberalism has consistently maintained a focus upon relations between individuals and statist (and non-statist) authority figures, with significant implications for the distribution of material resources as well as interpersonal and intergroup powers.

Classical liberals have refuted ontological visions of identity as essentialized, fixed, or non-subjective. Liberals such as Wilhelm von Humboldt and John Stuart Mill argued for the necessity of freedom to facilitate the development of individuals' unique personalities. A modern treatment of note is James Buchanan's ([1979] 1999) model of "artifactual man," in which individuality is not fixed but is, rather, the result of creative, novel choices that one can make throughout their life (also Marciano and Meadowcroft 2025). Our argument is that it is ontologically inadmissible to suggest that liberalism assumes fixity in identity, let alone expression.

In the market virtuosity thesis, markets are arenas through which individuals can engage in mutually beneficial material exchanges, contributing to expanding prosperity in aggregate. The operation of free and competitive markets allows for upward mobility for entrepreneurs and workers and facilitates improved living standards for consumers. The emancipative aspect of economic liberalism suggests that minorities, such as LGBTQ individuals, can prosper as competition dually lowers relative output prices and increases the relative cost of labor market discrimination.

The QCL position is that markets have generally played a range of beneficial roles in supporting queer lives. For example, Dennis Altman (1982: 21) argued that "[n]o other minority has depended so heavily on commercial enterprises to define itself." Additionally, "[o]ne of the ironies of American capitalism is that it has been a major force in creating and maintaining a sense of identity among homosexuals" (Altman 1982). Queer historians such as Jeffrey Escoffier and John D'Emilio have remarked upon the growth of goods and services, as well as commercial establishments, catering to the specific needs of gay men, lesbians, and other members of the queer community (D'Emilio 1983; Escoffier 1997).

In modern, advanced economies, heterotopic commercial spaces for LGBTQ individuals (e.g., gay bars, bathhouses, bookstores), as well as financial sponsorship and support for non-commercial spaces, have helped queer individuals and communities to flourish (e.g., Faderman and Timmons 2006; Gieseking 2020). LGBTQ individuals may take on entrepreneurial projects for socialized purposes – such as creating queer critical mass within local markets or to perform entrepreneurship to socially destigmatize undesired or noxious beliefs about LGBTQ people (e.g., Fletcher et al. 2024).

Finally, QCL sees reform as generally an enriching process for queer individuals and communities. Reforms such as decriminalizing sodomy, enabling transgender people to change gender markers on official documentation, and extending marriage rights to same-sex couples can be interpreted as being consistent with classical liberal ethics of respecting individual autonomy and non-interference with private decisions (Coates 2023). The cessation of police harassment and discriminatory judicial punishments are other important measures consolidating formal freedoms for LGBTQ people. Although in key respects the legal reform agenda remains incomplete throughout many parts of the world, liberalization has afforded greater dignity and empowerment along certain margins.

Countries that uphold the liberal rule of law doctrine may be seen as providing so-called "freedom space" for heterogeneous groups – such as the LGBTQ community – without undue interference of the state (in the case of non-profit organizations, see Wandel and Valentinov 2014). Even when constitutional safeguards fail, a democratic environment can lay the groundwork for LGBTQ associations, social movements, and other groups to press for liberatory change within the political realm (Goodman 2025).

QCL scholars tend to sympathize with the non-liberal, queer-theoretic view that changes to law are insufficient to bring about queer emancipation. Freedom in the liberal society is not limited to the ability to vote and petition for public policy liberalization. In the liberal society, individuals have a presumed right to organize with like-minded others to persuade, and reason with, others *outside of the domain of politics*. For example, the cultural normalization of queer lives has been an important feature of the reform agenda over recent decades, arguably yielding successes in terms of promoting greater acceptance of LGBTQ people (Stulberg 2018).

Overall, QCL extends the liberal priority of equality to LGBTQ community members – implying that queer individuals, who have been among the most marginalized in society, have the same freedoms, rights, and privileges as others. Therefore, QCL is argued to be the fullest realization of classical liberalism itself.

A short history of classical liberal engagement with LGBTQ issues

Previous classical liberal engagements on queer issues: Marginal, but nonetheless worthwhile, undertakings

Classical liberal engagements with LGBTQ issues are not a "null set." Although Google Scholar does not index all scholarly publications, in late October 2025, a Google Scholar search for the term "queer liberalism" returned approximately 149,000 results.[10] These results are likely to reflect academic literature that is *critical* of classical liberal understandings. Even so, the results tentatively suggest that the stock of *bona fide* classical liberal engagements with queer theory and LGBTQ issues is non-zero.[11]

Chronologically, debates for queer liberty initially focused upon decriminalization of consensual acts and amelioration of legal discrimination and harassment. Liberal thinkers prioritized non-interference, or "negative liberty," arguments. Later, classical liberals and libertarians augmented previous perspectives with insights favoring empowerment of LGBTQ communities through the emancipating aspects of market and civil societal processes (which include, to some extent, "positive freedom" arguments).

Many of the liberal ideas conveyed in the past, as well as in the present, are historically and sociologically situated perspectives that do not necessarily represent a coherent, or whole, intellectual "system" about queer issues. Even so, many of these positive and normative contributions have helped to establish the QCL framework. We provide a selective summary of some of the major classical liberal, and libertarian, contributions to understanding issues affecting LGBTQ people.

Pre-twentieth century classical liberal insights

Cesare Beccaria (1738–1794) was an Italian jurist who is widely recognized as a precursor of modern criminology. In *An Essay on Crime and Punishments*, published in 1764, he argued that many criminal punishments were excessively applied, and perhaps arbitrarily so in a way that flouts the principles of equality under the law. Beccaria outlined a principle of "proportional punishment" corresponding to the severity of crimes proven (based on judicial trials in which the accused is, *ex ante*, presumed innocent) to have been committed. Beccaria argued against the criminalization of consensual acts of sodomy between gay men. He viewed sodomy as a crime that is difficult to prove, tending to be "proven by argument or by weak or equivocal evidence" (Beccaria [1764] 2009: 83).

Beccaria's doctrines of crime and punishment inspired British philosopher Jeremy Bentham (1748–1832), although Bentham's own writings regarding the criminalization of sodomy remained unpublished until the late twentieth century. In his essay "On Pederasty," Bentham described the legal treatment of sodomy as a case of disjunction between "punishment ... so severe" *versus* the notion that "the mischief of the offence ... [of sodomy] ... is so remote and even so problematical" (Bentham and Crompton 1978b: 93). Indeed, he would write in a utilitarian vein that such acts "produces pleasure" for individuals who consent to them (Bentham and Crompton 1978a: 390). As a general remark, Bentham (cited in Quinn 2014: 80) believed that "all-comprehensive liberty for all modes of sexual gratification not predominantly noxious" would be beneficial to humankind.[12]

Bentham argued that "[t]he mere fact that the custom was abhorrent to the majority of the community no more justified the persecution of sodomites than it did the killing of Jews, heretics, smokers, or people who ate oysters" (Bentham, cited in Dabhoiwala 2014). The exhaustive use of legal and regulatory instruments to detect, and then suppress, the "victimless crime" of sodomy also attracted Bentham's ire: "[i]f there be one idea more ridiculous than another" it would be that "of a legislator who, when a man and a woman are agreed about a business of this sort, thrusts himself in between them, examining situations, regulating times, and prescribing modes and postures" (Bentham and Crompton 1978b: 100–101).

In the late 1800s, the Irish playwright Oscar Wilde was arrested and jailed for "gross indecency" on account of sexual relations with other men. Wilde's arrest and trial aroused public controversy, but his case drew sympathies from libertarians such as Benjamin Tucker (1854–1939). Tucker criticized the court ruling that Wilde be jailed for two years. In an editorial, Tucker wrote:

> A man who has done nothing in the least degree invasive of any one; a man whose entire life, so far as known or charged, has been one of strict conformity with the idea of equal liberty; a man whose sole offence is that he has done something which most of the rest of us (at least such is the presumption) prefer not to do — is condemned to spend two years in cruel imprisonment at hard labor. ... Men who imprison a man who has committed no crime are themselves criminals.
>
> (Tucker, cited by Peron 2018)

Classical liberal discussions about the desirability of decriminalizing – or at least reducing the severity of punishments in response to – homosexual acts may be couched within broader ideational changes concerning sexual freedom. As Dynes

(2008: 461) noted, "[d]uring the 18th century, a group of libertine writers emerged, especially in France – among them Jean-Baptiste Boyer d'Argens, Jean-Charles Gervaise de Latouche, and the Marquis D. A. F. de Sade – who vividly highlighted the positive value of sexual expression." In her classic *The Vindication of the Rights of Woman*, the first-wave feminist Mary Wollstonecraft (1759–1797) nominated the ancient Greek poet, and lesbian icon, Sappho and the French trans woman Chevalière d'Éon as among those figures benefiting from an education afforded to men and, consequently, having been equipped (on a similar basis to men) with the virtues of "courage and resolution" (Wollstonecraft [1792] 2014).[13]

Twentieth-century insights

The struggles by LGBTQ people to assert their liberties and rights during the twentieth century had left an indelible imprint upon modern queer consciousness. Disaffection with a lack of legal equality and socio-cultural respect led to a variety of queer mobilizations against overly restrictive and unjust environments. During the 1950s in the United States, a variety of groups, such as the Mattachine Society and Daughters of Bilitis, pressed the case for gay and lesbian civil rights and societal acceptance. Arbitrary and humiliating police raids on queer spaces, such as bars and restaurants, eventually led to counter-responses such as rioting by LGBTQ groups. Perhaps the most prominent case was the Stonewall riot of June-July 1969, in which gay men, transgender women, and others protested police harassment (Stein 2019). Similar events preceded Stonewall in places such as Los Angeles and San Francisco (e.g., Boyd 2003; Self 2008).

In *The Constitution of Liberty*, leading liberal thinker Friedrich Hayek (1899–1992) wrote, "[b]ut where private practices cannot affect anybody but the voluntary adult actors, the mere dislike of what is being done by others, or even the knowledge that others harm themselves by what they do, provides no legitimate ground for coercion" (Hayek [1960] 2011: 212). He went on to footnote that

> [t]he most conspicuous instance of this in our society is that of the treatment of homosexuality ... private practice among adults, however abhorrent it may be to the majority, is not a proper subject for coercive action for a state whose object is to minimize coercion.
>
> (Hayek [1960] 2011: 212)

The Objectivist libertarian icon Ayn Rand (1905–1982) during the early 1970s remarked of her sense of detestation toward lesbian women, and the "women's liberation" movement, more generally (Rand [1971] 1999).[14] Despite her personal antipathies, she offered a principled argument for rejecting state discrimination and harassment of LGBTQ people: "[a]ll laws against homosexual acts should be repealed. I do not approve of such practices or regard them as necessarily moral, but it is improper for the law to interfere with a relationship between consenting adults" (Mayhew 2005: 18).[15]

Ralph Raico (1936–2016), a libertarian historian and activist within the Libertarian Party during the 1970s, produced a pamphlet articulating a libertarian approach to gay rights. Raico ([1975] 2007: 2) decried the ill-effects of "Church-sanctioned State oppression" experienced by gays, indicating that discrimination and stigmatization called for an urgent focus upon gay liberation. Raico ([1975] 2007: 4) insisted that "sovereignty over oneself necessarily included self-sovereignty for gays as well." He proposed a broad swathe of reforms to ensure "gay people will have the same opportunity for meaning and dignity in their lives as all human beings" (Raico [1975] 2007: 12).[16]

Justin Raimondo (1951–2019), a libertarian activist who later described himself as a "conservative-paleo-libertarian," wrote two essays that subsequently appeared as the pamphlet "In Praise of Outlaws: Rebuilding Gay Liberation." In it, Raimondo (1979: 11) described the relationship between queer citizens and the state that governs over them as "a state of war." He then stated that "[t]he historical oppression of gays by the State defines the spirit of their class interests: the interests of the gay community are *never* served by any increase in State power, even if it is allegedly on its behalf" (Raimondo 1979: 13).

During the last quarter of the twentieth century, there were measurable shifts toward greater recognition and acceptability of LGBTQ people, especially in Western countries. Legal restrictions upon same-sex activities were relaxed at subnational and national levels, as were legislation prohibiting the public expressiveness of diverse and nonconforming gender identities. Homosexuality was removed from the *Diagnostic and Statistical Manual of Mental Disorders* in the early 1970s (McHenry 2022), signaling a crucial step in the de-pathologization of same-sex attraction.[17] These momentous changes in a liberalizing direction were forged through a combination of political pressures, efforts to increase the public visibility of LGBTQ people and, through it, promote social normalization, as well as rising community acceptance of gender identities and sexual orientations.

The mainstreaming of queer culture was becoming evident in fashion, literature, music, and television during the 1980s and 1990s. Non-liberal queer historian Jeffrey Escoffier (1997) wrote of the transitions – from a "closeted" to "liberated" queer economy – preceding the "pink dollar" consolidation of LGBTQ purchasing power in tandem with mainstream popularity of queer aesthetics as embodied in goods and services. However, the pace of liberalization was uneven and harassment and victimization still tragically occurred, and LGBTQ communities were severely impacted by the HIV-AIDS epidemic (Herek and Greene 1994).[18]

During the 1980s and 1990s, a range of classical liberal (and libertarian) voices emerged to articulate the case for LGBTQ legal freedoms and greater social respectability. The former Cato Institute executive vice-president David Boaz

(1953–2024) argued for legal equality between homosexual and heterosexual individuals and couples.[19] Although critical of Foucauldian and related influences upon queer theory and activism, conservative writer Andrew Sullivan (1995) wrote an influential tract arguing cases along classical liberal lines for legal equality for gays and lesbians.

Twenty-first-century insights

In the twenty-first century, legal liberalization has advanced in Western countries, and other regions such as East Asia, South America, and to a lesser extent, Africa. Issues such as same-sex marriage, child adoption by same-sex couples, and the ability of transgender individuals to change official documentation to reflect their gender status, have occupied the attention of classical liberals (and, similarly, libertarians). Scholars have also indicated their general interest in using liberal insights when studying the conditions and experiences of LGBTQ individuals and communities.

Arguably the most prominent twenty-first century classical liberal figure is Deirdre McCloskey, who undertook gender affirmation surgery in the late 1990s and has advocated for queer liberty for over 20 years. In a 2007 book chapter, for example, she argued that:

> the market is not the enemy of queers. The restaurants and bars from which the drag queens exploded in political action in the 1960s in San Francisco and then in New York were after all profit-making entities. The enemies were the gender cops, not the owners of coffee shops. States use conservative institutions, anti-queer institutions, anti-free institutions, institutions that keep citizens sitting where they can be taxed and won't cause trouble.
>
> (McCloskey 2007: 86)

In her autobiography, *Crossing: A Memoir*, McCloskey presents an intimate account of her gender transition experiences while couching them in the classical liberal presumption of human autonomy. As McCloskey stated in the afterword of the second edition, "[g]ender change I reckon is a freedom thing, one of a long line of liberations from 1776 on" (McCloskey 2019: 277). And in regard to the age-old accusation that "we all have an internal identity, fixed and ready made," McCloskey responded, "[w]e make ourselves, which is our freedom as human beings" (McCloskey 2019: 177–178).

A new generation of classical liberal scholars is using MPE to analyze queer issues in a wide variety of ways (see Berggren and Nilsson 2013, 2016; Cowen 2013; Goodman 2013, 2015, 2016a, 2016b, 2023, 2025; Novak and Copland 2014; Horwitz 2015; Novak 2015a, 2015b; Kuznicki 2017, 2023; Cheang 2019; Dalla Chiesa 2021; Malamet and Novak 2023; Powell 2025). Although we can only provide a partial summary of the literature, a pattern of classical liberal engagement has unfolded over time. This book builds upon these foundations to address LGBTQ issues, perspectives, and themes under a consistent framework of QCL.

Structure of the book

This book consists of 12 chapters from experts in economics, political economy, sociology, and related fields. The research topics highlight theoretical and applied insights using the prism of the QCL framework. Several contributions engage with non-liberal queer theories as well as adjacent ideas in fields such as critical studies, feminism, and gender and sexuality studies. The empirical cases are drawn from a variety of Western countries and beyond.

The book is demarcated into two parts. Chapters 2 to 6 inclusive are primarily conceptual in orientation, referring primarily (though not exclusively) to aspects of queer theory with reference to the mainline approach to political economy.

In Chapter 2, Alexander Craig provides a comparative analysis of economic, as well as certain extra-economic, conditions experienced by LGBTQ community members. The analysis is centered upon the prospects of flourishing queer life under "tradition," "planning," and "market," a tripartite distinction for societal organization previously applied by Austrian economist Don Lavoie ([1985] 2016). Traditional societies are assessed to generally stifle interpersonal differences and promote local cultural, economic, and social conformities, although Craig acknowledges queer studies suggesting that certain pre-modern societies tolerated (or accepted) diverse modes of gender and sexual expressions and identities. While the allure of planning lies in its promise of rationalizing human affairs in efficient or effective ways, this mode of organization is shown to severely limit the autonomy of minorities including LGBTQ individuals. Markets are superior to tradition and planning from the perspective of queer flourishing – especially on account of empowering LGBTQ people to realize their differentiated preferences and tastes, as well as ambitions and capabilities.

In Chapter 3, Jordan Lofthouse and Zane Willard show that liberal institutions promote entrepreneurial action, including by LGBTQ individuals, that has served as an important driver of change for queer emancipation. Because certain institutions promote entrepreneurship, and that entrepreneurship itself can reshape (both formal and informal) institutions, there is a bilateral relationship between entrepreneurship and institutions that have proven to be empowering for queer communities in the United States and elsewhere. Although the process of queer emancipation has been far from perfect, institutional quality is a significant factor in enabling entrepreneurs to discover opportunities that overall enhance the status of LGBTQ individuals.

Conventional queer theories assume that commercial activities corrode the commitments and values cherished by LGBTQ individuals, including the desire for queer communal life. In Chapter 4, Mikayla Novak uses conceptual developments in the intersectional spaces between MPE and economic sociology to challenge the prevailing "market corrosion" thesis. Drawing especially upon the insights of Virgil Storr (2008, 2009), Novak shows that LGBTQ community members have often used commercial settings to enlarge their social networks as well as affirm senses of shared identity and communal belonging. The "social appropriation" of queer commercial spaces has crucially served the function of affirming core values such as honesty, trust, and even love, with repressive cultural and legal environments. Markets can therefore provide "queer social spaces" to affirm LGBTQ expression and identity and have placed a larger role in fostering increasing societal tolerance over matters of gender and sexuality.

Modern philosophical precepts presume that government is necessary to protect individual rights and safety. But does the "protective state" necessarily protect LGBTQ individuals. In Chapter 5, Nathan Goodman outlines a critique of the protective state which indeed casts doubt upon its credibility as a guarantor of peace, order, and security benefiting LGBTQ individuals and community groups. Queer rights movements have fended off predation by law enforcement officials, but in recent decades there have been calls for the government to enact "hate crimes" legislation as well as efforts to enshrine rights through judicial decisions. Goodman uses public choice theory to critically examine the tensions that exist with respect to the uneven discharge of statist duties to protect queer people. The chapter applies ideas from polycentricity theory and "direct action studies" to point out that LGBTQ communities may seek non-state alternatives for protection (as well as mutual, intra-communal support).

Turning now to applications of QCL, Nathan Goodman and Jordan Lofthouse consider aspects of queer community life in Salt Lake City, Utah. In Chapter 6, the authors reflect on why Salt Lake City has emerged as a "queer-friendly" city, despite the dominant presence of the Church of Jesus Christ of Latter-Day Saints (LDS Church) in the region. The emergence of a robust civil society for LGBTQ people has produced a rich ecology of formal and informal groups to address a diversity of needs and challenges for queer Utahns. The queer communities in Salt Lake City benefit from having multiple venues for engagement, and even multiple models of pride. Robust self-governance within a broader polycentric order of association is shown to help LGBTQ individuals live healthier, happier, and more connected lives even when the dominant cultural norms are not particularly welcoming to gender and sexual diversity.

In Chapter 7, Carolina Dalla Chiesa and Yana Zaharieva introduce readers to the concept of a "queer digital information commons." LGBTQ community members are using online platforms and resources to share, and disperse, queer content, and build an audience as well as supporters who act as patrons of the emergent online spaces. Dalla Chiesa and Zaharieva investigate a range of queer-led projects on crowdfunding platforms such as Kickstarter and Patreon, as well as LGBTQ themed podcasts and YouTube videos. Characteristics of polycentricity are detected among the information sharing channels under consideration. Empirical qualitative evidence drawn from European cases suggests that Internet access is helping queer individuals and communities to obtain the goods, services, and knowledge that they need, including to navigate uncertain or hostile cultural and political environments.

In Chapter 8, Malia Dalesandry explores the relationships between criminalization, stigmatization, social capital, and resilience in a community of black transgender sex workers (and supporters) in Washington, DC. Semi-structured, open-ended interviews with community members revealed an array of emergent arrangements to help sex workers navigate their local environment. The chapter also identifies the formation of community identity surrounding a shared sense of repression but also collective narratives of resilience despite that repression. Sex worker communities created an array of institutions and practices for self-care, mutual support, as well as protection, bound together by social capital. This chapter showcases the use and value of ethnographic qualitative methods for working with stigmatized communities such as the black transgender sex worker community.

In Chapter 9, Byron "Trey" Carson considered the trade-offs between economic and social freedom, public health, and the well-being of queer communities. Freer societies are supposed to provide opportunities for people with resources to develop health infrastructure and practices to avoid infectious diseases, but more frequent interactions within freer societies might also spread disease and encourage other public health problems (e.g., Troesken 2015). These tensions have applicability to LGBTQ individuals who have faced specific public health problems, such as the HIV/AIDS epidemic and other sexually transmitted diseases, in addition to public health issues that affect the general population. Economic and social liberties generally tend to enhance the public health of queer communities, and in some cases the trade-offs between freedom and health are not so severe in the case of LGBTQ individuals. Restrictive public health institutions could unintentionally cause negative outcomes for public health throughout queer communities.

In Chapter 10, Elliot Bowers and Mikayla Novak examine the nature and effects of transphobia, and the importance of community-led solutions to an emergent, yet perverse, social phenomenon. The harms of transphobia are well known, culminating in situations in which the autonomy and dignity of transgender and gender non-conforming people are compromised. Transphobia arises through the actions and conduct of multitudes of people with respect to binary gendered socio-cultural norms, and with no central coordination involved. Transphobia's prevalence and persistence reflects how conventional, binary gender norms have consolidated through socialization, peer pressure, and moralizing. Bowers and Novak focus upon socio-cultural strategies deployed by transgender and gender non-conforming individuals and groups, and their allies, to challenge the incidence, and redress the effects, of transphobia. The chapter adds realism to social-scientific studies of emergent and spontaneous orders, raising questions to what extent such orders are necessarily beneficial to those impacted by them.

In Chapter 11, Bryan Cheang focuses on circumstances facing LGBTQ individuals in East and Southeast Asia, exploring how developments in governance and civil society from the 1970s onwards have influenced the trajectory of queer activism and rights in those regions. Certain communitarian cultures that prevail in Asia's East and Southeastern regions have elevated norms and values dedicated the preservation of a relatively static social order, which has been traditionally inimical to the expression of diverse gender and sexual identities. The existence of authoritarian institutions in several Asian countries that have also threatened queer liberties. Despite these challenges, Cheang finds that LGBTQ communities have actively pursued legal recognition, cultural acceptance, and solidarity building with some success where formal political freedoms are reinforced by liberal social practices. This chapter offers a crucial transnational perspective on concepts of QCL and specifically furthers our understanding of the intersection between politics, culture, and queer freedom in Asia.

The concluding chapter (Chapter 12) provides a summary of the key arguments and themes conveyed throughout the book, and it offers several suggestions regarding future research regarding queer theory and practices through liberal-philosophical and MPE-analytical lenses. The contributions in this book will not only motivate additional intellectual inquiries into classical liberal interpretations of queer life but inspire practical projects to promote the freedoms of queer communities.

Notes

1 Unless otherwise stated, this topical and analytical scope of this book will be focused upon these groups. Several contributors also discuss the role of Allyship (including from heterosexual people) in supporting queer individuals and groups. Nonetheless, it is acknowledged that certain other specific identities exist within the broader queer spectrum – such as Intersex, Pansexual, Non-Binary, Two-Spirit, etc. – that we largely reserve for future discussion and research inquiries.
2 In this volume, the terms "LGBTQ" and "queer" will be used interchangeably (unless otherwise specified). More finely grained distinctions will be made using references to specific groups (viz., lesbian, gay, bisexual, transgender), and to descriptive classifiers of behavior, expression, and identity such as "gender identity" and "sexual orientation."
3 Gallup (2025) polling shows a general trend of greater acceptability toward gays and lesbians in general, and approval of same-sex marriage, among U.S. respondents; however, specific issues such as the involvement of transgender people in sports. Minkin et al. (2025) report survey results indicating greater U.S. social acceptance of gay and lesbian, relative to transgender, individuals.
4 Later in this introduction, we refer to some notable classical liberal scholarly works on the subject, as well as a range of popular works produced by classical liberals (and libertarians).
5 In a certain nod to the Marxian frame of analysis, Foucault likewise identified the valorization of the social construct of heterosexuality as resting in the economic imperative of reproducing future generations of workers.
6 Foucault (1978: 69) offers

> a general working hypothesis. The society that emerged in the nineteenth century-bourgeois, capitalist, or industrial society, call it what you will-did not confront sex with a fundamental refusal of recognition. On the contrary, it put into operation an entire machinery for producing true discourses concerning it. Not only did it speak of sex and compel everyone to do so; it also set out to formulate the uniform truth of sex.

7 The contributions of Rich and other lesbian feminists (and queer theorists) point to the complex interlocking of "intersectional" forms of identity that can serve to marginalize

or oppress groups. The case in point here is that the experiences of lesbian women are affected by *both* the priorities of patriarchy and heterosexuality.

8 Consistent with a recognition of Hayek's (1949) ideas about the translation of pure theory into the realm of politics, the use of non-liberal approaches to retain recognizable academic boundaries for queer theory may furthermore serve as a source for activist energy resisting conventional perspectives about gender and sexuality matters.

9 While some of these radical classical liberals identify their position as "anarcho-capitalist," others identify as "anti-capitalist" on grounds that a radically freed market would dislodge existing forms of concentrated wealth and power (see Chartier and Johnson 2011).

10 Results based on the search of the "queer liberalism" term by Google Scholar (https://scholar.google.com).

11 We argue that such a conclusion is sustained even when recognizing that liberalism comes with many descriptors and labels – for example, classical liberalism, Rawlsian liberalism, progressive liberalism, liberal socialism, etc.

12 The philosophical thought of other utilitarians could similarly be deployed to argue against the criminalization of homosexual acts. Combining Mill's harm principle with the notion that "over himself, over his own body and mind, the individual is sovereign" (Mill [1859] 1985: 16) lends support against the criminal punishment of consenting sexual activities between same-sex-attracted individuals. For further discussion, see Basse (2024).

13 For discussions concerning the significance of Sappho to lesbian identity, see Andreadis (2014) and Mueller (2021). The life of Mme. d'Eon, including her connections with Wollstonecraft, are explored by Morris (2019), Bergès (2020), and Conlin (2025).

14 Anarcho-capitalist libertarian Murray Rothbard (1926–1995) conveyed similar views to that of Rand. For example, he was critical of the "widening rebellion against biological sex norms, as well as against natural diversity, … [that] … has been the recently growing call for bisexuality by Left intellectuals" (Rothbard 2000: 15).

15 Sciabarra (2003) presents a defense of homosexuality from a Randian ethical perspective.

16 Several of the key reforms nominated by Raico included: repealing laws against consensual sexual acts between adults; eliminating prohibitions against same-sex unions; removing cross-dressing prohibition laws; and abolishing restrictions against same-sex adoption rights.

17 Notable among the advocates of the psychiatric destigmatization of homosexuality was psychiatrist Thomas Szasz (1960). His 1960 work, *The Myth of Mental Illness*, referred to homosexuality as a mode of human behavior earmarked with an "illness" not based upon scientific evidence identifying a psychiatric disorder but, rather, owing to the social disapproval surrounding same-sex attraction and conduct. A brief discussion of Szasz's and related arguments that appeared during the 1960s is given by Varnell (2000). Caplan (2006) provides an economic generalization of Szasz's insights.

18 Novak (2021) discusses social movement responses to intellectual property restrictions upon the sale of generic pharmaceutical HIV-AIDS treatments.

19 Boaz's long-time partner, Stephen H. Miller, founded the "Independent Gay Forum."

References

Adam, Barry D. 1987. *The Rise of a Gay and Lesbian Movement.* Boston, MA: Twayne Publishers.

Alexander, Rustam. 2023. *The Hidden History of Gay Oppression in the USSR.* Manchester, UK: Manchester University Press.

Altman, Dennis. 1982. *The Homosexualization of America: The Americanization of the Homosexual.* New York, NY: St. Martin's Press.

An, David, and Kavita Batra. 2022. "Trends in Scientific Output on the Lesbian, Gay, Bisexual, and Transgender (LGBT) Community Research: A Bibliometric Analysis of the Literature." *Journal of Health and Social Sciences* 7 (1): 114–131.

Andreadis, Harriette. 2014. "The Sappho Tradition." In *The Cambridge History of Gay and Lesbian Literature*, edited by E. L. McCallum and Mikko Tuhkanen, 15–33. Cambridge, UK: Cambridge University Press.

Baber, Kristine M. 2009. "Postmodern Feminist Perspectives and Families." In *Handbook of Feminist Family Studies*, edited by Sally A. Lloyd, April L. Few and Katherine R. Allen, 56–58. Thousand Oaks, CA: SAGE Publications.

Basse, Benoît. 2024. "Utilitarianism and LGBT Rights." In *Research Handbook of Law and Utilitarianism*, edited by Guillaume Tusseau, 240–256. Cheltenham, UK: Edward Elgar.

Beccaria, Cesare. [1794] 2009. *On Crimes and Punishments*. London, UK: Routledge.

Becker, Gary S. 1971. *The Economics of Discrimination*. Second edition. Chicago, IL: University of Chicago Press.

Benson, Bruce L. 1990. *The Enterprise of Law: Justice Without the State*. San Francisco, CA: Pacific Research Institute for Public Policy.

Bentham, Jeremy, and Louis Crompton. 1978a. "Offences Against One's Self." *Journal of Homosexuality* 3 (4): 389–406.

Bentham, Jeremy, and Louis Crompton. 1978b. "Jeremy Bentham's Essay on "Paederasty" Part 2." *Journal of Homosexuality* 4 (1): 91–107.

Bergès, Sandrine. 2020. "A Female Body." Times Literary Supplement. https://www.the-tls.com/politics-society/social-cultural-studies/a-female-body.

Berggren, Niclas, and Therese Nilsson. 2013. "Does Economic Freedom Foster Tolerance?" *Kyklos* 66 (2): 177–207.

Berggren, Niclas, and Therese Nilsson. 2016. "Tolerance in the United States: Does Economic Freedom Transform Racial, Religious, Political and Sexual Attitudes?" *European Journal of Political Economy* 45 (Supplement): 53–70.

Boaz, David. 1997. *The Libertarian Reader: Classic and Contemporary Readings from Lao-tzu to Milton Friedman*. New York, NY: Free Press.

Boettke, Peter J. 1997. "Where Did Economics Go Wrong? Modern Economics as a Flight from Reality." *Critical Review* 11 (1): 11–64.

Boettke, Peter J. 2012. *Living Economics: Yesterday, Today, and Tomorrow*. Oakland, CA: Independent Institute.

Boettke, Peter J., and Nicholas A. Snow. 2014. "Political Economy and the Science of Association: A Suggested Reconstruction of Public Choice through the Alliance of the Vienna, Virginia, and Bloomington Schools of Political Economy." *Review of Austrian Economics* 27 (1): 97–110.

Boettke, Peter J., Stefanie Haeffele-Balch, and Virgil Henry Storr. 2016. *Mainline Economics: Six Nobel Lectures in the Tradition of Adam Smith*. Arlington, VA: Mercatus Center at George Mason University.

Boyd, Nan Alamilla. 2003. *Wide-Open Town: A History of Queer San Francisco to 1965*. Berkeley, CA: University of California Press.

Brechenmacher, Saskia. 2025. "The New Global Struggle Over Gender, Rights, and Family Values." Carnegie Endowment for International Peace. https://carnegieendowment.org/research/2025/06/the-new-global-struggle-over-gender-rights-and-family-values.

Brennan, Geoffrey, and James M. Buchanan. 1988. "Is Public Choice Immoral? The Case for the 'Nobel' Lie." *Virginia Law Review* 74 (2): 179–189.

Brown, Gavin, Kath Browne, Rebecca Elmhirst, and Simon Hutta. 2010. "Sexualities in/of the Global South." *Geography Compass* 4 (10): 1567–1579.

Buchanan, James M. 1987. "The Constitution of Economic Policy." *American Economic Review* 77 (3): 243–250.

Buchanan, James M. [1979] 1999. "Natural and Artifactual Man." In *The Logical Foundations of Constitutional Liberty. The Collected Works of James M. Buchanan*, Volume 1, edited by Geoffrey Brennan, Hartmut Kliemt, and Robert D. Tollison, 246–259. Indianapolis, IN: Liberty Fund.

Butler, Judith. 1990. *Gender Trouble: Feminism and the Subversion of Identity*. New York, NY: Routledge.

Butler, Judith. 2024. *Who's Afraid of Gender?* New York, NY: Farrar, Straus & Giroux.
Caplan, Bryan. 2006. "The Economics of Szasz: Preferences, Constraints and Mental Illness." *Rationality & Society* 18 (3): 333–366.
Carrera-Fernández, Maria Victoria, and Renée DePalma. 2020. "Feminism Will Be Trans-inclusive or It Will Not Be: Why Do Two Cis-hetero Woman Educators Support Transfeminism?" *Sociological Review* 68 (4): 745–762.
Chartier, Gary. 2012. *Anarchy and Legal Order: Law and Politics for a Stateless Society*. New York, NY: Cambridge University Press.
Chartier, Gary, and Charles W. Johnson. 2011. *Markets, Not Capitalism: Individualist Anarchism Against Bosses, Inequality, Corporate Power, and Structural Poverty*. New York, NY: Minor Compositions.
Chasin, Alexandra. 2000. *Selling Out: The Gay and Lesbian Movement Goes to Market*. New York, NY: Palgrave.
Cheang, Bryan. 2019. *Free-Market Humanitarianism: A Primer*. St. Paul, MN: Ally Press.
Cloud, Dana. 2022. "Queer Liberation and Socialism: Learning from the Stories of a Movement." Tempest, June 21. https://tempestmag.org/2022/06/queer-liberation-and-socialism.
Coates, Russell. 2023. "How Classical Liberalism Played a Crucial Role in Advancing LGBTQ+ Rights." Learn Liberty, June 28. https://www.learnliberty.org/blog/how-classical-liberalism-advanced-lgbt-rights.
Conlin, Jonathan. 2025. "Adventurer, Saint, Celebrity: The Chevalière Deon's Transgender Selves." *Australian Feminist Studies*. https://doi.org/10.1080/08164649.2025.2549702.
Cowen, Nick. 2013. "What Would Hayek Say About Gendered Violence?" In *What Would Hayek Say Today (Really)?*, edited by Legatum Institute, 27–29. London, UK: Legatum Institute.
Crenshaw, Kimberle. 1989. "Demarginalizing the Intersection of Race and Sex: A Black Feminist Critique of Antidiscrimination Doctrine, Feminist Theory and Antiracist Politics." *University of Chicago Legal Forum* 1: 139–167.
Dabhoiwala, Faramerz. 2014. "Of Sexual Irregularities by Jeremy Bentham – Review 2014." The Guardian, June 26. https://www.theguardian.com/books/2014/jun/26/sexual-irregularities-morality-jeremy-bentham-review.
Dalla Chiesa, Carolina. 2021. "Crowdfunding the Queer Museum: A Polycentric Identity Quarrel." In *Governing Markets as Knowledge Commons*, edited by Erwin Dekker and Pavel Kuchař, 238–255. London, UK: Cambridge University Press.
D'Emilio, John. 1983. "Capitalism and Gay Identity." In *Powers of Desire: The Politics of Sexuality*, edited by Ann Snitow, Christine Stansell and Sharon Thompson, 100–113. New York, NY: Monthly Review Press.
Downs, Jim. 2016. "Red-hot Gay Marriage." Aeon, April 19. https://aeon.co/essays/the-radical-roots-of-gay-liberation-are-being-overlooked.
Drucker, Peter. 2011. "The Fracturing of LGBT Identities under Neoliberal Capitalism." *Historical Materialism* 19 (4): 3–32.
Drydakis, Nick. 2024. "The Economics of Being LGBT. A Review: 2015–2020." In *The Routledge Handbook of LGBTQ Identity in Organizations and Society*, edited by Julie A. Gedro and Tonette S. Rocco, 200–213. New York, NY: Routledge.
Dworkin, Andrea. 1974. *Woman Hating*. New York, NY: E. P. Dutton.
Dynes, Wayne. 2008. "Sexuality." In *The Encyclopedia of Libertarianism*, edited by Ronald Hamowy, 461–462. Thousand Oaks, CA: SAGE Publications.
Escoffier, Jeffrey. 1997. "The Political Economy of the Closet: Notes Toward an Economic History of Gay and Lesbian Life before Stonewall." In *Homo Economics: Capitalism, Community, and Lesbian and Gay Life*, edited by Amy Gluckman and Betsy Read, 123–134. New York, NY: Routledge.
Faderman, Lillian, and Stuart Timmons. 2006. *Gay L.A.: A History of Sexual Outlaws, Power Politics, and Lipstick Lesbians*. New York, NY: Basic Books.
Fletcher, Luke, Valerio Incerti, and Caroline Essers. 2024. "A Social Identity Perspective on Lesbian, Gay, Bisexual and Transgender (LGBT) Entrepreneurs' Networking Behavior." *Journal of Enterprising Communities: People and Places in the Global Economy* 18 (5): 1126–1146.

Floyd, Kevin. 2009. *The Reification of Desire: Toward a Queer Marxism*. Minneapolis, MN: University of Minnesota Press.
Foucault, Michel. 1978. *The History of Sexuality: Volume 1*. New York, NY: Vintage.
Friedman, David D. 1973. *The Machinery of Freedom: Guide to a Radical Capitalism*. New York, NY: Arlington House.
Gallup. 2025. "LGBTQ+ Rights." https://news.gallup.com/poll/1651/gay-lesbian-rights.aspx.
Gaus, Gerald F. 1983. "Public and Private Interests in Liberal Political Economy, Old and New." In *Public and Private in Social Life*, edited by S. I. Benn and G. F. Gaus, 183–221. New York, NY: St. Martin's Press.
Gieseking, Jen Jack. 2020. *A Queer New York: Geographies of Lesbians, Dykes, and Queers*. New York, NY: New York University Press.
Gleeson, Jules Joanne, and Elle O'Rourke. 2021. *Transgender Marxism*. London, UK: Pluto Press.
Goodman, Nathan. 2013. "Chelsea Manning and the State's Abusive Transphobia." Center for a Stateless Society, August 24. https://c4ss.org/content/21003.
Goodman, Nathan. 2015. "Queer Liberation and Jury Nullification." Center for a Stateless Society, June 11. https://c4ss.org/content/38208.
Goodman, Nathan. 2016a. "Book Review: *Queering Anarchism: Addressing and Undressing Power and Desire*." Molinari Review 1 (1): 99–103.
Goodman, Nathan. 2016b. "The Promise of Agora-Feminism." Center for a Stateless Society, September 9. https://c4ss.org/content/45995.
Goodman, Nathan P. 2023. "Commerce, Spontaneous Order, and Gender Freedom Movements." *Cosmos + Taxis* 11 (11+12): 24–36.
Goodman, Nathan P. 2025. "A Radical Liberal Approach to LGBTQ Emancipation." In *Liberal Emancipation: Explorations in Political and Social Economy*, edited by Mikayla Novak, 229–258. Cham, Switzerland: Palgrave Macmillan.
Han, Enze, and Joseph O'Mahoney. 2018. *British Colonialism and the Criminalization of Homosexuality: Queens, Crime and Empire*. London, UK: Routledge.
Hayek, Friedrich A. 1945. "The Use of Knowledge in Society." *American Economic Review* 35 (4): 519–530.
Hayek, Friedrich A. 1949. "The Intellectuals and Socialism." *University of Chicago Law Review* 16 (3): 417–433.
Hayek, Friedrich A. 1989. "The Pretence of Knowledge." *American Economic Review* 79 (6): 3–7.
Hayek, Friedrich A. [1960] 2011. *The Constitution of Liberty*. In *The Collected Works of F. A. Hayek: Volume 17*, edited by Ronald Hamowy. Chicago, IL: University of Chicago Press.
Hennessy, Rosemary. 2017. *Profit and Pleasure: Sexual Identities in Late Capitalism*. New York, NY: Routledge.
Herek, Gregory M., and Beverly Greene. 1994. *AIDS, Identity, and Community: The HIV Epidemic and Lesbians and Gay Men*. Thousand Oaks, CA: SAGE Publications.
Herek, Gregory M., and John P. Capitanio. 1996. ""Some of My Best Friends": Intergroup Contact, Concealable Stigma, and Heterosexuals' Attitudes Toward Gay Men and Lesbians." *Personality and Social Psychology Bulletin* 22 (4): 412–424.
Horwitz, Steven. 2015. *Hayek's Modern Family: Classical Liberalism and the Evolution of Social Institutions*. New York, NY: Palgrave Macmillan.
Jay, Karla, and Allen Young. 1972. *Out of The Closets: Voices of Gay Liberation*. New York, NY: Douglas.
Jeffreys, Sheila. 1997. "Transgender Activism: A Feminist Response." *Journal of Lesbian Studies* 1 (3–4): 55–74.
Jeffreys, Sheila. 2014. *Gender Hurts: A Feminist Analysis of the Politics of Transgenderism*. London, UK: Routledge.
Koyama, Emi. 2021. "The Transfeminist Manifesto." In *Feminist Theory Reader: Local and Global Perspectives*. Fifth edition, edited by Carole R. McCann, Seung-kyung Kim and Emek Ergun, 83–90. New York, NY: Routledge.

Kuznicki, Jason. 2017. "Gender as Art." Liberal Currents, June 6. https://www.liberalcurrents.com/gender-as-art.

Kuznicki, Jason. 2023. "Gender as Essence and as Economic Choice." *Cosmos + Taxis* 11 (11+12): 80–91.

Lavoie, Don. [1985] 2016. *National Economic Planning: What Is Left?* Arlington, VA: Mercatus Center at George Mason University.

Lewis, Holly. 2016. *The Politics of Everybody: Feminism, Queer Theory, and Marxism at the Intersection*. London, UK: NBN International.

Macedo, Stephen. 1991. *Liberal Virtues: Citizenship, Virtue, and Community in Liberal Constitutionalism*. Oxford, UK: Clarendon Press.

MacKinnon, Catherine A., Finn Mackay, Mischa Shuman, and Sandra Fredman. 2024. "Exploring Transgender Law and Politics." *Signs: Journal of Women in Culture and Society* 50 (1): 279–318.

Malamet, Akiva, and Mikayla Novak. 2023. "Gender as a Discovery Procedure: Social Construction, Markets, and Gender." *Cosmos + Taxis* 11 (11+12): 9–23.

Marciano, Alain, and John Meadowcroft. 2025. "Buchanan's Theory of Emancipation: Artifactual Man in Perspective." In *Liberal Emancipation: Explorations in Political and Social Economy*, edited by Mikayla Novak, 57–78. Cham, Switzerland: Palgrave Macmillan.

Mason, Corinne L. 2018. *Routledge Handbook of Queer Development Studies*. London, UK: Routledge.

Mayhew, Robert. 2005. *Ayn Rand Answers: The Best of Her Q&A*. New York, NY: New American Library.

McCann, Hannah, and Whitney Monaghan. 2020. *Queer Theory Now: From Foundations to Futures*. London, UK: Red Globe Press.

McCloskey, Deirdre. 2007. "Introduction: Queer Markets." In *Media Q – Media/Queered: Visibility and Its Discontents*, edited by Kevin G. Barnhurst, 83–88. New York, NY: Peter Lang Publishing.

McCloskey, Deirdre. 2019. *Crossing: A Transgender Memoir*. Chicago, IL: University of Chicago Press.

McHenry, Sara. 2022. ""Gay is Good": History of Homosexuality in the *DSM* and Modern Psychiatry." *American Journal of Psychiatry Residents' Journal* 18 (1): 4–5.

Mill, John Stuart. [1859] 1985. *On Liberty*. Penguin Classics edition. London, UK: Penguin.

Minkin, Rachel, Juliana Horowitz, Luona Lin, and Dana Braga. 2025. "The Experiences of LGBTQ Americans Today." Pew Research Center. https://www.pewresearch.org/wp-content/uploads/sites/20/2025/05/ST_2025.5.29_LGBTQ-experiences_report.pdf.

Mirowski, Philip, and Dieter Plehwe. 2015. *The Road from Mont Pèlerin: The Making of a Neoliberal Thought Collective*. Cambridge, MA: Harvard University Press.

Mises, Ludwig von. [1920] 1935. "Economic Calculation in the Socialist Commonwealth." In *Collectivist Economic Planning: Critical Studies on the Possibilities of Socialism*, edited by Friedrich A. Hayek, 87–130. London, UK: Routledge & Kegan Paul.

Morgensen, Scott Lauria. 2012. "Theorising Gender, Sexuality and Settler Colonialism: An Introduction." *Settler Colonial Studies* 2 (2): 2–22.

Morris, Marilyn. 2019. "The Chevalière d'Eon, Transgender Autobiography and Identity." *Gender & History* 31 (1): 78–90.

Mueller, Melissa. 2021. "Sappho and Sexuality." In *The Cambridge Companion to Sappho*, edited by P. J. Finglass and Adrian Kelly, 36–54. Cambridge, UK: Cambridge University Press.

Novak, Mikayla. 2015a. *Gender Identity and Libertarianism*. Center for a Stateless Society. https://c4ss.org/wp-content/uploads/2015/06/GIandLib.pdf.

Novak, Mikayla. 2015b. "The Condition of Transgender Women: Libertarian Perspectives." Cato Institute libertarianism.org, May 12, https://www.libertarianism.org/columns/condition-transgender-women-libertarian-perspectives.

Novak, Mikayla. 2021. *Freedom in Contention: Social Movements and Liberal Political Economy*. Lanham, MD: Lexington Books.
Novak, Mikayla. 2025. *Liberal Emancipation: Explorations in Political and Social Economy*. Cham, Switzerland: Palgrave Macmillan.
Novak, Mikayla, and Simon Copland. 2014. "Is Libertarianism the Best Friend of Queer Communities?" The Guardian (Australia), May 23. https://www.theguardian.com/commentisfree/2014/may/24/is-libertarianism-the-best-friend-of-queer-communities.
Olive, James L. 2015. "Queering the Intersectional Lens: A Conceptual Model for the Use of Queer Theory in Intersectional Research." In *Intersectionality in Educational Research*, edited by Dannielle Joy Davis, Rachelle J. Brunn-Bevel and James L. Olive, 19–30. New York, NY: Routledge.
Ostrom, Elinor. 1990. *Governing the Commons: The Evolution of Institutions for Collective Action*. Cambridge, UK: Cambridge University Press.
Ostrom, Elinor. 1998. "A Behavioral Approach to the Rational Choice Theory of Collective Action: Presidential Address, American Political Science Association, 1997." *American Political Science Review* 92 (1): 1–22.
Ostrom, Elinor. 2005. *Understanding Institutional Diversity*. Princeton, NJ: Princeton University Press.
Ostrom, Vincent, Charles M. Tiebout, and Robert Warren. 1961. "The Organization of Government in Metropolitan Areas: A Theoretical Inquiry." *American Political Science Review* 55 (4): 831–842.
Peron, James. 2018. "Benjamin Tucker in Defense of Oscar Wilde." https://medium.com/the-radical-center/benjamin-tucker-in-defense-of-oscar-wilde-e777fc96abf1.
Powell, Aaron. 2025. "David Boaz and Trans Rights." Liberty Fund, Online Library of Liberty. Liberty Matters, June 5. https://oll.libertyfund.org/publications/liberty-matters/2025-06-05-david-boaz-and-trans-rights.
Quinn, Michael. 2014. "Popular Prejudices, Real Pains: What Is the Legislator to Do When the People Err in Assigning Mischief?" In *Bentham's Theory of Law and Public Opinion*, edited by Xiaobo Zhai and Michael Quinn, 63–89. Cambridge, UK: Cambridge University Press.
Rahman, Momin. 2010. "Queer as Intersectionality: Theorizing Gay Muslim Identities." *Sociology* 44 (5): 944–961.
Raico, Ralph. [1975] 2007. *Gay Rights: A Libertarian Approach*. Arizona: Stonewall Libertarians.
Raimondo, Justin. 1979. *In Praise of Outlaws: Rebuilding Gay Liberation*. San Francisco, CA: Students for a Libertarian Society.
Rand, Ayn. [1971] 1999. *The Return of the Primitive: The Anti-Industrial Revolution*. New York, NY: Penguin.
Rao, Rahul. 2015a. "Echoes of Imperialism in LGBT Activism." In *Echoes of Empire: Identity, Memory and Colonial Legacies*, edited by Kalypso Nicolaidis, Berny Sèbe and Gabrielle Maas, 353–370. London, UK: I. B. Taurus.
Rao, Rahul. 2015b. "Global Homocapitalism." *Radical Philosophy* 194: 38–49.
Rao, Rahul. 2020. *Out of Time: The Queer Politics of Postcolonality*. New York, NY: Oxford University Press.
Raymond, Janice. 1980. *The Transsexual Empire: The Making of the She-Male*. London, UK: Women's Press.
Renn, Kristen A. 2010. "LGBT and Queer Research in Higher Education: The State and Status of the Field." *Educational Researcher* 39 (2): 132–141.
Rich, Adrienne. 1980. "Compulsory Heterosexuality and Lesbian Existence." *Signs: Journal of Women in Culture and Society* 5 (4): 631–660.
Rothbard, Murray N. 1973. *For a New Liberty: The Libertarian Manifesto*. New York, NY: Macmillan.

Rothbard, Murray N. 2000. *Egalitarianism as a Revolt Against Nature and Other Essays*. Second edition. Auburn, AL: Ludwig von Mises Institute.
Saguy, Abigail C. 2022. *Come Out, Come Out, Whoever You Are*. New York, NY: Oxford University Press.
Samuels, Jacinth. 1999. "Dangerous Liaisons: Queer Subjectivity, Liberalism and Race." *Cultural Studies* 13 (1): 91–109.
Schiapponi, Martina. 2024. "The Neglected Transgender Experience in Judith Butler's Theory." Unpublished manuscript. https://doi.org/10.13140/RG.2.2.27298.64963.
Sciabarra, Chris Matthew. 2003. *Ayn Rand, Homosexuality, and Human Liberation*. Cape Town, South Africa: Leap Publishing.
Self, Robert O. 2008. "Sex in the City: The Politics of Sexual Liberalism in Los Angeles, 1963–79." *Gender & History* 20 (2): 288–311.
Shaw, Ari. 2023. "The Global Assault on LGBTQ Rights Undermines Democracy." Chatham House, June 2. https://www.chathamhouse.org/publications/the-world-today/2023-06/global-assault-lgbtq-rights-undermines-democracy.
Simon, William. 1996. *Postmodern Sexualities*. London, UK: Routledge.
Skipworth, Sue Ann, Andrew Garner, and Bryan J. Dettrey. 2010. "Limitations of the Contact Hypothesis: Heterogeneity in the Contact Effect on Attitudes toward Gay Rights." *Politics & Policy* 38 (5): 887–906.
Smith, Adam. [1759] 2002. *The Theory of Moral Sentiments*. Cambridge, UK: Cambridge University Press.
Spade, Dean. 2015. *Normal Life: Administrative Violence, Critical Trans Politics, and the Limits of Law*. Durham, NC: Duke University Press.
Stein, Marc. 2019. *The Stonewall Riots: A Documentary History*. New York, NY: New York University Press.
Stock, Kathleen. 2021. *Material Girls: Why Reality Matters for Feminism*. London, UK: Fleet.
Storr, Virgil Henry. 2008. "The Market as a Social Space: On the Meaningful Extraeconomic Conversations that Can Occur in Markets." *Review of Austrian Economics* 21 (2): 135–150.
Storr, Virgil Henry. 2009. "Why the Market? Markets as Social and Moral Spaces." *Journal of Markets and Morality* 12 (2): 277–296.
Stulberg, Lisa M. 2018. *LGBTQ Social Movements*. Cambridge, UK: Polity Press.
Sullivan, Andrew. 1995. *Virtually Normal: An Argument About Homosexuality*. New York, NY: Alfred A. Knopf.
Szasz, Thomas S. 1960. *The Myth of Mental Illness: Foundations of a Theory of Personal Conduct*. New York, NY: Hoeber-Harper.
Tadlock, Barry L., Andrew R. Flores, Donald P. Haider-Markel, Daniel C. Lewis, Patrick R. Miller, and Jami K. Taylor. 2017. "Testing Contact Theory and Attitudes on Transgender Rights." *Public Opinion Quarterly* 81 (4): 956–972.
Thelwall, Mike, Tracey Jayne Devonport, Meiko Makita, Kate Russell, and Lois Ferguson. 2023. "Academic LGBTQ+ Terminology 1990–2021: Increasing Variety, Increasing Inclusivity?" *Journal of Homosexuality* 70 (11): 2514–2538.
Tschantret, Joshua. 2020. Revolutionary Homophobia: Explaining State Repression against Sexual Minorities. *British Journal of Political Science* 50 (4): 1459–1480.
Troesken, Werner. 2015. *The Pox of Liberty: How the Constitution Left Americans Rich, Free, and Prone to Infection*. Chicago, IL: University of Chicago Press.
Varnell, Paul. 2000. "Gay Rights on the Right." https://www.szasz.com/varnell.htm.
Wagner, Richard E. 2010. *Mind, Society, and Human Action: Time and Knowledge in a Theory of Social Economy*. London, UK: Routledge.
Wandel, Jürgen, and Vladislav Valentinov. 2014. "The Nonprofit Catallaxy: An Austrian Economics Perspective on the Nonprofit Sector." *Voluntas: International Journal of Voluntary and Nonprofit Organizations* 25 (1): 138–149.

Welzel, Christian. 2013. *Freedom Rising: Human Empowerment and the Quest for Emancipation*. New York, NY: Cambridge University Press.
Whitney, Elizabeth. 2006. "Capitalizing on Camp: Greed and the Queer Marketplace." *Text and Performance Quarterly* 26 (1): 36–46.
Wollstonecraft, Mary. [1792] 2014. *A Vindication of the Rights of Woman*. Penguin Classics edition. London, UK: Penguin.
Yeo, Jiin-Yih, Sue-Hie Ting, and Collin Jerome. 2024. "A Bibliometric Analysis of the Research on Social Attitudes Towards LGBT Community (2002–2022)." *Journal of Homosexuality* 71 (7): 1684–1702.

2

PLAN COORDINATION, LGBTQ IDENTITIES, AND THE EXTENT OF THE MARKET

Alexander W. Craig

It is darkly amusing to note that in the twentieth century, all three leading combatants in World War II accused each other of being the origin of or corrupted by homosexuality. Members of the German Nazi Party denounced homosexuality as both "sexual Bolshevism" (Hekma et al. 1995) and a product of "degenerate individualism" (Giles 2002). Under Stalin, the USSR re-criminalized homosexual activity, which was said to originate within fascism and bourgeois capitalists (Frencia and Gaido 2020). In the United States, homosexuals were accused of having a "psychological maladjustment that led people towards communism" during the Lavender Scare (Johnson 2023: 16) and, later, of comprising a large proportion of the Nazi party (Jensen 2002). Whether fascist, communist, or (at least nominally) capitalist, societies of many organizational types have abused LGBTQ people. It need hardly be added that LGBT people faced significant difficulties in medieval Europe's heavily tradition-based society (Karras 2017).[1] Nonetheless, it is worthwhile to investigate what kind of broad societal institutions facilitate LGBTQ freedom, however imperfectly, and special attention to their economic system may be revealing.

A queer classical liberal orientation suggests that the mechanisms behind economic coordination in different societies are likely to play a role in the extent and expansion of LGBTQ freedom. In the contemporary United States, a broadly market-based society, LGBTQ freedoms have rapidly expanded since the 1990s, and before their decriminalization and eventual legal recognition, LGBTQ communities were able to, if not exactly flourish, at least form a sufficient critical mass to provide mutual support and catalyze a movement toward greater freedom. This was never the case in Nazi Germany or Soviet Russia. After the fall of the Nazi regime, East and West Germany decriminalized homosexuality, but it would be several decades before a reunified, economically liberalized Germany eventually legalized

DOI: 10.4324/9781003615781-2

same-sex marriage in 2017. Post-Soviet Russia continues to starkly oppress LGBTQ individuals (Edenborg 2020) and has never reached above its 2017 score of 6.58 out of 10 in the Fraser Institute Index of Economic Freedom, making it the 94th freest country in the world for that year. By contrast, the United States in that year reached 8.43 and Germany reached 8.02, ranking 5th and 16th, respectively. In at least these three cases, economic freedom and market-based economic orders seem to correlate with LGBTQ freedom.

Beyond the United States, Russia, and Germany, economic freedom is known to causally increase development (Grier and Grier 2021), and development and LGBTQ freedom are correlated with each other both around the world and within subregions of the global economy (Badgett et al. 2019). Economic freedom may not be the most important factor in determining the degree of LGBTQ freedom in a country, but globally the two seem to be related. Statistical tests of the relationship are likely to be frustrated by both (1) the concurrent long-term upward trends in LGBTQ freedom and economic freedom as well as (2) the slow-moving, multi-step mechanisms likely involved in large cultural changes. The more qualitative, theoretical political economy approach taken in this chapter is more likely to arrive at insights that, though imprecise, are important.

I will argue that economic freedom, the ability to rely on market-based coordination of one's economic life, is more likely to facilitate LGBTQ freedom and well-being than other modes of plan coordination on which a society might rely. Following the ideas of mainline political economist Don Lavoie ([1985] 2016), I will contrast market-based coordination with tradition- and planning-based coordination mechanisms. Market-based coordination empowers individuals to make decisions within their well-defined and limited sphere of influence, relying on exchange, prices, contracts, property rights, and similar institutions to reconcile actors' plans. Tradition-based systems assign decision-making powers and even decision rules to individuals in particular social positions, relying on historic norms to set expectations and coordinate plans. Whereas Market- and Tradition-based systems rely predominantly on emergent mechanisms, Planning-based systems are relatively more top-down.[2] Planning-based systems place certain actors in key decision-making positions over many others, assigning them the power to produce and enforce an overarching plan to achieve social coordination.

Of these, the space for experimentation, extensive specialization, wealth-generation capacity, and many other features mean the market-based coordination system best facilitates LGBTQ freedom. More intense market activity produces the wealth, product variety, and disciplining effects of competition that both enable LGBTQ individuals to have their particular needs and desires met but also for LGBTQ communities to advocate for their own freedom and flourishing. Furthermore, a greater extent of Market-based plan coordination gives greater flexibility for individuals to choose their own life course, both because Tradition lacks the resources to enable such experimentation and Planning, besides devolving into many of the drawbacks of Tradition, relies heavily on the limited conceptual toolkit of the planners.

This chapter will proceed as follows. The next section will explicate the three forms of social coordination alluded to above, explaining their necessity and noting that likely every society relies on all three, though varying in the composition of which activities are coordinated by which mechanism. This is followed by a defense of the claim LGBTQ freedom is best advanced and preserved within societies that give extensive room for individual decision-making and plan coordination via negotiation.

Then I discuss the "intensive margin", highlighting a variety of ways LGBTQ interests are advanced and become easier to advance in a society with larger markets, for example, markets with greater numbers of participants. Next, I describe how greater reliance on markets on the "extensive margin" increases LGBTQ freedom and well-being. For markets to coordinate more activities, the other mechanisms must cede those social arenas, so I will then contrast the market-based coordination system with tradition- and planning-based societies vis-à-vis LGBTQ issues, contending that although no coordination system can ever guarantee LGBTQ rights, market-based systems are more consistent with them.

I conclude with thoughts on the future of LGBTQ freedom, making recommendations for means to advance LGBTQ interests and predictions concerning future trends.

Social coordination: Tradition, planning, and market

Every society needs some means of coordinating plans between its members. Arguably, this is a prerequisite for any assemblage of human individuals to constitute a society. Without the ability to ensure that one's plans will be possible to execute without frustration by the actions of another, no plan of any kind is likely to succeed, irrespective of content. A social setting of constant incompatibility between the courses of action individuals take is really a setting wherein individuals find themselves in constant conflict, again irrespective of those plans' objectives. Individuals purely motivated to pursue the well-being of others could not achieve their goal if in the process of their good deeds they were perpetually frustrating the similarly altruistic goals of others. Even those who were perfectly informed of others' plans would need some means of deciding whose plans to revise if those plans were not *ab initio* coordinated so as to never conflict. Identical, perfectly informed, morally unimpeachable agents might know exactly the best means of reconciling their plans, but, unrealism aside, this only implies that the conjunct of perfect information and moral rectitude entails plan coordination. Relax either of these assumptions and the necessity of some further mechanism arises.

One can imagine three possible "poles" of coordination mechanisms: (1) do what has always been done, come what may, (2) delegate global planning to a specialized social position, (3) leave coordination to individual agents, anticipating the need to revise local plans as conflicts between them become apparent. In *National*

Economic Planning: What is Left? Lavoie presents a tripartite classification schema of coordination mechanisms that lines up with these three extremes. He terms them (1) Tradition, (2) Planning, and (3) Market. Noting that with the possible exception of Tradition, none seem to have operated entirely on their own, he argues for the impossibility of their simultaneous use in coordinating any given area of social activity. In places where two of these mechanisms meet, there is some amount of discoordination. This may be entirely worthwhile, as different mechanisms may so outperform one another in their respective arenas that discoordination at the boundary between those areas may be a worthwhile cost, as when traditions may specify the content of intergenerational obligations but markets specify how one earns the income needed to satisfy one's familial duties. The rest of this section examines each of the coordination mechanisms' internal logics, emphasizing elements that are relevant for the specific concerns of LGBTQ freedom and flourishing examined in subsequent sections.

Tradition

One means of coordinating plans is to simply avoid changing them. Although this presents problems for making any plans at the dawn of society, subsequently one can be sure that plan discoordination is impossible, as, having been achieved once, coordination need never be re-established. Lavoie refers to this means of coordinating plans as "Tradition", noting the arrival of Tradition in human evolution introduced a novel, Lamarckian force shaping humanity. Instead of being dependent on the biological evolution of genetic formatting to address contemporary survival needs, what might be thought of as selection on biological hardware, humans could use socially transmitted survival techniques, a culture software, according to traditional norms. When these failed, a society would disappear, be replaced, assimilate to another, etc.

The obvious challenge for this mechanism is that although it may not endogenously require plan revision, exogenous shocks to the system are impossible to proactively adjust to. If used alone and without deviation, experimentation in light of novel circumstances becomes impossible. Lavoie goes so far as to say agriculture is the "highest productive achievement of Tradition" which, if accurate, demonstrates the limits to which such an inflexible mechanism can be put. Though far superior to Darwinian selection on genetic mutations, Tradition still struggles with novelty.

Other significant drawbacks to Tradition include its limited ability to handle large numbers and varieties of agents, resources, technologies, and so on. Although in principle one can imagine traditions accreted over millennia that address how to handle innumerable situations, in reality the limited ability of a society to convey traditional norms means Tradition can only process a limited number of people. Most people must be able to identify each other individually or by social position, remember the prescribed norms of interaction, and execute the assigned scripts. Famously, Robin Dunbar argued that there is a cognitive limit to the number of people with whom a human individual can maintain a personal relationship, approximately 150. Because Tradition supplies societies with relatively blunt tools for paring down the cognitive burden of navigating the world, this number becomes far more significant than under systems that can sustain anonymous cooperation, as in many contemporary markets in the developed world. The cognitive burden of behaving in accordance with a traditional system can be considerable, never mind the difficulty of transmitting these norms across generations.

Here, it ought to be emphasized that the inability of Tradition to facilitate complex social organization in heterogenous societies does not imply it is undesirable in general nor that any action ought to be taken to replace it where it is currently in use. Some social norms serve important functions that a society depends on and that would be extremely costly to renegotiate. One can imagine a discovery that, due to the prevalence of right-handedness, a social norm of driving on this or that side of the road is generally safer than the other. Such a discovery would not imply that a given society ought to switch which side of the road they use, as the costs of doing so and the degree of pre-coordination already achieved would be too great to be worth upending. It might, however, imply a desirable choice for new transportation networks or for certain kinds of subcommunities, like vehicle racing enthusiasts.

Although the foregoing discussion takes the purest form of Tradition to involve no change at all, real world traditions are obviously more flexible. Circumstances sometimes force change on traditions, yet the resulting "new traditions" are recognizably continuous with the previous ones. Taking conceptual inspiration from existing Traditions to handle novel challenges is commonplace, and accretions around existing traditions often build novel means of coordinating plans to solve various societal problems. Crego and Salter explore this process in the development of a hierarchical clergy in the early Christian church (Crego and Salter 2025). In clarifying a distinction that Hayek leaves muddled, Hasnas argues that customary law is a form of traditional law as the unintentional product of "the formation of interactional expectancies" (Hasnas 2005: 83), whereas the modern common law is the form of law practiced in the United States and the United Kingdom that takes legal precedents as binding. In this sense, customary law is the traditional set of rules as they are found out in the world, whereas the common law is the systematized version that may well be imposed on those whom it binds. Both can be looked at as traditional systems in different senses, but they are only Tradition as a plan coordination mechanism to the extent that they do, in fact, coordinate agents' plans. When traditions need to change, they are necessarily not coordinating plans, though their influence may guide some of the decision-making about future norms, providing a weaker form of plan coordination at a meta-level. Mostly, changing traditions requires either an unintentional selection mechanism or deliberate planning.

Planning

Another mechanism for coordination would be to assign the ability to make plans to a specialized position, group, or individual who will then consciously deliberate and issue an overall plan for society. The most dramatic example of this form of coordination is that of a centrally planned economy such as the USSR during the War Communism period (Boettke 2001, ch. 6). In such a system, the individual(s) in charge of planning achieve coordination by only permitting a single plan. Individuals' actions are meant to fit into such a plan as components, and therefore discoordination is eliminated by never arising in the first place. The deliberate planning of society as a whole obviates the need for any endogenous plan revision. Unlike Tradition, Planning has, at least in principle, the capacity to respond to exogenous shocks by means other than acquiescence. Planners, observing the shock, can issue a plan revision wherein individuals alter their course of action in a manner appropriate to address the novel circumstances. Under conditions of perfect knowledge on the part of the planners, there is no need for individuals to endogenously alter their own plans in this case, as the new overall plan can be constructed so as to optimally respond to the novel circumstances in whole and in part. This also bears on the scale of the system. Whereas traditions are necessarily a feature of a specific group's cultural particulars, a societal plan can be as all-encompassing as the planners aspire to make it and can feasibly enforce.

Planning purports to put human intelligence to use in organizing society as a whole, whereas Tradition leaves it significantly subject to random chance. In multiple respects, however, it is a fragile system. Most obviously, the knowledge of the planners in understanding the broad forces at play in a society is limited. Even if, contrary to Adam Smith's Man of System observation, individual decision-making per se were brought under the control of the planners, there remains the issue of comprehending the objectives and constraints of such a large body as a modern society. The most famous economic arguments against central planning turn predominantly on the difficulty of procuring and using knowledge concerning, and likely embedded in, a particular time and place (Mises [1920] 1935; Hayek 1945, 1948; Boettke 2001, ch. 3), but it can equally well be argued that central planners' conception of the world is likely to be unproductively homogenous and limited (Boettke 2002). For example, one might reasonably ask how the technocratic Soviet experiment with comprehensive central planning ca. 1918 was expected to succeed when the formal theory of optimal allocation under perfect information was not complete for several decades, never mind the theories of imperfect information, search theory, and incompleteness.

Karl Marx remains the standard exemplar of a planning theorist, but he was notably hesitant to state how planners would do the planning. Furthermore, he was far from the first proponent of central planning. As Lavoie points out, it was actually figures such as Henri de Saint-Simon who originated the idea of planning society, which for him meant organizing it along the model of a military. Furthermore, the actual implementation of planning in various societies did not arise from anything like the Marxist or even the Saint-Simonian program (though it was clearly cloaked in Marxist-Leninist rhetoric in the USSR). It was, rather, an opportunity for large economic entities to entrench their privileged positions using the militarization of various world powers' economies during World War I (Lavoie [1985] 2016, ch. 7). Planning thus both arose as an idea and was implemented not as the economic liberation of a class but as the militarization and regimentation of a society.

Planning, however, did not disappear with the centrally planned societies of the twentieth century. In contemporary developed societies, technocratic states often impose significant but partial planning on the economies within their jurisdictions. As the title of his 2019 book alludes to, Jeffrey Friedman has characterized the technocratic state as exerting *Power Without Knowledge*, or of needing much more knowledge to achieve its technocratic ends than it is really capable of marshalling (Friedman 2019). This knowledge must be an understanding of how people will behave, that is, of what their plans are. Without perfect or near perfect knowledge, the state struggles to achieve its ends. In a similar vein, Koppl has argued that much contemporary policy sets the state up as a "big player", an entity that shapes the behavior of its environment by necessitating that other entities predict its behavior, as when a monetary or fiscal authority's policy stance sets short-term expectations on the parts of others in their society (Koppl 2002). In this sense, it "plans" for others, and they must adjust their plans within the range of options the big player leaves for them.

Market

If Tradition is best described as "no plan" (only evolutionary selection) and Planning is best described as "one plan" (issued by a specific class, organization, or person), then Lavoie's last form of social organization might best be described as "many plans", which at first blush seems to fly in the face of the idea of any social coordination being achieved at all. Lavoie refers to this means of coordination as the Market. For Lavoie, Market-based organization involves "rivalrous competition in the pursuit of money profits" (Lavoie [1985] 2016: 37). As individuals pursue their individual plans, they express their assessment of the choice-worthiness of the options available to them by means of monetary valuation of what is available for purchase. If they can take resources that others assess as being low value and reallocate them to high value uses, they may keep some of the created value as entrepreneurial profits. Prices thus reflect relative valuations, resource scarcities, expectations about the future, and more while incentivizing the revision of plans to continually "improve" the use of society's limited resources and coordinate the dispersed plans of countless individuals.

Although Lavoie's focus on the cash nexus is appropriate as an illustration of the most powerful means of plan coordination in Market-based societies, a more comprehensive approach would extend the concept to involve more than competition in the cash nexus. What distinguishes markets from Planning and Tradition is the presence of a distributed mechanism for plan coordination that introduces an adaptive, evolutionary mechanism. Unlike Tradition, the Market mechanism endogenously encourages plan revision in a coordination-enhancing direction. Thus, recent work in the Austrian tradition on social learning has emphasized that while they cannot replace "competition in the pursuit of money profits" there are other mechanisms that can, to an extent, take advantage of dispersed knowledge by rewarding discovery and plan revision (Chamlee-Wright 2007, 2008, 2010; Chamlee-Wright and Myers 2008; Storr et al. 2015, 2017). These mechanisms are likely to be especially important in contexts where markets are too costly to rely on.

Achieving coordination via this mechanism requires that each individual has a delimited sphere of influence wherein they are free to make decisions as they see fit. It is a mistake to imagine that the Market eliminates planning (Hayek [1944] 2007, ch. 8). Rather, within their institutionally defined sphere of influence, each individual makes their own plans based on signals and incentives they face as the result of others' actions and interactions. In an ideal implementation, each individual is subject to the same rules defining their sphere of influence and these spheres may be voluntarily altered with the consent of the relevant parties (Hayek [1960] 2011, ch. 10). The highly abstract nature of this definition of one's sphere of influence is deliberate. The more general the rules, the less an individual's particular identity or circumstances enter into defining their rights, the more one may do as one sees fit in one's circumstances. This permits a highly experimental pattern of behavior within one's sphere and with others who consent to participate in the experiment. This is part of the basis for markets' permissiveness with regard to social norms, lifestyles, and identity expression. On the other hand, as the legal boundaries between persons become less general and abstract, they become more command-like, inching a society closer to Planning, which requires codification, categorization, and some amount of forced homogenization (Scott 1998; Lofthouse and Boettke 2025).

When they meet

It ought to be noted that finding Tradition, Planning, or Market in isolation from the others is rare to the point of likely non-existence in the contemporary world. Certainly, no large contemporary country lacks for bodies with the power to issue commands at their discretion to profit-seeking economic decision-makers, as in the case of any regulatory body issuing case-by-case approvals, such as the Competition Commission of India, community planning boards in US municipalities, or medical technology approvals by the European Medicines Agency. Furthermore, many societies combine traditional norms with market-oriented activities with nontrivial economic consequences, as documented with respect to familial norms by Fukuyama (1995).

However, wherever these different means of coordination do meet, they cannot, except by chance, result in plan coordination. It is impossible to rely on the principle "Do what has always been done" at the same time as "Do as commanded by a planner" or "Do as best you see fit within your sphere of control". Two different scenarios present themselves for how these principles might meet: one might be embedded in and subordinate to another, or they may abut one another at the edges of their respective arenas. If one is embedded within another, it can simply acquiesce to the demands of the other whenever they conflict. Firms can issue business plans, but markets can force businesses to alter their plans or else face bankruptcy. Bond markets can force sovereign Planners to wholly abandon their ambitions. Traditions can dictate the markets be closed on certain days or never used for certain activities. This kind of subordination of one mechanism to another presents no real challenge.

A more considerable problem arises when two mechanisms meet one another, and neither is obviously subordinated to the other. Consider a religious good, such as mosque's Friday prayer services, provided within a Market-based society. These are not directly organized or provided by market means, irrespective of how much narrow economic efficiency that might bring. It is simply accepted that the traditions involved are either more worthwhile in themselves or better suited to achieving the relevant goals of the Muslim community. To the extent that markets would induce a set of plans that differs from that actually used, there may simply be discoordination. The immovable timing of Friday prayers may make it difficult for Muslims in non-Muslim societies to maintain market-organized employment, with its variable demands on one's time, while also regularly attending the prayer service, forcing them to pick which set of irreconcilable plans to pursue in order to resolve the discoordination.

Given that every society uses Tradition, Planning, and Markets, every society has some degree of discoordination. Except when expanding coordination into hitherto uncoordinated activities, more expansive use of one means of coordination can only be achieved through less reliance on another. Some discoordination is sometimes worthwhile in a manner reminiscent of Grossman and Stiglitz (1980). It is the cost of using multiple means of coordination, what Wagner (1998) refers to as a "clash" along "fault lines" on a "tectonic landscape", an apt metaphor given that living along a fault line is often well worth the risk of earthquakes, unpleasant as they may be.

Markets and LGBTQ flourishing: The intensive margin

Markets promote LGBTQ flourishing. This section and the next discuss several means by which they do so. In this section, I will focus on how more intense use of markets, for example, greater wealth, larger populations, or higher degrees of specialization, enables LGBTQ freedom and flourishing. Here, it bears repeating that although the language of "the Market" has been adopted from Lavoie, what is under discussion includes a broader set of arrangements than monetary exchange, including any mechanism where plans are made and reconciled using individual spheres of control and a universal set of consistent rules (i.e., the rule of law).

The most obvious respect in which markets promote LGBTQ flourishing is in their enabling of wealth generation. Markets endogenously generate wealth by incentivizing product innovation, productive specialization, discovery of productive resources, and more. Although this is not a channel of benefits unique to LGBTQ concerns, it is nonetheless important. Even were there another system that established substantially greater degrees of respect, inclusion, legal recognition, personal security, etc. for LGBTQ individuals, if it endogenously generated little to no wealth, that mechanism would be undesirable for LGBTQ people. Without the means to obtain them, the theoretical possibility and permissibility of many LGBTQ goods is worthless.

Beyond the existential security and material comfort provided by wealth, often it can promote greater personal freedom, as noted by Sen (2011) among others. When a society exists close to the edge of survival, even mild variability of individual circumstances can pose an existential threat by pushing one's production below subsistence. Thus, norms that incentivize rigid adherence to others' expectations can be necessary. With a greater level of wealth, a society can tolerate greater deviation from these norms, "purchasing" individual freedom. This may partially explain why some poorer societies, like India and Bangladesh, have highly institutionalized gender roles for LGBTQ people, such as the hijra, while richer members of those societies opt to join the global LGBTQ community rather than adopt the norms of the traditional categories (Hossain 2022: 25). It is also notable that businesses oriented toward serving LGBTQ patrons are likely to have the goal of de-stigmatizing LGBTQ behavior, inclinations, culture, etc. both within the minds of their patrons (who often may feel shame or fear as a result of internalizing the hostility of a broader culture) and within the broader culture at large.

Markets also promote product variety in a manner that benefits LGBTQ people. Market economies often exhibit nonlinearities in scale, with product variety tied to economies of scale after the manner of a monopolistically competitive industry. As more firms can be sustained by more consumers, greater varieties of products can be brought to market, enabling consumers to tailor their mix of products to their preferences more closely. This mechanism enables LGBTQ individuals to find or even to produce more goods specific to their desires. Whereas a municipality of less than 50,000 residents is unlikely to be able to sustain an LGBTQ bar, a city of 5,000,000 may be able to have not only multiple such bars but bars catering to specific segments of that demographic, whether by age, income, gender, relationship status, or non-demographic characteristics of consumer demand. This same mechanism applies to many other LGBTQ-related varieties of goods and services such as healthcare, movies, clothing, matchmaking, literature, and home décor.

The greater variety of LGBTQ products and the greater wealth of LGBTQ persons can depend on there being a critical mass of LGBTQ people able to monetarily express their economic demands, which implies a benefit from a greater population, assuming a constant or rising proportion of LGBTQ persons in the population. Markets and the attendant institutions that facilitate them have been critical for the development of such levels of wealth and technologies as make the large populations of developed societies sustainable. Although a significant amount of the fall in mortality that came with modern economic development actually resulted from significant public health projects undertaken by governments (Deaton 2013). it was the same institutional changes that facilitated markets that also induced those governments to make such public health investments. Furthermore, other aspects of sustaining a large population are dependent on market organization, like producing large quantities of food, clothing, and shelter.

As classically articulated by Becker (1957), more competitive environments strongly disincentivize discrimination on the basis of factors irrelevant to the standard on which agents compete. In more competitive environments, employers will have little choice but to avoid discriminating against LGBTQ job applicants or face a more limited applicant pool, meaning fewer potentially productive employees. Although this will not necessarily eliminate employer discrimination, as some employers may simply be willing to take lower profits in exchange for indulging their desire to discriminate, it does force employers to bear much of the costs of such discrimination and reward non-discriminatory employers. There is empirical evidence that the wage gap between straight and gay men is smaller in more economically free (and presumably therefore more competitive) regions among US regions where anti-gay discrimination is common (Christafore and Leguizamon 2019). This mechanism does not eliminate discrimination on the part of consumers, but a related mechanism may, as discussed below.

Societies with more intensive use of markets are likely to be wealthier, have greater product variety, larger LGBTQ populations, less reliance on restrictive social norms, and less employment discrimination on the basis of LGBTQ status, but the discussion so far has not mentioned the ability LGBTQ individuals (and/or their allies) have to promote their own freedom and acceptance. All of the above contribute to their ability to do so. As discussed by Rojas (2024), wealth is simply a necessity for producing social change. It is borderline tautologous to state that greater resources enable groups to achieve their ends. Markets' capacity for wealth generation gives LGBTQ individuals greater resources with which to promote social change, for instance by financing lawsuits, providing salaries for professional activists, or purchasing media space to raise visibility. Greater product variety can include representative media, social movement symbols (e.g., pride flags), spaces for community building and organization, etc. all of which can be tools for promoting LGBTQ interests. Greater LGBTQ population enables larger amounts of interpersonal support within LGBTQ communities and a lower average fixed costs for many activities. It becomes more feasible to cluster geographically to take advantage of scale-related nonlinearities, as these might not be worth moving to exploit if the resultant population were smaller.

Reduced reliance on traditional norms lowers the cost of changing people's expectations about how LGBTQ people will behave, making provocative activism and negotiation of individualized social expectations less costly. To the extent that employers might hire LGBTQ individuals in spite of consumers' desire to discriminate, this may expose consumers to LGBTQ individuals and reduce their hostility by demonstrating the potential for mutually beneficial interactions. A similar mechanism is described in Coyne et al. (2007) with respect to the racial integration of professional baseball players. More intensive use of markets certainly empowers LGBTQ communities to promote their own well-being.

Markets and LGBTQ freedom: The extensive margin

In addition to higher volume, more competitive, more specialized markets providing benefits, a greater extent of reliance on markets in any given society facilitates LGBTQ freedom. When markets coordinate more activities, LGBTQ people have greater freedom to do as they see fit. Necessarily, for one area of social activity to become coordinated by markets, the other mechanisms must give way, so this section will compare the LGBTQ freedom permitted by the alternative coordination mechanisms to that permitted by markets.

Tradition versus the market

Though a Eurocentric perspective may overlook it, it is not impossible for Tradition to permit a variety of institutionalized LGBTQ roles. These may be more permissive than the wholesale suppression characteristic of the normative stance of historic Anglo-American and European societies. Institutionalized third genders exist in a variety of cultures including the *hijra* of South Asia (Reddy 2005; Sharma 2009); *calalai*, *calabai*, and *bissu* in Indonesia (Davies 2010); *travestis* in Brazil (Diehl et al. 2017); *muxes* in Mexico (Ramirez and Munar 2022); *fa'afafine* in Samoa (Schmidt 2010); and many others. Many of these identities may be quite fulfilling for the individuals who take them on, and they may coordinate plans effectively while enabling total fulfillment of an individual's LGBTQ interests. However, the social recognition of these genders should not be taken as a sign of historic or contemporary acceptance of individuals who express them (Chisholm 2018). Many members of these groups face social stigmatization, a variety of kinds of discrimination, distinct health challenges, social isolation, and more difficulties in spite of their recognized traditional identity and role. Recognition of a social category and expectations aligned in accordance with that role do not necessitate respect for the occupants of those positions, much less their flourishing.

Because, unlike the Market, Tradition lacks robust mechanisms for endogenous social change, LGBTQ freedom is impossible to promote while strictly adhering to it for coordinating plans. Tradition must assign individuals social roles that dictate their life plan, permitting little to no deviation. This implies that such social roles must be transmitted across generations, and the complexity of life-plans and the structure of society as a whole is therefore limited by humans' ability to transmit norms. Highly tailored roles that closely match what the transfeminist activist and biologist Julia Serrano calls "intrinsic inclinations" (Serano 2016) are therefore difficult for Tradition to sustain.

By contrast, market societies permit an enormous variety of social roles, and the experimentation with gender and sexuality they facilitate can endogenously create enormously varied sets of social categories for individuals to perform in the sense described by Judith Butler (1990). Although, as mentioned, Tradition can contain roles for those outside the cisheterosexual majority, those roles, in addition to often being marginalized, are not as varied as the labels seen in market societies: butch women, transgender nonbinaries, lesbian separatists, gay femboys, queer asexuals ... in short, all the identities glossed in the "+" suffix to the LGBT label.

Tradition, in order to maintain the homogeneity necessary for intergenerational norm transmission, also requires relatively small communities. This is both because others' social positions must be readily recognizable and because Tradition can only supply the means to sustain relatively small populations. As mentioned earlier, larger populations enable greater specialization and the production of goods more specific to even minority populations, partially by spreading fixed costs over larger groups. To the extent that a social arena requires small groups of relatively homogenous agents, less specialized patterns of activity are possible and permanent minority groups like LGBTQ communities are unlikely to have their needs met as well as is possible in that arena under Market organization.

Lastly, the type of overarching rules governing the Market simply permits greater varieties of choices than Tradition. Because markets require predictable, general rules that enable individual decision-making, their institutional prerequisites are more permissive than the relatively specific dictates of traditional norms. One's life plan can be flexible, permitting experimentation with or even open defiance of social convention. The term "queer", when not used as a slur, arguably refers to a pattern of behavior that defies categorization under traditional norms and is therefore definitionally incompatible with a strictly Tradition-based coordination mechanism. Markets, on the other hand, permit anything from adherence to historic, gendered traditions to ignoring them completely to using them as a substrate for manipulation in a subversive gender performance. Markets are not totally neutral with respect to a society's moral beliefs and normative lifestyles, but they do permit greater freedom of individual expression.

Planning versus markets

In the contemporary developed world, it is unlikely that Tradition would be seriously proposed as a means for coordinating whole societies, but Planning is more likely to be put forward both as a means to coordinate society and as a means to LGBTQ liberation. Non-comprehensive planning of the type advocated by most members of the contemporary political left is particularly popular. Markets, nonetheless, are superior to Planning in permitting LGBTQ freedom and promoting LGBTQ individuals' flourishing. Non-comprehensive planning falls prey to many of the problems that arise in comprehensive planning, only on a smaller scale and with greater intrinsic instability due to social discoordination at Planning's interface with the Market (Ikeda 2004).

Here, it might be objected that LGBTQ inclusion in markets is merely a form of "homonormativity" or "homocapitalism" that, rather than pursuing liberation, simply reifies, commodifies, and profits from the exploitation of LGBTQ identities to which the capitalists are in reality indifferent, if not actively seeking to disarm through assimilation (Stoffel 2021).[3] However, Markets require less legibility and categorization than does Planning (and, of course, substantially less than does Tradition). It may be true that for mass production of LGBTQ goods to occur, there must be legibility in some sense, but the fact that Markets enable individuals to plan their lives as they see fit subject to the same rules as anyone else means LGBTQ individuals and communities can invent novel categories, put them forward to a kind of test in the eyes of those whom they care to interact with, and thereby endogenously introduce novel categorical schema. Mass culture likely requires categorization irrespective of coordination mechanism, but because markets permit the freedom for individuals to introduce novel categories without the permission of a societal planner, they permit the upset of standard expectations in ways other systems do not. Furthermore, to the extent that homocapitalism is problematic because it needs the neoliberal state, Markets do not contribute to homocapitalism, as Market organization is inconsistent with the planning power of the state and expansion of markets is diminution of the state.

Among the biggest weaknesses of Planning in general is the limited knowledge of planners. This leads to centrally planned systems failing to deliver significant improvement in the standard of living offered to their residents, but, relatedly, it means planners will struggle to know what the needs of unusual populations will be. While markets incentivize specialization, Planning requires knowledge that can only be obtained via specialization in specific areas while at the same time requiring that those planning society specialize only in activity of planning. This leads to a situation where although the planners may know the general nature of the general goods most people require (food, clothing, shelter, healthcare, entertainment) they do not know the way to provide these in particular local instances or according to the needs of atypical consumers like LGBTQ populations.

Many of the deficiencies of Planning for LGBTQ populations are ways Planning, in practice, differs less from Tradition than is often recognized. Beyond the lack of knowledge of the particular circumstances of time and place that both systems exhibit, both have a problem of a limited conception of possibilities. Planning not only lacks the ability to muster detailed knowledge, it limits the social system to patterns of behavior of which the planners conceive. The limited conceptual perspective of the planners can impose boundaries on the pattern-disruption famously attendant to freer social systems (Nozick 1974, ch. 7). The USSR can be interpreted as a form of Russian empire under Communist, rather than Tsarist, rule (Grigor and Martin 2001). In addition to promoting minority ethnic groups' national identities (Martin 2001) the Soviets promoted Russian nationalism and folk heroes as a means of promoting patriotic sentiment (Brandenberger 2001). These illustrate the way Planning requires the regimentation of society. The regimentation of society requires adherence to a manageable set of conceptual roles within the social order. The limitation of social roles leads to suppression of transgressive identities, including LGBTQ identities. Given the extreme improbability of substantive LGBTQ representation among planners, not to mention the internal heterogeneity of LGBTQ identities, planners ought to be the object of deep wariness when it comes to LGBTQ liberation. The biases and prejudices of the planners inevitably seep into social planning, leading to such fatuous claims as those listed at the beginning of this chapter, that homosexuality and fascism or homosexuality and communism are ineluctably linked.

Historical examples of planned societies' treatment of LGBTQ illustrate the point. In the *Queer Encounters with Communist Power*, the author argues that "The Communist Party of Czechoslovakia of course did not support diversity and feared identities that questioned the ideological foundations of state socialism" (Sokolová 2021: 16). This was, notably, not something particular to the state's treatment of LGBTQ people, who were not formally targeted by the state more than any other group perceived as such a threat. Although Sokolová argues this is evidence that the state did not oppress LGBTQ people in particular, it is nonetheless an example of how "Historically rooted homophobic sentiments of mainstream society … blended together with the systematic destruction of freedoms and individuality, affecting all people regardless of their sexual orientation". Even if a planned society nominally commits itself to equal rights for LGBTQ people, the political economy of Planning often still requires quelling demands for the state to live up to that supposed commitment.

As already mentioned in the introduction, the USSR re-criminalized homosexuality under Stalin. In the flurry of institutional changes in 1917, the Bolsheviks had removed the tsarist laws against sodomy, but by 1934 Stalin had been convinced by the chief of the secret police that it was necessary to recriminalize it to prevent Nazi infiltration of young male Soviet social circles (Alexander 2023: 6). When a Scottish self-identified communist wrote to him pleading for better treatment for homosexuals, Stalin's reaction was to write label him an "idiot and degenerate" and dismiss his letter entirely (Alexander 2023: 23).

As in Czechoslovakia, the Russian state attempted to stamp out all challenges to its ideology, and its commitment to Stalin as the personal embodiment of the society's aspirations was so strong that Freudian psychoanalysis was banned. Nonetheless, some homosexual men were so desperate to escape persecution and internalized shame that they sought out illegal Freudian therapy in Siberia to attempt to become heterosexual (Alexander 2023, ch. 6). The situation for LGBTQ people did not substantially improve even after Stalin's death. Punishment for homosexual behavior in the Gulag colonies was made more intense during Khrushchev's rule. New psychotherapeutic "cures" were attempted. Soviet doctors were in the dark about AIDS at a time when US and European doctors were well aware of the poorly understood condition. When LGBTQ communities in the West were organizing to demand rights and public concern for their fight against AIDS, the Soviets doubled down on entrapping, blaming, and jailing LGBTQ people.

As part of a national social engineering campaign, Communist Cuba in the 1970s undertook to force those deemed threats to the Revolution to transform into model citizens through socially useful labor (Madero 2016). Homosexuals were categorized into different groupings depending on the degree to which their homosexuality manifested in socially disapproved ways, with one needing to behave "normally" and not desire to leave Cuba in order to qualify as the least concerning type. Many homosexuals were explicitly regarded as counterrevolutionaries and understood to be insufficiently masculine, with the solution drawn from Mao Zedong's writings to make them work in order to convert them into "new men" or, similarly, to masculinize them through forced labor in military production camps. Again, the need to enforce conformity to a single societal plan and the power over economic production that a planning state can wield rapidly becomes a powerful threat to those who are socio-culturally disfavored.[4]

Comprehensive planning may be more prone to regimentation and outright failure than non-comprehensive planning, but the latter is not immune from it. Austrian economists have argued that partial planning is unstable, its practical implementation leading to a continuous lurching toward and away from comprehensive planning (Ikeda 2004), and its justificatory logic lacking any stopping point that would negate its entailment of autocratic, comprehensive planning (Hayek [1944] 2007). Notably, by politicizing large areas of an economic system, partial planning can still remove autonomy from LGBTQ individuals and hinder their flourishing.

One example of these "dynamics of interventionism" and their complicating effect on LGBTQ groups' well-being, one may consider the healthcare industry. Before legal recognition of gay marriages in the United States, health insurance coverage of unmarried LGBT partners was a significant problem. Where a heterosexual couple might have been able to extend health insurance coverage through one spouse's employer to cover the other spouse (and thereby obtain tax-exempt insurance benefits), same-sex couples might have had to get coverage for one member of the couple in the tightly regulated, artificially scarce insurance "market". If the US healthcare market were less regulated and insurance coverage worked like catastrophic insurance (rather than a complex maze of financial regulations, healthcare provision regulations, subsidies, state and federal programs, industry lobbying groups, and more), it is easy to imagine the provision of LGBTQ healthcare services in a manner much less dependent on state recognition of LGBTQ relationships. The debate over the reasonableness of gender affirmation care for minors continues, but it should be of little doubt that the competence for evaluating it lies more with doctors and parents than with legislatures.

However, for all the problems of partial planning that do exist in the United States and Western Europe, it is worth noting that these are predominantly market-based societies with robust LGBTQ cultures and communities. They are, in many cases, some of the world's societies with the longest exposure to Market-based plan coordination and some of the most commerce-friendly societies on Earth. The fact that they are also sites of some of the most well-developed LGBTQ communities and markets is unlikely to be a coincidence.

Conclusion

Every society requires a means of coordinating its members' plans. Tradition and Planning supply neither the ability to sustain a complex society nor the flexibility to attempt experiments in living that enable minority communities, especially transgressive minorities like LGBTQ populations, to achieve their own ends and advocate for their own causes. Markets, on the other hand, provide both of these. More activities being Market-coordinated and greater amounts of activity in those social arenas would facilitate LGBTQ freedom and flourishing.

Neither the Market nor LGBTQ freedom and flourishing are automatically expanding, though they can be mutually reinforcing. The degree of freedom obtained in some developed countries should be taken as a good sign for the future of those in developing societies. The demonstration that a wealthy society can afford to not only tolerate but substantially include LGBTQ populations may generate a cultural spillover effect to developing nations that can escape the stultifying norms of Tradition as they become wealthier. At the same time, we should expect authoritarian states to continue to suppress LGBTQ identities, as recently seen in China (Ellis-Petersen 2016; Economist 2024; Wang 2024). To the extent that such authoritarian states and Market coordination are inconsistent in the long run, there may yet be hope for LGBTQ communities if the successes of marketization lead to declines in support for authoritarian governance. For this reason, LGBTQ advocates ought to support intercultural exchange, both metaphorical and literal, with such societies, as exposure to a culture of openness, trade, and ongoing experimentation may undermine such authoritarian states.

The headwinds running counter to LGBTQ freedom and flourishing may also come from less intensive use of markets. As the global population is expected to fall over the next century, fewer LGBTQ individuals in absolute terms may mean worse treatment as the average fixed costs of advocacy and specialized goods rise. In this sense, the wealth produced in markets and the consequent population decline due to the demographic transition may actually work counter to LGBTQ interests. However, if Markets are sustained or expanded enough to continue to provide a rising standard of living in some societies, it may be that those higher average costs are smaller as a percentage of the average LGBTQ person's income, or new tools may be invented that reduce those costs. As suggested by mainline political economy, LGBTQ entrepreneurial alertness within the Market may provide the means to LGBTQ liberation even in the face of substantial challenges.

Notes

1 Attitudes in the medieval Islamic world were more permissive, though certainly not approving.
2 It may be tempting to say Planning is monocentric and top down, whereas Tradition and Markets are polycentric and bottom-up. This is close to the truth, but it is an oversimplification, as even centrally planned economies often decentralize their planning to at least some extent by delegating planning to subcomponents of the state or having the two sides of a pair in a hierarchical relationship adjust their plans around each other's abilities, information, and constraints (Roberts 1969).
3 Aside from the main point made in this paragraph, it is also worth noting that the alternative to having large economic entities seek to profit from interacting with a minority group is having them regard interactions with those groups as either threatening or things indifferent. Regarding others as potential benefactors is likely preferable.
4 It is worth acknowledging at this point that market-based societies were not innocent of mistreatment of homosexuals during this period, but they were often less harsh in a variety of ways. The United States was faster but more piecemeal than the Soviet Union in removing and relaxing enforcement of sodomy laws, for example. What makes Planned societies especially dangerous in this regard is the power the state has to repress agitation for acceptance.

References

Alexander, Rustam. 2023. *Red Closet: The Hidden History of Gay Oppression in the USSR*. Manchester, UK: Manchester University Press.

Badgett, M. V. Lee, Kees Waaldijk, and Yana van der Meulen Rodgers. 2019. "The Relationship Between LGBT Inclusion and Economic Development: Macro-Level Evidence." *World Development* 120: 1–14.

Becker, Gary S. 1957. *The Economics of Discrimination*. Chicago, IL: University of Chicago Press.

Boettke, Peter J. 2001. *Calculation and Coordination: Essays on Socialism and Transitional Political Economy*. New York, NY: Routledge.

Boettke, Peter J. 2002. "Information and Knowledge: Austrian Economics in Search of Its Uniqueness." *Review of Austrian Economics* 15 (4): 263–274.

Brandenberger, David. 2001. "It is Imperative to Advance Russian Nationalism as the First Priority" Debates within the Stalinist Ideological Establishment, 1941–1945." In *A State of Nations: Empire and Nation-Making in the Age of Lenin and Stalin*, edited by Ronald Grigor and Suny Terry Martin, 275–299. Oxford, UK: Oxford University Press.

Butler, Judith. 1990. *Gender Trouble: Feminism and the Subversion of Identity*. New York, NY: Routledge.

Chamlee-Wright, Emily. 2007. "The Long Road Back: Signal Noise in the Post-Katrina Context." *Independent Review* 12 (2): 235–259.

Chamlee-Wright, Emily. 2008. "Signaling Effects of Commercial and Civil Society in Post-Katrina Reconstruction." *International Journal of Social Economics* 35 (8): 615–626.

Chamlee-Wright, Emily. 2010. *The Cultural and Political Economy of Recovery: Social Learning in a Post-Disaster Environment*. London, UK: Routledge.

Chamlee-Wright, Emily, and Justus A. Myers. 2008. "Discovery and Social Learning in Non-Priced Environments: An Austrian View of Social Network Theory." *Review of Austrian Economics* 21 (2): 151–166.

Chisholm, Jennifer. 2018. "Muxe, Two-Spirits, and the Myth of Indigenous Transgender Acceptance." *International Journal of Critical Indigenous Studies* 11 (1): 21–35.

Christafore, David, and Susane Leguizamon. 2019. "Taste-Based Discrimination, Tolerance and the Wage Gap: When Does Economic Freedom Help Gay Men?" *Kyklos* 72 (3): 21–35.

Coyne, Christopher J., Justin P. Isaacs, Jeremy T. Schwartz, and Anthony M. Carilli. 2007. "Put Me In, Coach, I'm Ready to Play." *Review of Austrian Economics* 20 (4): 237–246.

Crego, David, and Salter, Alexander. 2025. "Clement Counsels Corinth: Efficient Hierarchy and the Rise of Christianity." *Public Choice*, https://doi.org/10.1007/s11127-025-01341-x.

Davies, Sharyn Graham. 2010. *Gender Diversity in Indonesia: Sexuality, Islam and Queer Selves*. London, UK: Routledge.

Deaton, Angus. 2013. *The Great Escape: Health, Wealth and the Origins of Inequality*. Princeton, NJ: Princeton University Press.

Diehl, Alessandra, Denise Leite Vieira, Marina Milograna Zaneti, Ana Fanganiello, Pratap Sharan, Rebecca Robles, and Jair de Jesus Mari. 2017. "Social Stigma, Legal and Public Health Barriers Faced by the Third Gender Phenomena in Brazil, India and Mexico: Travestis, Hijras and Muxes." *International Journal of Social Psychiatry* 63 (5): 389–399.

Economist. 2024. "Roxie, One of China's Few Lesbian Bars, Closes Its Doors." June 27, https://www.economist.com/china/2024/06/27/roxie-one-of-chinas-few-lesbian-bars-closes-its-doors.

Edenborg, Emil. 2020. "Russian LGBT Politics and Rights." *Oxford Research Encyclopedias: Politics*. Oxford, UK: Oxford University Press.

Ellis-Petersen, Hannah. 2016. "China Bans Depictions of Gay People on Television." Guardian, March 4, https://www.theguardian.com/tv-and-radio/2016/mar/04/china-bans-gay-people-television-clampdown-xi-jinping-censorship.

Frencia, Cintia, and Daniel Gaido. 2020. "Marxismo y Liberación Homosexual: Magnus Hirschfeld, La Socialdemocracia Alemana de Preguerra y El Gobierno Soviético Temprano." In *Historia Del Socialismo Internacional*, edited by Daniel Gaido, Manuel Quiroga and Velia Luparello, 89–120. Santiago, Chile: Ariadna Ediciones.

Friedman, Jeffrey. 2019. *Power Without Knowledge: A Critique of Technocracy*. New York, NY: Oxford University Press.

Fukuyama, Francis. 1995. *Trust: The Social Virtues and the Creation of Prosperity*. New York, NY: Free Press.

Giles, Geoffrey J. 2002. "The Denial of Homosexuality: Same-Sex Incidents in Himmler's SS and Police." *Journal of the History of Sexuality* 11 (1/2): 256–290.

Grier, Kevin B., and Robin M. Grier. 2021. "The Washington Consensus Works: Causal Effects of Reform, 1970–2015." *Journal of Comparative Economics* 49 (1): 59–72.

Grigor, Ronald, and Suny Terry Martin. 2001. *A State of Nations: Empire and Nation-Making in the Age of Lenin and Stalin*. Oxford, UK: Oxford University Press.

Grossman, Sanford J., and Joseph E. Stiglitz. 1980. "On the Impossibility of Informationally Efficient Markets." *American Economic Review* 70 (3): 393–408.

Hasnas, John. 2005. "Hayek, the Common Law, and Fluid Drive." *New York University Journal of Law & Liberty* 1: 79–110.

Hayek, Friedrich A. 1945. "The Use of Knowledge in Society." *American Economic Review* 35 (4): 519–530.

Hayek, Friedrich A. 1948. "The Meaning of Competition." In *Individualism and Economic Order*, edited by Friedrich A. Hayek, 92–106. Chicago, IL: University of Chicago Press.

Hayek, Friedrich A. [1960] 2011. "The Constitution of Liberty." In *The Collected Works of F. A. Hayek: Volume 17*, edited by Ronald Hamowy. Chicago, IL: University of Chicago Press.

Hayek, Friedrich A. [1944] 2007. "The Road to Serfdom: Text and Documents." In *The Collected Works of F. A. Hayek: Volume 2*, edited by Bruce Caldwell. Chicago, IL: University of Chicago Press.

Hekma, Gert, Ossterhuis Harry, and James Steakley. 1995. "Leftist Sexual Politics and Homosexuality: A Historical Overview." *Journal of Homosexuality* 29 (2–3): 1–40.

Hossain, Adnan. 2022. *Beyond Emasculation: Pleasure and Power in the Making of Hijra in Bangladesh*. Cambridge, UK: Cambridge University Press.

Ikeda, Sanford. 2004. "The Dynamics of Interventionism." *Advances in Austrian Economics* 8: 21–57.

Jensen, Erik N. 2002. "The Pink Triangle and Political Consciousness: Gays, Lesbians, and the Memory of Nazi Persecution." *Journal of the History of Sexuality* 11 (1/2): 319–349.

Johnson, David K. 2023. *The Lavender Scare: The Cold War Persecution of Gays and Lesbians in the Federal Government*. Chicago, IL: University of Chicago Press.

Karras, Ruth Mazo. 2017. *Sexuality in Medieval Europe: Doing Unto Others*. New York, NY: Routledge.

Koppl, Roger. 2002. *Big Players and the Economic Theory of Expectations*. New York, NY: Palgrave Macmillan.

Lavoie, Don. [1985] 2016. *National Economic Planning: What Is Left?* Arlington, VA: Mercatus Center at George Mason University.

Lofthouse, Jordan K., and Peter J. Boettke. 2025. "Governance with, Not Government Over Citizens." *European Economic Review* 179: 105147.

Madero, Abel Sierra. 2016. "'El Trabajo Os Hará Hombres': Masculinzación Nacional, Trabajo Forzado y Control Social En Cuba Durante Los Años Sesenta." *Cuban Studies* 44 (1): 309–349.

Martin, Terry. 2001. "An Affirmative Action Empire: The Soviet Union as the Highest Form of Imperialism." In *A State of Nations: Empire and Nation-Making in the Age of Lenin and Stalin*, edited by Ronald Grigor and Suny Terry Martin, 67–90. Oxford, UK: Oxford University Press.

Mises, Ludwig von. [1920] 1935. "Economic Calculation in the Socialist Commonwealth." In *Collectivist Economic Planning: Critical Studies on the Possibilities of Socialism*, edited by Friedrich A. Hayek, 87–130. London, UK: Routledge & Kegan Paul.

Nozick, Robert. 1974. *Anarchy, State, and Utopia*. New York, NY: Basic Books.

Ramirez, Jacobo, and Ana María Munar. 2022. "Hybrid Gender Colonization: The Case of Muxes." *Gender, Work & Organization* 29 (6): 1868–1889.

Reddy, Gayatri. 2005. *With Respect to Sex: Negotiating Hijra Identity in South India*. Chicago, IL: University of Chicago Press.

Roberts, Paul Craig. 1969. "The Polycentric Soviet Economy." *Journal of Law & Economics* 12 (1): 163–179.

Rojas, Fabio. 2024. "Race, Freedom, and Social Change." In *Sociology and Classical Liberalism in Dialogue: Freedom Is Something We Do Together*, edited by Fabio Rojas and Charlotta Stern, 45–66. Lanham, MD: Lexington Books.

Schmidt, Johanna. 2010. *Migrating Genders*. London, UK: Routledge.

Scott, James C. 1998. *Seeing Like a State: How Certain Schemes to Improve the Human Condition Have Failed*. New Haven, CT: Yale University Press.

Sen, Amartya. 2011. *Development as Freedom*. New York, NY: Random House.

Serano, Julia. 2016. *Whipping Girl: A Transsexual Woman on Sexism and the Scapegoating of Femininity*. New York, NY: Seal Press.

Sharma, Satish Kumar. 2009. *Hijras: The Labelled Deviants*. New Delhi, India: Gyan Publishing.

Sokolová, Věra. 2021. *Queer Encounters with Communist Power: Non-Heterosexual Lives and the State in Czechoslovakia, 1948–1989*. Prague, Czech Republic: Karolinum Press.

Stoffel, Alexander. 2021. "'Homocapitalism': Analytical Precursors and Future Directions." *International Feminist Journal of Politics* 23 (1): 173–178.

Storr, Virgil Henry, Stefanie Haeffele-Balch, and Laura E. Grube. 2015. *Community Revival in the Wake of Disaster*. New York, NY: Palgrave Macmillan.

Storr, Virgil Henry, Stefanie Haeffele-Balch, and Laura E. Grube. 2017. "Social Capital and Social Learning after Hurricane Sandy." *Review of Austrian Economics* 30 (4): 447–467.

Wagner, R. E. 1998. "Social Democracy, Societal Tectonics, and Parasitical Pricing." *Constitutional Political Economy* 9 (2): 105–111.

Wang, Vivian. 2024. "Xi Jinping's Recipe for Total Control: An Army of Eyes and Ears." New York Times, May 25, https://www.nytimes.com/2024/05/25/world/asia/china-surveillance-xi.html.

3

QUEER LIBERATION THROUGH ENTREPRENEURSHIP

Jordan K. Lofthouse and Zane Austin Willard

Since the founding of the United States, social and political life has been nominally based on the liberal principles of limited government, equality under the law, and broad individual freedom. However, the rights and privileges of a truly liberal society were withheld from many groups of people—including women, people of color, Native Americans, immigrants, and LGBTQ individuals—until recently. Of course, many challenges still exist in fully realizing the promises of a liberal society, but there has been undeniable progress in the expansion of individual freedom and equality under the law (Boettke 2021; Novak 2021).

Like other oppressed groups in the United States, queer people lacked many rights and privileges, experiencing discrimination, stigmatization, and violence. To contend with these problems, the LGBTQ rights movement has focused on two main goals: (1) securing formal legal rights for autonomy in self-expression and personal relationships, and (2) achieving broader acceptance from mainstream society. Since the 1960s, queer liberation has had many successes within formal and informal contexts. The American Psychiatric Association no longer classifies homosexuality as a mental disorder. Conversion therapy has been banned in many states. Many churches are changing their rhetoric regarding LGBTQ people. The U.S. Supreme Court declared sodomy laws unconstitutional in Lawrence v. Texas in 2003. The "Don't Ask, Don't Tell" policy in the U.S. military was repealed in 2010. Queer cultural products are highly popular across non-queer audiences. Many large corporations now explicitly cater to LGBTQ customers and have so zealously signaled their openness to queerness that they have been accused of "pandering" and "rainbow washing" (Ginder and Byun 2015; Ciszek and Lim 2021; Schopper et al. 2025). Such tectonic social shifts in only a few decades are remarkable, even though many ongoing challenges still exist.

DOI: 10.4324/9781003615781-3

In the queer studies literature, no clear consensus exists regarding how queer people have gained rights and privileges over time. Scholars have identified several overlapping processes shaping queer liberation, including grassroots mobilization, coalitional politics, so-called "assimilationist" strategies, normalization through visibility, political pressure, and judicial activism. Many queer studies scholars have therefore expressed skepticism toward framing queer liberation as a straightforward march of progress, emphasizing instead its unevenness, exclusions, and setbacks (see D'Emilio 1983; Walters 2001; Armstrong 2002; Freeman 2010; Eng 2010; Franke 2015; Fischer 2019).

We agree that queer liberation has been shaped by multiple, overlapping processes and that progress has not been uniformly experienced. However, queer studies scholarship has tended to underemphasize the institutional frameworks and agents of change that have contributed to the expansion of queer rights and privileges. In particular, despite a rich body of work on LGBTQ rights and visibility, the field has largely underexamined the role of market processes in queer social change. Much of queer studies' critical attention has focused on the state, law, normativity, and discourse, with markets most often framed as sites of commodification, depoliticization, or assimilation under the banner of neoliberalism (Walters 2001; Duggan 2002; Puar 2007; Eng 2010). While these critiques offer important insights into the limits of queer progress, they often treat markets as secondary or corrosive forces rather than as institutional contexts through which social change unfolds. As a result, queer studies has rarely examined how markets, entrepreneurial activity, and processes of exchange have contributed to shifts in visibility, community formation, and cultural legitimacy for LGBTQ individuals. This omission does not negate the field's critical contributions—instead, it points to an analytical gap regarding the institutional mechanisms through which queer liberation has advanced. By bringing insights from liberal political economy into conversation with queer studies, this chapter supplements existing accounts by theorizing markets—and the entrepreneurs who operate within them—as consequential for institutional and cultural change.

In this chapter, we supplement the existing queer studies literature by introducing useful insights from mainline political economy (MPE) and queer classical liberalism, particularly the insights about institutions and entrepreneurship. We argue that the extension of liberal rights and privileges to queer individuals has happened relatively quickly due to entrepreneurs who have reshaped formal and informal institutions. Entrepreneurs play a critical role in social progress because they are the agents of change in a society who are alert to and seize previously undiscovered opportunities. In the economics literature, entrepreneurship has been well theorized in market settings, and scholars associated with MPE have built on that foundation by theorizing about nonmarket entrepreneurship in political, social, cultural, and ideological settings (Kirzner 1973, 1997; Dees et al. 2001; Boettke and Coyne 2002, 2003; Alvord et al. 2004; Shockley et al. 2006; Storr et al. 2015; Aligica 2019; Cheang and Palmer 2023).

All entrepreneurship occurs within institutional and cultural contexts. Institutions, as formal and informal social rules, shape expectations and specify the incentives and constraints that individuals face. Additionally, culture is a shared set of meanings that shape how people interpret the world around them and how they evaluate opportunities. Entrepreneurs act *within* institutional and cultural contexts, but entrepreneurs can also *reshape* institutions and culture over time. In other words, entrepreneurial action can shift and steer a society's shared meanings, beliefs, ideologies, rules, and organizations. Thus, theories of social change must incorporate entrepreneurship, institutions, and culture (Geertz 1973; North 1990, 2005; Boettke and Coyne 2002; Ostrom 2005; Boettke et al. 2008; Aligica and Boettke 2011; Grube and Storr 2015; Cheang and Palmer 2023).

This chapter provides an overview of five categories of entrepreneurship, and then examines how they have changed formal and informal institutions to bring about social change for the benefit of LGBTQ individuals. Market entrepreneurs have used the profit motive to cater to the needs and wants of queer individuals, providing them with goods and services, as well as increasing cultural visibility and acceptance. Political entrepreneurs have advocated for and facilitated legal reforms that have eliminated discriminatory laws. Social entrepreneurs have created clubs, associations, organizations, and nonprofits that have advocated for social change and provided community for queer individuals. Cultural entrepreneurs have shifted the way that queer people have been presented in popular culture, which has led to the mainstreaming of traditionally queer artforms and queer expressions. Ideological entrepreneurs have helped to shift mindsets and beliefs, leading to broader tolerance and acceptance of queer people.

However, entrepreneurship does not guarantee social progress. Within certain institutional or cultural contexts, entrepreneurship can be unproductive or destructive (Baumol 1990; Sobel 2008; Smith and Yandle 2014; Holcombe 2018). In recent years, entrepreneurship has been responsible for backsliding that has curtailed LGBTQ rights in some places. For example, political entrepreneurs have implemented a slate of explicitly anti-trans laws since the 2010s, such as North Carolina's 2016 infamous "Bathroom Bill," the Trump administrations' trans military bans, and legislation banning access to gender-affirming healthcare for trans youth. These are political wins in primarily conservative areas, and such laws have negative impacts on the physical and mental well-being of queer people (Horne et al. 2022; Barbee et al. 2022; Brightman et al. 2024).

By orienting itself within the broader framework of queer classical liberalism, this chapter offers two distinct contributions to the queer studies literature. First, it provides a theoretical basis for the successes of the queer rights movement by synthesizing ideas regarding entrepreneurship, institutional analysis, critical media studies, and queer studies. Using a multidisciplinary approach, the chapter examines how entrepreneurs across market and nonmarket domains have led to social and legal progress for queer individuals. Second, the chapter provides a rich collection of real-world examples illustrating how different types of entrepreneurship have contributed to LGBTQ liberation in the United States.

In the next section, we review the literature on entrepreneurship to provide a theory of institutional reform and social change as it relates to queer liberation. Following that, we examine many real-world cases of how entrepreneurs in market and nonmarket contexts have served as the agents of queer liberation in the United States. Then, we discuss the potential tradeoffs and dark sides of entrepreneurship as they relate to queer liberation, especially unproductive or destructive forms of entrepreneurship. Finally, we conclude with the implications of this research.

Social change through entrepreneurship

Social change is the transformation of cultural, social, economic, or political activity over time, which can happen at various speeds and levels (Novak 2021). Social change may be desirable or repugnant, depending on the normative framework used for evaluating both means and outcomes. From a liberal perspective, social change is desirable when it expands individual freedom, promotes legal equality, upholds the rule of law, places limitations on arbitrary government action, and increases toleration within society.

Using the framework of liberal political economy—sometimes called MPE—social change arises from the interactions of entrepreneurs, institutions, and culture (see Boettke 2012; Storr et al. 2015; Grube and Storr 2015; Boettke et al. 2016; Aligica et al. 2019; Novak 2021). Entrepreneurs are the agents of change in a society who are alert to and seize previously unrecognized or unexploited opportunities. As economists Virgil Henry Storr, Stefanie Haeffele-Balch, and Laura E. Grube (2015: 11) argue, the entrepreneur is

> a central figure in most episodes of social change. Of course, the legal environment in which entrepreneurs must operate, the budget constraints that delimit their options, and the social ties and other factors they must consider before they can choose a course of action, all shape entrepreneurial activity.

Institutions are formal and informal social rules that shape expectations and specify the incentives and constraints that individuals face (North 1990; Ostrom 2005). The term "culture" has many connotations, but for the purposes of this chapter, we adopt the definition of a socially shared set of meanings that shape how people, including entrepreneurs, interpret the world around them and how they evaluate opportunities (Geertz 1973; Grube and Storr 2015). Entrepreneurs are culturally embedded and operate within an institutional context, but they can also change institutions and shift cultural meanings. In short, entrepreneurship *is shaped by* and also *shapes* institutions and culture.

The academic literature has identified at least five kinds of entrepreneurship: market, political, social, cultural, and ideological. Regardless of the kind, all entrepreneurs are alert to advantageous opportunities. Entrepreneurial alertness is an omnipresent feature of all humans, but bringing an entrepreneurial idea to fruition requires action. Choosing to exploit a potential entrepreneurial discovery will depend on a variety of factors, such as costs, preferences, and cultural meanings. When entrepreneurs implement their discoveries, they necessarily disrupt existing systems or paradigms because they provide new goods, challenge current norms, reshape institutions, influence public policy, and shift cultural values. In other words, all entrepreneurs break down old traditions and bring forth new lifestyles. Thus, a core feature of any kind of entrepreneurship is the challenging of power or status (Pennington 2025).

The distinctions between different kinds of entrepreneurship are not always stark, and a single action might simultaneously exhibit characteristics of different types of entrepreneurship. As Storr et al. (2015: 27–28) argue,

> [T]he boundaries that separate different types of entrepreneurs are very porous. To be sure, the different designations of entrepreneurs are meant to capture what are supposedly very important differences (1) in the nature of the opportunities noticed and the type of social change the entrepreneur intends and actually brings about, as well as (2) in the nature of the rules that govern their behavior in the different spheres where they operate and the knowledge surrogates, feedback, or learning mechanisms that they can rely on to guide their behavior.

In other words, the types of opportunities that entrepreneurs will be alert to and potentially seize will depend on the institutional and cultural context in which they find themselves. Thus, some entrepreneurial actions may fall under only one category—such as "market" or "political" or "social"—but many span across different domains simultaneously. For tractability, Table 3.1 provides a brief overview of each type of entrepreneurship, its core characteristics, the relevant feedback mechanisms, and some real-world examples.

The broad literature in economics has defined market entrepreneurship as either (1) alertness to opportunities or (2) innovation. These two concepts are not mutually exclusive, and they are likely complements. Entrepreneurs are alert to and recognize profit opportunities that others have overlooked, such as unmet consumer needs, inefficiencies, or underutilized resources (Kirzner 1973, 1985, 1997). After recognizing a profit opportunity, a market entrepreneur can choose to take action by implementing that idea. Often, the implementation disrupts existing industries in socially productive ways. This process of "creative destruction" leads to innovations that add value, facilitating economic growth. Additionally, creative destruction causes production processes

TABLE 3.1 Types of entrepreneurship

Type of entrepreneurship	*Core characteristics*	*Feedback mechanisms*	*Examples*
Market	Alert to and exploit opportunities for monetary profit through market exchange	Prices; profit and loss	For-profit firms
Political	Alert to and exploit opportunities for political profit through political exchange	Votes; campaign contributions; power; discretion; prestige; rents	Politicians; bureaucrats; judges; special interest groups
Social	Alert to and exploit opportunities to create social value or produce social change	Donations; membership; social influence	Clubs; associations; nonprofit organizations; religious groups
Ideological	Alert to and exploit opportunities to create new conceptions of how the world can or should work	Intellectual influence; shifts in public opinion	Thought leaders; public intellectuals
Cultural	Alert to and exploit opportunities to shape narratives that influence societal beliefs and attitudes	Popularity; engagement; acceptance	Influencers; cultural first-movers

Source: Authors' illustration.

to become more efficient, leading to goods and services that better satisfy the wants of consumers (Schumpeter 2008). Truly innovative goods and services erode the dominance of established corporations or industries, shifting power toward new players.

Market entrepreneurs have two important feedback mechanisms that allow them to navigate uncertainty and dynamic conditions. First, market prices are critical because they allow for the aggregation and communication of knowledge that is dispersed and tacit (Hayek 1945; Kirzner 2018a). Second, profit and loss serve as a signal about the social usefulness of an entrepreneur's choices. If an entrepreneur is making profits, that is generally an indication that the entrepreneur is meeting the needs and wants of consumers. If an entrepreneur is incurring losses, that is a signal that resources could be deployed more profitably elsewhere. The combination of prices and profit-and-loss leads to two dynamic feedback mechanisms that communicate to entrepreneurs how they should change their behavior. However, these feedback mechanisms facilitate the fulfilling of consumers' desires only when markets are relatively free, meaning that prices emerge without government interference and companies only profit when they provide goods that consumers willingly want to buy. Interventions into markets disrupt the feedback mechanisms, leading to distortions and inefficiencies (Kirzner 2018b).

Political entrepreneurs, also known as public sector entrepreneurs, operate within the political sphere of government. As Storr et al. (2015: 19) describe, political entrepreneurs are "politicians or officials who are alert to, and work to, exploit opportunities to enact political profits (i.e., political and bureaucratic power)." In other words, they attempt to leverage political processes or government systems to create or exploit opportunities for gain by finding innovative ways to influence policy decisions or institutional reforms (Shockley et al. 2006). In the broadest sense, political entrepreneurs can be elected officials, bureaucrats, activists, interest group leaders, or lobbyists. The commonality among all these various types of people is they can act as catalysts for social change through the government when they mobilize public support, build political coalitions, lobby for particular policies, craft new policies, and challenge the political-bureaucratic status quo.

Market and political entrepreneurs are similar in that they are rationally self-interested and are looking for advantageous opportunities. However, they are different because they operate within different institutional contexts. Market entrepreneurs must entice consumers to choose their goods and services voluntarily. Political entrepreneurs, on the other hand, have the coercive power of the state at their disposal, which complicates matters. The exercise of this coercive power can be socially beneficial or socially harmful. Political entrepreneurs can be agents of positive social change by introducing new policies or reforms that address social, economic, or political problems. For example, political entrepreneurs can enhance social welfare by mobilizing previously marginalized groups, promoting political participation, increasing transparency, and developing accountability. They can also subvert entrenched power structures by mobilizing new constituencies or undermining dominant coalitions, shifting power from established elites to new players or marginalized groups.

However, political entrepreneurs can also use the coercive power of government to exacerbate domination of marginalized groups or bestow privileges on a favored group at the expense of less favored groups, among other socially harmful actions. As the public choice literature has indicated, one of the most significant potential harms of political entrepreneurship is rent-seeking, where political entrepreneurs use the political process to secure economic advantages without creating social value. The processes of rent-seeking diffuse costs on a larger group and concentrate benefits on a smaller group, but the costs to the larger group outweigh the gains to the smaller one (Tullock 2004). Rent-seeking often comes in the forms of favorable regulations, tax breaks, or subsidies, which distort market competition and create economic inefficiencies. Political entrepreneurs can also generate or exploit moral panics, using fear and misinformation to advance agendas that restrict individual freedoms, such as exploiting fears of immigrants or queer individuals (Wagner 1966, 2016; Smith and Yandle 2014; Holcombe 2018).

Other forms of nonmarket entrepreneurship include social, cultural, and ideological. The literature on these forms of entrepreneurship is less developed, but such nonmarket entrepreneurs are, at their core, instigators of bottom-up change who engage in cultural creative destruction (Cheang and Palmer 2023; Pennington 2025). Social entrepreneurs—unlike market entrepreneurs whose primary goal is profit maximization—prioritize creating social value or producing social change. In many cases, social entrepreneurs attempt to bridge existing gaps where both governments and markets have failed (Dees et al. 2001; Sullivan Mort et al. 2003; Alvord et al. 2004; Shockley and Frank 2011). Storr et al. (2015: 20–21) have observed that the literature provides multiple definitions of social entrepreneurship, but the definitions generally agree that

> a focus on social aims is essential for characterizing an activity as social entrepreneurship. … Think of individuals, motivated by religious or secular social aims, who established enterprises to give food, shelter, and clothing to the very poor. Think of the social activists and community organizers who have championed some particular social cause and are trying, through their protests, advocacy, and lobbying, to convince others of their views and win others to their cause.

Social entrepreneurs often start new civil groups, such as clubs, associations, or nonprofits to accomplish their aims. However, it can be difficult for social entrepreneurs to know whether their efforts are effectively serving their ends. Unlike market entrepreneurs who can rely on prices and the profit-and-loss mechanism, social entrepreneurs have different (and often more nebulous) feedback mechanisms, such as donations, membership numbers, or social influence. Just as profit indicates to market entrepreneurs that they are effectively serving consumers, social entrepreneurs can interpret increasing or decreasing levels of donations or membership as an indication on how to proceed with their ventures.

Ideological entrepreneurs are, as North (2005) describes, people who seek to change the rules of the game by changing people's minds. In North's view, ideological entrepreneurs must convince others that the ideological underpinnings of the existing institutional structure are unjust. However, as Storr (2008: 100) argues, "[T]he ideological entrepreneur remains an underdeveloped concept in North's work on institutional change." Other scholars have expanded on the concept, such as Storr et al. (2015: 24), who define it as

> entrepreneurship aimed at ideological change, a necessary precursor to any institutional change. […] Any would be institutional entrepreneur must also be an ideological entrepreneur. Nothing, of course, guarantees that an ideological entrepreneur will be able to convince others to accept her new ideology.

Thus, an ideological entrepreneur is a

> bold innovator who creates new conceptions of how the world works or combines and presents existing models of how the world works in new ways (i.e., to promote ideological development). She would work to capture the ideological marketplace, competing fiercely against other ideological entrepreneurs as well as against the weight of existing public opinion and conventions.
>
> (Storr et al. 2015: 25; see also Storr 2008).

Ideological entrepreneurs often take the form of thought leaders or public intellectuals. They have some idea about how the world can or should work. To know whether their rhetoric is effective and whether their ideas are catching on, ideological entrepreneurs need feedback mechanisms, which might include observable shifts in public opinion or other indications of intellectual influence. If an ideological entrepreneur does not observe a shift in public opinion, that indicates that she should use different rhetorical approaches to persuade people. However, such feedback mechanisms are highly nebulous, and it can be unclear whether the rhetoric is ineffective or whether the entrepreneur's ideas are undesirable.

The concept of cultural entrepreneurship is also disputed in the literature, with some definitions treating cultural entrepreneurs as market entrepreneurs who specialize in cultural goods/services, while other definitions treat cultural entrepreneurs as similar to ideological entrepreneurs who shift people's tastes, preferences, and ways of thinking (see McCloskey 2010, 2016; Klamer 2011; Gehman and Soublière 2017; Lounsbury and Glynn 2019; Dobreva and Ivanov 2020). Despite tensions or disagreements within the various definitions, a cultural entrepreneur is a person who is embedded in a cultural context with local and tacit knowledge about social values and meanings that unite a group of people. As Klamer (2011: 153) argues,

> The economy is about the realization of values. Economic values stand for the income and other revenues that allow people to realize the important social and cultural values. In case of social values, think of relationships, social status, an identity and the like, and cultural values refer to spiritual, esthetic, and other values that convey a sense of meaningfulness to life.

Thus, a cultural entrepreneur's discoveries and actions can shape narratives that influence societal beliefs, attitudes, and identities.

Cultural entrepreneurs are similar to ideological entrepreneurs in some ways and social entrepreneurs in others, so the distinctions between these categories are not clear cut. Cultural entrepreneurs may take the form of influencers or cultural first-movers who shape the shared narratives among individuals. Like other types of entrepreneurs, cultural entrepreneurs need feedback mechanisms to know whether their means are accomplishing their desired ends. For cultural entrepreneurs, feedback mechanisms are relatively fuzzy and ambiguous, such as popularity, engagement, or social acceptance. Such feedback mechanisms are difficult to measure and quantify, meaning that interpreting how to adapt one's actions is much more of an art than a science. Despite the relatively unclear feedback mechanisms, cultural entrepreneurs are often at the forefront of social change because they challenge cultural and social power structures by amplifying voices that have been historically marginalized or by challenging mainstream values and ideologies.

Entrepreneurs as agents of queer liberation

As discussed above, social change arises from the actions of entrepreneurs in a variety of market and nonmarket contexts, leading to a shift in cultural meanings, ideologies, preferences, and institutional rules. In the case of the LGBTQ rights movement in the United States, entrepreneurs have helped bring about the previously unrealized liberal principles that people want to live under. In what follows, we give a variety of real-world examples of entrepreneurship in market and nonmarket contexts that have led to greater rights, freedom, and toleration of queer people.

Market entrepreneurs in queer liberation

Market entrepreneurs have provided the goods, services, and platforms necessary for the flourishing and social inclusion of LGBTQ individuals. One of the most prominent and well-known forms of market entrepreneurship has been the creation of bars and clubs for queer people, which have played a pivotal role in advancing LGBTQ rights and privileges (Hildebrand 2023). In addition to providing a social venue and a place for entertainment, queer bars and clubs served—and continue to serve—as critical hubs for community-building, activism, cultural expression, and political organizing.

One of the oldest and most influential sites of LGBTQ activism is the Black Cat Tavern, a gay bar in Silver Lake, Los Angeles. On New Year's Eve in 1967, police raided the Black Cat Tavern and arrested its patrons. The raid on the Black Cat sparked protests, making it one of the earliest organized demonstrations for gay rights, predating the Stonewall Riots by almost a year and a half. The raid caused the owners and patrons of the bar, along with activists, to legally challenge California's anti-sodomy laws. The protests and the legal challenge highlighted the police abuse of queer people to a wider audience. Thus, the entrepreneurs behind the Black Cat Tavern provided both a space for entertainment and a social platform for resistance and legal challenges that laid the groundwork for future LGBTQ advocacy (Nash 2022).

The Stonewall Inn in Greenwich Village, New York, is now famous for being a pivotal site in the LGBTQ rights movement. The Inn was originally a mafia-owned bar that provided a space for queer people to gather. The owners had tacit agreements with the police to turn a proverbial blind eye in exchange for bribes. However, on June 28, 1969, a routine police raid turned violent at the Inn. Patrons fought back, sparking riots that marked the beginning of the modern LGBTQ rights movement in the United States. The riots led to the formation of groups such as the Gay Liberation Front, the Gay Activists Alliance, and other advocacy groups (Carter 2004; Notaro 2017).

In addition to for-profit bars and clubs, many other corporations have been at the forefront of queer liberation. Ben Cohen and Jerry Greenfield started the ice cream company Ben & Jerry's, which has been a longtime supporter of LGBTQ rights. In 1989, they became one of the first companies to extend benefits to same-sex partners. The company was acquired by Unilever in 2000, but the acquisition agreement created an independent Board of Directors that allows the company to prioritize its various social missions, including advocacy for marriage equality and anti-discrimination legislation (Ball 2019; Szyndlar and Wąsikiewicz-Firlej 2019; Parsons and Perreault 2022; Ben & Jerry's 2024).

PayPal has been an advocate for LGBTQ rights, including offering full benefits to same-sex couples and refusing to do business in regions with discriminatory laws. PayPal refused to operate in North Carolina after the passage of HB2 (the so-called "bathroom bill"), using its economic influence to protest discriminatory legislation. Paypal's influence pushed governments and other businesses to reconsider their stances due to the financial risks of supporting anti-LGBTQ laws (Lopez 2016; Kasperkevic 2016).

In 2022, the Walt Disney Company made a public statement denouncing Florida's HB 1557, the "Parental Rights in Education Act" colloquially known as the "Don't Say Gay Bill." The bill limits discussions of gender identity and sexual orientation in Florida's public school system, infringing on the first amendment rights of public-school teachers and increasing censorship in public education under the guise of "parental rights" (Fowler and Mountz 2024; Regutti et al. 2025). In this public statement, Disney reminded the public they would continue fighting for the LGBTQ community in Florida and in the United States. Then-Disney CEO Bob Chapek signed the statement and shared in an interview he called Florida Governor Ron DeSantis to express his disdain for the legislation (Blair 2022).

Political entrepreneurs in queer liberation

Political entrepreneurs have also played key roles in advocating for legal reforms, challenging discriminatory policies, and building coalitions to expand LGBTQ rights. One of the most prominent examples is Harvey Milk, who was one of the first openly gay elected officials in the United States when he was elected to the San Francisco Board of Supervisors in 1977. Milk focused on building alliances across various marginalized communities and advocating for LGBTQ rights. Milk was instrumental in the defeat of California's Proposition 6 (i.e., the Briggs Initiative), which would have banned LGBTQ individuals from teaching in public schools. He laid the foundation for LGBTQ political organizing and advocacy in the United States (Reynolds 2019). In more recent years, openly LGBTQ politicians such as former U.S. Secretary of Transportation Pete Buttigieg and Sarah McBride, a transwoman and Congresswoman form Delaware, have been highly visible elected and appointed public officials.

Margarethe Cammermeyer became a political entrepreneur when she challenged the military's policy that banned LGBTQ individuals from serving openly. Cammermeyer was openly lesbian and a U.S. Army colonel, which led to her dismissal from the military in 1992. The ensuing legal battle eventually overturned her discharge, which highlighted the injustice of discriminatory military policies. This high profile incident made discrimination in the military more widely known, and it helped to contribute to the eventual repeal of "Don't Ask, Don't Tell" (Baldwin 1995).

President Barack Obama and leaders in his administration were political entrepreneurs by initiating the repeal of the military's "Don't Ask, Don't Tell" policy in 2010 (Lee 2013; Neff and Edgell 2013; Letendre and Abramson 2022). Additionally, Obama's public support for marriage equality in 2012 helped shift public opinion, which was a prerequisite for the Supreme Court's landmark 2015 decision in *Obergefell v. Hodges*, legalizing same-sex marriage nationwide (Stewart-Winter 2018; Tsai 2018).

In addition to single individuals, many organizations have acted entrepreneurially in a political context. Lambda Legal, a nonprofit organization founded in 1973, has been a leader in legal battles for LGBTQ rights in the United States. It played a central role in numerous landmark cases, including Lawrence v. Texas (Spindelman 2004; Lambda Legal n.d.). Another example is the Human Rights Campaign (HRC), which is the largest LGBTQ civil rights organization in the United States. Founded in 1980, HRC has engaged in political entrepreneurship by lobbying for legislative reforms, endorsing pro-LGBTQ candidates, and mobilizing grassroots activism. HRC has been instrumental in passing major pieces of legislation that benefit LGBTQ individuals, including the Matthew Shepard and James Byrd Jr. Hate Crimes Prevention Act (2009) and the repeal of "Don't Ask, Don't Tell." Through its lobbying efforts and political advocacy, HRC has successfully shifted public institutions toward greater legal protections for LGBTQ people at both the state and federal levels (Human Rights Campaign n.d.).

Social, cultural, and ideological entrepreneurs in queer liberation

Since social, cultural, and ideological entrepreneurs have significant overlap, we discuss them here as one group. Together, these types of entrepreneurs have been instigators of bottom-up social change for queer individuals. Social entrepreneurs, for instance, have created organizations for institutional and cultural reform, advocated for policy changes, and provided social connections for stigmatized individuals. For example, the GSA (Gay-Straight Alliance) Network, founded in 1998 by Carolyn Laub, is a national organization that empowers LGBTQ youth and allies to create safe spaces in schools through the formation of GSA clubs. GSA Network has helped establish thousands of GSA clubs across the United States, fostering supportive environments for LGBTQ students in both urban and rural areas. By empowering young activists to engage in advocacy at the school level, GSA Network has pressured public school systems to implement policies that protect LGBTQ students (Russell et al. 2009, 2010; Baams et al. 2020; GSA Network 2024).

Also founded in 1998, The Trevor Project is a nonprofit organization that provides crisis intervention and suicide prevention services to LGBTQ youth. Through its 24/7 crisis hotline, chat, and text services, The Trevor Project has helped reduce instances of self-harm and suicide, while its educational programs have raised awareness about the mental health challenges faced by LGBTQ youth (Phillips 2022). Founded in 2003, the Transgender Legal Defense & Education Fund (TLDEF) similarly advances the well-being and legal recognition of transgender people by providing legal support, advocating for policy change, and raising public awareness about trans rights issues. TLDEF's Name Change Project has assisted thousands of transgender individuals in legally changing their names, a crucial step toward achieving both legal and social recognition (Thaler et al. 2009). Together with these targeted interventions, longstanding institutions such as the Los Angeles LGBT Center—established in 1969 by Morris Kight, Don Kilhefner, and others—demonstrate the breadth of social entrepreneurship in queer liberation. As the largest LGBTQ social services organization in the world, the Center provides comprehensive healthcare, legal advocacy, housing, and educational services, and has partnered with local governments and public agencies to deliver inclusive care and housing solutions.

Many cultural and ideological entrepreneurs have shifted widespread perceptions and beliefs about queer people. Media has served as a powerful tool for advancing the rights of queer communities. Taking a note from cultural studies and critical media scholarship, media has long been the catalyst for advancing public understandings of cultural others. Representation is important because people construct meaning of the material world through representational systems of signs and concepts that they come to know through their interactions with visual culture such as popular media, including film, television, news media, and social media (Hall 1997). Early queer and trans media studies scholarship examined the use of media in advancing public perception about the early gay rights movement (Gross 2001) and the AIDS crisis (Treichler 1999). This works two-fold: entrepreneurs such as Ellen DeGeneres and RuPaul are celebrities the public only understand through their media consumption of their cultural products, as well as cultural products of media organizations like television series and films about queer people.

In 1997, Ellen DeGeneres came out as a lesbian both on her sitcom Ellen and in real life—a groundbreaking moment in mainstream U.S. television. Ellen's public coming out and subsequent career as a successful talk show host made queer identities more visible and accepted by mainstream audiences (Reed 2005; Skerski 2007; Armstrong et al. 2020). Also in the 1990s was the premiere of the sitcom *Will & Grace*, which became one of the first mainstream U.S. television series to feature openly gay main characters on network television. *Will & Grace* played a pivotal role in shifting public perceptions of queerness by normalizing LGBTQ relationships and presenting gay characters as relatable and complex. Scholars argue that series such as Will & Grace help reduce homophobia by exposing audiences to positive depictions of LGBTQ individuals (Cooper 2003; Mitchell 2005; Silverman 2013). However, by inviting mainstream audiences to read the program within familiar televisual frames, *Will & Grace* can be read as reinforcing heterosexism and, thus, can be seen as heteronormative (Battles and Hilton-Morrow 2002), or rather homonormative. Coined by Lisa Duggan (2002), homonormativity refers to the appropriation of the gay and lesbian into conforming to heteronormative values of monogamy and sexual normativity. In other words, the proper gay subject behaves just like their heterosexual counterparts but have a romantic partner of the same sex.

More recent mainstream representations have broadened to include queer and transpeople of color. Most notably, Black trans activist and actress Laverne Cox was a regular on the Netflix series *Orange is the New Black* (2013–2019). Cox was later featured on the cover of TIME's March 2014 issue "The Transgender Tipping Point" (Steinmetz 2014). Other notable representations of trans and queer people of color in popular media include the Academy-Award winning motion-picture, *Moonlight* that tells the story of a young Black queer man grappling with the complexities of his racial, sexual, and class identities (Flood 2021; Rudrow and Edgar 2023). The FX series *Pose* (2018–2021) received praise for its representations of Black and Latinx queer and trans people during the AIDS crisis. In 2024, *Emilia Perez* (2024) a musical crime film received praise for its representation of Latinx trans identity, as well as criticism from LGBTQ audiences for its lack of nuance in the film's depiction of trans identity. The film's lead actress, Karla Sofia Gascon, became the first transwoman to be nominated for Best Actress at the 97th Academy Awards in 2025.

One of the most transgressive sites of cultural entrepreneurship advancing the inclusion of LGBTQ identities in the mainstream is the competitive reality TV series, *RuPaul's Drag Race* (2009–present). *Drag Race* straddles the worlds of cultural and market entrepreneurship, illustrating how for-profit entertainment can be used to shift public perceptions of queerness. The series showcases drag culture—long considered an underground or subversive art form—but now broader audiences consume the artform *en masse*. Since the series premiered in 2009, *Drag Race* has expanded into a global media brand with 22 different international franchises. The international franchises are available to stream on *Drag Race*'s parent company's platform WOW Presents Plus which exclusively produces LGBTQ content. *Drag Race* uses personal interviews with the contestants to offer insight into the lives of LGBTQ communities. By sharing stories related to coming out, homophobia, transphobia, and self-acceptance, *Drag Race* has induced a broader sense of sympathy for the struggles and success of queer people. Viewers who might not have been previously familiar with or open to drag or queer culture are now exposed to it in a way that makes it more accessible, to greater cultural acceptance of queer identities (Brennan and Gudelunas 2017).

Beyond *Drag Race*, reality TV has been a progressive site for LGBTQ representation since the 2000s. The reality TV genre democratizes media by presenting "real" people living their "real" lives in front of a camera (Andrejevic 2004). As critical scholars of reality TV contend, this is a performance that only presents itself as "real" through an editing and production process that packages reality TV into compelling storylines in episodic formats (Dubrofsky 2011). Yet, for this same reason, reality TV has often been ahead of the curve in representing marginalized communities, as opposed to mainstream narrative film and television (Murray and Ouellette 2009).

One example in the early 2000s is *Queer Eye for the Straight Guy* (2003–2007), in which five gay men who are lifestyle experts "make over" straight men by teaching them how to decorate, cook, dress, groom, and educating them about culture. In 2018, the series was rebooted on Netflix as *Queer Eye* with a new cast and expanded their makeovers beyond straight men to include women and queer people. Other series such as TLC's *I am Jazz* (2015–2023) documented Jazz Jennings transition as a young transwoman; similarly, Caitlyn Jenner's docuseries *I am Cait* (2015–2016) documented her adjustment to living as a woman after coming out publicly in 2015. Taken together, reality TV is a productive site for cultural and ideological entrepreneurs by presenting LGBTQ communities in nuanced ways that offer insights to audiences who may not have immediate relationships with queer people. Relatedly, films and television series alike featured trans characters and storylines such as *Transparent* and *Grey's Anatomy*.

Like reality TV, social media (or social networking sites) are also a democratizing medium that gained popularity at the beginning of the 2000s (Dubrofsky 2011), where reality TV audiences and social media users have more immediate access to celebrities. Trans celebrities have used social media as cultural entrepreneurs to share their transitions, such as actor Elliott Page and NBA Hall of Famer Dwayne Wade's daughter Zaya, who entered the mainstream as an activist for trans youth (Willard and Menzies 2024). For queer people, particularly queer and trans youth, social media has been a useful tool for exploring one's queer identity, finding community, and accessing LGBTQ content.

Potential tradeoffs and dark sides of entrepreneurship

Economists have discussed how entrepreneurship can become unproductive and destructive under institutions that promote negative-sum action over positive-sum action (Wagner 1966; Baumol 1990; Sobel 2008; Choi and Storr 2019). Even with all the progress, entrepreneurs can find ways to use existing antipathy toward queer people to benefit themselves. Central to the progress of these entrepreneurs for queer liberation is a commitment to advancing visibility for LGBTQ communities and issues in politics and popular culture. For marginalized communities, increased visibility has long been associated with advancing broader cultural acceptance, yet alongside increased visibility is increased violence against these communities. By making queer people more legible by the state invites the surveillance of queer people (see Kafer and Grinberg 2019; Willard 2026). To become visible means to become a "thing" something or someone that is now seen and counted, which has often prompted increased violence and surveillance of queer and trans people (Aizura 2017). Mia Fischer (2019) traces the relationship between increased violence against trans communities alongside their increased visibility. Fischer recognizes the benefits of increased representation in politics and culture but warns activists to not rest on representational politics alone, that physical and epistemic violence will persist.

For instance, no bills targeting drag performers have been given the national spotlight until Tennessee's conservative lawmakers introduced legislation in March 2023. Subsequently, five other states introduced similar legislation. These bills are marketed as banning drag in public places for the sake of children. Yet, they are written in a manner such that they could apply to trans people through language such as "male or female impersonators," where a trans person could be framed as such by law enforcement (see Williams and Ringel 2026). This occurs at the same time as the massive success of *RuPaul's Drag Race*, drag culture entering the mainstream, and the increased visibility of trans people in culture. While same-sex marriage is a success for gay and lesbian couples, trans people continue to be under scrutiny by the state with legislation such as drag bans and legislative assaults and political attacks like bills banning trans youth's access to gender-affirming healthcare and access to athletics and sports. In 2017, the Trump administration announced a ban on transgender individuals serving in the U.S. military, citing concerns about military readiness and costs associated with transgender healthcare (Pepin-Neff and Cohen 2021; Nagourney and Peters 2023).

Ideologically, these successes are limited to the extent they promote normative ideas of citizenship for LGBTQ people. As noted above, one pervasive ideology encoding the gay and lesbian subject is homonormativity, the notion that the appropriate gay and lesbian subject conforms to heteronormative values of monogamy, marriage, and family (Duggan 2002). Gays and lesbians who do not conform to the homonormative ideal such as rejecting marriage, having polyamorous relationships, and participating in kink and fetish sexual practices are ostracized. Although marriage equality advanced protections for gay and lesbian couples, which was particularly salient following the AIDS crisis where those whose partners were dying of AIDS-related illnesses did not have authority over their partner's medical choices. Critics note the institutionalization of same-sex marriage limited the radical potential for queer politics (Brandzel 2016; Franke 2015). This is what Mary

Bernstein (2018: 1941) describes as the "assimilationist dilemma" which suggests that gaining acceptance into mainstream institutions such as marriage will diminish the salience of lesbian or gay identity. By framing the paramount of gay liberation as marriage equality, the continued fight for protections for trans and queer people is diminished as the coalition for LGBTQ equality shrinks from the loss of gay and lesbian activists satisfied with their rights to marriage.

In the cultural space, normative discourses about gender and sexuality persist not only in television series like *Will & Grace* and *Queer Eye* as we note above, but also on *Drag Race* and in representations of queer celebrities in media. While *Drag Race* has provided a platform for queer people to express gender and sexuality in expansive and nuanced ways, critical scholars note these progressive representations are limited to white and western participants across the global franchise (Upadhyay 2019; Willard and Dubrofsky 2024). Like many representations of gay and lesbians are encoded with homonormativity, depictions of trans people in media are symptomatic of transnormativity in culture. Transnormativity is the notion that the appropriate way to be transgender is to have a "complete" medical and visual transition from one gender to another, upholding the gender binary and alienating those whose trans identity is expressed along the spectrum of gender identity such as non-binary and other fluid gender performances (Johnson 2016). Critical scholars note how this unfolds in seemingly positive representations of trans people on series such as *Orange is the New Black* (Thomas 2020) and *Euphoria* (Price 2022) and with trans celebrities in reality TV (Li 2019; McIntyre et al. 2023) and social media (Willard and Menzies 2024).

Conclusion

The rapid expansion of rights, privileges, and tolerance for LGBTQ people in the United States is a remarkable phenomenon. While many ongoing challenges for queer people still exist, liberal political economy provides a way for scholars of queer issues to understand how such massive social changes come about. Entrepreneurs in market and nonmarket settings have been the agents of change who have played crucial roles in advancing individual liberty and expanding rights. Entrepreneurs have also challenged established norms and promoted social tolerance.

This chapter has focused specifically on the United States, but the arguments here are applicable to other contexts, such as the Global South or nondemocratic, nonliberal societies. However, there is no guarantee that the processes of social change that have led to the liberation of queer individuals in the United States will happen at the same rate or in the same ways in other locations. Entrepreneurs in the United States have benefited from a foundation of wealth and established liberal institutions, which suggests that entrepreneurs in less affluent countries or those lacking a tradition of liberal institutions may face greater challenges. Despite the seemingly daunting challenges, many opportunities exist for market and nonmarket entrepreneurs to shift and shape institutions and culture in ways that promote queer liberation. Entrepreneurs can use their dispersed and tacit knowledge to discover previously undiscovered opportunities for change. The specific forms of entrepreneurship will likely have different characteristics than the U.S. context because of different formal and informal institutions, as well as different cultures and ideologies. The fact that queer liberation has happened in many places gives hope that it can happen in others.

This research pushes back against the literature that condemns liberalism—particularly the ill-defined specter of "neoliberalism"—for harming queer people and their interests. If by "neoliberalism" people mean commodification and market exchange, there are most certainly tradeoffs. No panaceas exist for addressing complex social issues. However, perhaps scholars and activists have been too hasty to disparage commodification and market exchanges. Markets have been the source, or at least the setting, of much of the progress for queer liberation. The research here suggests that scholars should be more circumspect in their analysis of the actual role of markets and market entrepreneurs in the progress of queer individuals. Of course, markets will have power imbalances due to wealth or influence, but power imbalances exist in government and civic life as well. Markets have their own shortcomings, but as the queer classical liberalism approach suggests they can also be tools of progress and subverting the arbitrary exercise of power.

References

Aizura, Aren Z. 2017. "Unrecognizable: On Trans Recognition in 2017." *South Atlantic Quarterly* 116 (3): 606–611.

Aligica, Paul Dragos. 2019. *Public Entrepreneurship, Citizenship, and Self-Governance*. Cambridge, UK: Cambridge University Press.

Aligica, Paul Dragos, and Peter J. Boettke. 2011. "Institutional Design and Ideas-Driven Social Change: Notes from an Ostromian Perspective." *The Good Society* 20 (1): 50–66.

Aligica, Paul Dragos, Peter J. Boettke, and Vlad Tarko. 2019. *Public Governance and the Classical-Liberal Perspective*. Oxford, UK: Oxford University Press.

Alvord, Sarah H., L. David Brown, and Christine W. Letts. 2004. "Social Entrepreneurship and Societal Transformation: An Exploratory Study." *Journal of Applied Behavioral Science* 40 (3): 260–282.

Andrejevic, Mark. 2004. *Reality TV: The Work of Being Watched*. Lanham, MD: Rowman & Littlefield.

Armstrong, Elizabeth A. 2002. *Forging Gay Identities: Organizing Sexuality in San Francisco, 1950-1994*. Chicago, IL: University of Chicago Press.

Armstrong, Cory L., Jue Hou, and Kylie McLeod. 2020. "Is Ellen DeGeneres a 'DeGenerate?': How TV's First Out Lesbian Connects to Public Support for Same-Sex Marriage." *Electronic News* 14 (1): 3–21.

Baams, Laura, Amanda M. Pollitt, Carolyn Laub, and Stephen T. Russell. 2020. "Characteristics of Schools with and without Gay-Straight Alliances." *Applied Developmental Science* 24 (4): 354–359.

Baldwin, Holly. 1995. "'Don't Ask, Don't Tell': Lesbians Challenge the New Military Policy." *Berkeley Women's Law Journal* 10: 148–155.

Ball, Carlos A. 2019. *The Queering of Corporate America: How Big Business Went from LGBTQ Adversary to Ally*. New York, NY: Beacon Press.

Barbee, Harry, Cameron Deal, and Gilbert Gonzales. 2022. "Anti-Transgender Legislation – A Public Health Concern for Transgender Youth." *JAMA Pediatrics* 176 (2): 125–126.

Battles, Kathleen, and Wendy Hilton-Morrow. 2002. "Gay Characters in Conventional Spaces: Will and Grace and the Situation Comedy Genre." *Critical Studies in Media Communication* 19 (1): 87–105.

Baumol, William J. 1990. "Entrepreneurship: Productive, Unproductive, and Destructive." *Journal of Business Venturing* 11 (1): 3–22.

Ben & Jerry's. 2024. "About Us." https://www.benjerry.com/about-us?through-the-decades=tab-2000s.

Bernstein, Mary. 2018. "Same-Sex Marriage and the Assimilationist Dilemma: A Research Agenda on Marriage Equality and the Future of LGBTQ Activism, Politics, Communities, and Identities." *Journal of Homosexuality* 65 (14): 1941–1956.

Blair, Elizabeth. 2022. "After Protests, Disney CEO Speaks Out Against 'Don't Say Gay' Bill." NPR, March 10. https://www.npr.org/2022/03/08/1085130633/disney-response-florida-bill-dont-say-gay.

Boettke, Peter J. 2012. *Living Economics: Yesterday, Today, and Tomorrow*. Oakland, CA: Independent Institute.

Boettke, Peter J. 2021. *The Struggle for a Better World*. Arlington, VA: Mercatus Center at George Mason University.

Boettke, Peter J., and Christopher J. Coyne. 2002. "Context Matters: Institutions and Entrepreneurship." *Foundations and Trends in Entrepreneurship* 5 (3): 143–159.

Boettke, Peter J., and Christopher J. Coyne. 2003. "Entrepreneurship and Development: Cause or Consequence." *Advances in Austrian Economics* 6: 67–87.

Boettke, Peter J., Christopher J. Coyne, and Peter T. Leeson. 2008. "Institutional Stickiness and the New Development Economics." *American Journal of Economics and Sociology* 67 (2): 331–358.

Boettke, Peter J., Stefanie Haeffele-Balch, and Virgil Henry Storr. 2016. *Mainline Economics: Six Nobel Lectures in the Tradition of Adam Smith*. Arlington, VA: Mercatus Center at George Mason University.

Brandzel, Amy L. 2016. *Against Citizenship: The Violence of the Normative*. Urbana, IL: University of Illinois Press.

Brennan, Niall and David Gudelunas. 2017. *RuPaul's Drag Race and the Shifting Visibility of Drag Culture*. Cham, Switzerland: Palgrave Macmillan.

Brightman, Sara, Emily Lenning, Kristin J. Lurie, and Christina DeJong. 2024. "Anti-Transgender Ideology, Laws, and Homicide: An Analysis of the Trifecta of Violence." *Homicide Studies* 28 (3): 251–269.

Carter, David. 2004. *Stonewall: The Riots That Sparked the Gay Revolution*. New York, NY: St. Martin's Press.

Cheang, Bryan, and Tom G. Palmer. 2023. *Institutions and Economic Development: Markets, Ideas, and Bottom-Up Change*. Singapore: Springer.

Choi, Seung Ginny, and Virgil Henry Storr. 2019. "A Culture of Rent Seeking." *Public Choice* 181 (1):101–126.

Ciszek, Erica, and Hayoung Sally Lim. 2021. "Perceived Brand Authenticity and LGBTQ Publics: How LGBTQ Practitioners Understand Authenticity." *International Journal of Strategic Communication* 15 (5): 395–409.

Cooper, Evan. 2003. "Decoding Will and Grace: Mass Audience Reception of a Popular Network Situation Comedy." *Sociological Perspectives* 46 (4): 513–533.

Dees, J. Gregory, Jed Emerson, and Peter Economy. 2001. *Enterprising Nonprofits: A Toolkit for Social Entrepreneurs*. New York, NY: Wiley.

D'Emilio, John. 1983. *Sexual Politics, Sexual Communities: The Making of a Homosexual Minority in the United States, 1940-1970*. Chicago, IL: University of Chicago Press.

Dobreva, Nevena, and Stanislav Ivanov. 2020. "Cultural Entrepreneurship: A Review of the Literature." *Tourism & Management Studies* 16 (4): 23–34.

Dubrofsky, Rachel E. 2011. "Surveillance on Reality Television and Facebook: Authenticity to Flowing Data." *Communication Theory* 21 (2): 111–129.
Duggan, Lisa. 2002. "The New Homonormativity: The Sexual Politics of Neoliberalism." In *Materializing Democracy: Toward a Revitalized Cultural Politics*, edited by Russ Castronovo, Dana D. Nelson and Donald E. Pease, 175–194. Durham, NC: Duke University Press.
Eng, David L. 2010. *The Feeling of Kinship: Queer Liberalism and the Racialization of Intimacy*. Durham, NC: Duke University Press.
Fischer, Mia. 2019. *Terrorizing Gender: Transgender Visibility and the Surveillance Practices of the U.S. Security State*. Lincoln, NE: University of Nebraska Press.
Flood, Maria. 2021. *Moonlight: Screening Black Queer Youth*. London: Routledge.
Fowler, Megan Marie, and Sarah Mountz. 2024. "Discipline, Erasure, and Silenced Subjectivities: A Critical Discourse Analysis of Florida's 2022 Parental Rights in Education Act." *Affilia: Feminist Inquiry in Social Work* 39 (1): 24–41.
Franke, Katherine. 2015. *Wedlocked: The Perils of Marriage Equality*. New York, NY: New York University Press.
Freeman, Elizabeth. 2010. Time Binds: *Queer Temporalities, Queer Histories*. Durham, NC: Duke University Press.
Geertz, Clifford. 1973. *The Interpretation of Cultures*. New York, NY: Basic Books.
Gehman, Joel, and Jean-François Soublière. 2017. "Cultural Entrepreneurship: From Making Culture to Cultural Making." *Innovation* 19 (1): 61–73.
Ginder, Whitney, and Sang-Eun Byun. 2015. "Past, Present, and Future of Gay and Lesbian Consumer Research: Critical Review of the Quest for the Queer Dollar." *Psychology & Marketing* 32 (8): 821–841.
Gross, L. (2001). *Up from Invisibility: Lesbians, Gay Men, and the Media in America*. New York, NY: Columbia University Press.
Grube, Laura E., and Virgil Henry Storr, 2015. *Culture and Economic Action. New Thinking in Political Economy*. Cheltenham, UK: Edward Elgar.
GSA Network. 2024. "Leadership Is Our Legacy." https://gsanetwork.org/updates/leadership-is-our-legacy.
Hall, Stuart. 1997. *Representation: Cultural Representations and Signifying Practices*. London: Sage Publications.
Hayek, Friedrich A. 1945. "The Use of Knowledge in Society." *American Economic Review* 35 (4): 519–530.
Hildebrand, Lucas. 2023. *The Bars are Ours: Histories and Cultures of Gay Bars in America, 1960 and After*. Durham, NC: Duke University Press.
Holcombe, Randall G. 2018. *Political Capitalism: How Economic and Political Power Is Made and Maintained*. New York, NY: Cambridge University Press.
Horne, Sharon G., Mallaigh McGinley, Nedim Yel, and Meredith R. Maroney. 2022. "The Stench of Bathroom Bills and Anti-Transgender Legislation: Anxiety and Depression Among Transgender, Nonbinary, and Cisgender LGBQ People During a State Referendum." *Journal of Counseling Psychology* 69 (1): 1–13.
Human Rights Campaign. n.d. "About." https://www.hrc.org/about.
Johnson, Austin H. 2016. "Transnormativity: A New Concept and Its Validation through Documentary Film About Transgender Men." *Sociological Inquiry* 86 (4): 465–491.
Kafer, Gary and Daniel Grinberg. 2019. "Editorial: Queer Surveillance." *Surveillance & Society* 17 (5): 592–601.
Kasperkevic, Jana. 2016. "PayPal Cancels North Carolina Center in Protest of Law That 'denies Equal Rights." Guardian, April 5. https://www.theguardian.com/technology/2016/apr/05/paypal-cancels-north-carolina-center-charlotte-law-lgbt-discrimination.
Kirzner, Israel M. 1973. *Competition and Entrepreneurship*. Chicago, IL: University of Chicago Press.
Kirzner, Israel M. 1985. *Discovery and the Capitalist Process*. Chicago, IL: University of Chicago Press.

Kirzner, Israel M. 1997. "Entrepreneurial Discovery and the Competitive Market Process: An Austrian Approach." *Journal of Economic Literature* 35 (1): 60–85.

Kirzner, Israel M. 2018a. *Competition, Economic Planning, and the Knowledge Problem*. In *The Collected Works of Israel M. Kirzner*, edited by Peter J. Boettke and Frédéric Sautet. Indianapolis, IN: Liberty Fund.

Kirzner, Israel M. 2018b. "The Perils of Regulation: A Market-Process Approach." In *Reflections on Ethics, Freedom, Welfare Economics, Policy, and the Legacy of Austrian Economics. The Collected Works of Israel M. Kirzner*, edited by Peter J. Boettke and Frédéric Sautet, 418–455. Indianapolis, IN: Liberty Fund.

Klamer, Arjo. 2011. "Cultural Entrepreneurship." *Review of Austrian Economics* 24 (2): 141–156.

Lambda Legal. n.d. "Our History." https://lambdalegal.org/history.

Lee, Jonathan L. 2013. "The Comprehensive Review Working Group and Don't Ask, Don't Tell Repeal at the Department of Defense." *Journal of Homosexuality* 60 (2–3): 282–311.

Letendre, Linell A., and Hal Abramson. 2022. "Negotiating Social Change: Backstory Behind the Repeal of Don't Ask, Don't Tell." *University of Florida Journal of Law and Public Policy* 32 (2): 157–252.

Li, Minjie. 2019. "Transitioning Together: Negotiating Transgender Subjectivity with Family and Other Trans People on Reality Television." *Journal of Homosexuality* 68 (3): 496–521.

Lopez, German. 2016. "PayPal Makes It Official: North Carolina's Anti-LGBTQ Law Will Cost the State Jobs." Vox, April 5. https://www.vox.com/2016/4/5/11369334/paypal-lgbtq-north-carolina.

Lounsbury, Michael, and Mary Ann Glynn. 2019. *Cultural Entrepreneurship: A New Agenda for the Study of Entrepreneurial Processes and Possibilities*. Cambridge, UK: Cambridge University Press.

McCloskey, Deirdre N. 2010. *Bourgeois Dignity: Why Economics Can't Explain the Modern World*. Chicago, IL: University of Chicago Press.

McCloskey, Deirdre N. 2016. *Bourgeois Equality: How Ideas, Not Capital or Institutions, Enriched the World*. Chicago, IL: University of Chicago Press.

McIntyre, Joanna, Damien W. Riggs, and Clare Bartholomaeus. 2023. "Jazz Jennings and Evie Macdonald: Trans Child Celebrities, Transnormativity, and Childhood 'Innocence.'" *Celebrity Studies* 14 (2): 214–226.

Mitchell, Danielle M. 2005. "Rhetorically Contained: The Construction and Incorporation of Difference in Will & Grace." *Journal of Popular Culture* 38 (6): 1050–1068.

Murray, Susan and Laurie Ouellette. 2009. *Reality TV: Remaking Television Culture*. New York, NY: New York University Press.

Nagourney, Adam, and Jeremy W. Peters. 2023. "How a Campaign Against Transgender Rights Mobilized Conservatives." New York Times, April 18. https://www.nytimes.com/2023/04/16/us/politics/transgender-conservative-campaign.html.

Nash, Katelyn. 2022. "A Forgotten 'Riot': Discovering the Black Cat Tavern Raid's Place in Queer History." *Armstrong Undergraduate Journal of History* 12 (3): 81–93.

Neff, Christopher L., and Luke R. Edgell. 2013. "The Rise of Repeal: Policy Entrepreneurship and Don't Ask, Don't Tell." *Journal of Homosexuality* 60 (2–3): 232–249.

North, Douglass C. 1990. *Institutions, Institutional Change, and Economic Performance*. New York, NY: Cambridge University Press.

North, Douglass C. 2005. *Understanding the Process of Economic Change*. Princeton, NJ: Princeton University Press.

Notaro, Sheri R. 2017. "The Stonewall Riots: Moving from the Margins to the Mainstream." *Advances in Education in Diverse Communities: Research, Policy and Praxis* 12: 143–164.

Novak, Mikayla. 2021. *Freedom in Contention: Social Movements and Liberal Political Economy*. Lanham, MD: Lexington Books.

Ostrom, Elinor. 2005. *Understanding Institutional Diversity*. Princeton, NJ: Princeton University Press.

Parsons, Becky, and Mildred F. Perreault. 2022. "Queer Marketing, Who Is It Really For?: Identifying a Strategy for Authentic Approaches to LGBTQ+ Branded Messages." In *LGBTQ Digital Cultures: A Global Perspective*, edited by Paromita Pain, 116–129. New York, NY: Routledge.

Pennington, Mark. 2025. *Foucault and Liberal Political Economy: Power, Knowledge, and Freedom.* Oxford, UK: Oxford University Press.

Pepin-Neff, Christopher, and Aaron Cohen. 2021. "President Trump's Transgender Moral Panic." *Policy Studies* 42 (5–6): 646–661.

Phillips, Kat. 2022. "We Are All Human: A Review of the Trevor Project and the It Gets Better Project." *Journal of Consumer Health on the Internet* 26 (1): 82–91.

Price, Sarah F. 2022. "Proving authentic femininity: Transnormative health narratives in television." *Communication and Critical/Cultural Studies* 19 (2): 197–215.

Puar, Jasbir K. 2007. *Terrorist Assemblages: Homonationalism in Queer Times*. Durham, NC: Duke University Press.

Reed, Jennifer. 2005. "Ellen DeGeneres: Public Lesbian Number One." *Feminist Media Studies* 5 (1): 23–36.

Regutti, Kailin, Zane Austin Willard, and Mahuya Pal. 2025. "Regimes of Visibility in Disney's CSR: Corporate Wokeness, Neoliberalism, and Promotional Industries." In *The Sage Handbook of Promotional Cultures and Society*, edited by Lee Edwards, Clea Bourne, Jason Vincent A. Cabañes and Gisela Castro, 205–216. Thousand Oaks, CA: Sage.

Reynolds, Andrew. 2019. *The Children of Harvey Milk: How LGBTQ Politicians Changed the World.* New York, NY: Oxford University Press.

Rudrow, Keven James, and Amanda Nell Edgar. 2023. "Reading Moonlight, Reading the Other." *Communication and Critical/Cultural Studies* 20(1): 270–287.

Russell, Stephen T., Anna Muraco, Aarti Subramaniam, and Carolyn Laub. 2009. "Youth Empowerment and High School Gay-Straight Alliances." *Journal of Youth and Adolescence* 38 (7): 891–903.

Russell, Stephen T., Russell B. Toomey, Jason Crockett, and Carolyn Laub. 2010. "LGBT Politics, Youth Activism, and Civic Engagement." In *Handbook of Research on Civic Engagement in Youth*, edited by Lonnie R. Sherrod, Judith Torney-Purta, and Constance A. Flanagan, 471–494. Hoboken, NJ: John Wiley & Sons.

Schopper, Tiziana, Anna Berbers, and Lukas Vogelsang. 2025. "Pride or Rainbow-Washing? Exploring LGBTQ+ Advertising from the Vested Stakeholder Perspective." *Journal of Advertising* 54 (2): 233–250.

Schumpeter, Joseph A. 2008. *Capitalism, Socialism and Democracy*. Third edition. New York, NY: Harper Perennial Modern Thought.

Shockley, Gordon E., and Peter M. Frank. 2011. "The Functions of Government in Social Entrepreneurship: Theory and Preliminary Evidence." *Regional Science Policy & Practice* 3 (3): 181–199.

Shockley, Gordon E., Roger R. Stough, Kingsley E. Haynes, and Peter M. Frank. 2006. "Toward a Theory of Public Sector Entrepreneurship." *International Journal of Entrepreneurship and Innovation Management* 6 (3): 205–223.

Silverman, Rachel E. 2013. "Comedy as Correction: Humor as Perspective by Incongruity on Will & Grace and Queer as Folk." *Sexuality & Culture* 17 (2): 260–274.

Skerski, Jamie. 2007. "From Prime-Time to Daytime: The Domestication of Ellen DeGeneres." *Communication and Critical/Cultural Studies* 4 (4): 363–381.

Smith, Adam C., and Bruce Yandle. 2014. *Bootleggers and Baptists: How Economics Forces and Moral Persuasion Interact to Shape Regulatory Politics*. Washington, DC: Cate Institute.

Sobel, Russell S. 2008. "Testing Baumol: Institutional Quality and the Productivity of Entrepreneurship." *Journal of Business Venturing* 23 (6): 641–655.

Spindelman, Marc. 2004. "Surviving Lawrence v. Texas." *Michigan Law Review* 102 (7): 1615–1667.

Steinmetz, Katy. 2014, "The Transgender Tipping Point." TIME, May 29. https://time.com/135480/transgender-tipping-point.

Stewart-Winter, Timothy. 2018. "The Gay Rights President." In *The Presidency of Barack Obama: A First Historical Assessment*, edited by Julian Zelizer, 95–110. Princeton, NJ: Princeton University Press.

Storr, Virgil Henry. 2008. "North's Underdeveloped Ideological Entrepreneur." *Annual Proceedings of the Wealth and Well-Being of Nations* 1: 99–115.

Storr, Virgil Henry, Stefanie Haeffele-Balch, and Laura E. Grube. 2015. *Community Revival in the Wake of Disaster: Lessons in Local Entrepreneurship*. New York, NY: Palgrave Macmillan.

Sullivan Mort, Gillian, Jay Weerawardena, and Kashonia Carnegie. 2003. "Social Entrepreneurship: Towards Conceptualisation." *International Journal of Nonprofit and Voluntary Sector Marketing* 8 (1): 76–88.

Szyndlar, Marta, and Emilia Wąsikiewicz-Firlej. 2019. "The LGBT Community as a Stakeholder in Communicating Corporate Social Responsibility: An Analysis of Selected Case Studies." *Scripta Neophilologica Posnaniensia* 19:191–221.

Thaler, Cole, Flor Bermudez, and Susan Sommer. 2009. "Legal Advocacy on Behalf of Transgender and Gender Nonconforming Youth." In *Social Work Practice with Transgender and Gender Variant Youth*, edited by Gerald P. Mallon, 153–176. New York City: Routledge.

Thomas, Victoria E. 2020. "Gazing at "It": An Intersectional Analysis of Transnormativity and Black Womanhood in Orange is the New Black." *Communication, Culture & Critique* 13 (4): 519–535.

Treichler, Paula A. 1999. *How to Have Theory in an Epidemic: Cultural Chronicles of AIDS.* Durham, NC: Duke University Press.

Tsai, Robert L. 2018. "Obama's Conversion on Same-Sex Marriage: The Social Foundations of Individual Rights." *Connecticut Law Review* 50 (1): 1–60.

Tullock, Gordon. 2004. "Virginia Political Economy." In *The Selected Works of Gordon Tullock, Volume 1*, edited by Charles K. Rowley. Indianapolis, IN: Liberty Fund.

Upadhyay, Nishant. 2019. "'Can You Get More American than Native American?': Drag and Settler Colonialism in RuPaul's Drag Race." *Cultural Studies* 33 (3): 480–501.

Wagner, Richard E. 1966. "Pressure Groups and Political Entrepreneurs: A Review Article." *Papers on Non-Market Decision Making* 1 (1): 161–170.

Wagner, Richard E. 2016. *Politics as a Peculiar Business: Insights from a Theory of Entangled Political Economy*. Cheltenham, UK: Edward Elgar.

Walters, Suzanna Danuta. 2001. *All the Rage: The Story of Gay Visibility in America.* Chicago, IL: University of Chicago Press.

Willard, Zane Austin. 2026. "Confronting and Subverting LGBTQIA+ Surveillance." In *Oxford Research Encyclopedias: Science, Technology, and Society*, edited by Rayvon Fouché. Oxford, UK: Oxford University Press.

Willard, Zane Austin, and Rachel E. Dubrofsky. 2024. "RuPaul's Drag Race: Queer Authenticity and Strategic Westernness." *Communication, Culture and Critique* 17 (3): 170–176.

Willard, Zane Austin, and Alisha L. Menzies. 2024. "Fashioning Zaya Wade in the Press: Authenticity, Black Femininity, and Transnormativity." *Journal of Communication Inquiry* 48 (4): 581–598.

Williams, Clay M., and Evan Ringel. 2026. "A Review of Anti-Drag Legislation and Its Implications for Drag performers' Mental Health." *Journal of Homosexuality* 73 (7): 1742–1765.

4

THE MARKET AS A QUEER SOCIAL SPACE

Mikayla Novak

Queer accounts of economic life tend to be, though not exclusively, critical of the impact of markets upon gay, lesbian, bisexual, transgender, and queer (LGBTQ) people. In a series of critiques that parallel communitarian thought, or the earlier identified tensions between community-minded *Gemeinschaft* and commercial-minded *Gesellschaft* (Tönnies [1887] 1957), certain queer theorists have considered markets as being corrosive of societal functioning and vitality more generally, and specifically detrimental to the aspirations and needs of diverse gender and sexual minorities. This position puts aside the objections to mainstream economic assumptions and methodological commitments which are labeled by queer economists as being unrealistic. In particular, the *homo economicus* model is seen to present a reductive version of human agency that ignores the socio-cultural (and not to mention, economic) implications of transgressive identity and desire (Cornwall 1997).

The queer-theoretic objection to markets may be interpreted as consisting of two interrelated elements. There are concerns that markets, and in particular the expansion of commercial enterprises selling products with notes of queer aesthetic and symbolism, have the effect of "colonizing" queer life, and in turn draining LGBTQ communities of their diverse vitalities. Guidotto (2006: 1, 2) cynically refers to an assimilationist so-called "McQueer phase" that suggests "what many are toting as 'liberation' is nothing short of being sold (out) in a Styrofoam container with a side of fries." Meanwhile, Clark (1993) refers to a "normalization pressure" upon LGBTQ people as the likes of "lesbian chic" diffuse through consumer markets. Similarly, the competitive striving of economic entrepreneurs to appeal to conventional tastes via the production of outputs, and specifically the development of a "gay market," is seen as unlikely to nullify the need for political activism that seeks recognition of gendered and sexual differences. For example, Skover and Testy

DOI: 10.4324/9781003615781-4

(2002) juxtapose the valorizing potentials of gender and sexual identity commodification with the political struggles to overcome stigma and devaluation in legal and political contexts.

The argument in this chapter is not to suggest that queer life in the market is not without its problems. As has been identified by decades of scholarship under the rubric of queer economics, LGBTQ people have experienced economic discrimination to some extent, and with certain sub-groups with the community often finding themselves toward the wrong end of income inequality distributions (Jacobsen and Zeller 2008; Badgett et al. 2021). However, queer objections concerning the social implications of markets are argued here to overlook those elements of economic activities which *are not* antagonistic toward the LGBTQ community. For a start, empirical evidence has been produced which gives some comfort to economic liberals concerning the capacity of market interactions to foster attitudes which are not antithetical or hostile toward gender and sexual minorities. For example, Berggren and Nilsson (2013) report a positive correlation between economic freedom and toleration toward homosexuals. More recently, Storr and Choi (2019: 176) report that "individuals residing in market societies are more likely to be open toward religious, sexual, and cultural differences. In fact, respondents from market societies are more likely to be accepting of homosexuality."[1] These alternative perspectives may be interpreted as part of the intellectual groundwork for a queer classical liberal framing of the role and function of markets in LGBTQ lives.

Scholars have recently contributed to the literature on the sociality of markets by integrating the insights of Austrian economics, economic sociology, and cultural science (Storr 2008, 2009; Chamlee-Wright and Storr 2015; Storr and John 2020). Attributable to the novel research efforts of Virgil Storr and his colleagues at George Mason University, the market has come to be identified as a *social space* wherein participants congregate and emergently build connections of personal intimacy and friendship going beyond what is necessary to consummate commercial transactions. Not only are these social connections owing to the unique contexts in which they are forged, but they are potentially deep connections thus contrasting the usual attribution of markets with fleeting and ephemeral interpersonal encounters. I henceforth refer to these pro-social implications of market processes as "Storrian effects."

Storr and colleagues have depicted markets as social spaces in a variety of applications, including life in developing countries (Chamlee-Wright 1997), how people interact economically to rebuild their lives post-disaster (Storr et al. 2015), and friendship in the commercial sphere during a pandemic (Storr et al. 2023). There is an underexplored angle which can refer to markets as *queer social spaces*, which is the central focus of this chapter.

In many places around the world, commercial venues emerged that enabled LGBTQ people to meet one another and develop friendships and even romantic relations. There are other, indirect, channels through which market activities helped to foster queer sociality. A host of economic intermediaries took advantage of technological developments, such as communication and information technologies, to reduce informational asymmetries about where members of the queer community could meet, thus reducing isolation. The entangled nature of social life, with associational opportunities that criss-cross economic, political, and social domains (Wagner 2016), provided further opportunities for friendships and intimacies – for example, as people organized and maintained LGBTQ business associations and similar interest organizations. Markets as queer social spaces assisted LGBTQ people to resist, if not overcome, senses of prejudice and stigma traditionally attached to diverse gender identities and sexual orientations.

The structure of the chapter is as follows. The next section will present an outline of the characteristics and implications of Storrian effects, with linkages also drawn to adjacent literature in economic sociology and political economy (Zelizer 1994, 2011; Ostrom 1998). This is followed by a series of case studies highlighting the many ways through which market activities promoted queer social relationships in major North American cities. Examples of pro-social market interactions beyond the North American case will also be discussed. The chapter will then conclude, highlighting how queer individuals took advantage of economic opportunity to actively build social connectivity and solidarities with one another.

Storrian effects: Understanding the sociable economic life

To comprehend an explicitly social dimension underlining market activities, it is appropriate to initially turn to the contributions of Virgil Storr and his colleagues. Storr is an active scholarly contributor toward what is the modern intellectual representation of the so-called "mainline" tradition of political economy (e.g., Boettke 2012), which is attached to a legacy stretching from Smith and Menger to Mises and Hayek and to Buchanan, Vincent and Elinor Ostrom, and Don Lavoie. The mainline approach emphasizes the epistemic dimensions of, and contributions of entrepreneurship toward, market processes; both economic and political activities as exchange processes; and the possibilities of emergent social coordination and self-governance as foundations of human flourishing. The distinct contributions of Storr, and those of his colleagues, within this mainline political economy project is to integrate concepts from political economy, cultural studies, and economic sociology to affirm market processes in ways previously underappreciated in mainstream thinking. Specifically, as told by Storr (2009: 279), "the market is a space that encourages the development of social bonds."

To some extent, the idea of the market as a social space is posed as a critique. More precisely, mainline intellectual efforts to recognize the sociability which permeates market relations is, to some extent, a response to perceived inadequacies surrounding treatments of the social in economics. Embodying the human agent as a representative being with fixed preferences and omniscience makes for analytical and empirical tractability, insofar as the frictions and complications of social relationality can be swept aside (Granovetter 1985). Critics argue that the mainstream strategy stretches ontological credibility: "[i]n effect, *homo economicus* is an emotionless, compassionless, uncompromising, friendless and calculating being, and the market is a space populated with agents who are identical to her" (Choi and Storr 2022: 121). The charge that the neoclassical economic actor is effectively an unsociable entity has certain affinities with queer critics of mainstream economics, such as Cornwall (1997) who castigates the orthodoxy for evading the economic implications of desire. Similar critical statements may be extended to the oversimplifications of mainstream reception to questions of identity (Davis 2011).

Austrian economics is regarded by proponents of mainline political economy as being more robust in its accounting of socially contextualized individuals. Mises and Hayek, the figureheads of the twentieth-century Austrian school, gave affirming nods to the market as a social phenomenon and how individuals are economically influenced by socio-cultural precepts. While it is true that "the agent in Austrian economics is not an isolated individuals without any socially meaningful relationship, roaming about in institution-less deserts" (Choi and Storr 2022: 121), it could also be said that the Austrians failed to provide a systematic intellectual account of the social as they prioritized other issues, such as economic calculation, distributed knowledge, and processual aspects of the market. Perhaps the generic lack of Austrian recognition about the importance of social activities is revealed by Hayek's (1979) rather sheepish acknowledgement of the civil societal studies of Richard Cornuelle, but the point here has even more to do with the perception that "[n]oncommercial activities and noncommercial relations are seen as epiphenomena" (Storr 2008: 142) by the Austrians.

The novel point of difference that Storr and colleagues wish to emphasize is that "meaningful market relationships also add value to our social lives" (Choi and Storr 2022: 131). This is because, "the market is not *merely* a social body, a social phenomenon, nor a process; the market is also a social space" (Choi and Storr 2022: 130). Since the time of Adam Smith, mainline economists have recognized the significance of speech acts within economic exchange contexts. Far from being delimited to mere enunciation of bids by consumers, and simple "yes/no" responses to them by suppliers, "conversations between socially bonded market participants concerned with more than simply making a deal happen frequently between market participants" (Storr 2010: 189). Indeed, the communicative property of market interaction, as an aspect of Storrian effects in the main, goes beyond bartering, negotiation, and other guises of higgling on the market, as I shall outline shortly.[2] Equally attuned to another Smithian idea – that of the innate tendencies by humans toward sociability with their fellows – an implication of Storr's intellectual project is the finding that "many beneficial social relationships are buttressed by markets and would not exist if markets did not exist" (Storr 2010: 189).

Storr and his colleagues, including students and research peers, have cataloged an array of examples to illustrate how markets facilitate social connections among heterogeneous individuals. Some examples are arguably more obvious than others.

Family businesses may be a more obvious case, with strong social connections that have the potential to span years, if not decades, owing to the presence of intergenerational entrepreneurship. Business owners and managers can develop friendships, and potentially even more, with their supply chain partners, with such social relations likely to galvanize over time. As will be noted later in this section, even market competitors can develop meaningful relationships of a social dimension with one another, through business associations, lobbying efforts, and commercial events bringing people together.

The idea that markets exert social effects is not limited to these examples. Storr (2010) refers to how coworkers can develop strong relationships with one another, and even romances that are separate from harassment cases and other forms of improper conduct. In stating that coworkers "often develop strong bonds because of their common experiences and circumstances" (Storr 2008: 145), such attachments could yield positive effects such as the dilution of drudgery that has sometimes been attributed to specialization and the rigors of work. Additionally, there are supplier-customer or principal-client relations throughout the economy. The exchange of pleasantries between staff and customers may not necessarily be contrived, as claimed by Hochschild (1983) with her concept of "emotional labor," but be, instead, organic and genuinely expressed and shared between parties, especially as they come to know one another through repeated exchanges.

What is significant about Storr's categorization of market-facilitative social deepening is his inclusion of consumption experiences. There seems little doubt that certain consumer items – such as Birkenstocks, Doc Martens, Absolut vodka, Calvin Klein, and Subaru cars – have been labeled, at least by some, as gay and lesbian products (Kates 1998; Mayyasi and Priceonomics 2016). Similarly, LGBTQ community members have been stereotyped as "excessive" shoppers, or conspicuous shoppers of niche fashion and other items (e.g., Penaloza 1996). However, Storrian effects refer to something else about consumption: its capacity to forge customer-customer relationships. Indeed, "[s]hopping and consuming can be social activities that provide an opportunity for friends to deepen their bonds" (Storr 2008: 146). As noted below, purchasing goods and services also serves as a means for individuals to signal their affiliation and support for the community. Storrian effects open the possibility that members of gender and sexual minority groups, too, engage in shared consumptive experiences among small groups of friends, having the beneficial effect of producing common experiences and strengthening social ties.

The upshot of the market as social space is that relationships are economically widespread, and they commonly evolve from merely acquaintance statuses. Storr and colleagues identify deep friendships, mentorship relationships, and even romantic relations wherein market participants share their innermost aspirations and concerns with one another, and oftentimes in a state of high trust. In this context, "commercial friendships, similar to other friendships, involve affection, intimacy, social support, loyalty, and reciprocal gift giving" (Price and Arnould, cited by

Storr 2010: 189). The relationships may manifest themselves within workplaces or other commercial venues, as well as outside those settings; for example, "[t] hink of the coworkers on the factory floor that also bowl and barbeque together" (Storr 2008: 137). The sincerity of friendships and other social connections within the market indicates that these shared experiences are not simply the instrumental accumulation of "social capital" (Coleman 1990), but genuine human bonds of affection, camaraderie, and solidarity whose breakage or cessation would likely cause deep emotional and psychological harms to those detrimentally affected by the relational losses.

Previously, I referred to the market as a social *space*. What does this mean, and what are the implications of space for the instantiation of Storrian effects? Drawing upon the Marxist anthropology of Henri Lefebvre, Storr refers to the use of physical spaces for the conduct of human activities that, furthermore, are imbued with intersubjective meanings and understandings with respect to legitimized purposes and uses of such spaces. The concept of space is simultaneously the result of social practice, as produced and reproduced by social activity, and a site of social life as inhabited by participating individuals (Storr 2008: 141). Crucial to Storr's theoretical construction is the proposition that the market itself is a benign kind of social space whereby "commercial relationships can grow into beneficial social bonds" (Storr 2010: 187). The Storrian appropriation of Lefebvre's anthropological appreciation of space as a locus for economically facilitated relationality problematizes the perception of the market as an abstraction with colonizing potential. It is also distinct from, but potentially complementary to, Ikeda's (2012) reference to an "action space" being the spatialized dimension of the exercise of economically entrepreneurial activities.

To briefly foreshadow what is to follow, the emergence of LGBTQ districts in urban areas is often seen as galvanizing a sense of community orchestrated around diverse gender identities and sexual orientations. In a similar vein to Lefebvre and Storr, Kates (1998: 13) describes these districts as possessing "spatial boundaries, all basic social services, a concentration of like-minded (in certain limited but significant respects) people, a reproduction of all functions of an entire society (i.e., a microcosm), and a collective memory." In the next section, I will illustrate how commercial enterprises within such locations have enabled gender and sexual minorities to undertake "expressive" spending for empathic or sympathetic purposes with, and for, other LGBTQ community members to, *inter alia*, retain a localized, sub-cultural circulation of funds. Alongside the desire to keep spending "queer and local," so to speak, are the distinct possibilities that individuals strategically shop for items that help them semiotically express their identities to others, reducing the search costs of finding other members of the LGBTQ community.

In his works, Storr largely refers to meaningful social connections through face-to-face interactions in economic contexts. But Storrian effects are inclusive of technological intermediation, notably communications, that provide individuals with information about the social environment which, in turn, has the potential to encourage subsequent face-to-face interactions. As noted by Behr and Storr (2022: 296), a "greater ability to communicate and greater access to information both allow for easier association." Storr (2008: 146) has also noted that transportation services are also instrumental "in building communities and cementing relationships across sometimes great distances." Of note is that communications and transportation infrastructure, and the services associated with them, may "allow individuals to be more selective by making it easier for them to find and communicate with the groups that they want to be associated with" (Storr 2009: 282).

The capacity of intermediation to facilitate *discoveries* of social opportunities by LGBTQ individuals is significant. Gender and sexual minorities have, much like everybody else, an innate desire to associate with like-minded, and similarly identified, people. However, the capacity for association by members of the community has long been suppressed by social norms that privilege cisgender and heterosexual lifestyles and prerogatives, coupled with severe legal restrictions including criminalization of homosexual sex and gender nonconformity. Communicative outlets, such as gay and lesbian newspapers and magazines, radio transmissions, and, more recently, the provision of LGBTQ websites, social media, and other digital platforms, helped reduce isolation within queer communities. Meanwhile, the availability of transportation has enabled gender and sexual minorities to physically come together at certain locations to build affections and friendship bonds, as well as escape intolerant mainstream communities. The value of technological intermediation in bringing marginalized groups together has also been affirmed in respect of racial minorities, for example, the role of Sears catalogs and the "Green Book" travel guide enabling African Americans to circumvent institutionalized discrimination in the Jim Crow American South (Magness 2018; Scott 2021).

Another social dimension of economic life that may be added to the panoply of Storrian effects concerns the influence of human organization in not only reducing transaction costs but providing an avenue for association. Storr refers to commercial enterprises, but economic agents can also develop and nurture social relationships within and through economic associations, such as business representative organizations and similar mercantile interest groups. It is likely that intra-organizational collaborations would strengthen social ties, given that organizations "function as filters resulting in attitudinally similar employees which may, in turn, increase the potential for romantic initiations" (Price et al., cited by Storr 2010: 189). While students of the social implications of markets should be mindful as to whether economic associations encourage productive (profit seeking) or unproductive (rent seeking) entrepreneurship (Chamlee-Wright and Storr 2011), identification of social connectivity within such entities is in keeping with Storr's (2008: 141) elemental point that "real relationships that are not merely commercial relationships and meaningful contacts that cannot be reduced to mere business contacts are also developed and nurtured in markets."

In summary, Storr (2008: 141) indicates that markets are "vibrant, colorful social spaces where real relationships and meaningful contacts are developed and nurtured." This socialized interpretation of market effects, filled with personal bonding, bantering, congeniality, and even affection given circumstances of time and place, is consistent with empirical observations to the effect that "[f]ew real world exchanges ... are anonymous or even impersonal" (Storr 2008: 147). The idea that market processes can sustain human connections and communal feeling is in sharp contrast with ideas articulated by certain queer theorists, and others, that markets somehow encroach upon or devour sociality: "[t]he death of social bonds does not appear to be a cost of the growth of market relationships" (Storr 2009: 281). To the extent that Storrian effects are upheld both theoretically and empirically, these phenomena advance a novel, and indeed compelling, case for market activities in addition to the standard mainline case of the market as an economic order promoting effective coordination among diverse, heterogeneous individuals.

Markets as queer social spaces: North American case studies

The articulation of Storrian effects demonstrates that "the market is not a cold, impersonal space" (Storr and John 2020: 54). Rather, the market is "a deeply meaningful space (like the home or the church), where people's lives play out, where people build relationships, and where people develop their character, identities, and aspirations" (Storr and John 2020). The social implications of market activity are evident from a reading of historical literatures of both LGBTQ communities, and of personal lives within those communities. From the preceding discussions, I identify three kinds of Storrian effects of relevance to the queerly lived experience: (i) personal relationships developed within commercial settings and in the context of market activity; (ii) the usage of commercial sites (including intermediary services) to galvanize larger-scale associations, as well as building social experiences and collective memories; and (iii) the deliberate purposing of funds and resources, created by generic market growth and economic development, for specific community-oriented projects.

What follows is a presentation of selective case studies from secondary literature that illustrate the presence of Storrian effects within the LGBTQ context. The case studies are further restricted to those of major North American cities with large LGBTQ population shares, such as New York, San Francisco, Los Angeles, Chicago, Toronto, Montreal, and others (Conron et al. 2021; Statistics Canada 2021). It must be noted that the cases should not necessarily be construed as being representative of *all* queer communities in North America (or elsewhere), or of the array of social effects of market interaction in other contexts. There are numerous sites of concentrated LGBTQ residencies and economic activity in Europe, Australasia, and elsewhere, some of which will also be discussed in this chapter.

It is also important to appreciate that LGBTQ history is unlikely to be fully accessible for this (or any other) research, for stigmatization and marginalization effects are presumed to have deterred many community members from publicly (including on an anonymous or pseudonymous basis) discussing their life experiences. With this qualification in mind, I focus much of my attention upon the social effects of economic interactions by LGBTQ people from the years following World War II to roughly the 1990s,[3] the latter commonly identified as the commencement of the "mainstreaming" of queer culture and economy (e.g., Lukenbill 1995; Walters 2001; Seidman 2002). I not only wish to show that Storrian effects existed to the benefits of gender and sexual minorities, with markets providing the capacity to produce a range of social benefits, but that such effects were evident *even during a period of legal repression and social conformity.*

Commercial sites and building personal relations

The effects of commercial enterprises in facilitating queer relationalities and shared senses of identity have been recognized. For example, Dennis Altman (1982: 21) argued that "[n]o other minority has depended so heavily on commercial enterprises to define itself," and, similarly, "[o]ne of the ironies of American capitalism is that it has been a major force in creating and maintaining a sense of identity among homosexuals." An iconic example of this is the gay bar or nightclub. Numerous ethnographic testimonies attest to the existence of such commercial venues as sites of self-discovery and self-realization for individual gays and lesbians. The 1960s homophile activist Otto Bremerman recalled that his first visit to a San Francisco gay bar felt like "home" (Smith 2021). Kates (1998) reports that first-time visits to Toronto nightclubs by gay men led to revisions of certain negative stereotypes about same-sex sociality as reported in mainstream media outlets and through previous peer-to-peer communications.

The communal feeling of interacting within for-profit bars and nightclubs was not restricted to first-time, "rite of passage" visitors. Testimonials chronicled by researchers also indicated that bars and nightclubs provided a persistent sense of equivalence (or a near-equivalence) between interacting within these venues and being with family. One lesbian reported that frequenting a Los Angeles beer bar with white and Latina lesbians "was like going to a friend's home or a community center" (Faderman and Timmons 2006: 90). Arguably this perception is reinforced by the availability of multi-faceted services, as a given bar may also serve "as a loan office, restaurant, message reception center, telephone exchange, and so forth" for patrons (Achilles [1967] 1998: 175). Others, such as Cartier (2013), described how frequenting bars were for some LGBTQ community members akin to being in a religious-type congregation. The significance of this point is reflective in other studies suggesting that interactions within commercial environments engendered collective effloresence between LGBTQ individuals (e.g., Harry and DeVall 1978). Within this, repeated interactions within bars and nightclubs contributed to the emergence of clearly delineated sub-cultures, such as butch-femme dynamics in lesbian spaces, the leather or motorcycle appreciation scene in others, and so on (e.g., Harry 1974; Armstrong 2002; Cartier 2013). As stated by Smith (2021: 130), "[g]ay bars were, and are, hubs for socializing, political organizing, and experiencing oneself as a joyous being connected to one's desired cultures, subcultures, and communities."

Commercial spaces of LGBTQ socialization were not limited to the bars and nightclubs.[4] Cafes and restaurants are an obvious place wherein LGBTQ community members mingle and form not only acquaintances but solidify more meaningful relationships (Podmore 2001; Faderman and Timmons 2006: 149–150). Alvarez (2008) draws upon interviews and surveys to highlight how gyms represent a social space for gay men, with friendships and relationships being commonplace within those venues. Bookstores, with either general offerings or adults-only publications, have been important in facilitating encounters between individuals, for example, lesbian feminists (Meeker 2006). Even spaces facilitating seemingly fleeting interactions, such as gay bathhouses, have been seen as "important locations for the constitution and building of gay male communities" (Nash 2014: 86). Not only did bathhouses provide reasonably safe spaces for intimate encounters to realize same-sex attraction, but they helped establish a socio-cultural environment among patrons and management as illustrated by Chauncey's (1994, ch. 8) discussion of the "social world of the baths."

Storrian effects emphasize that individuals interact within commercial venues, and use such locations, to help forge a variety of social relationships. Queer literature suggests that in addition to customer-customer relationships, such as those consummated within the bar and nightclub scenes, other durable interactions have been formed – specifically, relationships between suppliers and customers, and coworkers, and business partnerships. Achilles ([1967] 1998) referred to the crucial role of bartenders not only in symbolically projecting the preferred clientele of a gay bar but engendering a "following" between the business and customer. Indeed, it has been known that clients would switch their bar attendances based upon the inter-firm mobility of a popular bartender. Cartier (2013) and Canaday (2023) refer to coworker relationships formed among women within the nursing profession and in manufacturing industries wherein same-sex-attracted people congregated. Meeker (2006) and Johnson (2019) refer to the partnerships between Hal Call and Don Lucas in founding and operating Pan-Graphic press which produced homophile publications, and the example of gay couple Randolph Benson and John Bullock who published the *Grecian Guild Pictorial* physique magazine.

Economic intermediation and developing associations

Analysis of LGBTQ economic history indicates that a growing assembly of entrepreneurs provided more than direct goods and services to community members. During the second half of the twentieth century, a host of commercial enterprises provided indirect services to gays, lesbians, bisexual, transgender, and queer people, notably by acting as intermediaries between suppliers and demanders of products. Earlier, I referred to how certain bars provided additional services for their customers, "such as taking messages, lending money, or providing a bottle of milk for the cat" (Achilles [1967] 1998: 181). In an interesting example during the during the repressive era of the "closeted economy" prior to the 1970s, the former bartender of the Chicago "Lost and Found" lesbian nightclub recounted how she presided over same-sex marriages (Cartier 2013: 10). Later in this chapter, I will provide examples of commercial enterprises providing donations (cash and in-kind) for certain LGBTQ causes.

Business associations generically serve the function of economizing transactions, and certain other, costs which would otherwise be borne by individual establishments. In 1962, a coalition of gay bar owners and liquor wholesalers established the Tavern Guild to, in part, protect members from the economic and financial instabilities resulting from regular bar raids by law enforcement personnel in San Francisco. This objective had a clear political dimension which is, in turn, suggestive of the deeply entangled character of LGBTQ intermediary activities during this period. As noted by Boyd (1998: 1362–1363), "[t]he Tavern Guild used queer economic resources in the 1960s to achieve limited political alliances and expanded civil rights without relying on a politic of mainstream visibility." The efforts of the Guild, in tandem with individual activists and emerging social movements, in overturning the bar raid regime (and similar attempts at repressing economic activity) helped to increase confidence in the queer business sector and, from there, deepened the LGBTQ market. About a decade later in the same city, Harvey Milk was involved in establishing the Castro Village Merchants Association in response to the exclusion of gay-operated businesses by the then-existing Eureka Valley Merchants Association (Harry and DeVall 1978; Alan 2023).

Intermediation that has had the effect of undergirding relationships was not only evident at the local level. LGBTQ people were actively involved in developing their own communications network, and experimented with systems, to support cheaper and easier informational transfers between individuals over longer distances. Several researchers have investigated the profound effects of guidebooks in enabling individuals to overcome isolation and find others within the LGBTQ community. Weightman (1981: 110) noted, for example, that

> [i]f one is a stranger in a city, a bar guide or perhaps a newspaper will point the way to a bar, a restaurant, gay community centers or some other facility where the stranger can meet people and make new acquaintances.

The sense of community associated with expanding communication is not restricted to the knowledge gained by those parties receiving information. It has been indicated that guidebook preparation was an ongoing, co-productive process between the suppliers and readers of information contained therein. Meeker (2006: 203) says that numerous guidebooks "were compiled as both small-scale do-it-yourself projects and as collaborative works in which the line between author and reader was quite permeable." An example is Bruce Baird's *Le Guide Gris* (Grey Guide) of gay-friendly accommodation and services outside of the United States:

> as the guidebook gained additional readers and it achieved wider distribution, readers started to assist Baird in the collecting of information by correcting mistakes from previous editions and by offering dispatches from places around the globe that Baird had yet to visit, including locations in Africa, the Middle East, and Asia.
> (Meeker 2006: 207)

Even without mobility to places with concentrated LGBTQ economic and social activities, the provision of books, guides, magazines, newsletters, and newspapers had the effect of fostering the development of an "imagined community" among gays, lesbians, and other gender and sexual minorities across the United States. For example, Johnson's (2019) historical account of physique magazines demonstrated that members of a community need not be in close physical proximity to one another. In the case he describes, individuals merely require a shared interest – in this case, in male bodybuilding and modeling – to be (or at least have the potential to be) counted as a community. Developments in respect of community organization (e.g., hosting pride festivals in major global cities), symbolic recognition (e.g., origination and use of the rainbow pride flag), and even legal victories (e.g., same-sex marriage in several developed countries) have further consolidated the sense that non-cisgender and non-heterosexual individuals can belong to an LGBTQ community of shared consciousness and solidarity (Formby 2017).[5]

Considerable attention has been accorded to the emergence of certain localities in major North American cities as concentrated sites of LGBTQ residency, commercial, and social activity. Some examples of these include Greenwich Village in New York City, the Castro area of San Francisco, Boystown in Chicago, Toronto's Church and Wellesley area, and the Gay Village of Montreal. These locations not only include commercial shopfronts and physical amenities that incorporate signs and symbols of accommodation toward LGBTQ community members. Gay-friendly locales are perceived by people to be shared "action spaces" (Weightman 1981; Ikeda 2012) wherein gender and sexual minorities can express themselves, as well as interact with like-minded others, in relative openness and safety.

In an area such as Boulevard St. Laurent in Montreal, even visibility is viewed as crucial to generating a sense of shared communal space. For lesbians,

> Boul. St-Laurent was an important 'place' in their own everyday geographies because of this visibility and sociability to and with each other. By frequenting

> the street itself and some of its institutions and businesses, they, on some level, 'queer' particular sites for themselves.
>
> (Podmore 2001: 348)

Whereas past debates centered over what extent the co-presence of LGBTQ community members in specific districts was, itself, constraining (e.g., Wittman 1970), it seems that generic tendencies in the direction of greater public toleration of diverse gender and sexual activity and expression, and traces of LGBTQ interactivity beyond so-called "ghettoes" of spatial concentration, have tempered the force of earlier discussions.

Market resources and leveraging community interests

In contrast to the idea that LGBTQ community members have, or should, reject any form of engagement with the commercial sphere, there is considerable anecdotal evidence that gender and sexual minorities have undertaken the opposite. Not only have individuals established their own businesses and forms of economic intermediation, but they have actively sought to engage with commercial enterprises owned by LGBTQ community members or those situated within gay-friendly districts. As an illustration of this "buy gay" mentality, one respondent in Kates's study of consumption by gay males in Toronto said: "I buy in the gay community because I like to put my money where the gay people are" (Kates 1998: 125). Similarly, a Toronto gay community activist once quipped, "gay money is damned good money," urging members of the community to use their buying power to support gay-owned businesses and demand superior service quality (Nash 2014).

It is also important to bear in mind that people have repurposed funding and assets generated from economic exchanges for the benefit of building LGBTQ civic capital and social infrastructures. The diversity of ways in which this has been achieved, and the prevalence of the redeployment of monies and property over decades past, has been striking. Bars, hotels, nightclubs, and restaurants were not only used to host club and community meetings for LGBTQ groups, but it is well known that commercial enterprises have provided donations, sponsorship money, and goods in-kind to support social activities for LGBTQ groups. San Francisco's gay bars donated food and drinks for Society for Individual Rights parties in the mid-1960s (D'Emilio 1983), while bars and other commercial premises in this area and elsewhere funded gay and lesbian sporting activities (Harry and DeVall 1978). Bérubé (2003: 40) noted that gay bathhouses organizing parties on public holidays "were a tremendous service to the gay men whose families had rejected them and for whom holidays represented a particularly depressing time of year."

A host of commercial outlets have been instrumental in funding local pride parades, both from their inception and to today. For example, as to the question regarding who funded the first Long Beach Pride Festival, a former board member noted:

"that the money for our first Festival *was lesbian bar money* is undisputed" (cited in Cartier 2013: 150). The Lambda Rising bookstore in Washington, D.C., sponsored that city's first gay and lesbian pride celebrations (Johnson 2019: 78). Many of the contemporary debates concerning the appropriateness of commercial sponsorships of LGBTQ pride festivals tend to overshadow the realities of funding from for-profit sources in the establishment of what are now significant symbolic events that publicly project the existence of, and issues pertaining to, LGBTQ communities.

The economic history of LGBTQ is exemplified by abundant efforts to self-finance and provide their own community amenities and social services. To some extent, the community benefited from the increasing wealth enjoyed by individuals, as legal, regulatory, and social restrictions eased, and economic discrimination tended to wane. Armstrong and Crage referred to promulgation of reforms as the product of an implicit, Stonewall-era alliance between affluent, educated, and politically connected gays with resources and with a proclivity to engage in legal challenges and poorer individuals who "often served as a source of innovation and a 'radical flank' of the movement" (Armstrong and Crage 2006: 744). Devor and Matte (2006) recall the life of Reed Erickson, a trans man who used his inheritance in part to fund education and research by the gay rights organization ONE Inc. (which published the ONE magazine from 1953 to 1969).

Community clubs and associations would also show little hesitation in activating fundraising initiatives to maintain their operations. For example, the New York-based Men of All Colors Together (MACT) social group would fundraise by organizing an annual dinner and dance onboard a circle line ship around Manhattan (Shokeid 2015). The Los Angeles Gay Women's Services Center, which provided the first social services agency exclusively for lesbians, would help pay for its operations by hosting a weekly dinner (Faderman and Timmons 2006). Of note is that even socialist and other radical community groups enjoined in the practice of fundraising – for example, certain collectives sought donations to fund HIV/AIDS awareness and education programs (Hobson 2016). Not every group enjoyed the same capacity to maintain their ventures, with gay and lesbian health clinics relying upon donations of second-hand resources (such as furnishings) from community members (Batza 2018).

Markets as queer social spaces elsewhere in the world

The following provides a selective sample of Storrian effects applicable to queer lived experiences in regions of the world outside of North America.

Europe (United Kingdom)

Much of the focus of queer studies in Britain is focused upon the great metropolis of London, although there have been considerable efforts to shed light upon the experiences of LGBTQ across the United Kingdom (e.g., Homfray 2007; Bengry et al. 2023). Within this literature there are several accounts of the importance of commercial enterprises in facilitating queer social life. In his accounting of London's LGBTQ scenes in the first half of the twentieth century, Matt Houlbrook describes a world in which:

> [c]ommercialized leisure ... created new opportunities for queer sociability. Men moved through a world that was deeply embedded in modern urban culture – that took hold in everyday sites and was shaped by the social, cultural, and economic landscape inhabited by all Londoners. Where they chose to socialize was informed by shared ideas of fashionability, and common financial constraints. As such, queer commercial sociability overlapped with that forged by disparate other groups. ... For some, consumerism opened up potentially *private* spaces, allowing them to meet friends discreetly in restaurants or bars while remaining invisible to onlookers. For others, it means access to sites of *public* sociability – venues where they could be openly different.
>
> (Houlbrook 2005: 69)

The extent of liberation that Houlbrook identifies with the emergence of LGBTQ commercialism is qualified by the entrenchment of class distinctions and other stratification markets during the period (Houlbrook 2005), however it is notable that the intersection of queerness and class probably contributed to the consolidation of areas such as Soho, in London's West End, as a spatial attractor for communal life among LGBTQ individuals and groups (Houlbrook 2005: 87–88; Bengry 2010; Joyce 2022).

The growth and extent of markets catering to LGBTQ people went beyond the nightclub scene or the maintenance of commercial venues allowing for sexual activities. Justin Bengry has written extensively upon the entrepreneurial development of British literary markets catering for a variety of queer readers – ranging from pornographic magazines to specialized publications catering to an array of interests and hobbies that may appeal to LGBTQ (and other) consumers. The *Film and Filming* magazine, for example, provided an expressive outlet for gay men encompassing "homosexually themes articles, advertising and contact ads" (Bengry 2013: 244). In some other instances, entrepreneurial insight has been implicated in the development of a queer reading audience, not to mention an identity for gay men, lesbian women, and others within the LGBTQ community. For example, the late nineteenth-century periodical, *The Artist and Journal of Home Culture*, "relied upon elite knowledge of Hellenic imagery and ideas of youthful masculine beauty to appeal to queer tastes while remaining palatable to its core heterosexual audience" (Bengry 2015: 25).

Oceania (Australia)

Arguably, the most iconic geographic hub of queer life in Australia is in Sydney, especially the inner suburban areas of Darlinghurst (and Oxford Street) and Newtown.

LGBTQ entrepreneurs in these spaces were implicated in reducing transaction costs, enabling consumers to enact exchanges with suppliers in Sydney's LGBTQ commercial scene. One of the ways they succeeded in doing so was to supply information about the availability of commercial activities, and the goods and services they provided. One case in point was that of Michael Glynn, an American expatriate who founded *The Sydney Star* (later *Sydney Star Observer*) newspaper in 1979. Published on a weekly basis, and made freely available in gay bars, bookstores, and certain other commercial premises,[6] Glynn's editorials expressed a destigmatizing motivation for the periodical – essentially, to use commercial media at a platform to build community awareness and pride (Calder 2016). It has been argued that the:

> newspaper played a critical role in the evolution, consolidation and survival of the Sydney gay and lesbian community through its affirmation of the 'coming out' narrative, through its articulation and promotion of sexual citizenship, and through its intervention in the homosexual law reform campaign and the fight against AIDS.
>
> (O'Grady 2012: 12)

Dowsett (1996: 240) refers to the anecdotal example of a young man who discovered an old copy of another publication (called *Campaign*) containing Sydney gay venue listings and uses this, and a newer copy of the same publication, to "read about the bars, venues, and events in the Oxford Street precinct. Three months later, he made his first furtive trip to Oxford Street." All in all, the provision of information through the gay press has been crucial in the commingled development of gay commerce and destigmatizing gay identity (Altman 1982; Wotherspoon 2016).

Storr's (2008: 283) description that "the market makes it easier for individuals to act on their social feelings and allows for a greater diversity of expressions" appears applicable to the pro-social attributes of Sydney's gay markets. People met others for short-term encounters or longer-term relationships in Sydney's gay bathhouses, bars, hotels, and other premises (e.g., Reynolds 2007). Recollections are also made of friendships forged in gay bars and other commercial venues, including one examples of a shared accommodation situation in inner-Sydney between one gay man and fellow bargoers (e.g., Dowsett 1996).

As important as markets have been as sites of connection, the compatibility between economic and social interactions and objectives has been contested. Nonetheless, instances can be found of LGBTQ communities engaging with finance and economics to help build community capacities. For example, the 1970s activist group Campaign Against Moral Persecution (CAMP) operated coffee shops and ran fundraising activities from their clubrooms in Sydney and elsewhere (Thompson 1985; Reynolds 2002). Another example has been the Oxford Street "Shop Yourself Stupid" event, with part of the proceeds from retail spending donated to leading HIV charitable concern the Bobby Goldsmith Foundation (Faro and Wotherspoon 2000).

Africa (South Africa)

South Africa is one of the more liberalized countries on the African continent in relation to LGBTQ rights, with constitutional protections for sexual orientation, same-sex marriage provisions, as well as adoption rights for same-sex couples. However, that country's history over the past century has been marred by the former apartheid regime, with its implications not only for racial relations but the treatment of people based upon gender identity and sexual orientation (e.g., Isaacs and McKendrick 1992; Jones 2008). The maintenance of apartheid was typically backed by heavy-handed (but inconsistent) police enforcement – including against gay-friendly venues found, or suspected to be supportive of, interracial intimacy and association (Leap 2004).

Even in these repressive contexts, LGBTQ communities were able to establish a meaningful presence in places such as the country's financial capital, Johannesburg, as well as the south-western coastal city of Cape Town. As indicated by Leap (Leap 2004: 139),

> interracial homosexuality was a visible part of Cape Town's gay scene, including … informal social exchange at several of the city's gay bars and clubs (although not all were willing to admit persons of color, even when licensing laws allowed them to do so).

Isaacs and McKendrick (1992) separately identify gay bars, gay clubs and other venues, and gay bookstores as among the distinct subsystems within Cape Town's LGBTQ commercial ecology. Although racial segmentation has remained evident during the post-apartheid era (Visser 2003; Tucker 2009), Cape Town has in modern times been promoted as the "gay capital" of not only South Africa but the entire African continent.

In addition to the existence of commercial premises fostering queer sociality, markets were used by LGBTQ South Africans to appropriate resources for social and political changes. Gevisser (1995) outlined how South Africans organized a "Law Reform" movement during the late 1960s to ward off legislative attempts to impose more severe punishments against sodomy. Fundraising was pivotal to this campaign for legal reform, according to one of the organizers: "fundraising drove the whole thing. The fundraising lists were the link between the grassroots and the organisers, and fundraising parties were the places where people meet" (cited in Gevisser 1995: 33). Fundraising was also perceived as an efficacious strategy to help amplify the voices and issues of black South Africans. By way of example, Simon Nkoli used fundraising as a technique to build a black interest group within the white-dominated Gay Association of South Africa (GASA) and, subsequently, to develop multiracial LGBTQ associations with as the Gay and Lesbian Organisation of the Witwatersrand (GLOW) (Gevisser 1995; Martin 2024).

Conclusion

Over the past decade or so, a team of researchers centered on Virgil Storr has originated scholarship that explicitly identifies markets as social spaces. Specifically, the perspective conveyed by this research effort is that "viewing the market as a social space emphasizes the social significance of economic relationships" (Storr 2008: 144). The idea that "meaningful social relationships … are buttressed by markets and could not develop if markets did not exist" (Storr 2010: 182) not only possesses analytical value but normative significance with respect to wider debates about the social implications of market interaction. This chapter has sought to extend the coverage of Storrian effects cited in literature through their specific application to the economic activities of members of the LGBTQ community.

It is hoped that this chapter will invite future research explorations among mainline political economists and queer classical liberals on the implications of markets for gender and sexual minorities. Mainline political economists have illustrated how trading relationships build connections between people over vast distances: "[o]ur market activities bring us into fellowship with people across the globe and across ethnicities and nationalities" (Storr 2009: 280). There is an opportunity to explore how globalization has affected the fortunes and sense of solidarity of local LGBTQ communities, especially those located in geographic hubs of queer flourishing. Perhaps a related issue is to explore how the advent of digital technologies is shaping LGBTQ association and community. The significance of this topic is that the advent of the Internet and social media has been cited as a causal factor in the decline of LGBTQ bars and nightclubs (Ghaziani 2014; Morgan 2019).

Aside from opportunities to produce additional applied research, there may be future opportunities to explore the sociological dimensions of queer markets. For example, researchers have explored the queer nighttime economy as examples of "subcultural incubators" (Mattson 2015) or "cultural fields" (Ghaziani 2025), which are concepts that may be productively interpreted through a mainline political economy lens. Meanwhile, opportunities await to use Viviana Zelizer's (2011) ideas to further develop a notion of "queer circuits of commerce," illustrating the complex and dynamic ways in which minorities such as members of the LGBTQ community interact with markets.

It is also important to consider how the growth of LGBTQ markets and the onset of social openness along gender and sexual lines, especially in developed countries, have affected the quality of social relations between LGBTQ and non-LGBTQ communities. Has the entrenchment of Storrian effects among LGBTQ people influenced broader community tolerance toward diverse gender and sexual expression and identity? If so, how? Finally, Storr and his colleagues have shown how markets propagate morals within society (Choi and Storr 2019). Have markets been an effective moral teacher for members of the LGBTQ community? In what respects have market-facilitative moral teachings diffused among this constituency? The specification of such questions suggests that this chapter should be seen as a first step in a living research agenda exploring the ways in which markets benefited historically oppressed gender and sexual minorities.

Notes

1 Also noteworthy is the findings of Badgett et al. (2019) of a positive correlation between legal rights for lesbian, gay, bisexual, and transgender persons and economic development. An implication of this result is that legal rights, themselves, emerge in environments exhibiting greater socio-cultural tolerance toward diversity with respect to gender identity and sexual orientation.

2 Social scientists have also recognized the significance of physical cues as heuristic aids for economic agents in discerning, *inter alia*, the trustworthiness (or otherwise) of potential counterparties to a given exchange (e.g., Scharlemann et al. 2001; Manzini et al. 2009).

3 This period corresponds with Escoffier's (1997) identification of four phases of evolution of the U.S. gay-lesbian economy – a post-war "closet economy" of small-scale enterprises on the borderlines of legality, followed by a late 1960s "liberation economy" of business growth consistent with legal and cultural liberalization, then a late 1970s "territorial economy" of gentrification and LGBTQ district development, and, finally, the 1980s "AIDS economy" that incentivized the growth of a gay services economy together with social and political organizations.

4 It has been argued in queer studies literature that bars and nightclubs were the primary sites for LGBTQ sociability during the mid-twentieth century period of legal and social restrictions. "For most of the 20th century, bars, nightclubs, and cafés were often the only place to meet other queer people" (Bailey 2021: 20). Nor should the use of private residences as locations for socializing be ignored during this period. Even so, liberalization during the 1960s and beyond certainly appears to have assisted the growth in the size and scope of commercial enterprises catering to LGBTQ community needs.

5 It is noted that some individuals who may identify as gay, lesbian, bisexual, or transgender may not identify with a broader "rainbow" LGBTQ community or may otherwise wish to distance themselves from perceived negative attributes attached to such a community (e.g., Winer 2022). Tensions among the various components of the LGBTQ community have contributed in recent years to the formation of sub-groups with strong exclusion boundaries. Notable among these is the LGB Alliance which excludes transgender individuals from its organizational and other activities.

6 It has been noted that Glynn formatted the printing size of the newspaper such that it could sit neatly on top of cigarette vending machines in bars, clubs, and hotels servicing gay customers (Calder 2015).

References

Achilles, Nancy [1967] 1998. "The Development of the Homosexual Bar as an Institution." In *Social Perspectives in Lesbian and Gay Studies: A Reader*, edited by Peter M. Nardi and Beth E. Schneider, 175–182. New York, NY: Routledge.

Alan, Terrance. 2023. "Harvey, the Merchants, and the Theater." Bay Area Reporter, April 19. https://www.ebar.com/story.php?ch=news&sc=news&id=324657.

Alvarez, Erick. 2008. *Muscle Boys: Gay Gym Culture*. New York: Haworth Press.

Altman, Dennis. 1982. *The Homosexualization of America: The Americanization of the Homosexual*. New York, NY: St. Martin's Press.

Armstrong, Elizabeth A. 2002. *Forging Gay Identities: Organizing Sexuality in San Francisco, 1950–1994*. Chicago, IL: University of Chicago Press.

Armstrong, Elizabeth A., and Suzanna M. Crage. 2006. "Movements and Memory: The Making of the Stonewall Myth." *American Sociological Review* 71 (5): 724–751.

Badgett, M. V. Lee, Kees Waaldijk, and Yana van der Meulen Rodgers. 2019. "The Relationship between LGBT Inclusion and Economic Development: Macro-level Evidence." *World Development* 120: 1–14.

Badgett, M. V. Lee, Christopher S. Carpenter, and Dario Sansone. 2021. "LGBTQ Economics." *Journal of Economic Perspectives* 35 (2): 141–170.

Bailey, Eliza Jane. 2021. "Personal Narratives: Discovering San Francisco's Changing Spaces for Queer Women." San Francisco State University, Master of Arts in Geography Thesis.

Batza, Katie. 2018. *Before AIDS: Gay Health Politics in the 1970s*. Philadelphia, PA: University of Pennsylvania Press.

Behr, Rachael K., and Virgil Henry Storr. 2022. "Tocquevillean Association and the Market." In *The Cambridge Companion to Democracy in America*, edited by Richard Boyd, 278–305. New York, NY: Cambridge University Press.

Bengry, Justin. 2010. "Peacock Revolution: Mainstreaming Queer Styles in Post-War Britain, 1945–1967." *Socialist History* 36: 55–68.

Bengry, Justin. 2013. "Films and Filming: The Making of a Queer Marketplace in Pre-decriminalisation Britain." In *British Queer History: New Approaches and Perspectives*, edited by Brian Lewis, 244–266. Manchester, UK: Manchester University Press.

Bengry, Justin. 2015. "Who is the Queer Consumer? Historical Perspectives on Capitalism and Homosexuality." In *Consuming Behaviours: Identity, Politics, and Pleasure in Twentieth-Century Britain*, edited by Erika Rappaport, Sandra Trudgen Dawson and Mark J. Crowley, 21–36. London, UK: Bloomsbury.

Bengry, Justin, Matt Cook, and Alison Oram. 2023. *Locating Queer Histories: Places and Traces Across the UK*. London, UK: Bloomsbury Academic.

Berggren, Niclas, and Therese Nilsson. 2013. "Does Economic Freedom Foster Tolerance?" *Kyklos* 66 (2): 177–207.

Bérubé, Allan. 2003. "The History of Gay Bathhouses." *Journal of Homosexuality* 44 (3–4): 33–53.

Boettke, Peter J. 2012. *Living Economics: Yesterday, Today, and Tomorrow*. Oakland, CA: Independent Institute.

Boyd, Nan Alamilla. 1998. "Shopping for Rights: Gays, Lesbians, and Visibility Politics." *Denver University Law Review* 75: 1361–1373.

Calder, Bill. 2015. "Gay Lifestyle Publications: Drawing the Crowds to Grow the Bar Scene." *Media International Australia* 156 (1): 39–49.

Calder, Bill. 2016. *Pink Ink: The Golden Era for Gay and Lesbian Magazines*. Newcastle upon Tyne, UK: Cambridge Scholars Publishing.

Canaday, Margot. 2023. *Queer Career: Sexuality and Work in Modern America*. Princeton, NJ: Princeton University Press.

Cartier, Marie. 2013. *Baby, You Are My Religion: Women, Gay Bars, and Theology Before Stonewall*. London, UK: Routledge.

Chamlee-Wright, Emily. 1997. *The Cultural Foundations of Economic Development: Urban Female Entrepreneurship in Ghana*. London, UK: Routledge.

Chamlee-Wright, Emily, and Virgil Henry Storr. 2011. "Social Capital, Lobbying and Community-based Interest Groups." *Public Choice* 149 (1/2): 167–185.

Chamlee-Wright, Emily, and Virgil Henry Storr. 2015. "Social Economy as an Extension of the Austrian Research Program." In *The Oxford Handbook of Austrian Economics*, edited by Peter J. Boettke and Christopher J. Coyne, 247–271. New York, NY: Oxford University Press.

Chauncey, George. 1994. *Gay New York: Gender, Urban Culture, and the Making of the Gay Male World, 1890–1940*. New York, NY: BasicBooks.

Choi, Ginny Seung, and Virgil Henry Storr. 2019. *Do Markets Corrupt Our Morals?* Cham, Switzerland: Palgrave Macmillan.

Choi, Ginny Seung, and Virgil Henry Storr. 2022. "The Social and Moral Aspects of Markets." In *A Modern Guide to Austrian Economics*, edited by Per L. Bylund, 121–141. Cheltenham, UK: Edward Elgar.

Clark, Danae. 1993. "Commodity Lesbianism." In *The Lesbian and Gay Studies Reader*, edited by Henry Abelove, Michèle Aina Barale, and David M. Halperin, 186–201. New York, NY: Routledge.

Coleman, James S. 1990. *Foundations of Social Theory*. Cambridge, MA: Belknap Press of Harvard University Press.

Conron, Kerith J., Winston Luhur, and Shoshana K. Goldberg. 2021. *LGBT Adults in Large US Metropolitan Areas*. Williams Institute. https://williamsinstitute.law.ucla.edu/publications/lgbt-us-msa.

Cornwall, Richard R. 1997. "Deconstructing Silence: The Queer Political Economy of the Social Articulation of Desire." *Review of Radical Political Economics* 29 (1): 1–130.

Davis, John B. 2011. *Individuals and Identity in Economics*. New York, NY: Cambridge University Press.

D'Emilio, John. 1983. *Sexual Politics, Sexual Communities: The Making of a Homosexual Minority in the United States, 1940–1970*. Chicago, IL: University of Chicago Press.

Devor, Aaron H., and Nicholas Matte. 2006. "ONE Inc. and Reed Erickson: The Uneasy Collaboration of Gay and Trans Activism, 1964–2003." In *The Transgender Studies Reader*, edited by Susan Stryker and Stephen Whittle, 387–406. New York, NY: Routledge.

Dowsett, Gary W. 1996. *Practicing Desire: Homosexual Sex in the Era of AIDS*. Stanford, CA: Stanford University Press.

Escoffier, Jeffrey. 1997. "The Political Economy of the Closet: Notes Toward an Economic History of Gay and Lesbian Life before Stonewall." In *Homo Economics: Capitalism, Community, and Lesbian and Gay Life*, edited by Amy Gluckman, and Betsy Read, 123–134. New York, NY: Routledge.

Faderman, Lillian, and Stuart Timmons. 2006. *Gay L.A.: A History of Sexual Outlaws, Power Politics, and Lipstick Lesbians*. New York, NY: Basic Books.

Faro, Clive, and Garry Wotherspoon. 2000. *Street Seen: A History of Oxford Street*. Carlton South, Victoria: Melbourne University Press.

Formby, Eleanor. 2017. *Exploring LGBT Spaces and Communities: Contrasting Identities, Belongings and Wellbeing*. New York, NY: Routledge.

Gevisser, Mark. 1995. "A Different Fight for Freedom: A History of South African Lesbian and Gay Organisation – The 1950s to the 1990s." In *Defiant Desire: Gay and Lesbian Lives in South Africa*, edited by Mark Gevisser and Edwin Cameron, 14–86. Oxford, UK: Taylor & Francis Group.

Ghaziani, Amin. 2014. *There Goes The Gayborhood?* Princeton, NJ: Princeton University Press.

Ghaziani, Amin. 2025. "The Cultural Field of Queer Nightlife: Organizations, Artists, and Curatorial Activism." *Sociological Quarterly* 66 (4): 724–747.

Granovetter, Mark. 1985. "Economic Action and Social Structure: The Problem of Embeddedness." *American Journal of Sociology* 91 (3): 481–510.

Guidotto, Nadia. 2006. "Cashing in on Queers: From Liberation to Commodification." *Canadian Online Journal of Queer Studies in Education* 2 (1): 1–28.

Harry, Joseph. 1974. "Urbanization and the Gay Life." *Journal of Sex Research* 10 (3): 238–247.

Harry, Joseph, and William B. DeVall. 1978. *The Social Organization of Gay Males*. New York, NY: Praeger.

Hayek, Friedrich A. 1979. *Law, Legislation and Liberty, Volume 3: The Political Order of a Free People*. Chicago, IL: University of Chicago Press.

Hobson, Emily K. 2016. *Lavender and Red: Liberation and Solidarity in the Gay and Lesbian Left*. Oakland, CA: University of California Press.
Homfray, Mike. 2007. *Provincial Queens: The Gay and Lesbian Community in the North-West of England*. Bern, Switzerland: Peter Lang.
Hochschild, Arlie Russell. 1983. *The Managed Heart: Commercialization for Human Feeling*. Berkeley, CA: University of California Press.
Houlbrook, Matt. 2005. *Queer London: Perils and Pleasures in the Sexual Metropolis, 1918–1957*. Chicago, IL: University of Chicago Press.
Ikeda, Sanford. 2012. "Entrepreneurship in Action Space." *Advances in Austrian Economics* 16: 105–139.
Isaacs, Gordon, and Brian McKendrick. 1992. *Male Homosexuality in South Africa: Identity Formation, Culture, and Crisis*. Cape Town, South Africa: Oxford University Press.
Jacobsen, Joyce, and Adam Zeller. 2008. *Queer Economics: A Reader*. London, UK: Routledge.
Johnson, David K. 2019. *Buying Gay: How Physique Entrepreneurs Sparked a Movement*. New York, NY: Columbia University Press.
Jones, Tiffany F. 2008. "Averting White Male (Ab)normality: Psychiatric Representations and Treatment of 'Homosexuality' in 1960s South Africa." *Journal of Southern African Studies* 34 (2): 397–410.
Joyce, John-Pierre. 2022. *Odd Men Out: Male Homosexuality in Britain from Wolfenden to Gay Liberation*. Manchester, UK: Manchester University Press.
Kates, Steven M. 1998. *Twenty Million New Customers! Understanding Gay Men's Consumer Behavior*. Binghampton, NY: Haworth Press.
Leap, William L. 2004. "Language, Belonging, and (Homo)sexual Citizenship in Cape Town, South Africa." In *Speaking in Queer Tongues: Globalization and Gay Language*, edited by William L. Leap and Tom Boellstorff, 134–162. Urbana, IL: University of Illinois Press.
Lukenbill, Grant. 1995. *Untold Millions: Positioning Your Business for the Gay and Lesbian Consumer Revolution*. New York, NY: HarperBusiness.
Magness, Phillip W. 2018. "The Economic Color Blindness of the Sears Catalog." American Institute for Economic Research. https://www.aier.org/article/the-economic-color-blindness-of-the-sears-catalog.
Manzini, Paola, Abdolkarim Sadrieh, and Nicolaas J. Vriend. 2009. "On Smiles, Winks and Handshakes as Coordination Devices." *Economic Journal* 119 (537): 826–854.
Martin, Yasmina. 2024. "Simon Nkoli, GLOW, and the Anti-Apartheid Struggle." Black Perspectives, April 30. https://www.aaihs.org/simon-nkoli-glow-and-the-anti-apartheid-struggle.
Mattson, Greggor. 2015. "Bar Districts as Subcultural Amenities." *City, Culture and Society* 6 (1): 1–8.
Mayyasi, Alex, and Priceonomics. 2016. "How Subarus Came to Be Seen as Cars for Lesbians." The Atlantic, June 22. https://www.theatlantic.com/business/archive/2016/06/how-subarus-came-to-be-seen-as-cars-for-lesbians/488042.
Meeker, Martin. 2006. *Contacts Desired: Gay and Lesbian Communications and Community, 1940s–1970s*. Chicago, IL: University of Chicago Press.
Morgan, Richard. 2019. "The American Gay Bar Is Down, But Don't Count It Out Just Yet." Bloomberg, June 28. https://www.bloomberg.com/news/articles/2019-06-28/the-american-gay-bar-is-down-but-don-t-count-it-out-just-yet.
Nash, Catherine J. 2014. "Consuming Sexual Liberation: Gay Business, Politics, and Toronto's Barracks Bathhouse Raids." *Journal of Canadian Studies* 48 (1): 82–105.
O'Grady, Dominic. 2012. "Preaching to the Perverted: Michael Glynn and the Sydney Star." University of Sydney, Ph.D. Thesis.
Ostrom, Elinor. 1998. "A Behavioral Approach to the Rational Choice Theory of Collective Action: Presidential Address." *American Political Science Review* 92 (1): 1–22.

Penaloza, Lisa. 1996. "We're Here, We're Queer, and We're Going Shopping!" *Journal of Homosexuality* 31 (1–2): 9–41.
Podmore, Julie A. 2001. "Lesbians in the Crowd: Gender, Sexuality and Visibility Along Montréal's Boul. St-Laurent." *Gender, Place and Culture: A Journal of Feminist Geography* 8 (4): 333–355.
Reynolds, Robert. 2002. *From Camp to Queer: Re-making the Australian Homosexual*. Melbourne, Australia: Melbourne University Press.
Reynolds, Robert. 2007. *What Happened to Gay Life?* Sydney, NSW: University of New South Wales Press.
Scharlemann, Jörn P. W., Catherine C. Eckel, Alex Kacelnik, and Rick K. Wilson. 2001. "The Value of a Smile: Game Theory with a Human Face." *Journal of Economic Psychology* 22 (5): 617–640.
Scott, Michael. 2021. *The Green Book*. Cato Institute. https://www.libertarianism.org/articles/green-book.
Seidman, Steven. 2002. *Beyond The Closet: The Transformation of Gay and Lesbian Life*. New York, NY: Routledge.
Shokeid, Moshe. 2015. *Gay Voluntary Associations in New York: Public Sharing and Private Lives*. Philadelphia, PA: University of Pennsylvania Press.
Skover, David M., and Kellye Y. Testy. 2002. "LesBiGay Identity as Commodity." *California Law Review* 90 (1): 223–255.
Smith, Tegan. 2021. "Gay Bars in Pre-Stonewall San Francisco: "Walk-In Closets" as the Source of a Surprisingly Divergent Queer Activism." *Historical Perspectives: Santa Clara University Undergraduate Journal of History* 26: 107–131.
Statistics Canada. 2021. "LGBTQ2+ Communities in Canada: A Demographic Snapshot." https://www150.statcan.gc.ca/n1/pub/11-627-m/11-627-m2021062-eng.htm.
Storr, Virgil Henry. 2008. "The Market as a Social Space: On the Meaningful Extraeconomic Conversations that Can Occur in Markets." *Review of Austrian Economics* 21 (2): 135–150.
Storr, Virgil Henry. 2009. "Why the Market? Markets as Social and Moral Spaces." *Journal of Markets and Morality* 12 (2): 277–296.
Storr, Virgil Henry. 2010. "Hayek and Lefebvre on Market Space and Extra-catallactic Relationships." In *Economic Pluralism*, edited by Robert Garnett, Erik K. Olsen, and Martha Starr, 181–193. London, UK: Routledge.
Storr, Virgil Henry, and Ginny Seung Choi. 2019. *Do Markets Corrupt Our Morals?* Cham, Switzerland: Palgrave Macmillan.
Storr, Virgil Henry, and Arielle John. 2020. *Cultural Considerations within Austrian Economics*. Cambridge, UK: Cambridge University Press.
Storr, Virgil Henry, Stefanie Haeffele-Balch, and Laura E. Grube. 2015. *Community Revival in the Wake of Disaster: Lessons in Local Entrepreneurship*. New York, NY: Palgrave Macmillan.
Storr, Virgil Henry, Rachael K. Behr, and Michael R. Romero. 2023. "Commercial Friendship During a Pandemic." *Review of Austrian Economics* 36 (3): 357–382.
Thompson, Denise. 1985. *Flaws in the Social Fabric: Homosexuals and Society in Sydney*. Sydney, NSW: Allen & Unwin.
Tönnies, Ferdinand. [1887] 1957. *Community & Society*, translated and edited by Charles P. Loomis. East Lansing, MI: Michigan State University Press.
Tucker, Andrew. 2009. *Queer Visibilities: Space, Identity and Interaction in Cape Town*. Chichester, UK: Wiley-Blackwell.
Visser, Gustav. 2003. "Gay Men, Leisure Space and South African Cities: The Case of Cape Town." *Geoforum* 34: 123–137.
Wagner, Richard E. 2016. *Politics as a Peculiar Business: Insights from a Theory of Entangled Political Economy*. Cheltenham, UK: Edward Elgar.
Walters, Suzanna Danuta. 2001. *All the Rage: The Story of Gay Visibility in America*. Chicago, IL: University of Chicago Press.

Weightman, Barbara A. 1981. "Towards a Geography of the Gay Community." *Journal of Cultural Geography* 1 (2): 106–112.
Winer, Canton. 2022. "Solidarity, Disdain, and the Imagined Center of the Gay Imagined Community." *Sociological Inquiry* 92 (S1): 710–732.
Wittman, Carl. 1970. "Refugees from Amerika: A Gay Manifesto." https://libcom.org/article/gay-manifesto-carl-wittman.
Wotherspoon, Gary. 2016. *Gay Sydney: A History*. Sydney, Australia: NewSouth Publishing.
Zelizer, Viviana A. 1994. *The Social Meaning of Money*. New York, NY: Basic Books.
Zelizer, Viviana A. 2011. *Economic Lives: How Culture Shapes the Economy*. Princeton, NJ: Princeton University Press.

5

THE PROTECTIVE STATE AND LGBTQ RIGHTS

Nathan P. Goodman

In June 1969, the police raided a gay bar in Greenwich Village. Patrons at the Stonewall Inn were searched, harassed, scrutinized, and assaulted by police, all because of their sexuality and gender expression. This type of police harassment and repression was a common occurrence for gay, lesbian, bisexual, and gender non-conforming people at the time. But what happened next was less common. The bar patrons fought back. The resulting "Stonewall Riots" became a symbol, a focal point for the burgeoning Gay Liberation movement. To this day, pride festivals and pride parades are typically held in June in commemoration of this resistance to anti-LGBTQ police violence (Armstrong and Crage 2006; Goodman 2023).

Years later, Congress passed the Matthew Shepard and James Byrd, Jr. Hate Crimes Protection Act of 2009. This law expanded federal hate crimes statutes to make sexual orientation a protected class. This means that if violent criminals target someone based on their sexual orientation, that crime can be treated as a federal crime and subjected to enhanced penalties. It also means that additional federal resources are given to police departments to address hate crimes (Bassichus et al. 2015; U.S. Department of Justice Civil Rights Division 2023).

These two landmark moments in LGBTQ history illustrate the complexity of the relationship between LGBTQ people and the criminal justice system. Police, courts, and prisons have often been used to repress, harass, and brutalize LGBTQ people for consensual sex, gender non-conforming expression, and other activities that ought to be no business of the law. Yet at the same time, LGBTQ people have faced harassment and violence from criminals. Many LGBTQ people have therefore often wanted the state to empower police, courts, and prisons to enforce laws against such abuse. The challenge that LGBTQ people face in this regard is a special case of what constitutional political economists call "the paradox of government." That is, a government that has sufficient power to protect people's rights

DOI: 10.4324/9781003615781-5

also may use that power to violate those rights. The question, then, is whether it is possible to simultaneously empower and constrain the state. Can we empower state agents to protect individual rights without also empowering them to violate individual rights? Likewise, can we empower state agents to protect LGBTQ people without empowering them to brutalize LGBTQ people?

These are institutional questions in line with the normative and philosophical concerns of queer classical liberalism. To answer these questions, I draw on a tradition in political economy that analyzes institutions, focusing on how alternative institutional arrangements shape cooperation among fallible, flawed, purposive human actors. Because these themes have been crucial to political economy since the time of Adam Smith, they form the core of what some scholars call "mainline political economy" (MPE) (Boettke 2012; Boettke et al. 2016).

Various agents of the state, including police, prosecutors, judges, bailiffs, prison guards, and soldiers, are entrusted with coercive powers. Classical liberals often advocate that they retain and use these powers to protect individuals' rights to their persons and property. Public choice economist and Nobel laureate James M. Buchanan dubbed these elements of the state "the protective state." This can be contrasted with "the productive state," which produces public goods, and "the predatory state," which abuses and violates rights and secures rents for special interest groups (Buchanan 1975). Buchanan famously advocated a "politics without romance," in which analysts carefully consider the incentives that imperfect and self-interested state agents have. Yet in some of his treatments of the protective state, Buchanan seemed relatively romantic about it. He still was aware of dangers and incentive problems, but he seemed optimistic that the right set of constitutional rules can keep the protective state from devolving into the predatory state. Buchanan's analysis is a seminal contribution to MPE. But other scholars in the MPE tradition have challenged his perspective.

Christopher Coyne (2018) offers a more pessimistic view of the protective state. He argues that the image of the protective state as an impartial referee outside the game is unrealistic. Employees of the protective state are active players. So are private firms that they contract with as well as voters and politicians that they answer to. Each of these actors has a range of goals, and as such they respond to incentives and may act opportunistically when they can get away with doing so. They are not merely referees neutrally enforcing fixed rules. Instead, they are trying to improve their own well-being and standing in a world where some of them have the power to coerce in the name of enforcing the rules. One response a constitutional political economist may offer is that constitutional constraints can limit the discretionary power of the protective state and its agents. Yet Coyne points out that the uncertainty of our dynamic world limits the effectiveness of this response. The designer of a constitution cannot anticipate all future threats. If state agents are going to effectively respond to those threats, they therefore require some range of discretionary power to adapt to new threats. Yet this discretionary power means opportunities to abuse power. Designing a constitution that effectively binds the agents of the protective state is therefore a wicked problem. Despite the best intentions of constitutional political economists like Buchanan, the protective state threatens individual liberty.

Coyne's analysis of the protective state fits into a broader literature that applies public choice theory to analyze the institutions, incentives, and knowledge that shape policing, incarceration, judicial decision-making, and the national security state. Coyne himself has made substantial contributions to our understanding of the incentives that influence individuals in the military and the national security state (Coyne 2015; Coyne and Hall Blanco 2016a) as well as the militarization of domestic policing (Hall and Coyne 2013; Coyne and Hall-Blanco 2016b; Coyne and Hall 2018). Other public choice scholars have analyzed the incentives of police under alternative institutional arrangements. For instance, Elinor Ostrom and her colleagues used fieldwork to examine municipal police performance under consolidated arrangements as well as more polycentric arrangements (Ishak 1972; Ostrom et al. 1973a, 1973b; Rogers and Lipsey 1974; Parks 1979; Ostrom and Whitaker [1974] 1999).

This chapter aims to contribute to this literature on public choice analysis of the protective state by focusing on the relationship between the protective state and LGBTQ rights. What institutions, if any, can effectively empower the state to protect LGBTQ people from predation and rights violations, while simultaneously constraining the state from violating LGBTQ rights? This question is vitally important at a normative level, and it is also a fascinating social scientific question. To answer it, this chapter draws on historical and contemporary examples to illustrate the ways states can both protect and threaten LGBTQ rights. In addition, I examine non-state mechanisms of protecting LGBTQ rights. If the state is a dangerous organization that is all too likely to become predatory and oppressive, perhaps non-state alternatives can be more congenial to LGBTQ rights. My analysis here builds on the work of radical queer and trans scholars and activists who have sharply critiqued and organized against police violence and the prison industrial complex (Daring et al. 2012; Spade 2015; Stanley and Smith 2015; Spade 2024).

The chapter proceeds as follows. First, I argue that even a state with formal constitutional limits aimed at protecting rights is likely to become a threat to these rights. Then I discuss some ways LGBTQ activists have attempted to empower the protective state to protect LGBTQ rights. I follow this with the other side of the ledger, a discussion of ways the nominally protective functions of the state have often enabled state-agents to egregiously violate the rights of LGBTQ people. Given the threats posed by agents of the protective state, I then discuss non-state mechanisms for providing protection, as well as experiments with such alternatives within the LGBTQ community. I conclude by discussing avenues for future research on the protective state and LGBTQ rights.

Dynamics of the protective state

James M. Buchanan recognized that people could use politics for a variety of ends. For instance, they might use politics to produce public goods that are difficult to provide on the market. He called this the "productive state." They might also use the state to seize wealth from others or secure special privileges at the expense of others. Public choice scholars use a variety of terms to refer to this, including the "redistributive state," the "predatory state," and the "rent-seeking society." But to Buchanan, perhaps the most important function of the state was enforcing some basic rules of the game. By protecting individual rights, the state would give individuals the space to make their own life plans and pursue voluntary exchange and cooperation with one another. It would also deter predatory action that might, in the limit, render extended social cooperation untenable. Ideally, the state in this capacity would act as a neutral referee, simply enforcing general rules rather than acting to benefit some at the expense of others. Buchanan (1975) termed this function of the state "the protective state."

Ideally, the protective state would act as a neutral referee. However, in practice, those tasked with enforcing rules are people. Even if they are interested in enforcing general rules neutrally, they also have other interests. These other interests mean that they can at times have incentives to deviate from neutral enforcement of a fixed set of rules. These incentives may be driven by material self-interest or may be driven by various ideological or other-regarding preferences. In either case, they can give rise to biased enforcement of rules, or interpretations of rules in predatory ways.

Buchanan emphasized constitutional solutions to these problems. Establishing strong constitutional constraints could limit the discretionary power of governmental decision-makers, including those tasked with interpreting and enforcing rules. However, constraints that bind too tightly could, in principle, prevent desirable forms of collective-decision-making, provision of public goods, or enforcement of rules. There are therefore significant tradeoffs associated with constitutional design. As Buchanan and Tullock (1962) noted, rules that reduce the costs of making decisions tend to increase the expected scale of political externalities, while rules that reduce the expected scale of political externalities increase the costs of making decisions. Individuals may disagree about how to negotiate these tradeoffs. At the level of setting the constitutional framework, Buchanan and Tullock advocated something closer to a unanimity rule, so that the constitutional rules would have buy-in and be seen as legitimate by almost everyone. Meanwhile, they favored a lower threshold for day-to-day collective decisions, so that decision-making costs would be lower and government could operate effectively.

In practice, however, we cannot fully separate day-to-day collective decision-making or implementation of decisions from the constitutional rules. Everyday practice may influence how constitutional rules are *interpreted*. Rather than being self-enforcing, constitutional rules must be interpreted by judges, citizens, and government employees. The interpretation that seems plausible will be shaped by daily practice. Moreover, daily practice may alter the incentives and constraints facing government officials in a manner that eventually expands their power in ways those who initially crafted the constitution did not anticipate. For instance, practicing a particular form of coercion can create both human capital (skills) and physical capital (tools) that can be used coercively in various ways that diverge from the initial intention of those who authorized the coercion (Coyne 2018; Coyne and Hall 2018; Coyne and Goodman 2022; Hall et al. 2024; Goodman 2024). Skills and tools initially used for protective activities within constitutional constraints can thus all too easily be turned toward predatory uses beyond the scope of prior constitutional constraints. For instance, military hardware might initially be used to fight off a foreign military that is attacking people. However, that same hardware may eventually be wielded by police officers kicking down a civilian's door to carry out a no-knock raid to search for prohibited narcotics. Within an open-ended system, we see the protective state evolve in unanticipated directions that expand the scale and scope of state power (Coyne 2018). This leads to endogenous evolution that constitutional designers cannot anticipate (Devins et al. 2015), or what Salter (2017) calls "constitutional drift."

Buchanan writes that "If politics could be restricted to the exercise of these minimal or protective state functions (the night watchman state), little or no concern need be expressed about coercive political intrusions on the liberties of citizens" (Buchanan 1995: 261). However, the protective state functions tend to involve the accumulation of substantial capacities for violent coercion. The protective state therefore contains within itself the seeds of the predatory state. Buchanan is therefore surely right that "politics is almost certain to extend beyond any such limits" aimed at restraining politics to protective coercion (Buchanan 1995).

Does the protective state protect LGBTQ people?

Various LGBTQ people have sought recognition and protection of their rights via the state's formal legal system. The amount of coercion this entails can vary. For instance, recognition of a gay couple's marriage is quite unlikely to lead police to coerce or arrest anyone. Instead, this legal recognition enables the couple to coordinate their plans, more easily share property, share custody if they choose to raise children together, and so on. This is an instance of the protective state protecting LGBT rights, but it's not a particularly coercive instance. It relies on the courts rather than on police, prisons, or soldiers. We could imagine similar protections arising from the evolution of common or customary law that is not directed by the state.

However, some uses of the protective state to protect LGBTQ rights rely on police, prosecutors, and prisons. For example, consider hate crimes legislation. Many LGBTQ rights organizations support hate crimes legislation as a way of protecting people from often brutal homophobic and transphobic violence. This is understandable. Assaulting, beating, or killing someone for who they are can strike fear into entire communities. Using the law to challenge this interpersonal violence can, at least in principle, create a safer and more free society. However, I argue that there are several dangers associated with hate crimes legislation. More generally, these illustrate the dangers of empowering the state to protect people.

To understand these issues with hate crimes legislation, we first need to understand what hate crimes laws are. While definitions of hate crimes can vary, "hate crimes are generally defined as criminal acts committed against people, property, and/or organizations because of the group they identify with/belong to or are perceived to belong to (e.g., Black, Jewish, Muslim, sexual minority …)" (Bills and Vaughn 2023: 116). The Federal Bureau of Investigation (FBI) defines a hate crime as "a committed criminal offense which is motivated, in whole or in part, by the offender's bias(es) against a race, religion, disability, sexual orientation, ethnicity, gender, or gender identity" (FBI, n.d., cited in Bills and Vaughn 2023). However, in addition to federal hate crimes legislation, state governments throughout the United States also implement hate crimes legislation. American federalism therefore creates a situation where hate crime laws can vary substantially across jurisdictions (Bills and Vaughn 2023).

There are several federal hate crimes statutes in the United States. In 1994, "the Hate Crimes Sentencing Enhancement Act (HCSEA, 1994) made committing a hate crime a federal offense and augmented existing penalties for hate crime offenders" (Bills and Vaughn 2023: 117). In other words, this law established sentencing guidelines that meant harsher and more punitive sentences were recommended for hate crimes than for similar crimes that were not characterized as hate crimes. Ultimately, however, classifying an offense as a "hate crime" requires subjective judgments about the mindset, beliefs, and motives of the offender. This can be especially challenging in cases where the defendant appears to have multiple motives. In practice, this means that there is substantial discretion for police officers and prosecutors to decide whether to pursue hate crimes charges and the corresponding sentencing enhancements. "The inherent subjectivity of this process invites arbitrary and uneven application of penalty enhancements" (Franklin 2002: 158). While the ostensible purpose of hate crimes legislation is to protect members of marginalized groups, this discretionary power means that police and prosecutors may selectively use hate crimes enhancements against members of marginalized groups. Franklin argues that:

> One particularly pernicious consequence is that the laws appear to be contributing to increased criminal penalties against African Americans, one of the groups they were designed to protect. … Given the well-documented race and class biases within the legal system … it is not surprising that without explicit attention to issues of social power, hate crime laws will end up replicating the very power imbalances and inequalities they were designed to ameliorate.
>
> (Franklin 2002: 167)

Hate crimes legislation is therefore a double-edged sword. It can be used to protect marginalized people from interpersonal violence. However, its mechanism for doing so is increasing the severity of penalties inflicted by the criminal justice system. These harsher penalties are imposed at the discretion of the actual agents who work together as part of the protective state. If these individuals are biased against the marginalized group that the hate crimes laws were written to protect, then the sentencing enhancements may be disproportionately wielded against members of that marginalized group.

An additional objection often given to hate crimes legislation relates to its implications for free expression. Various scholars have raised concerns about the First Amendment implications of hate crimes laws (see Gellman 1992; Gerstenfeld 1992; Jacobs and Potter 1998; Bell 2002; Franklin 2002: 166). Sentencing enhancements for hate crimes are closely tied to the beliefs and thoughts of the perpetrator, rather than just the perpetrator's actions. This means that people can face additional imprisonment and other coercive, state-imposed punishment based on thoughts and speech, rather than actions.

In 1993, the U.S. Supreme Court assessed some of these First Amendment issues in their ruling in *Wisconsin v. Mitchell.* In this case, Todd Mitchell, a black man who beat a white man based on his race, received an enhanced sentence under a Wisconsin hate crimes law. Steven Gey summarizes the facts of the case:

> The *Mitchell* facts provide a relatively pure example of a case covered by hate crime enhancement statutes. On the evening of the crime, at an apartment complex in Kenosha, Wisconsin, Todd Mitchell and a group of other young black men discussed a scene from the movie "Mississippi Burning," in which a white man attacks a black child. At some point Mitchell said to the group, "Do you all feel hyped up to move on some white people?" After the group moved outside, a young white boy approached on the opposite side of the street. Mitchell said to the group, "You all want to fuck somebody up? There goes a white boy; go get him." The group then caught and severely beat the victim, who remained in a coma for four days.
>
> (Gey 1997: 1016)

Mitchell was convicted of aggravated battery. The jury also concluded that he had committed a hate crime, which meant that under Wisconsin's sentencing enhancement law he faced a longer sentence than the usual maximum sentence for aggregated battery. Mitchell's attorneys challenged the hate crime enhancement law on First Amendment grounds. The Wisconsin Supreme Court ruled in favor of Mitchell, but the U.S. Supreme Court overturned their ruling and upheld the sentencing enhancement. According to the U.S. Supreme Court, this sentencing enhancement did not violate Mitchell's First Amendment rights.

A ruling like *Wisconsin v. Mitchell* does not merely uphold hate crimes laws and sentencing enhancements. It provides precedent, thereby shaping future court rulings on other First Amendment issues. Whenever "a policy expands the scope of government … it creates institutional precedent that can have subsequent wide-reaching consequences for civil liberties, especially when the policy is evaluated and upheld by the Supreme Court" (Goodman et al. 2021: 546). By 1996, judges had "already cited *Mitchell* to justify punishing political and social dissent in several contexts outside the realm of racial hate speech" (Gey 1997: 1065). *Mitchell* was used multiple times to uphold the *Don't Ask, Don't Tell* policy, which prohibited openly gay soldiers from serving in the U.S. military. "*Mitchell* is cited in these cases as support for the proposition that the government may use speech (i.e., verbal admissions of homosexuality) as the basis for imposing sanctions against prohibited action (i.e., homosexual actions)" (Gey 1997: 1066).

The *Mitchell* ruling was also cited by the Oregon Supreme Court to uphold punitive damages against environmental activists who trespassed while protesting logging. "The court rejected the demonstrators' free speech claims, citing *Mitchell's* principle that expressive activities 'that produce special harms distinct from their communicative impact ... are entitled to no constitutional protection'" (Gey 1997: 1067). These precedents are examples of "a politically progressive speech-regulation theory that ends up providing the government with an excellent justification for suppressing politically progressive speech" (Gey 1997: 1015). More broadly, however, they illustrate how entrusting the protective state with broader powers can easily lead to expansions of their powers for uses that many would find predatory and unjustly coercive. You can never grant the state power that will only be used in ways you like. The powers you give to state agents to protect you can easily be turned against you.

Efforts to police hate and bigotry present similar problems in other countries. Many of these countries have laws prohibiting *hate speech*, not just hate crimes. While First Amendment jurisprudence prevents the United States from adopting hate speech laws, many other countries have enacted them. Yet by prohibiting and punish various forms of speech, hate speech prohibitions prevent the open discourse that enables emancipatory social change. Throughout Europe, hate crimes laws have been used to censor and penalize speech critical of religion, for instance (Greenwald 2017). Given that many religions promulgate anti-LGBT bigotry, this could easily be used to stifle some forms of LGBT activism. This is not hypothetical. In France, "judges fined Laure Pora, the former head of the Paris chapter of ACT UP, 2,300 euros for using the term ['homophobe'] during a 2013 demonstration against the pro-life group Lejeune Foundation and La Manif Pour Tous" (Lang 2016, cited in Greenwald 2017).

In the United States, the Matthew Shepard and James Byrd, Jr. Hate Crimes Protection Act of 2009 expanded federal hate crimes laws to apply them to sexual orientation, gender, and gender identity. As a result, the law received substantial support from many LGBT rights activists. However, the Sylvia Rivera Law Project (SRLP), which provides legal services to poor transgender and gender nonconforming people, opposed the legislation. They declared

> As an organization that centers racial and economic justice in our work and that understands mass imprisonment as a primary vector of violence in the lives of

> our constituents, we believe that hate crimes legislation is a counterproductive response to the violence faced by LGBT people.
>
> (Sylvia Rivera Law Project, n.d.)

They also lamented that the Matthew Shepard Act was passed as part of the same bill as the U.S. military budget:

> We are also dismayed by the joining of a law that is supposedly about "preventing" violence with the funding for continued extreme violence and colonialism abroad. This particular bill was attached to a $680-billion measure for the Pentagon's budget, which includes $130 billion for ongoing military operations in Iraq and Afghanistan. Killing people in Iraq and Afghanistan protects no one, inside or outside of U.S. borders.
>
> (Sylvia Rivera Law Project, n.d.)

This opposition reflects their recognition that the protective state often inflicts serious predatory violence upon vulnerable people. SRLP has many members and stakeholders who have been incarcerated or otherwise faced state violence. The organization was founded by Dean Spade, a transgender legal scholar and activist who has written extensively about state violence and the case against hate crimes legislation (Spade and Willse 2000; Spade 2015; Spade 2024).

While hate crimes legislation can generate serious costs by entrenching and expanding state violence, it is also important to consider the potential benefits of hate crimes laws. The goal of hate crimes legislation is to protect people from violence, especially violence motivated by hate and bigotry against their identity. This naturally raises a question. How effective are hate crimes laws at deterring interpersonal violence against members of the LGBTQ community? Incentives matter, so in principle raising the cost of an action, including a crime, should provide some deterrence on the margin (Becker 1968). However, the magnitude of this deterrence effect is an empirical question. Making a prison sentence longer imposes costs years in the future. Crimes are often committed by people who are shortsighted, impulsive, or impatient, so sentencing enhancements may deliver relatively little deterrence. Indeed, the available evidence suggests that consistency and certainty of accountability does more to deter than increased severity does (Kleiman 2010; Tabarrok 2015). Moreover, incarceration can make reoffending more likely and more severe (Mueller-Smith 2015). In the case of hate crimes, being sent to prison may increase risk of reoffending because the "likelihood that enhancements will strengthen offenders' bias is even greater if they are sent to prison, where virulent racism and homophobia are the norm" (Franklin 2002: 164). This is not to say that hate crimes laws provide no deterrence, but simply that there are good reasons to doubt that the deterrence has sufficient magnitude to justify the costs.

It is understandable to use the protective state to protect LGBTQ rights. Many people think of the protective state as the primary mechanism for securing justice in our society. However, examining hate crimes legislation illustrates how efforts aimed specifically at challenging bigoted violence can empower the state in ways that are directly counterproductive to the progressive and protective ends that reformers seek.

The protective state's long history of repressing LGBTQ people

The raid on the Stonewall Inn in 1969 was not an isolated incident. The police officer, the prison guard, the prosecutor, and the judge have all too often approached LGBTQ people not to protect them, but to attack and repress them. This is not merely a historical phenomenon of bygone days, but a current reality. It is a reality that some queer and trans people feel in their bodies, which have been scarred and injured by police officers' batons, tasers, tear gas, and fists. It is a reality that haunts the memories of those humiliated, degraded, and sometimes even raped by police officers and prison guards (Amnesty International USA 2005; Stanley and Smith 2015; Stauffer 2016). It is a reality that holds true across national borders, across economic systems, and across historical eras.

In other words, the protective state has a long history of attacking LGBTQ people. Sometimes these attacks are a result of deliberate policies aimed at criminalizing homosexuality, gender nonconformity, or other perceived deviance. For instance, in the United States, sodomy laws directly prohibited and punished consensual gay sex. While some leftist commentators may want to blame capitalism for these U.S. policies, anti-gay state repression has also occurred under socialist states. For example, in Cuba,

> [b]etween 1959 and 1980, gay men endured experiences ranging from limited job opportunities to detention in street sweeps to incarceration in labor camps. Having long hair or flamboyant hairstyles, wearing tight pants or colorful shirts, and exhibiting mannerisms perceived to be effeminate were sufficient to place one under suspicion of being gay.
>
> (Majied 2015: 30, cited in Goodman 2025: 244)

While homosexuality is not criminalized in China, media featuring LGBTQ characters and themes faces state censorship (Chia 2019). These cases involve targeting LGBTQ people as a matter of policy. However, in other cases, members of the LGBTQ community are especially vulnerable to police violence or prison violence as an unintended consequence of policies that are not homophobic or transphobic on their face.

Let's begin with some instances of repression that look a lot like the Stonewall raid. In December 1978, the "Toronto Police Morality Squad executed a pre-dawn raid on Barracks Bathhouse" (Nash 2014: 83). This use of vice laws and morality statutes to criminalize a gay business and meeting space struck fear into the community and provoked political resistance. A few years later, in 1981, there were "raids on four Toronto bathhouses that resulted in close to 300 charges being laid" (Nash 2014). These types of raids illustrate how the state attacks businesses that provide community hubs, violently attempting to break up the crucial nexus between markets and queer civil society.

Some readers may hope that these types of raids are a thing of the past, at least in advanced liberal democracies. After all, the 2003 U.S. Supreme Court ruling in *Lawrence v. Texas* determined that sodomy laws were unconstitutional. This ended *explicit* criminalization of consensual homosexual sex in the United States. However, it did not end state violence against LGBTQ people.

For example, there have been multiple police raids against gay bars in the United States since *Lawrence v. Texas.* As recently as May 2, 2025, police with Pittsburgh's Nuisance Bar Task Force (NBTF) "raided the Pittsburgh gay bar P Town during a drag show featuring trans icon Amanda Lepore" (Monteil 2025). According to Mayor Ed Gainey, this raid was based on "a report to the city's Bureau of Fire, specifically asking for a check on overcrowding" (cited in Monteil 2025). On June 28, 2009, officers from the Fort Worth Police Department and the Texas Alcoholic Beverage Commission raided the Rainbow Lounge, a gay bar in Fort Worth, Texas. The raid involved use of significant force against bar patrons, with one hospitalized with a brain injury he still suffered from over a decade later (CBS News Texas 2012; Starling 2023). Both raids illustrate how enforcement of facially neutral laws can function to strike fear into communities and attack their social spaces.

In addition to attacks on LGBT community spaces such as gay bars, LGBTQ individuals are also often vulnerable to state violence. For instance, a nationwide 2015 survey of transgender respondents found that

> [r]espondents who interacted with the police either while doing sex work or while the police mistakenly thought they were doing sex work reported high rates of police harassment, abuse, or mistreatment, with nearly nine out of ten (86%) reporting being harassed, attacked, sexually assaulted, or mistreated in some other way by police.
>
> (James et al. 2016: 14)

The same survey found that many trans people were kicked out of their homes, denied employment opportunities, or otherwise put in economically vulnerable positions due to discrimination. This places them in vulnerable positions where they're more likely to interact with police, whether for making their living in the black market, sleeping outside, stealing, or otherwise engaging in what some term "survival crimes." Indeed,

> One in five (20%) have participated in the underground economy for income at some point in their lives—including 12% who have done sex work in exchange

> for income—and 9% did so in the past year, with higher rates among women of color.
>
> (James et al. 2016)

As a result, police sometimes profile trans people, especially transgender women of color, as sex workers. This profiling then feeds into the aforementioned abuse.

Police officers are not the only state agents who abuse LGBTQ people. Once queer and trans people are incarcerated, they're vulnerable to abuse by guards as well as fellow inmates. All too often these are mutually reinforcing. Guards often incarcerate transgender women and other transfeminine (transfem) people in men's prisons, which makes them vulnerable to rape by fellow inmates. Worse still, sometimes guards deliberately facilitate this abuse.

> In some cases, transfems are subject to 'V-coding' where they are roomed with aggressive and sexually violent inmates as a means of pacifying him or rewarding him for good behavior, both of which keep overall violence down, but result in the transfem inmate being sexually and physically assaulted.
>
> (Compton 2024: 19; see also Oparah 2012; Kulak 2018)

In these contexts, transgender women are not treated as individual people whose rights are being respected. Rather, they are treated as means to an end, pieces of property that guards can use as a bargaining chip. Guards sell them into sexual slavery in exchange for less disruptive behavior from sexually violent inmates. In addition, guards sometimes directly sexually exploit, assault, and humiliate transgender inmates. The ostensible agents of the protective state here become agents of the sexually predatory state.

The state's treatment of LGBTQ people varies around the world. Many states, especially in Africa and Asia, still overtly criminalize and punish consensual homosexual sex and other aspects of LGBTQ life (Lee and Ostergard 2017; ILGA n.d.). This overt, deliberate criminalization of LGBTQ love and life has become much rarer in developed, wealthy, Western liberal democracies. However, when queer and trans people flee illiberal societies, wealthy, Western, liberal democracies often exclude them via immigration restrictions. The enforcement of these immigration restrictions often involves violent arrests, detention in inhumane conditions, and deportation back to danger and repression (Flores and Sprague 2025). In this way, overt criminalization in some countries is reinforced via immigration restrictions in other countries. By limiting free movement, states reinforce one another's monopolistic power, enabling predation and repression to persist.

Protection without the state

Many people believe that the state should have a territorial monopoly on the legitimate use of force. As a result, they often believe that the state should be the *only* organization that provides protection.

However, when people fear the police rather than trusting them as protectors, they are likely to seek out alternatives. And in fact, many LGBTQ people have done just that. This has taken various forms, some better than others. For instance, at the Stonewall Inn, security was handled by the mafia. This has all sorts of problems, but when various aspects of your life are criminalized, organized criminals are often those who are skilled at bribing and evading law enforcement. Devising alternative governance arrangements is one important aspect of running an illicit business. Governance within black markets is imperfect. Indeed, it is often deeply flawed. Yet at the same time, black markets are not *ungoverned*. Sometimes, governance in black markets comes from formal organizations with constitutions, written rules, and elaborate systems of violent sanctions. Skarbek (2014) documents how prison gangs engage in this type of governance. Yet he also notes that social norms and reputation mechanisms provided governance within prisons until the population grew too large for people to know one another's reputation (Skarbek 2014). Among queer and trans sex workers, this type of informal governance and use of reputation tends to play a significant role. For instance, sex workers often warn each other about abusive clients (Brouwers 2022). Some sex workers prescreen clients and prefer to work with regular repeat clients to protect their safety (McBride et al. 2022). Sex workers will also often work together and offer sessions with multiple workers together, so that they can keep each other safe (Brouwers 2022). Transgender sex workers watch out for each other in various ways, providing protection from street criminals, abusive clients, and police (Mecca 2015; see also Dalesandry in this volume).

Sometimes LGBTQ people engage in political organizing in civil society to create community-based alternatives to the police. For instance, the Audre Lorde Project, an organization run by trans people of color, created the Safe Outside the System (SOS) Collective that worked to address violence without calling the police. Recognizing that responding to violence and deescalating violent situations is a product of human action, they worked to cultivate skills in these efforts among ordinary people. For example, they offer training resources such as a "Safe Party Toolkit," which explains the types of violence that often occur at parties and offers guidance on how to prepare for deescalation and rapid response. They also offer direct services to survivors of violence (Rodriguez 2021). These efforts illustrate how civil society and voluntary association help people build up the skills necessary for self-governance, rather than encouraging passive submission to and reliance upon state authority.

These scattered examples of queer and trans people organizing to keep each other safe, rather than relying on the protective state, are suggestive of what's possible. Rather than assuming that state-provided security is the *only* form of security, we can recognize that people's lives are governed by a polycentric archipelago of private and public associations, and that people can form new associations to adaptively address challenges. When people cannot rely on or trust the state, they do not passively sit by. Instead, they act creatively to strive to improve their lives. This often means forming alternatives to the protective state. As a result, we observe polycentric defense, rather than defense and security delivered solely by a state monopoly (Coyne and Goodman 2020).

A substantial body of scholarly literature analyzes the various ways that people form rules endogenously when they cannot rely on state-provided governance (Leeson, 2014). Peter Boettke calls this research program "analytical anarchism" (Boettke 2005, 2025; Boettke and Candela 2020). We've already mentioned reputation mechanisms as one part of this. Yet these are often assumed to only work in small groups. However, endogenous rule formation and self-governance have been observed in cases that involve large groups of people, including those who many would not expect to act well. As Boettke explains,

> Functioning and sustainable social order has been found among the least likely candidates—e.g., stock traders (Stringham, 2003), pirates (Leeson, 2007), and prisoners (D'Amico, 2010; Skarbek 2014, 2020)—and we have seen institutional evolution coming out of natural disasters such as Katrina (Storr et al., 2015) and man-made disasters such as war (Coyne, 2008).
>
> (Boettke 2025: 13)

For many LGBTQ people, the state is a threat rather than a protector. As a result, they are experimenting with non-state means of protecting each other. Further research should use the insights of analytical anarchism for in-depth case studies on these non-state governance arrangements. Researchers should engage in careful comparative institutional analysis between different means of protection. This comparative institutional analysis expands the range of institutional possibilities that we can consider. Rather than assuming the protective state is inevitable and necessary, we can consider anarchist possibilities as well. Some queer classical liberal (QCL) scholars will aim to reform the protective state, seeing a reformed protective state as the best way to protect individual rights. But other QCL scholars, including me, are interested in anarchist alternatives. Many queer liberation activists have embraced anarchism (Daring et al. 2012). MPE, particularly the positive political economy of analytical anarchism, offers us tools to analyze their proposals, and to contrast them with proposed reforms to the protective state.

Conclusion

Many liberals dream of a state that protects rights rather than violating them. Many states have nominally accepted liberal principles, and this has led to real improvements. Yet all actually existing states have retained significant predatory elements. In practice, the protective state has thus far been inseparable from the predatory state. The state's predation tends to fall most harshly on people who are stigmatized and marginalized. This often means that queer and trans people face significant risks of state violence. In this context, building up the state's coercive capacity in an effort to protect the rights of LGBTQ people is quite a dangerous gambit.

Yet queer and trans people are creative. Rather than sitting idly by as both the state and individual bigots target them with violence, they seek out and devise ways to protect themselves and each other. These efforts offer hopeful glimmers of a wider array of institutional alternatives. They suggest that the liberal project of protecting individual rights need not be tethered to the state.

References

Amnesty International USA. 2005. *Stonewalled: Police Abuse and Misconduct Against Lesbian, Gay, Bisexual, and Transgender People in the United States*. New York, NY: Amnesty International.

Armstrong, Elizabeth A. and Suzanna M. Crage. 2006. "Movements and Memory: The Making of the Stonewall Myth." *American Sociological Review* 71 (5): 724–751.

Bassichus, Morgan, Alexander Lee, and Dean Spade. 2015. "Building an Abolitionist Queer and Trans Movement with Everything We've Got." In *Captive Genders: Trans Embodiment and the Prison Industrial Complex*, edited by Eric Stanley and Nat Smith, 15–40. Oakland, CA: AK Press.

Becker, Gary S. 1968. "Crime and Punishment: An Economic Approach." *Journal of Political Economy* 76 (2): 169–217.

Bell, Jeannine. 2002. "Deciding When Hate Is a Crime: The First Amendment, Police Detectives, and the Identification of Hate Crime." *Rutgers Race and the Law Review* 4: 33–76.

Bills, Matthew A. and Michael S. Vaughn. 2023. "A Contemporary Review of Hate Crimes Legislation in the United States." *Criminal Justice Policy Review* 34 (2): 115–139.

Boettke, Peter J. 2005. "Anarchism as a Progressive Research Program in Political Economy." In *Anarchy, State, and Public Choice*, edited by Edward Stringham, 206–220. Cheltenham, UK: Edward Elgar.

Boettke, Peter J. 2012. *Living Economics: Yesterday, Today, and Tomorrow*. Oakland, CA: Independent Institute.

Boettke, Peter J. 2025. "Toward a Genuine Institutional Economics." *Constitutional Political Economy*, https://doi.org/10.1007/s10602-025-09496-x.

Boettke, Peter J. and Rosolino Candela. 2020. "The Positive Political Economy of Analytical Anarchism." In *The Routledge Handbook of Anarchy and Anarchist Thought*, edited by Gary Chartier and Chad Van Schoelandt, 222–234. New York, NY: Routledge.

Boettke, Peter J., Stefanie Haeffele-Balch, and Virgil Henry Storr. 2016. *Mainline Economics: Six Nobel Lectures in the Tradition of Adam Smith*. Arlington, VA: Mercatus Center at George Mason University.

Brouwers, Lilith. 2022. "'I Feel Safe When I'm Working with Her': Sex Workers' Experiences of Management and Wider Work Relations." PhD diss., University of Leeds.

Buchanan, James M. 1975. *The Limits of Liberty: Between Anarchy and Leviathan*. Chicago, IL: University of Chicago Press.

Buchanan, James M. 1995. "Federalism and Individual Sovereignty." *Cato Journal* 15 (2–3): 259–268.

Buchanan, James M. and Gordon Tullock. 1962. *The Calculus of Consent: Logical Foundations of Constitutional Democracy*. Ann Arbor, MI: University of Michigan Press.

CBS News Texas. 2012. "Rainbow Lounge Raid Documentary Premieres in Fort Worth." March 15. https://www.cbsnews.com/texas/news/rainbow-lounge-raid-documentary-premieres-in-fort-worth.

Chia, Joy L. 2019. "'What's Love Got to Do with It?' LGBTQ Rights and Patriotism in Xi's China." *Australasian Journal of Asian Law* 20(1) 27–37.
Compton, Olivia. 2024. "A Transgender Economists Guide to Writing About Transgender and Gender Diverse People." University Library of Munich, MPRA Paper No. 122855. https://mpra.ub.uni-muenchen.de/122855.
Coyne, Christopher J. 2008. *After War: The Political Economy of Exporting Democracy*. Stanford, CA: Stanford University Press.
Coyne, Christopher J. 2015. "Lobotomizing the Defense Brain." *Review of Austrian Economics* 28 (4): 371–396.
Coyne, Christopher J. 2018. "The Protective State: A Grave Threat to Liberty." In *Buchanan's Tensions: Reexamining the Political Economy and Philosophy of James M. Buchanan*, edited by Peter J. Boettke and Solomon Stein, 147–169. Arlington, VA: Mercatus Center at George Mason University.
Coyne, Christopher J., and Nathan Goodman. 2022. "U.S. Border Militarization and Foreign Policy: A Symbiotic Relationship." *Economics of Peace and Security Journal* 17 (1): 5–16.
Coyne, Christopher J. and Nathan P. Goodman. 2020. "Polycentric Defense." *Independent Review* 25 (2): 279–292. Full pdf available here: https://www.independent.org/wp-content/uploads/tir/2020/09/tir_25_2_08_coyne.pdf
Coyne, Christopher J., and Abigail R. Hall. 2018. *Tyranny Comes Home: The Domestic Fate of U.S. Militarism*. Stanford, CA: Stanford University Press.
Coyne, Christopher J., and Abigail R. Hall Blanco. 2016a. "Empire State of Mind: The Illiberal Foundations of Liberal Hegemony." *Independent Review* 21 (2): 237–250.
Coyne, Christopher J., and Abigail R. Hall-Blanco. 2016b. "Foreign Intervention, Police Militarization, and Minorities." *Peace Review* 28 (2): 165–170.
D'Amico, Daniel J. 2010. "The Prison in Economics: Private and Public Incarceration in Ancient Greece." *Public Choice* 145 (3–4): 461–482.
Daring, C.B., J. Rogue, Deric Shannon, and Abbey Volcano. 2012. *Queering Anarchism: Addressing and Undressing Power and Desire*. Oakland, CA: AK Press.
Devins, Caryn, Roger Koppl, Stuart Kauffman, and Teppo Felin. 2015. "Against Design." *Arizona State Law Journal* 47: 609–681.
Flores, Andrew R., and Laurel D. Sprague. 2025. *Impact of Mass Deportations on LGBT People*. UCLA Williams Institute Brief. https://williamsinstitute.law.ucla.edu/wp-content/uploads/Mass-Deportations-EO-Feb-2025.pdf.
Franklin, Karen. 2002. "Good Intentions: The Enforcement of Hate Crime Penalty-Enhancement Statutes." *American Behavioral Scientist* 46 (1): 154–172.
Gellman, Susan. 1992. "Hate Crime Laws Are Thought Crime Laws." *Annual Survey of American Law* 1992/1993: 509–532.
Gerstenfeld, Phyllis B. 1992. "'Smile When You Call Me That!' The Problem with Punishing Hate Motivated Behavior." *Behavioral Sciences & the Law* 10 (2): 259–285.
Gey, Steven G. 1997. "What if *Wisconsin v. Mitchell* Had Involved Martin Luther King Jr.? The Constitutional Flaws of Hate Crime Enhancement Statutes." *George Washington Law Review* 65 (6): 1014–1070.
Goodman, Nathan P. 2023. "Commerce, Spontaneous Order, and Gender Freedom Movements." *Cosmos+Taxis* 11 (11+12): 24–36.
Goodman, Nathan P. 2024. "Border Militarization and Domestic Institutions." *Constitutional Political Economy*, https://doi.org/10.1007/s10602-024-09440-5.
Goodman, Nathan P. 2025. "A Radical Liberal Approach to LGBTQ Emancipation." In *Liberal Emancipation: Explorations in Political and Social Economy*, edited by Mikayla Novak, 229–258. Cham, Switzerland: Palgrave Macmillan.
Goodman, Nathan P., Christopher J. Coyne, and Abigail Devereaux. 2021. "Infectious Diseases and Government Growth." *Independent Review* 25 (4): 537–550.
Greenwald, Glenn. 2017. "In Europe, Hate Speech Laws Are Often Used to Suppress and Punish Left-Wing Viewpoints." *The Intercept*, August 29. https://theintercept.

com/2017/08/29/in-europe-hate-speech-laws-are-often-used-to-suppress-and-punish-left-wing-viewpoints.

Hall, Abigail R. and Christopher J. Coyne. 2013. "The Militarization of U.S. Domestic Policing." *Independent Review* 17 (4): 485–504.

Hall, Abigail R., Miriam A. Reyes Sandoval, Karla Segovia, and Nathan P. Goodman. 2024. "U.S. Intervention and Coercion-Enabling Capital: Evidence from El Salvador." *Eastern Economic Journal* 51: 87–111.

ILGA. n.d. "ILGA World Database." https://database.ilga.org/en.

Ishak, Samir. 1972. "Consumers' Perception of Police Performance: Consolidation vs. Deconcentration: The Case of Grand Rapids, Michigan Metropolitan Area." Ph.D. diss., Indiana University.

Jacobs, James B., and Kimberly Potter. 1998. *Hate Crimes: Criminal law and identity politics*. New York, NY: Oxford University Press.

James, Sandy E., Jody L. Herman, Susan Rankin, Mara Keisling, Lisa Mottet, and Ma'ayan Anafi. 2016. *The Report of the 2015 U.S. Transgender Survey*. Washington, DC: National Center for Transgender Equality.

Kleiman, Mark A.R. 2010. *When Brute Force Fails: How to Have Less Crime and Less Punishment*. Princeton, NJ: Princeton University Press.

Kulak, Ash Olli. 2018. "Locked Away in SEG 'For Their Own Protection': How Congress Gave Federal Corrections the Discretion to House Transgender (Trans) Inmates in Gender Inappropriate Facilities and Solitary." *Indiana Journal of Law and Social Equality* 6 (2): 300–325.

Lang, Nico. 2016. "French Hate Crime Ruling Sets a Dangerous Precedent for LGBT People: It's Now Illegal to Call Someone a 'Homophobe' in France." *Salon*, November 7. https://www.salon.com/2016/11/07/french-hate-crime-ruling-sets-a-dangerous-precedent-for-lgbt-people-it-is-now-illegal-to-call-someone-a-homophobe-in-France.

Lee, Chelsea, and Robert L. Ostergard. 2017. "Measuring Discrimination Against LGBTQ People: A Cross-National Analysis." *Human Rights Quarterly* 39 (1): 37–72.

Leeson, Peter T. 2007. "An-Arrgh-chy: The Law and Economics of Pirate Organization." *Journal of Political Economy* 115 (6): 1049–1094.

Leeson, Peter T. 2014. *Anarchy Unbound: Why Self-Governance Works Better Than You Think*. New York, NY: Cambridge University Press.

Majied, Kamilah F. 2015. "Racism and Homophobia in Cuba: A Historical and Contemporary Overview." *Journal of Human Behavior in the Social Environment* 25 (1): 26–34.

McBride, Bronwyn, Kate Shannon, Jennie Pearson, Andrea Krüsi, Melissa Braschel, and Shira M. Goldenberg. 2022. "Seeing Pre-screened, Regular Clients Associated with Lower Odds of Workplace Sexual Violence and Condom Refusal Amidst Sex Work Criminalization: Findings of a Community-based Cohort of Sex Workers in Metro Vancouver, Canada (2010–2019)." *BMC Public Health*: 22: 519.

Mecca, Tommi Avicolli. 2015. "Brushes with Lily Law." In *Captive Genders: Trans Embodiment and the Prison Industrial Complex*, edited by Eric A. Stanley and Nat Smith, 57–62. Oakland, CA: AK Press.

Monteil, Abby. 2025. "Police Raid a Pittsburgh Gay Bar, Then Reportedly Ask for Photos With Amanda Lepore." *Them*, May 6. https://www.them.us/story/ptown-pittsburgh-lgbtq-bar-police-raid-amanda-lepore.

Mueller-Smith, Michael. 2015. "The Criminal and Labor Market Impacts of Incarceration." University of Michigan, Institute for Research on Poverty Working Paper. https://sites.lsa.umich.edu/mgms/wp-content/uploads/sites/283/2015/09/incar.pdf.

Nash, Catherine J. 2014. "Consuming Sexual Liberation: Gay Business, Politics, and Toronto's Barracks Bathhouse Raids." *Journal of Canadian Studies* 48 (1): 82–105.

Oparah, J. C. 2012. "Feminism and the (Trans)gender Entrapment of Gender Nonconforming Prisoners." *UCLA Journal of Gender and Law* 18 (2): 239–271.

Ostrom, Elinor, William Baugh, Richard Gaurasci, Roger Parks, and Gordon Whitaker. 1973a. *Community Organization and the Provision of Police Services*. Beverly Hills, CA: Sage Publications.

Ostrom, Elinor, Richard Parks, and Gordon Whitaker. 1973b. "Do We Really Want to Consolidate Urban Police Forces? A Reappraisal of Some Old Assertions." *Public Administration Review* 33 (5): 423–432.

Ostrom, Elinor, and Gordon Whitaker. [1974] 1999. "Community Control and Governmental Responsiveness." In *Polycentricity and Local Public Economies: Readings from the Workshop in Political Theory and Policy Analysis*, edited by Michael D. McGinnis, 203–231. Ann Arbor, MI: University of Michigan Press.

Parks, Roger. 1979. "Assessing the Influence or Organization on Performance: A Study of Police Services in Residential Neighborhoods." Ph.D. diss., Indiana University Bloomington.

Rodriguez, S.M. 2021. "Queer Abolitionist Alternatives to Criminalising Hate Violence." In *The Routledge International Handbook of Penal Abolition*, edited by Michael J. Coyle and David Scott, 190–200. New York, NY: Routledge.

Rogers, Bruce and C. McCurdy Lipsey. 1974. "Metropolitan Reform: Citizen Evaluations of Performances in Nashville-Davidson County, Tennessee." *Publius* 4 (4): 19–34.

Salter, Alexander William. 2017. "Constitutional Drift and Political Dysfunction: Underappreciated Maladies of the Political Commons." *Independent Review* 21 (4): 569–585.

Skarbek, David. 2014. *The Social Order of the Underworld: How Prison Gangs Govern the American Penal System*. New York, NY: Oxford University Press.

Skarbek, David. 2020. *The Puzzle of Prison Order*. New York, NY: Oxford University Press.

Spade, Dean. 2015. *Normal Life: Administrative Violence, Critical Trans Politics, and the Limits of Law*. Durham, NC: Duke University Press.

Spade, Dean. 2024. "No Cops, Courts, or Cages Means no State." In a "Critical Exchange" on "Police Abolition: Geo Maher, *A World Without Police: How Strong Communities Make Cops Obsolete*. London. Verso. 2022." *Contemporary Political Theory* 23 (1): 114–145.

Spade, Dean and Craig Willse. 2000. "Confronting the Limits of Gay Hate Crimes Activism: A Radical Critique." *Chicano-Latino Law Review* 21: 38–52.

Stanley, Eric A., and Nat Smith. 2015. *Captive Genders: Trans Embodiment and the Prison-Industrial Complex*. Oakland, CA: AK Press.

Starling, Nick. 2023. "June 28 Marks 14 Years Since the Police Raid of a Fort Worth Gay Bar." *CBS News*. June 28. https://www.cbsnews.com/texas/news/14-years-since-police-raid-fort-worth-gay-bar.

Stauffer, Brian. 2016. "Do You See How Much I'm Suffering Here? Abuse Against Transgender Women in U.S. Immigration Detention." Human Rights Watch, March 23. https://www.hrw.org/report/2016/03/23/do-you-see-how-much-im-suffering-here/abuse-against-transgender-women-us.

Storr, Virgil Henry, Stefanie Haeffele-Balch, and Laura E. Grube. 2015. *Community Revival in the Wake of Disaster: Lessons in Local Entrepreneurship*. New York, NY: Palgrave Macmillan.

Stringham, Edward. 2003. "The Extralegal Development of Securities Trading in Seventeenth-century Amsterdam." *Quarterly Review of Economics and Finance* 43 (2): 321–344.

Sylvia Rivera Law Project. n.d. "SRLP on Hate Crimes Laws." https://srlp.org/action/hate-crimes.

Tabarrok, Alex. 2015. "What Was Gary Becker's Biggest Mistake?" *Marginal Revolution*. September 16. https://marginalrevolution.com/marginalrevolution/2015/09/what-was-gary-beckers-biggest-mistake.html.

U.S. Department of Justice Civil Rights Division. 2023. "The Matthew Shepard And James Byrd, Jr., Hate Crimes Prevention Act Of 2009." May 30. https://www.justice.gov/crt/matthew-shepard-and-james-byrd-jr-hate-crimes-prevention-act-2009-0

6

POLYCENTRIC SOLUTIONS TO STIGMATIZATION IN SALT LAKE CITY'S QUEER COMMUNITIES

Nathan P. Goodman and Jordan K. Lofthouse

Salt Lake City, Utah, is famously the home of the headquarters of the Church of Jesus Christ of Latter-day Saints (also known as the LDS Church or the Mormon Church). The LDS Church is dominant throughout the so-called "Mormon Belt"—a geographic region in the western United States that encompasses all of Utah, as well as the adjacent regions in southern Idaho, western Wyoming, eastern Nevada, and northern Arizona. Members of the LDS Church predominate in this region due to historical settlement patterns, and today the majority of the population in many of these towns and cities are members of the Church (Meinig 1965; Yorgason 2003; Public Religion Research Institute 2024).

The LDS Church's cultural and political influences in this region are strong. Per the Church's doctrines and practices, average citizens and political leaders in the region frequently oppose same-sex romantic and sexual relationships, refuse to recognize the moral legitimacy of same-sex marriages, and oppose social and medical transition for transgender individuals (Kimball 1969; Abbott and Byrd 2009; Ballard 2015; The Church of Jesus Christ of Latter-day Saints 2024; Associated Press 2024a, 2024b).

Despite the prevailing cultural and political trends in the wider Mormon Belt, the spiritual, cultural, and economic hub of Salt Lake City is—perhaps surprisingly—a queer-friendly place with many robust formal organizations and informal groups that provide friendship, mutual assistance, and other forms of social support for LGBTQ individuals.

Our core argument is that polycentric social arrangements can help LGBTQ individuals live healthier, happier, and more connected lives when a dominant culture is not particularly welcoming. Polycentric systems are defined by many decision-making centers at a variety of scales, scopes, and levels. These various centers are overlapping and nested with one another, and they are independent on many margins, but

DOI: 10.4324/9781003615781-6

interdependent on others (Aligica and Tarko 2012). Three core attributes of polycentric systems are (1) the potential for contestation among different decision-making centers, (2) the ability to cooperate and collaborate among different decision-making centers, and (3) the availability of alternative choices when one center fails or becomes oppressive.

When liberal institutions protect markets and civil society from undue encroachment by a dominant political majority, a polycentric social order can emerge (Aligica et al. 2019). Within that polycentric social order, minority groups, including LGBTQ individuals, can create their own businesses, organizations, clubs, nonprofits, political associations, and informal communities to meet their needs. In Utah, queer individuals have engaged in Tocquevillian self-governance by creating formal and informal groups to address a diversity of challenges. They have used civil society and markets to address political and social pressures that are sometimes antagonistic to their preferences and interests. To name just a few examples, the Utah Pride Center facilitates youth and family programs, provides education/training, promotes community health, and organizes the city's pride festival. The Utah LGBTQ+ Chamber of Commerce, Equality Utah, Stonewall Sports Salt Lake, and UAF Legacy Health are other groups that provide goods, services, and social connections to queer individuals who have moved to Salt Lake City or travel there from outlying areas.

The unique contribution of this chapter is to tie together the literature in mainline political economy on polycentric governance (Ostrom 2005; McGinnis 2016; Aligica et al. 2019) with the literature on Mormon and queer issues (Bradshaw et al. 2015a, 2015b; Barker et al. 2016; Prince 2019). To date, these two literatures have not been synthesized, leaving a conspicuous gap. By understanding the role that liberal institutions play in setting up a polycentric social order, scholars, policymakers, and activists can better understand how minority communities, such as the queer communities in Salt Lake City, can provide the goods, services, and social connections that they need.

This chapter is structured in the following way. In the next section, we discuss the theory of polycentricity and how it can address complex social problems through processes of contestation and collaboration. Next, we describe the stigmatization that queer individuals face in the Mormon Belt that necessitates businesses, organizations, and communities that cater to them. Then we analyze how a polycentric web of overlapping organizations and social networks provides necessary goods, services, and connections for queer individuals in Salt Lake City. The following section discusses contestation and competition among LGBTQ groups in Salt Lake City. We then conclude with the implications of this research.

Polycentric solutions to complex policy problems

The theory of polycentricity was pioneered by scholars like Michael Polanyi, Vincent Ostrom, and Elinor Ostrom, and it has been advanced by more recent scholars working in the tradition of the Bloomington school of political economy (Polanyi

1951, 1964; Ostrom et al. 1961; Ostrom 1971, 1991, 2005, 2010; McGinnis 2000, 2016; Aligica et al. 2019). In polycentric systems, decision-making occurs at multiple levels, scales, and scopes. The various decision-making centers overlap and are nested, making them independent on some margins and interdependent on others. Examples of polycentric systems include federalist systems of government, competitive markets, civil society, and the scientific community. These systems are polycentric because they have many centers of decision-making in which power is divided along many margins, not just hierarchically.

Within a constitutional framework of the rule of law, legal equality, and individual liberty, a polycentric social order can emerge. Under illiberal and authoritarian institutions, dominant centers of power can coercively suppress new entrants and thereby maintain their monopoly power. Those with power may suppress voluntary associations that threaten their rule. Constitutional constraints that restrict these types of authoritarian power can help maintain a society where individuals are free to form diverse voluntary associations at multiple scales. As people form such associations, cooperative and competitive relationships will form between these associations. The emergent result is a polycentric social order.

One of the most important aspects of a polycentric social order is contestation, which refers to the "pushback" that one decision-making center can exert on another. One of the most common forms of contestation is competition. Competition is often envisioned as a negative-sum conflict, which may be true in some cases. For instance, if two groups compete for resources by physically fighting each other, scarce resources will be spent on destruction rather than creation. However, economists working in the tradition of mainline political economy note that some institutional arrangements channel competition toward pro-social ends. For example, often different organizations *compete for the opportunity to cooperate with others*. When organizations must compete for the chance to cooperate with someone, this gives each organization stronger incentives to treat that potential cooperator well.

In addition, the fact that multiple people and groups are free to compete enables them to discover new and better ways to serve others. Competition within markets is well theorized and well-documented in the economics literature. In competitive market settings, competition induces producers to create higher quality goods at lower costs, as well as engaging in innovation. However, competition also operates in non-market settings. For example, governments engage in interjurisdictional competition because taxpayers are likely to flee to other jurisdictions with preferable policies. This competition constrains the harmful impulses of policymakers. Civil society groups, like nonprofits and community organizations, compete among themselves for members and donors' money. In polycentric systems, whether market or non-market, competition between various groups increases the pressure that decision-makers in organizations feel so that they provide the services that members and donors want.

Another form of contestation in polycentric systems is institutional checks and balances, as well as back-stops. Since one entity can push back against another, this process mitigates abuses of power or imprudent choices. For example, nonprofit advocacy groups can push back against public policies that might be detrimental to a minority group. Different branches of government or levels of government can also lower the likelihood that political power is abused. Judges, for instance, may rule that executive actions are unlawful. Powers may be divided between different branches or levels of government. A state government may challenge the federal government, or *vice versa*.

Another aspect of a polycentric social order is collaboration, which refers to the ability of various decision-making centers to "band together" when their interests align. Sometimes this collaboration might result from formal agreements or contracts between organizations. Often, however, collaborations will be more informal in nature. Individuals with ties to multiple decision-making centers may share information or leverage their social ties within multiple organizations. Whether formal or informal, such collaboration can increase the complexity of a polycentric social order. Moreover, it shows that a polycentric order is not just one where individuals are atomized or associations must always be small. Starting from the bottom-up does not preclude large-scale cooperation to achieve big goals.

A polycentric social order has many alternative choices from which people can choose, leading to a diverse range of opportunities for contestation and collaboration. If one decision-making center fails to achieve its goals, becomes tyrannical, or does not fit the preferences of a person under that center, that individual can choose to leave and find another option. In competitive markets, a consumer can choose another producer if the goods and services do not meet the consumer's preferences or expectations. In government, citizens can "vote with their feet" to find the jurisdictions that meet their preferences for taxation and public spending, among other considerations (Tiebout 1956; Ostrom et al. 1961). In civil society, individuals can find the clubs, organizations, religious groups, mutual aid societies, and nonprofits that most closely align with their preferences, and they can defect to other groups if they are unsatisfied with their current affiliations.

However, choosing an alternative comes with a cost, and those costs may be relatively high. Physically moving to another political jurisdiction can be costly in terms of money, which is why voice and exit are often paired together (Hirschman 1970). Citizens can attempt to make their voices heard in a variety of ways, such as voting and protest, but if political change through voice is insufficient, exit provides at least another option. Real-world evidence shows that despite the costliness of voting with one's feet, millions of people do it every year, such as the tens of thousands of migrants who attempt to cross the southern border of the United States annually (Amuedo-Dorantes and Bucheli 2023).

Relatedly, the costs of defecting from one religious organization can be especially high, but the costs of defection may still be outweighed by the benefits, which can only be evaluated subjectively by an individual. Religious organizations are often tied together with worldviews, social capital, and intimate relations with family and friends. Having alternative choices, even with high exit costs, is a superior option to having no alternative choices at all.

Polycentricity is no panacea. There is no guarantee that any given polycentric system will satisfy our ideals. However, each of the mechanisms discussed in this section offers paths through which individuals and groups can discover and seek better lives. These mechanisms encourage social learning, discovery, adaptation, and evolution toward outcomes that are more satisfactory for those within polycentric systems.

Stigmatization of queer people in the Mormon Belt

The cultural, economic, and spiritual core of the Mormon Belt is Salt Lake City, which is the largest city in roughly a 300-mile radius. Salt Lake City is in the center of a relatively dense urban region called the Wasatch Front, which is a 100-mile-long string of cities along the Wasatch Range, with a population of approximately 2.5 million people. The rest of the Mormon Belt is relatively rural.

Whether in the dense urban core of the Wasatch Front or the rural hinterlands, the dominant cultural and political entity is the LDS Church. According to the Pew Research Center, 55 percent of Utah's population identifies as Mormon/LDS. About 35 percent of adults in Utah think that homosexuality should be discouraged, and 45 percent of adults in Utah oppose or strongly oppose same-sex marriage (Pew Research Center 2024). The LDS Church is socially conservative and has a theologically exclusive belief system, which leads to "a strong sense of group cohesiveness and a devaluation of those who are not part of the group" (Lefevor et al. 2022: 290). Part of the modern LDS belief system is that marriage is between one cisgender man and one cisgender woman, and any sexual contact outside of marriage is a sin. Viewing pornography is heavily forbidden. Any behaviors that do not conform to heterosexuality or cisgender identities are morally condemned.

The LDS Church has encouraged LGBTQ individuals to make efforts at changing their sexual orientation by focusing on living a very religious life. However, empirical evidence suggests this often has negative consequences. Those who fail to alter their sexual orientation reported suffering emotionally and spiritually, and they also reported that their level of faith in God and their church decreased (Dahl and Galliher 2012; Bradshaw et al. 2015a, 2015b). Although the LDS Church has softened its rhetoric regarding LGBTQ individuals in recent years, queer individuals are still discouraged from "living authentic lives, particularly in terms of having healthy sexual, romantic, and family relationships" (Shuler et al. 2024: 1203). These conditions lead to a profound sense of stigmatization.

In the sociology literature, the concept of "stigma" was pioneered by Erving Goffman, who theorized stigma as personal attributes that others view as deeply discrediting or devaluing. Stigma is, at its core, a relational judgment between individuals. Stigma is the result of perceived problems with one's physical attributes, personal characteristics, or associations that lead to a devaluation. For instance, a wide variety of characteristics can lead to stigmas, such as gender, age, disability, sexual orientation, mental disorders, race, ethnicity, or nationality. For Goffman, stigma is centered on a "spoiled identity" that is dependent on place and time, which can differ between social groups.

Goffman's work on stigma is related to Howard S. Becker's insights on deviance. Mainstream society excludes stigmatized individuals from full social acceptance because they deviate from their society's categories of normality. This deviance is used to justify discrimination. As Becker (1963: 34) writes,

> One tends to be cut off, after being identified as deviant, from participation in more conventional groups, even though the specific consequences of the particular deviant activity might never of themselves have caused the isolation had there not also been the public knowledge and reaction to it. For example, being a homosexual may not affect one's ability to do office work, but to be known as a homosexual in an office may make it impossible to continue working there.

Stigmatized individuals often internalize feelings of shame; however, they can respond by finding creative ways to reframe the stigma or even embrace it. Stigma is not static, and over time, strategic actions from the stigmatized individuals or groups can recalibrate how others perceive them, granting them more social value and approbation (Becker 1963; Goffman 1963; Aranda et al. 2023).

Empirical evidence indicates that many queer LDS individuals experience a sense of stigma, feel that they cannot live authentic lives, and cannot fully participate in Church society. Research indicates that some parents will not

> allow their children's gay or transgender friends in their home and they may even forbid their children from having LGBT friends because they believe this will prevent their children from being gay. Many parents believe that the best way to help their gay or transgender children thrive as teens and adults is to pressure them to have only heterosexual friends.
>
> (Ryan and Rees 2012: 8)

Other forms of stigmatization come in the form of parents attempting to change their child's sexual orientation or gender identity. Parents, despite perceiving their own actions as rooted in love or care, are often "surprised and even shocked to learn that their gay children experience these reactions as rejection or abuse. Young people feel that by rejecting their core identity, their parents are rejecting them" (Ryan and Rees 2012: 8).

While these feelings and practices are not unique to the LDS Church, the Church's unique belief structure and dense social capital networks make it especially difficult for queer individuals to remain in the communities in which they were raised. Many queer LDS individuals make the painful decision to separate themselves from the Church and Church-related social circles (Grigoriou 2014; Bradshaw et al. 2015a, 2015b; Dehlin et al. 2015; Lefevor et al. 2020, 2022; Shuler et al. 2024).

Stigmatization of LGBTQ people in LDS communities can have tragic consequences. For some, the pain is so great that they attempt to end their own life:

> Suicides in the fifteen to nineteen age range in Utah have doubled since 2011. While Utah doubled its rate of suicides among teens, the rest of the country did not see a substantial increase in their suicide rate [...]. Suicide has become the leading cause of death in this age group in Utah. Of course, correlation does not prove causation, but it is important to look at correlating factors to determine which of these might explain causation. The time frame for this doubling of teen suicides does correspond to an increased focus in the media on LGBTQ issues, especially in Utah as the debate on same-sex marriage played out. That clearly led to a backlash, including frequent Church statements criticizing same-sex marriage or the LGBTQ community. It stands to reason that these statements have reinforced conflicts within congregations and families over the issue and has unleashed an increase of demonstrated homophobia and anti-LGBTQ feelings within families. It can easily be inferred that this chain of events exacerbated family rejection of vulnerable LGBTQ teens, thereby increasing their risk of suicide attempts as described earlier.
>
> (Barker et al. 2016: 8–9)

This illustrates the severe consequences that stigma can have for mental and emotional health.

Polycentric social order and queer communities in Salt Lake City

Due to the stigmatization of queer individuals throughout the Mormon Belt, Salt Lake City has become a hub for LGBTQ communities in the region. The city has become a refuge, and many queer people move there to exit the conservative communities where they grew up. Salt Lake City has substantially more religious diversity than other parts of the Mormon Belt. For example, according to the 2023 PRRI Census of American Religion, 89 percent of respondents in Madison County, Idaho, identified as LDS, which is one of Idaho's more populous counties. Similarly, 81 percent of respondents in Utah County, Utah's second most populous county with over 700,000 people, identified as LDS (Public Religion Research Institute 2024: 26). By contrast, journalists reported in 2018 that Salt Lake County had become "minority Mormon," citing data from Church records that showed "Salt Lake County's population is now 48.91 percent Latter-day Saint, the lowest since at least the 1930s, according to the available records" (Canham 2018).

This religious diversity means that it is comparatively easy to meet people who dissent from the Mormon Belt's dominant ideology once one moves to Salt Lake.

The population density, walkability, and transit options associated with living in a city rather than a suburb also enable associational life.

That said, the LGBTQ community in Salt Lake City substantially predates the rise in the city's religious diversity, and after World War II, a "small, urban gay subculture began to emerge" (Anderson 2017: 7). In the late 1940s and early 1950s, members of this community largely found each other at several bars that cautiously accepted them as customers (Anderson 2017). The community began to coalesce in a more recognizable form in Salt Lake City after 1969, as the Gay Liberation movement emerged (Anderson 2017: 8). Since then, the community has grown substantially, creating a robust and flourishing array of commercial, civil, and political associations.

As a result, many LGBTQ people who are stigmatized by the LDS Church flee to the very city where the LDS Church's headquarters is located. There, they find like-minded people with whom they build communities. They do so through many forms of associational life, from formally organized non-profit organizations to informal friend groups to commercial enterprises to political associations and social movements. These different forms of associational life coexist, and individuals may participate in some associations and not others. At times, the associations may cooperate with each other. Contestation can happen internally, as part of a process of internal voice and deliberation, or via criticism and competition between groups.

Commercial society as a bedrock of LGBTQ civil society

Commercial action and for-profit firms are one part of a polycentric social order, and they are not a panacea for social ills, but the profit motive provides one potential avenue for catering to populations that are stigmatized (see Chapter 3 in this volume). It is undeniable that markets have both strengths and weaknesses, as do governments and civil society. These spheres of human action are components of a broader polycentric arrangement, and the cooperation and contestation between entities in these different spheres allows the beneficial aspects of each of the spheres to arise, while also constraining or mitigating the weaknesses. For instance, there is a possibility that markets might replicate or perpetuate monopolistic structures rather than enhance diversity. However, if there is a constitutional framework that facilitates the rule of law, legal equality, and individual liberty, then markets will provide incentives and knowledge that enable entrepreneurs to serve the desires of consumers. As part of this process, niche markets emerge to cater to small minorities, even those that are stigmatized or who have preferences that diverge from the majority of a given population.

In a market order, rationally self-interested individuals act entrepreneurially to cater to consumers' preferences so that they can profit through mutually beneficial exchange. Anyone can be an entrepreneur, as long as they are alert to and seize previously unrealized or unexploited opportunities. Potential entrepreneurs use their tacit and local knowledge of people's subjective values, and in the queer context, they can profit by serving individuals whose preferences fall outside mainstream convention. Markets tend to be socially beneficial because entrepreneurs are alert to and search for opportunities for mutual gain. When many different firms compete with one another, they may also differentiate themselves from each other by appealing to a different clientele. This latter form of competition and experimentation can be especially useful for members of marginalized groups. If a group is underserved, this means that an entrepreneur can make a profit by serving that group. Therefore, in a world where LGBTQ people lack spaces to express themselves, an entrepreneur can profit by creating such a space (Goodman 2023). Thus, markets promote social diversity because entrepreneurs have an incentive to provide a wide array of goods and services to the vast spectrum of preferences.

Bars have been an incredibly important example of commercial entrepreneurship. In Utah, gay bars began opening in the 1970s, though some bars welcomed sexual minorities as early as the 1940s. As Anderson explains:

> In 1973, Joe Redburn … opened the Sun Tavern, the first gay bar in the state with a sign. Perky's had opened on North Temple [in Salt Lake City] as a bar for women but was more discreet. Bars in the gay and lesbian movement have done more than just provide a place to drink; they have also functioned as miniature community centers. Gay bars in Salt Lake City were no different. Throughout the 1970s, the Sun Tavern became the foremost social gathering location for the community.
>
> (Anderson 2017: 25)

This illustrates the way that markets can be social spaces (Storr 2008). Commercial establishments that serve as queer social spaces remain an important part of LGBTQ life in Salt Lake City. As of 2025, Salt Lake City has several gay bars and clubs that serve the dual roles of commercial space and social space (Visit Salt Lake 2025).

In addition to bars, there are various other commercial enterprises that function as community spaces. Bookstores have often served this role. For instance, in 1967

> Steven Jones and Sherm Clow opened the Cosmic Aeroplane … an alternative bookstore that … sold gay-themed books and magazines, advertised in the *Salt Lick* and the *Open Door* [local gay publications], and attracted a clientele of poets, musicians, artists, antiwar protestors, gay rights activists, and feminists.
>
> (Anderson 2017: 32)

Today, bookstores continue to create space for discourse and community action for LGBT people in Utah. For example, Under the Umbrella is a bookstore and café dedicated to "sharing and celebrating queer books written by queer authors and offering a safe, sober, and accessible space for 2SLGBTQIA+ people to gather" (Under the Umbrella Bookstore 2025).[1]

Another bookstore and coffee shop, Legendarium, specializes in science fiction, fantasy, and tabletop role playing games. The owners are transgender and emphasize the importance of providing a space for queer community. A reporter from the Daily Utah Chronicle asked Legendarium co-founder Steph Blatter about what they see as important about the shop. They replied, "I think community honestly, especially coming out of the pandemic. We wanted to create a safe and inclusive space for queer people and nerds and really anybody who loves books and wants to find community and belonging" (Marler 2023). Legendarium is a sober and all-ages space, which means that it can serve LGBTQ people who would not be able to find community at a gay bar.

An important organization for queer people in Salt Lake City is the Utah LGBTQ+ Chamber of Commerce. Its mission is "to create long lasting partnerships between key organizations and businesses, ensuring both growth and visibility for the LGBTQ+ community and allies in Utah." The Chamber represents "approximately 300 small business, corporate, and nonprofit members who share the values of promoting equity, diversity, inclusion and belonging in the workplace" (The Utah LGBTQ+ Chamber of Commerce 2024). The Utah LGBTQ+ Chamber of Commerce's activities illustrate how civil society and commercial life are entangled, with businesses often banding together to participate in civil society.

Civil society groups as the nexus for social change

While commercial life offers crucial social spaces, there is also a rich associational life outside the commercial sector. The LDS Church has often been quite hostile to LGBTQ people, but queer individuals have organized civil society groups to advocate for greater dignity and acceptance within the Church. This activism can be traced back to the late 1970s, with one especially influential person being Stephen Zacharias (going by the name Matthew Price). In 1977, Zacharias and several Mormon and ex-Mormon gays and lesbians, founded Affirmation: Gay Mormons United in Salt Lake City to persuade church members and church leadership to be more accommodating and accepting of queer individuals (Anderson 2017: 29).

More recently, Mormons Building Bridges was formed in 2012, aiming "to ease some of the tensions between the LDS and LGBTQ communities" (Fletcher Stack 2020). The group brought together "more than 300 church members dressed in their Sunday best to march in that year's Utah Gay Pride Parade" (Fletcher Stack 2020). Different members of Mormons Building Bridges had disagreements about whether to challenge the Church's stances on homosexuality. Erika Munson, who cofounded Mormons Building Bridges, eventually left the group to form a new organization called Emmaus. This group, cofounded with a leader of Affirmation, aims to support LGBTQ people in the Church without challenging the Church's authority or stances (Fletcher Stack 2020).

Although some groups have tried to reconcile with the LDS Church, many other civil society organizations cater to the broader queer population, including queer individuals who want to distance themselves from LDS beliefs and culture. For instance, the Utah Pride Center is organized as a 501(c)3 non-profit organization that works to "unite, empower and celebrate Utah's diverse LGBTQIA+ community with safe, accessible, and inclusive programs, events, and services." The Utah Pride Center organizes the Utah Pride Festival, as well as a variety of youth and community programs (Utah Pride Center 2024). The Pride Festival, held each June, is their most visible and high-profile event. Each year, the festival brings together numerous LGBTQ people and allies for parades, marches, live performances, food and drink, and revelry. Businesses, community groups, and political parties have booths at the annual Pride Festival, simultaneously showing their support and advertising their respective projects to festival attendees. While the event was once quite small, "the Utah Pride Festival has grown to become the second-largest civic event in the state" (Anderson 2017: 94).

But while the Utah Pride Festival is the Utah Pride Center's best-known activity, the Pride Center hosts a variety of programming all year. This includes youth programming, which provides LGBTQ youth with a respite from schools and families where they may not feel safe to express themselves. It also includes a variety of community groups and support groups for a wide range of subgroups within the LGBTQ community. In this sense, the Pride Center serves as a hub and a platform within which a wide variety of smaller voluntary associations are formed to serve diverse wants and needs. Many activist and community projects have begun within the Pride Center. For instance, Dominique Storni "started Transgender Education and Awareness Month (TEAM) in November 2002 at the Gay and Lesbian Community Center of Utah (later renamed the Utah Pride Center)" (Anderson 2017: 79).

Another important organization is Equality Utah, which has a mission "to secure equal rights and protections for LGBT Utahns and their families." Equality Utah is an example of a political association, in which people come together to influence elections and legislation. It is a 501(c)(4) organization and is the state's largest LGBTQ civil rights organization. Organizing LGBTQ people and allies as an interest group offers a counterweight to the political action of the LDS Church and other socially conservative interest groups in Utah politics. It sponsors LGBTQ legislation and opposes negative bills; lobbies elected officials; builds coalitions; and empowers individuals and organizations alike to engage in the legislative process. It also publishes a voter guide full of candidates and endorses specific candidates who are champions for equality (Equality Utah 2023).

In terms of public health, UAF Legacy Health, formerly known as Utah AIDS Foundation, has the mission of providing "cross-culturally responsive healthcare for LGBTQ+ Utahns, people living with HIV, and their allies" (UAF Legacy Health 2024). Before 2023, Utah AIDS Foundation had a clinic that only provided testing for HIV/AIDS and sexually transmitted infections, but it had to refer patients to outside clinicians for other services. In 2023, the organization rebranded itself as UAF Legacy Health and expanded into a full-service, LGBTQ-focused primary care clinic. It provides a variety of health services in-house, such as HIV/AIDS and STI testing and other healthcare services, as well as support groups and mental health services (Harkins 2023).

The Utah AIDS Foundation formed alongside a broader network of grassroots organizations addressing the AIDS crisis in Utah. As Anderson explains:

> Grassroots efforts to assist people with AIDS were under way by 1985. Dr. Patty Reagan founded the Salt Lake AIDS Foundation; Duane Dawson, a nurse, formed AIDS Project Utah; David Sharpton founded the People With AIDS Coalition of Utah; Father Don Bramble started a support group for people with AIDS; and Dick Dotson founded Horizon House. The Royal Court of the Golden Spike Empire, a nonprofit pageant system established in 1976 to serve the needs of Utah's gay and lesbian community, began fundraising for people with AIDS in 1986. Under Emperor Scott Stites, the Royal Court raised over $10,000 from various gay community groups in Salt Lake City. Stites also created the first AIDS Awareness Week in Utah, a tradition observed to this day.
>
> (Anderson 2017: 35)

This illustrates how vulnerable, oppressed, and stigmatized people can come together and organize from the bottom-up to provide healthcare. The longevity and adaptation of UAF Legacy Health through the years further illustrates how social capital and organizational capacity built during crises can be used in pro-social ways long after the initial crisis.

Civil society organizations are also important spaces in which queer people can make new friends and engage in recreation. For instance, Stonewall Sports Salt Lake City was founded in 2018 as a completely volunteer-run organization, and its mission is "to provide an inclusive, low cost, high FUN sports league that is managed as a non-profit with a philanthropic heart" (Stonewall Sports SLC 2023). Other exclusively queer or queer-friendly recreation organizations exist, such as the Utah Gay Football League, Utah Gay Rodeo Association, Queer Utah Aquatic Club, Out Trails (for trail running), among others. This illustrates how civil society is not merely aimed at solving serious social problems, but also at providing enjoyable club goods for the members of civil associations.

Contestation and competition in LGBTQ civil society

Salt Lake City's LGBTQ residents are not a monolith. They do not all share the same ideas, values, or interests. The genuinely diverse rainbow of queer people can sometimes lead to conflict. In a polycentric system, this value heterogeneity, disagreement, and conflict can be addressed in multiple ways. Sometimes, it may be addressed through internal discussion *within* an organization. For instance, in any of the organizations discussed in this chapter, participants and members may discuss and deliberate as they try to influence the organization's direction. This involves the exercise of *voice* internally within a single organization.

However, in a polycentric system, people can also respond to their grievances in one organization by joining or forming another organization. Sometimes, this may take the form simply of *exit* or *competition*. In other cases, one organization may engage in contestation with another. One conflict of visions relates to what pride festivals should be. Major pride festivals, including the Utah Pride Festival, feature partnerships with and sponsorships from established businesses. Moreover, many pride events, including the Utah Pride Festival, partner with the police. This commercialization of pride is unappealing to some LGBTQ people, particularly those with leftist views. Many argue that this depoliticizes an event that grew out of what was once a radical political movement seeking liberation. Police involvement provokes still more ire. Pride events are held in June to commemorate the Stonewall Riots, during which patrons at a Greenwich Village gay bar called the Stonewall Inn fought back against the NYPD during a raid. Moving from this radical direct action to a corporate-sponsored, police-protected, and permitted event is seen as defanging the movement and losing the revolutionary, radical, and emancipatory spirit that once animated the Gay Liberation struggle. As Michael Aaron put it in the Salt Lake LGBTQ newspaper *Q Salt Lake*:

> The transformation of Pride from riot to revelry didn't happen overnight. After the Stonewall Uprising in 1969, the first Pride marches in the 1970s were acts of sheer courage: raw, loud, and radical. Marchers weren't asking for inclusion in the system; they were demanding that the system be changed. But over time, as social attitudes softened, so did Pride. By the 1990s and early 2000s, corporate interest in LGBTQ+ communities began to surge. Pride events became marketing opportunities. Companies like Target, American Airlines, and AT&T showed up with rainbow merchandise, floats, and sponsorships. Some of us cheered. Others worried about co-optation. But the money helped us throw bigger festivals, pay artists, fund local LGBTQ+ centers, and sustain nonprofits.
>
> (Aaron 2025)

This eloquently describes the transformation of Pride over the years, as well as the benefits and costs different people saw in that transformation, leading to different assessments of appropriate trade-offs.

In a polycentric system, individuals with different visions of pride are free to pursue their respective visions. Beginning in 2021, Salt Lake Community Mutual Aid has organized an annual event each June called "Pride Without Police"

(Vales 2024; Salt Lake Community Mutual Aid 2025). As the organizers explained in their event page for 2025:

> Our goal and purpose for the event remain the same. We oppose capitalist assimilation and call for queer liberation. We consider the Utah Pride Center's inclusion of police, real estate investors, petroleum refineries, and military contractors as directly inviting the very entities that drive our oppression. Instead, PWP is entirely community driven. All the groups involved with PWP are directly involved in local efforts to organize for a better world. Our goal for PWP is to provide an opportunity for people to take actual pride in who they are without the barriers imposed by the Pride Center.
>
> (Salt Lake Community Mutual Aid 2025)

One such barrier is the admission fee that the Utah Pride Festival charges attendees. As one attendee at Pride Without Police told a journalist, "The main Pride event for Utah Pride, run by the Utah Pride Center, is very expensive … I love that Pride Without Police is free, open to the public, and focused on being extremely accessible" (quoted in Vales 2024). Another attendee emphasized that Pride Without Police felt like a more genuine site of community engagement. Contrasting the event with the Utah Pride Festival's corporate sponsorships and commercial feel, they said, "Pride Without Police feels like an alternative to that, where we're taking care of each other; we're building community for each other; we're building alternative systems" (cited in Vales 2024).

While Pride Without Police criticizes the Utah Pride Center, they primarily show their dissent by organizing an alternative event. However, some disagreements among LGBTQ Utahns have resulted in more confrontational forms of contestation. One notable instance of such contestation relates to Jane Marquardt. She is a proud member of the LGBTQ community whose relationship with her wife Tami saw them committing to each other at various stages of the struggle for marriage equality (Marquardt 2015). In 2010, Equality Utah honored Jane and Tami Marquardt with the Allies in Equality Award (Vanderhooft 2010). As philanthropists, Jane and Tami had donated substantial sums to LGBTQ non-profits, including Equality Utah. Jane had also served on Equality Utah's board. She also used her talents as a lawyer to help LGBT Utahns, "offering seminars on establishing powers of attorney, wills and other directives to same-sex couples" beginning in 1982 (Vanderhooft 2010). Notably, Tami Marquardt had served as director of the Utah Pride Center (Vanderhooft 2010).

Yet in addition to this LGBTQ rights activism, Jane Marquardt was the board vice chair of the Management and Training Corporation (MTC). While MTC largely operates job training facilities for the federal government's Job Corps program, they also have operated prisons, jails, and ICE detention centers. These facilities are sites of state violence. This violence is harmful to all detainees and prisoners but can be especially severe for those who are LGBTQ. As Easton Smith (2019) asked in the *Salt Lake Tribune*, "How can Jane Marquardt be a 'a voice for the LGBTQ movement in Utah' when gay and transgender detainees at the MTC-run Otero County Processing Center in New Mexico face what lawyers called 'rampant sexual harassment, discrimination and abuse'?"

LGBTQ activists opposed to incarceration and detention have often drawn attention to this tension between Marquardt's stated values and her business. For example, in 2012 several activists with the Salt Lake City Prison Divestment Campaign disrupted a Utah Democratic Party Central Committee meeting where Jane Marquardt was running for vice chair of the Utah Democratic Party (Goodman 2012). They directly drew attention to the way that Marquardt's prisons harm vulnerable people, including LGBTQ people. Many of the activists were queer and emphasized their identity in their remarks. For instance, one queer activist shouted at Marquardt:

> As a queer woman [myself], you do not represent me. A lot of people overlook Jane's prison profits, because they say she is a strong supporter of LGBT rights. It may not be Jane's fault, and she may not like it, but LGBT kids are disproportionately more likely to be homeless than their peers. Yet homelessness is one of the leading contributors to LGBT people being criminalized and being placed in the United States' mass incarceration system. That's what Jane Marquardt does. She is not an advocate for LGBTQ people. As a queer woman, she is not a representative for me or LGBTQ people.
>
> (SLCPrisonDivestment 2012)

This disturbance prompted shouts in return from the crowd in attendance, who wanted the disruption to cease. One man violently grabbed papers out of the hand of the queer activist who was speaking out against Marquardt (SLCPrisonDivestment 2012).

There are many LGBTQ people in the world. A few of them own prisons, jails, and immigration detention centers, while many others are caged in those facilities. There is substantial disagreement among LGBTQ people in Salt Lake City about what standing a prison owner who has also engaged in philanthropy and activism for LGBTQ rights should have. Disputes about this have been contentious, illustrating a diversity of values and strategic judgments, and the challenge of acting in contexts of serious normative disagreement. Polycentric social arrangements are not panaceas for dealing with these disputes. However, they offer space for different people to voluntarily associate to advance their values and engage in contestation.

Conclusion

In the predominantly LDS region of the Mormon Belt, many children grow up hearing that homosexuality and gender nonconformity are sins. Yet despite these repeated messages, and the stigma they bring, many of them still grow up to be queer or trans. In Salt Lake City, these queer and trans people can find rich associational life in many forms, from sports leagues to bookstores, bars to activist groups.

This chapter has focused on Salt Lake City, but similar patterns have emerged in smaller or more rural Mormon Belt contexts. We have focused on Salt Lake City because it is the largest city in the Mormon Belt, which is one of the reasons it has the largest and most robust constellations of queer communities, meaning that it provides more options for queer people from smaller towns. But, like Salt Lake City, other towns have civil society groups and for-profit businesses that cater to queer people, allowing them to find meaningful connections. For example, Idaho Falls, Idaho, is a city of roughly 70,000 people, and being located 200 miles north of Salt Lake City, it is on the northern end of the Mormon Belt. Idaho Falls has several queer-friendly organizations and businesses, including the non-profit Idaho Falls Pride. Similarly, St. George, Utah, is a city of roughly 100,000 people located 300 miles south of Salt Lake City, putting it at the southern end of the Mormon Belt. Like Idaho Falls, St. George has several queer-friendly organizations and businesses, including Encircle St. George, which is a non-profit that provides a variety of mental-health and community-building services for queer people in southern Utah. Thus, polycentric social orders in communities of any size can expand the possibilities for the flourishing and de-stigmatization of queer people.

Utah is "The Beehive State," and the beehive symbolizes industry and hard work. Utah's industriousness in both the LDS community and the queer community is reminiscent of Tocqueville's observations in *Democracy in America*. Tocqueville marveled at how Americans had particular skill with the art of association. A robust civil society and a vibrant commercial society has allowed "Americans of all ages, all conditions, all minds [to] constantly unite" for a variety of reasons, including "religious, moral, serious ones, useless ones, very general and very particular ones, immense and very small ones … to celebrate holidays, established seminaries, build inns, erect churches, distribute books, send missionaries … create hospitals, prisons, and schools" (cited in Behr and Storr 2022: 282). In line with the insights of queer classical liberalism, the Tocquevillian tradition in America, and in Utah in particular, has expanded to queer communities who form their own associations to advance their own values and interests.

Monocentric organizational structures subordinate all their members to the edicts of a single center of decision-making that sits atop a hierarchy. Polycentricity enables people to form a rich tapestry of associational life, building meaningful social relationships that reflect diverse aims, values, goals, and lifestyles. People often refer to the "queer community" or the "LGBTQ community" as catchall terms, but referring to the "queer community" as a whole often mistakenly homogenizes it, as if it were monocentric. A more accurate term may be "queer *communities*" because of the diversity of beliefs and practices, which reflects the polycentric nature of how queer people actually organize themselves. Conceptualizing the queer community as many overlapping and nested communities is more analytically fruitful because it better reflects social reality. Thus, a polycentric social order allows different organizations and networks of queer people to cooperate with one another when they agree and contest against one another when they have different values.

In Salt Lake City's polycentric social order, some queer communities have worked to build inclusive, mainstream partnerships within existing power structures. Other communities have taken on a more radical, countercultural stance that challenges mainstream systems. Other communities are less politically oriented and seek to create an environment of inclusion and friendship through recreation or mutual assistance. In a polycentric social order, the diversity of divergent priorities is not a symptom of disarray. Instead, diversity and disagreement are part of a Tocquevillian republic in which people engage in democratic self-governance.

Of course, polycentric social orders are not panaceas, and they do not guarantee a utopia. Polycentric systems have the potential to reproduce existing inequalities in terms of resource access, especially for the most marginalized people. Additionally, exit from a community is costly, and it may be prohibitively costly when structural barriers prevent individuals from exercising meaningful choice. These concerns are legitimate, and there are at least two potential responses. First, polycentricity must be compared to the relevant alternative of monocentricity. When governance systems are hierarchical and centralized, the likelihood of inequalities and structural barriers is highest because there is minimal room for contestation. When power is decentralized, at least to some degree, there is more space to creatively find solutions to inequalities and more possibilities for exit. Second, the concept of polycentricity is not monolithic. Institutional rules and institutional configurations can be changed in an infinite number of ways. If polycentric governance systems have problems like inequalities of resources or structural barriers that prevent exit, rules and configurations can be changed on many margins to address the problems. New forms of collaboration or contestation may arise to address such problems. Thus, the queer communities in Salt Lake City benefit from having multiple venues for engagement, and even multiple models of pride festivals. In Salt Lake City, LGBTQ associational life operates in a rich, diverse, and complex network—a genuine rainbow.

Note

1 The acronym 2SLGBTQIA+ is inclusive of Two-Spirit (2S), Lesbian (L), Gay (G), Bisexual (B), Transgender (T), Queer (Q), Intersex (I), Asexual (A) identities, as well as other identities not otherwise listed (+).

References

Aaron, Michael. 2025. "Pride: From Protest to Party and Back Again." *QSaltLake*, June 16. https://www.qsaltlake.com/news/2025/06/16/pride-from-protest-to-party-and-back-again.

Abbott, Douglas A., and A. Dean Byrd. 2009. *Encouraging Heterosexuality: Helping Children Develop a Traditional Sexual Orientation.* Orem, UT: Millennial Press.

Aligica, Paul Dragos, Peter J. Boettke, and Vlad Tarko. 2019. *Public Governance and the Classical-Liberal Perspective: Political Economy Foundations*. Oxford, UK: Oxford University Press.

Aligica, Paul Dragos, and Vlad Tarko. 2012. “Polycentricity: From Polanyi to Ostrom, and Beyond.” *Governance* 25 (2): 237–262.

Amuedo-Dorantes, Catalina, and José R. Bucheli. 2023. “Implications of Restrictive Asylum Policies: Evidence from Metering along the U.S.-Mexico Border.” *Journal of Population Economics* 36 (3): 1941–1962.

Anderson, J. Seth. 2017. *LGBT Salt Lake*. Charleston, SC: Arcadia Publishing.

Aranda, Ana M., Wesley S. Helms, Karen D. W. Patterson, Thomas J. Roulet, and Bryant Ashley Hudson. 2023. “Standing on the Shoulders of Goffman: Advancing a Relational Research Agenda on Stigma.” *Business & Society* 62 (7): 1339–1377.

Associated Press. 2024a. “LGBTQ Advocates Say Mormon Church’s New Policies Marginalize Trans Members.” *U.S. News and World Report*, August 23. https://www.usnews.com/news/us/articles/2024-08-23/lgbtq-advocates-say-mormon-churchs-new-transgender-policies-marginalize-transgender-members.

Associated Press. 2024b. “Transgender Activists Flood Utah Tip Line with Hoax Reports to Block Bathroom Law Enforcement.” *NBC News*, May 8. https://www.nbcnews.com/nbc-out/out-news/transgender-activists-flood-utah-tip-line-hoax-reports-block-bathroom-rcna151226.

Ballard, M. Russell. 2015. “The Lord Needs You Now!” *Liahona*, September. https://www.churchofjesuschrist.org/study/liahona/2015/09/the-lord-needs-you-now?lang=eng.

Barker, Michael, Daniel Parkinson, and Benjamin Knoll. 2016. “The LGBTQ Mormon Crisis: Responding to the Empirical Research on Suicide.” *Dialogue* 49 (2): 1–24.

Becker, Howard S. 1963. *Outsiders: Studies in the Sociology of Deviance*. New York, NY: Free Press of Glencoe.

Behr, Rachael K., and Virgil Henry Storr. 2022. “Tocquevillean Association and the Market.” In *The Cambridge Companion to Democracy in America*, edited by Richard Boyd, 278–305. New York, NY: Cambridge University Press.

Bradshaw, Kate, John P. Dehlin, Katherine A. Crowell, Renee V. Galliher, and William S. Bradshaw. 2015a. “Sexual Orientation Change Efforts Through Psychotherapy for LGBQ Individuals Affiliated With the Church of Jesus Christ of Latter-Day Saints.” *Journal of Sex & Marital Therapy* 41 (4): 391–412.

Bradshaw, William S., Tim B. Heaton, Ellen Decoo, John P. Dehlin, Renee V. Galliher, and Katherine A. Crowell. 2015b. “Religious Experiences of GBTQ Mormon Males.” *Journal for the Scientific Study of Religion* 54 (2): 311–329.

Canham, Matt. 2018. “Salt Lake County Is Now Minority Mormon, and the Impacts Are Far Reaching.” *The Salt Lake Tribune*, December 9. https://www.sltrib.com/religion/2018/12/09/salt-lake-county-is-now.

Dahl, Angie, and Renee V. Galliher. 2012. “The Interplay of Sexual and Religious Identity Development in LGBTQ Adolescents and Young Adults: A Qualitative Inquiry.” *Identity* 12 (3): 217–246.

Dehlin, John P., Renee V. Galliher, William S. Bradshaw, and Katherine A. Crowell. 2015. “Navigating Sexual and Religious Identity Conflict: A Mormon Perspective.” *Identity* 15 (1): 1–22.

Equality Utah. 2023. “Mission and Vision.” https://www.equalityutah.org/mission.

Fletcher Stack, Peggy. 2020. “Proposed Name Change Exposes Divisions in Mormons Building Bridges, Spurs Creation of New LGBTQ Support Group.” *The Salt Lake Tribune*, May 13. https://www.sltrib.com/religion/2020/05/13/proposed-name-change.

Goffman, Erving. 1963. *Stigma: Notes on the Management of Spoiled Identity*. Englewood Cliffs, NJ: Prentice-Hall.

Goodman, Nathan P. 2012. “Jane Marquardt: ‘Progressive’ Prison Profiteer.” Center for a Stateless Society, December 11. https://c4ss.org/content/15179.

Goodman, Nathan P. 2023. "Commerce, Spontaneous Order, and Gender Freedom Movements." *Cosmos+Taxis* 11 (11–12): 24–36.

Grigoriou, Jennifer A. 2014. "Minority Stress Factors for Same-Sex Attracted Mormon Adults." *Psychology of Sexual Orientation and Gender Diversity* 1 (4): 471–479.

Harkins, Paighten. 2023. "Utah AIDS Foundation to Become State's First Full-Service LGBTQ Health Clinic." *The Salt Lake Tribune*, May 31. https://www.sltrib.com/news/2023/05/31/utah-aids-foundation-become-full.

Hirschman, Albert O. 1970. *Exit, Voice, and Loyalty: Responses to Decline in Firms, Organizations, and States*. Cambridge, MA: Harvard University Press.

Kimball, Spencer W. 1969. *The Miracle of Forgiveness*. Salt Lake City, UT: Bookcraft.

Lefevor, G. Tyler, Samuel J. Skidmore, James S. McGraw, Edward B. Davis, and Ty R. Mansfield. 2022. "Religiousness and Minority Stress in Conservatively Religious Sexual Minorities: Lessons from Latter-Day Saints." *International Journal for the Psychology of Religion* 32 (4): 289–305.

Lefevor, G. Tyler, Sydney A. Sorrell, Grace Kappers, Ashley Plunk, Ron L. Schow, Christopher H. Rosik, and A. Lee Beckstead. 2020. "Same-Sex Attracted, Not LGBQ: The Associations of Sexual Identity Labeling on Religiousness, Sexuality, and Health Among Mormons." *Journal of Homosexuality* 67 (7): 940–964.

Marler, Arlo. 2023. "Legendarium: Providing an Inclusive and Queer Alcohol-Free Space." Daily Utah Chronicle, April 17. https://dailyutahchronicle.com/2023/04/17/legendarium-book-store/.

Marquardt, Jane. 2015. "Here's Why I've Been Married 8 Times." *Huffington Post*, August 29. https://www.huffpost.com/entry/heres-why-ive-been-marrie_b_8033638.

McGinnis, Michael D. 2000. *Polycentric Games and Institutions: Readings from the Workshop in Political Theory and Policy Analysis*. Ann Arbor, MI: University of Michigan Press.

McGinnis, Michael D. 2016. *Polycentric Governance in Theory and Practice: Dimensions of Aspirations and Practical Limitations*. Indiana University, Working Paper. https://mcginnis.pages.iu.edu/polycentric%20governance%20theory%20and%20practice%20Feb%202016.pdf.

Meinig, D. W. 1965. "The Mormon Culture Region: Strategies and Patterns in the Geography of the American West, 1847–1964." *Annals of the Association of American Geographers* 55 (2): 191–220.

Ostrom, Elinor. 2005. *Understanding Institutional Diversity*. Princeton, NJ: Princeton University Press.

Ostrom, Elinor. 2010. "Beyond Markets and States: Polycentric Governance of Complex Economic Systems." *American Economic Review* 100 (3): 641–672.

Ostrom, Vincent. 1971. *The Political Theory of a Compound Republic: A Reconstruction of the Logical Foundations of American Democracy as Presented in the Federalist*. Blacksburg, VA: Center for Study of Public Choice.

Ostrom, Vincent. 1991. *The Meaning of American Federalism*. San Francisco, CA: ICS Press.

Ostrom, Vincent, Charles M. Tiebout, and Robert Warren. 1961. "The Organization of Government in Metropolitan Areas: A Theoretical Inquiry." *American Political Science Review* 55 (4): 831–842.

Pew Research Center. 2024. "Religious Landscape Study: Adults in Utah." https://www.pewresearch.org/religious-landscape-study/database/state/utah.

Polanyi, Michael. 1951. *The Logic of Liberty: Reflections and Rejoinders*. Chicago, IL: University of Chicago Press.

Polanyi, Michael. 1964. *Science, Faith, and Society*. Chicago, IL: University of Chicago Press.

Prince, Gregory A. 2019. *Gay Rights and the Mormon Church: Intended Actions, Unintended Consequences*. Salt Lake City, UT: University of Utah Press.

Public Religion Research Institute. 2024. "2023 PRRI Census of American Religion: County-Level Data on Religious Identity and Diversity." https://prri.org/wp-content/uploads/2025/05/PRRI_Dec_2024_Religion_final-1.pdf.

Ryan, Caitlin, and Robert A. Rees. 2012. *Supportive Families, Healthy Children: Helping Latter-Day Saint Families with Lesbian, Gay, Bisexual & Transgender Children*. San Francisco State University, Marian Wright Edelman Institute. https://familyproject.sfsu.edu/sites/default/files/documents/FAP%20LDS%20Booklet%20pst.pdf.

Salt Lake Community Mutual Aid. 2025. "Pride Without Police – 2025." https://web.archive.org/web/20250603194353/https://slcmutualaid.com/pride-without-police.

Shuler, Shay L., Korena Klimczak, and Amanda M. Pollitt. 2024. "Queer in the Latter Days: An Integrated Model of Sexual and Religious Identity Development Among Former Mormon Sexual Minority Adults." *Journal of Homosexuality* 71 (5): 1201–1230.

SLCPrisonDivestment. 2012. "Prison Profiteer Jane Marquardt Shut Down During Nomination Speech." https://www.youtube.com/watch?v=AphbBf-sY9Q.

Smith, Easton. 2019. "Commentary: Utah 'Philanthropists' Getting Rich by Locking up Immigrants." *The Salt Lake Tribune*, July 13. https://www.sltrib.com/opinion/commentary/2019/07/13/commentary-utah.

Stonewall Sports SLC. 2023. "About Stonewall Sports SLC." https://www.stonewallsports-saltlakecity.org/blank-1.

Storr, Vigil Henry. 2008. "The Market as a Social Space: On the Meaningful Extraeconomic Conversations That Can Occur in Markets." *Review of Austrian Economics* 21 (2/3): 135–150.

The Church of Jesus Christ of Latter-day Saints. 2024. "Individuals Who Identify as Transgender." In *General Handbook: Serving in The Church of Jesus Christ of Latter-Day Saints*. The Church of Jesus Christ of Latter-day Saints. https://www.churchofjesuschrist.org/study/manual/general-handbook?lang=eng.

The Utah LGBTQ+ Chamber of Commerce. 2024. "About Us." https://www.utahlgbtqchamber.org/about-us/.

Tiebout, Charles M. 1956. "A Pure Theory of Local Expenditures." *Journal of Political Economy* 64 (5): 416–424.

UAF Legacy Health. 2024. "Mission & Vision." https://uafhealth.org/mission-vision.

Under the Umbrella Bookstore. 2025. "About Us." https://www.undertheumbrellabookstore.com.

Utah Pride Center. 2024. "Vision and Misson." https://utahpridecenter.org/about/vision-mission.

Vales, Frank. 2024. "Alternative Pride Festival in Salt Lake City Promotes Community over Corporations." Globe SLCC, July 16. https://www.globeslcc.com/2024/07/16/pride-without-police-event-lgbtq-salt-lake.

Vanderhooft, JoSelle. 2010. "Allies Honored at Equality Utah Dinner." *Q Salt Lake*, September 16. https://www.qsaltlake.com/news/2010/09/16/allies-honored-at-equality-utah-dinner.

Visit Salt Lake. 2025. "Drink It In: Salt Lake's Gay Bar Scene Is Growing, Thriving, and Never Looking Back." https://www.visitsaltlake.com/things-to-do/nightlife-entertainment/gay-bars.

Yorgason, Ethan R. 2003. *Transformation of the Mormon Culture Region*. Urbana, IL: University of Illinois Press.

7

HOW DIVERSE IS DIVERSITY? AN ANALYSIS OF LGBTQ CONTENT ON DIGITAL PLATFORMS

Carolina Dalla Chiesa and Yana Zaharieva

The advancement of access to human and civil rights for marginalized groups, including so-called "rainbow communities," has enabled them to attain levels of acceptance, tolerance, and ultimately identity expression unseen before. Although these do not go without backlash from conservatives, in liberal democracies, LGBTQ individuals experience a greater openness to diversity, which translates into an ecosystem of cultural products and content dedicated to exploring the lives and struggles of such individuals. Historically, these communities have used independent media to represent individual experiences, for example, in video games (Ho et al. 2022), books, and movies (White 2012). More recently, online streaming, podcasts, and superstar icons representing queerness demonstrate a complex yet incomplete acceptance of difference.

Cultural content can reasonably express identities, histories and personal struggles. In the digital sphere, stories can be rather dispersed and diverse, with a proliferation of information sources beyond the typical "books, films, magazines." Podcasts, YouTube, Crowdfunding, Discord, Twitch, and other online channels enable a profusion of content from independent creators, amateurs, hobbyists, or professionals navigating the online economy. It is yet unclear whether LGBTQ online channels address LGBTQ-only topics or also a diversity of themes just like other social commentary channels. It is in these activities that a digital application of classical liberalism may be discerned.

To address this matter, this chapter takes an exploratory approach to content shared through specific creative platforms (namely, Kickstarter, Patreon, and podcasts via Spotify) to understand how narrow or diverse these digitally-nested content on LGBTQ is and how they promote polycentricity not only *structurally* (hence, their existence demonstrates how various centers of knowledge and information coexist), but also *content-wise* (by addressing topics other than LGBTQ-only). We

DOI: 10.4324/9781003615781-7

suppose that with greater liberties and social acceptance, content tends to spread more widely, less focused on socio-political topics, perhaps leaning into social commentary, generalities, and culture at large as well.

Our focus on the digital realms follows the proliferation of internet-based infrastructures transforming the dynamics of knowledge production, dissemination, and governance. Digitalization and the profusion of platform intermediaries facilitated the emergence of multiple, overlapping centers of information where power is more distributed: Wikipedia, Wikimedia Commons, crowdfunding, open-source coding platforms (e.g., GitHub), and media-driven outlets like YouTube and Twitch, among many others, have extensively collaborated to expand knowledge production in more diverse ways. This landscape is flourishing for various groups that benefit from less-controlled channels and that seek alternatives to traditional media provisioning models. Due to its historically marginalized roots, LGBTQ communities typically turn to bottom-up, grassroots, alternative, or less institutionalized intermediaries where content production and distribution are partially free. Pre-digitalization, these would have been "zines," "literary soirées," local bars, parties and pubs; currently, the online landscape adds up to those as audiences access major outlets from home. This has given rise to a complex ecosystem for online content production and information sharing, which is geographically dispersed, not only about queer agendas but also about a range of other topics – for example, Black Lives Matter, anti-war activism, immigration, women's rights, and non-marginalized topics such as typical social commentary.

Our main argument is that the processes of digitalization have enabled the *polycentricity* of centers of information production and distribution at large (in its forms and content), which stems from our adaptation of the term "polycentricity" used in public governance studies (Ostrom 1999) to contemporary decentralized informational landscapes. As a theoretical construct grounded in local realities, polycentricity typically thrives with diversity: it can only emerge when dispersed centers of knowledge, power, and governance exist and persist over time (Aligica and Tarko 2012). In essence, polycentricity posits that multiple, semi-autonomous decision-making units can interact, compete, and cooperate to generate adaptive, context-sensitive solutions to collective action problems. For LGBTQ communities, this notion can be particularly relevant, as the premise of diversity is present in its identity politics and in the possibility of "difference" or "otherness" from traditional norms. Without aiming to build overly simplistic arguments, we argue that *polycentricity* – in this specific case referring to various centers of information, knowledge, and content creation– can enable the flourishing of diverse identity commons.

Online information channels - typically characterized by lower entry barriers and minimal distribution costs typical of two-sided markets - can contribute to the formation of an ecosystem of digital information commons for LGBTQ communities. Through decentralized modes of content production and circulation, online channels (e.g., podcasts, YouTube channels, crowdfunding projects, and patronage) enable creators to bypass traditional gatekeepers while simultaneously building engaged audiences and securing financial support for their sustainability. This spontaneous arrangement not only diversifies the sources of knowledge production but is also expected to strengthen community resilience by distributing power across multiple nodes of creation, curation, and consumption. Although the polycentric arrangement we examine is not *per se* a planned form of decentralization akin to governmental structures, we suggest that online information ecosystems can operate similarly to idealized market-based spontaneous orders - as described by Michael Polanyi's (1951) *The Logic of Liberty* where centers of decision-making act independently – or to civil society's logics apart from markets and states (Ostrom, 2010).

The chapter first addresses the notion of information commons embedded in the online world, followed by an appraisal of various examples of LGBTQ projects making use online channels for their survival, information sharing and cultural expression about queer culture at large. We then explain the methodology employed in this study, unveil the findings, and conclude with an appraisal of the value of diverse digital commons for information ecosystems.

Digital information commons

Contemporary digital infrastructures have become essential enablers of intangible commons (e.g., identity, knowledge, information, culture) through non-rivalrous content sharing. Multiple users can download the same file, unlike, for example, waiting to check out a book that someone else is reading from a non-digital knowledge commons like an open library. Examples have included web boards, libraries, discussion forums, databases, blogging, file- and media-sharing platforms, social media, and wikis (see Fulk et al. 2004; Seal 2005; Mindel et al. 2018; Prainsack 2019). Furthermore, data-sharing commons for scientific research, open-source software development communities, and FOSS (free and open-source software) are also considered (Schweik and English 2013; Madison et al. 2018), as are more private "clouds" internal to specific organizations (Shiffman and Gupta 2013). Yet, there is very little literature on LGBTQ community members sharing content as a form of polycentric arrangement that benefits these communities. While scholars have examined the potential of information sharing (see Mehra and Braquet 2011; Cifor and Rawson 2023), the literature lacks an emphasis on online community spaces.

Yet, these achievements are not without their challenges. Digital enclosures, in the form of restrictive intellectual property regimes, platform monopolies, and state censorship, threaten the openness and sustainability of online commons. The increasing concentration of power in a few dominant platforms imposes risks of homogenization, surveillance, and arbitrary exclusion (Van Dijck et al. 2018). The circulation of cultural and informational resources essential to sustaining marginal cultural production and innovation (Von Hippel 2016), although intermediaries may not always favor this path.

Notably, the political economist Elinor Ostrom (2000) suggests that for natural common pool resources (such as water), self-governed commons may become harder to sustain as the number of appropriators increases over time. Unlike the traditional common pool resources, however, knowledge resources, such as ideas, data, creative works, and practices, are considered non-rivalrous and non-depletable (Bollier 2007). These goods do not deplete when more users participate in identity, culture, heritage expressions, or informational networks sharing intangible resources. Accessibility is considered one of the main characteristics of *information* shared as a commons, as it means that resources are easily accessible, free of charge, or at a lower nominal cost (Chander and Sunder 2004; Mindel et al. 2018). Yet, this only makes the question of excludability even more central to this discussion. Prainsack (2019) underlines the importance of excludability for digital commons and makes an argument for why it is problematic to conflate *Information Commons* with the *Public Domain.* She argues that Open Access and Public Domain regimes are susceptible to erosion by overuse – while communally governed, exclusive commons are not. Excludability helps prevent the issues of congestion and free riding that arise with Open Access, as those allowed into exclusive areas are those with an interest in and need for the information at hand and are likely to both benefit and contribute to it (Mindel et al. 2018).

Online-based infrastructures also facilitates the production of *value*, which can take the form of private, public, or non-market goods. Especially for public and non-market goods, the value is usually in the form of social benefits that are not immediately obvious and measurable. Frischmann (2012) details three types of infrastructures: (a) commercial, (b) public, and (c) social.[1] In both public and social infrastructure, the market mechanism cannot effectively gather information about social demand and externalities because the value they create is often diffuse and not directly observable. In theory, both the market mechanism and government intervention would fail to sustain social or public infrastructure, as they limit the potential positive externalities of a non-rivalrous resource. Open Access built on commons-based governance is potentially best suited to leverage non-rivalry to produce the most positive externalities.

One specific case in point is the WorldWideWeb infrastructure as a whole, which intertwines commercial, public, and social infrastructures at once. As it generates positive societal externalities, especially when users interact to produce and distribute public and non-market goods, mixed infrastructures exhibit both public good attributes and commercial features. For example, a low paywall can be applied for minimal monetization, still making the good widely accessible (Waldfogel 2017).

A "digital information commons" thus typically comprehends a heterogeneous, loosely coordinated network of media projects that collectively enable the production, dissemination, and preservation of knowledge and culture. Some online ecosystems can function as a "digital information commons," characterized by bottom-up governance, informal yet effective rules-in-use, and polycentric forms of coordination that support both the symbolic and material dimensions of cultural production.

LGBTQ grassroots initiatives worldwide

This chapter is based on the premise that a polycentric architecture of information is particularly important for the dynamics of participation among rainbow communities. Historically marginalized, criminalized, and often excluded from dominant public spheres, these communities have leveraged the affordances of digital infrastructures to build alternative spaces for expression, solidarity, and resistance. The proliferation of information-sharing centers facilitates the accommodation of diversity within LGBTQ communities themselves. These groups are not monolithic; however, they are differentiated by geography, language, class, race, gender identity, and political orientation, heavily stigmatized by socio-economic markers of low income (Drydakis 2024). A diverse information ecosystem likely enables the existence of multiple sub-communities, each with their own norms, practices, and priorities, while still enabling coordination and mutual recognition at broader scales. For instance, crowdfunding and subscription platforms such as Patreon and Kickstarter allow niche creators to cultivate direct patronage relationships with dispersed audiences, bypassing traditional gatekeepers which largely benefits queer agenda in need of collective support (see Dalla Chiesa 2021). Likewise, decentralized blog networks, podcasts, and independent publishers can foster a plurality of voices and perspectives, enriching and strengthening the so-called "cultural commons" (Bertacchini et al. 2012).

At the same time, greater institutional support, through the approval of legal frameworks and the recognition of rights, has potentially decreased the need for political content and rights activism. For example, Winkler (2021) examines how consuming media led people to become more supportive of the LGBTQ communities, while Woodford et al. (2018) analyze the correlation between LGBTQ-supportive institutional policies in universities and the well-being of queer students, finding that students' well-being increases with greater access to educational resources and institutional support. Ultimately, support from established institutions benefits queer communities and amplifies the impact of grassroots organizations. However, the extent of support varies across regions and is still contested by and large. Examples of queer book banning in the United States of America, repression in China, Iran, and the lack of sufficient recognition in Western democracies (to give a few illustrations) make this a contentious case of unstable policies whose rights become malleable. Marginalized communities are thus better off with a wide, bottom-up network of content creators, media outlets, and grassroots initiatives that can support people in the absence of or uncertainty about top-down policies.

In many cases where there is a lack of access to information and support for LGBTQ peoples, non-institutional channels are used as a replacement. Wexelbaum (2017), for instance, discusses how user-generated content (UGC) and social media are used as a substitute for central libraries by LGBTQ communities that lack access to official channels. In line with these findings, there has been recent scholarly attention to how queer people use the internet and digital media to socialize, find information, and ultimately seek support in their identity formation, given the lack of role models in cultural representation. Social media has often been seen as a tool for social and political activism by marginalized communities, as in China (Liao 2019) and Morocco (Vickery 2016). On content-sharing sites, users' perspectives can be examined through platforms such as YouTube, Facebook, Twitter, and others (Lovelock 2017; Miller 2017; Bond and Miller 2021).

Online platforms provide some of the only opportunities for LGBTQ peoples in otherwise conservative societies to interact with each other. Prinsloo (2011), for example, studied how trans people in South Africa built community and exchanged information through forums on the online platform Gender DynamiX. While transgenders are legally protected from discrimination in South Africa, social attitudes are rather conservative, with some communities seeing transgenders as a threat to local cultures and traditions (Luhur et al. 2021). Instead, many turned to online forums, such as the one Prinsloo describes, to engage in "Girl Talk" and "Boy Talk" – discussions around Male-to-Female and Female-to-Male gender transition. Winkler (2019) also shows how traditional media like radio and television in African countries have a negative or zero effect on LGBTQ's acceptance, which likely brings marginalized communities to online spheres. Roxburgh (2022), for example, describes how social media, particularly Facebook groups, act as the predominant online spaces for the queer community in the 2010s.

Media and literature with predominantly LGBTQ themes also thrive in countries with strong censorship laws. In China, for example, a literary genre of predominantly gay male romance and erotica literature, called Danmei (耽美), has spread and became widely commercialized, despite the government's crackdown on LGBTQ media (Ge 2024). Fans use various literature platforms, such as the volunteer-run Lucifer Club and the more commercial Jinjiang Literature City, where authors can earn income from their original work. Some authors opt to publish their work on Taiwanese platforms, where censorship is less strict than in mainland China (Yang and Xu 2017). However, the authors note that most fans who write and circulate Danmei fiction do so for free, maintaining an ecosystem of forums and websites for sharing and discussing these works voluntarily. Notably, many Danmei fans and distributors are heterosexual women who use it as a way of self-expression.

Also in countries considered "developed" by economic standards, institutional mechanisms can fail to allow formalized LGBTQ information channels due to social stigma. Bulgaria is a member of the European Union, but consistently scores low on indicators of LGBTQ equality and acceptance (ILGA World 2025). In 2024, an "Anti-LGBT propaganda in schools" law was introduced, which further limited the opportunity for information-sharing, especially among young people (ILGA Europe 2024). To compensate, online spaces like "Queer Sofia" have emerged, aiming to archive LGBTQ history and provide a platform for locals. The platform is run on submissions from contributors, patronage, and includes interviews on LGBTQ life in Bulgaria, as well as access to books and local events (Queer Sofia 2023).

The above examples demonstrate how online platforms both benefit from and contribute to LGBTQ communities by providing to socialize, share information, and engage with entertainment material despite frequent political backlash. Their emergence also supports the cultivation of social capital, trust, and norms of reciprocity among geographically dispersed participants, reinforcing the capacity for (digital) collective action even in the absence of centralized leadership or formal institutions.

Methodological note

We employed a qualitative content analysis strategy to identify explicit themes expressed in the online channels. This method can facilitate a deeper understanding of data related to meanings, interpretations, and content types (Zhang and Wildemuth 2009). We employ a "directed content analysis" (Hsieh and Shannon 2005) to categorize narratives, images, and projects into themes emerging from the data. To select platforms and LGBTQ-related content, we purposively sampled projects from Patreon, Kickstarter, and Spotify podcasts, in line with qualitative content analysis strategies (Zhang and Wildemuth 2009). The chosen platforms are selected for their facilitation in the use and spread of information through a mix of commercial, public, and social infrastructures (Frischmann 2012).

Patreon and Kickstarter are online patronage and crowdfunding platforms, respectively, where independent creators fund their projects and build audiences over time. By accessing LGBTQ-related content on these platforms, we were able to examine what kind of content creators produce. Podcasts, on the other hand, are a unique medium because they are often created and funded by independent creators, yet they have achieved enormous popularity and sometimes crossover with mainstream media (McHugh 2016; Llinares 2018). Furthermore, while collecting data from Patreon, we noticed that many creators were associated with a podcast channel, indicating an internal flow of information and projects between platforms.

The unit of analysis was the online project or online channel. For Patreon, it was the creator pages; for Kickstarter, it was funding calls for specific projects; for podcasts, it was the episodes hosted in a channel. We sampled the top 50 Patreon pages to achieve the most diverse possible sample. The sampling was done by taking the first 50 results when searching "LGBT" and "Queer" on Patreon.[2] For each Patreon page, we collected data from the page's available information, descriptions of the creator and their work, and the tiers of support available (see Table 7.1

TABLE 7.1 The three cases and their types of information

Source	*Unit of analysis*	*Number of observations*	*Information collected*
Patreon	Patronage campaigns	50 units	Number of supporters
Kickstarter	Funding calls	51 units	Number of supporters
Podcasts channels	Episodes	10 shows (1 episode per show)	Number of episodes

for a breakdown). For Kickstarter, the sampling was done by taking the first 50 projects when searching for "LGBT" and "Queer," sorted by popularity. Again, the specific criteria for popularity on Kickstarter are not known, as the projects varied in number of supporters and earnings, and some were still forthcoming.

For podcasts, we extracted the 10 most popular channels tagged "LGBT" from the platform's internal search engine. Here, too, it is unclear how podcasts are ordered, as there is no way to filter, and statistics such as the number of listeners are not available. Two of the podcasts were audio dramas, which we deemed not relevant to the research because we wanted to focus on unscripted podcasts rather than fictional ones. We therefore excluded them and added two additional podcasts sampled in the same way. For each podcast show, we collected data on the number of episodes, associated external products or creators, and the use of support mechanisms, sourced from the podcast or specific episode descriptions. The latest full episode of each podcast was sampled, and for each episode, we recorded the length, topics discussed, speaking tone, and promotion of support mechanisms. We also extracted quotes from each episode to exemplify how different topics were discussed, which features in the findings of this chapter.

In line with the thematic analysis method (Saldaña 2009), we analyzed the data by creating themes or categories that capture recurring patterns. The data were coded using 11 content characteristic categories (see Table 7.2 for a detailed description). Initially, seven characteristics were predetermined. These were formulated deductively, based on previous research about the use of online content by rainbow communities, such as political activism (Vickery 2016; Liao 2019), community-building (Craig and McInroy 2014; Bond and Miller 2021), information sharing (Craig and McInroy 2014; Fox and Ralston 2016; Miller 2017), sharing of personal experiences (Fox and Ralston 2016; Miller 2017), and discussing representation in media (Waggoner 2018). There were also categories created for the distribution of original content and discussion of non-LGBTQ-related themes, such as race and mental health, which were also expected, as they are common in online content. Four additional themes emerged during data collection and coding: social commentary, religion, charity, and co-creation. These were created inductively from recurring observations in the data. The previously collected data were then re-coded using the new categories to ensure consistency in category assignments across the data.

Thematic findings

Our analysis of 150 units across Patreon, Kickstarter, and Spotify podcasts reveals a rich tapestry of content types and thematic orientations. The thematic coding process identified 11 distinct categories of content, ranging from explicitly political advocacy to personal storytelling, creative production, and community-building initiatives. These categories emerged inductively from the data and reflect the multifaceted nature of queer content creation in digital spaces. Table 7.3 presents the

TABLE 7.2 The categories used for thematic coding

Category	*Definition*
1. Political topics	Related to laws and policies that affect the lives of LGBTQ people; Promoting a political view; Encouraging political action.
2. Community-related	Focused on providing and encouraging community interaction among LGBTQ people.
3. Content/product distribution	Distributing original works of art with LGBTQ themes, such as comics, web series, works of fiction, music, etc. or LGBTQ themed merchandise.
4. News/informative	Related to news stories and current events pertinent to the LGBTQ community; Informative and educational content about LGBTQ topics.
5. Personal stories	Regarding one's personal life, such as lifestyle, day-to-day activities, life updates, or sharing personal stories and memories.
6. Media and representation	Discussing LGBTQ representation in media such as movies and TV shows, and Media criticism.
7. Social commentary	Discussing and commenting on social issues and trends related to the LGBTQ community, as well as broadly LGBTQ related topics.
8. Other sensitive themes	Themes discussed that are not related to the LGBTQ community (e.g., race, disability, mental health, etc.).
9. Religion and spirituality	Discussing being an LGBTQ religious person, giving guidance and advice about practicing religion or spiritual practices as an LGBTQ person.
10. Charity and fundraising	Raising money/making donations for LGBTQ related charities and causes.
11. Co-production or co-creation	Related to co-producing and co-creating, this involves the audience participating in the creation process or engaging directly with the creator.

distribution of these themes across platforms, demonstrating both platform-specific patterns and cross-platform consistencies in how users share content and build audience engagement.

On Patreon, the most common categories were content distribution, co-creation, media and representation, and social commentary. For Kickstarter, it was similar, with the most commonly appearing categories being content and product distribution, co-creation, and charity causes. The most common themes in Podcast channels and episodes were personal, social commentary, discussions of media and representation, and a wide range of non-queer topics. Overall, the platforms were commonly used for the distribution of original content and products, co-creation and collaboration between creators and their audiences, and social commentary in various formats, in line with typical sociability interactions enabled by podcasts.

TABLE 7.3 The categories applied to the collected data

Category	*Patreon*	*Kickstarter*	*Podcast*	*Number of episodes*	*Total*
1. Political	1	1	1	1	4
2. Community-related	8	3	0	0	11
3. Content/product distribution	22	50	0	0	72
4. News/informative	5	5	4	3	17
5. Personal stories	6	4	6	10	26
6. Media and representation	12	2	5	7	26
7. Social commentary	12	0	7	10	29
8. Other sensitive themes	7	5	2	9	23
9. Religion and spirituality	2	2	0	0	4
10. Charity and fundraising	3	8	0	0	11
11. Co-production or co-creation	13	20	1	4	38
Total	*91*	*100*	*56*	*44*	*291*

Our examination also revealed distinct "platform affordances" (Morris 2020) shaping how creators engage with their audiences and mobilize resources. Each platform builds specific functions (algorithms, navigation systems, ranking systems, etc.): for example, subscription-based patronage platforms like Patreon facilitate sustained creator-audience relationships through recurring financial support; crowdfunding platforms such as Kickstarter enable project-based fundraising for discrete creative endeavors; and podcast platforms provide accessible venues for storytelling, community dialogue, and knowledge dissemination. These affordances reflect the specialized roles that different digital infrastructures play in sustaining communities' information commons. The goals and outcomes of using each platform were summarized in Table 7.4, along with example projects and their excludability/rivalry characteristics.

Content sharing and product distribution are the most popular uses of the platform we looked at. One way this manifested was in the case of Patreon creators who distribute media independently, such as authors *Onley James* and *Sheena Jolie (SJ Himes)*, who write romantic fiction and publish it independently. Due to Kickstarter's reward-tier system, there were numerous examples of content and product distribution on the platform. Those include pins (*LGBT Flower pins; Pride Pets – Cute LGBT+ Enamel Pins*), other merchandise (*Pride Heart Animal Keychains*) books (*Practice Makes Progress – An LGBT Inclusive Family Kids Book; Stitches: An LGBT+ Mystery Novel*), films (*"Me and Marcy" an LGBT themed short film*), other artistic projects, such as *Music Videos That Tell Our Story (LGBT) – Tom Goss.*

The second most common category was *co-creation and co-production.* This category was common in podcasts, where hosts respond to fan-submitted

TABLE 7.4 Main uses of each channel

	Subscription patronage	*Crowdfunding projects*	*Podcasts shows*
Main use 1	*External monetization* Supporting and monetizing another form of content creation, usually on social media, such as a YouTube channel or a Podcast, which can be viewed as a public good. Yet, rewards for subscription-based patronage are also club goods.	*Funding products* Funding one-off, rainbow-themed products (pins, jewelry, etc.) from existing businesses to cover upfront costs, and gauge interest in the product before manufacturing. Products and rewards from crowdfunding are most often private goods.	*(Para-)Socialization* Creating a community feeling and para-social relationship through a laid-back podcast format, including co-creation through responding to specific listener messages. Podcasts can be viewed as public goods as their main content is usually accessible for free and non-rivalrous.
Example 1	Jessie Gender – YouTube creator making educational, media commentary, and social commentary content (Gender 2025).	LGBT Flower Pins (Rachel 2022)	Just Break Up: Relationship Advice from Your Queer Besties is a casual, unscripted podcast where the hosts respond to listener-submitted questions about relationships.
Main use 2	*Independent publishing* Independently publishing LGBTQ art, such as comic books, fiction, video games, etc., with the support of patrons. The resulting projects can be considered any type of good, depending on the creator's willingness to monetize their creation.	*Funding cultural projects* Funding one-off LGBTQ artistic projects (such as movies, books, etc.) to cover labor and manufacturing costs, as well as to advertise and generate excitement. Rewards are often private or club goods, but the finished project may be a public good if it is made freely accessible.	*Information sharing* Sharing LGBTQ history, current events, pop culture, health facts, etc. Podcasts can be viewed as public goods as they are all accessible for free.

(*Continued*)

TABLE 7.4 (Continued)

	Subscription patronage	*Crowdfunding projects*	*Podcasts shows*
Example 2	Onley James – Author independently publishing LGBTQ romance books (James 2025)	LGBT films (House of Glitterific 2022)	Bad Gays – Podcast hosted by two historians
Main use 3	*Community spaces* Creating and maintaining online and offline community spaces that connect rainbow communities (sometimes associated with a charity). These spaces can be seen as public or club goods, depending on whether they are excludable or freely accessible.	*Charity fundraising* Fundraising for a charity donation or to support an LGBTQ organization for a specific project or goal. Usually, these are public goods, with specific campaign rewards configuring be private (pre-purchased) goods.	*Discussing representation* Media criticism and discussion – LGBTQ representation and themes in books, movies, TV shows, and other media. Podcasts can be viewed as public goods as they are usually accessible for free.
Example 3	Charlotte Gaymers Network – an organization creating a community of LGBTQ people on a common interest in games (Charlotte Gaymers Network 2025)	LGBT Detroit: The Renovation of a Safe, Brave Space (Lipscomb 2016)	Queer Movie Podcast – A Podcast where the hosts review movies with LGBTQ themes and discuss LGBTQ representation, sometimes with guests.
Outcomes	Sociability and community building (such as via associated Discord channels for many of the Patreon pages), continuous monetary support for independent LGBTQ content and works of culture/art.	Funding for the creation, manufacturing, distribution, and advertising of LGBTQ merchandise, creative products, and local events.	Entertainment via a sense of community-building, and representation for LGBTQ individuals, featuring more normative podcast content with queer themes and discussions about experiences.

questions. An example of this is *The Read* episode *The End is Boring*, where the hosts read out a story about a person's struggle with their relationship and respond:

> That sounds like your friend's issue to me. I don't necessarily think you have to cut her off.

Other podcasts like *Just Break Up* and *Gay-ish* have similar fan email segments, where they respond to whatever their listeners have sent in. On the other hand, on Kickstarter, higher-tier rewards for funding projects sometimes come with the opportunity to co-create with the creator. For example, a limited number of high-tier backers can create a custom character to be added to the book in *Adventuring with Pride: An LGBT 5E Supplement*. Others can get professional feedback on their own creative projects from the creators they support, such as poetry in the case of *Essential Queer Voices of U.S. Poetry*.

The next most popular category was *social commentary*. This was mostly present in podcasts, which were all unscripted and, to some extent, featured hosts freely sharing their thoughts on general societal trends and events, sometimes explicitly queer-related and sometimes not. For example, in the *Las Culturistas* episode *"The Bowen Yang Pokémon Experience" (w/Matt & Bowen)*, one of the hosts recounts an event he attended and comments on how society treats and exploits celebrities, a typical gossip topic.

> Let's just really think about whether we are making a decision for money or someone's well-being?

Similarly, the hosts and guests of *Queer as Fact* talk about the generational gap and changing language in the LGBTQ community, stating:

> You really notice that in, kind of, the changing language between the way that queer identities, and gender, and things like that, are talked about. The language changes almost to the point it's really hard to talk across that gap.

Similar topics seem to be the focus of YouTube channels tied to some of the Patreon pages we sampled. The following content characteristic category was *media and representation*. Creators often focus on commentary and criticism of this representation, promoting it to their audiences, but also combating harmful stereotypes and disrespectful portrayals. *BAIT: a queerbaiting podcast* is a show dedicated to discussing the concept of *queerbaiting*.[3] This idea is somewhat controversial within the community. For example, the hosts of BAIT say:

> Gay characters not doing what you want is not queerbaiting.

In addition to podcasts, many creators on Patreon have YouTube channels or podcast shows dedicated to discussing LGBTQ representation across different media, such as TV (Fandom Feels), comedy TV (Gayest Episode Ever), literature (LGBTQReads), Japanese anime and manga (YuriMother), and more.

Another popular category is content about the creators' *personal lives*. This is also popular in podcasts, due to the less restrictive format that allows audiences to develop a relationship with the hosts. Hosts often share personal updates or offer advice to LGBTQ people based on their own experiences. This can be very useful for people who are unable to access the community in person or do not know anyone who shares their specific experiences. For example, *Lesbian Chronicles: Coming Out Later in Life* is a podcast dedicated to the experiences of the hosts as women who were married to and had children with men before discovering their identities. They respond to audience questions and advise on navigating similar situations, such as:

> Maybe like once a week, agree to have a conversation and be like 'Okay, this is where I'm at right now'.

Some Patreon creators use a similar format, sharing personal life updates and vlogs on YouTube, like the couple *Paige and Holly.* The next category that emerged is *non-LGBTQ*-themed content that is not explicitly related to this community, though it often goes hand in hand with it. One of the most popular non-queer themes is race. In *Queer as Fact*, the guest talked about the representation of indigenous people in Australian history, specifically how she approached it in her own book:

> I thought to leave it out entirely, just because I was a white writer would also lend itself to a different sort of erasure, because you can't write about Australian history without referring to […] First Nations Cultures.

Furthermore, *mental health* emerges as an important sub-theme. The podcast *The Read* features a discussion of how people treat people with mental illness:

> There's still a lot of ignorance and therefore stigma about the mental illnesses that aren't easy or fun or palatable; the things that are hard to deal with.

The Patreon pages dedicated to content about mental health, like *Kya & Co,* state their goal as follows:

> We support charities and create art with strong messages of self-love, equality, and acceptance to inspire greater support and awareness of mental health conditions. We use our passion for raising awareness of mental health to create safe spaces for individuals affected by trauma and abuse.

The emergence of non-LGBTQ themes is not surprising, as LGBTQ identities often intersect with race, social class, mental health struggles, and disability, making individuals' experiences even more complex. The concept of intersectionality, introduced by Crenshaw (1989), refers to the fact that people's identities are multifaceted, and their experiences in society can be compounded and complicated by the intersection of those identities. The projects in this category have a unique quality of showing the experiences of people whose queer and non-queer identities intersect.

The following most popular characteristic was *news and informative content*. A variety of information is being shared, including recent news, historical facts, and relevant health and science information. Some examples include the hosts of the *Bad Gays* podcast, who provide well-researched historical context and analytical discussions of essential figures whose queerness is often overlooked, such as Benedetta Carlini. The *Gayish* podcast features a gay news segment that covers recent events pertinent to the LGBTQ community worldwide. Other Patreon pages were dedicated to spreading awareness and informing about LGBTQ groups, such as the *Dear Straight People* project, who document their struggles in Asia. Furthermore, independent journalists who use Patreon to fund their practice, such as Katelyn Burns, work to cover trans issues often disregarded by mainstream and alternative media channels alike.[4] In her Patreon page description, she writes:

> Your support here on Patreon is vital to my ability to continue as one of the rare few journalists who can cover trans issues full time.
>
> (Burns n.d.)

Among the less-represented project types is *charity*. There were a few projects dedicated solely to charity, such as the Kickstarter project *Mormon LGBT Safe Zone Pin: a Suicide Prevention Initiative*. However, other crowdfunding projects donated part of their earnings to charity. This was in the form of direct donations, such as in the cases of *Adventuring with Pride:* An LGBT 5E Supplement and Pride Pets – Cute LGBT+ Enamel Pins, or authors and publishers donating copies of their books to schools and libraries, such as Essential Queer Voices of U.S. Poetry.

Community-related projects looked about the same. In these projects, online communities crossed over to physical communities. The *Charlotte Gaymers Network* creates a community of queers around a common interest in games. For communities like this, the Patreon pages are usually just a means of financial support and are not a main place of interaction. For example, the *Queer Doula Network* is mostly housed in a private Facebook community and uses Patreon for some additional donations thus showing how online channels operate for financial sustainability while community building takes place elsewhere.

Surprisingly, one of the least represented themes was *socio-political* discussion. An episode of the *Queer Movie Podcast* featured the hosts commenting on anti-LGBTQ laws in Florida.[5] However, their tone was not authoritative, and even when discussing political issues, there was no call to action. There might be the impression that the hosts oppose oppressive laws, but this was not explicitly discussed. There was surprisingly little explicitly political content, given the historical and continuing political and social struggle of LGBTQ people. We will ponder some reasons for this phenomenon in our further analysis.

The other least represented topic was *religion.* We sampled two Patreon pages that distribute content about life as an LGBTQ Christian – *Matthias Roberts* and *Brian & Shay/Queer Theology,* who summarize their mission as follows:

> [We started this work] to connect our head and our heart, to spread the gospel message of justice and freedom, and to live into God's abundant love for us.
>
> (Brian & Shay n.d.)

There were only two other Kickstarter projects that discuss religion. Religion is a contentious theme, and there is still significant tension, which can explain why it is not something many creators dedicate their entire focus to, as it can cost them their audience.

The different channels we explored are part of an ecosystem of queer information online, encompassing many community goals. On Patreon, an organized community for each creator is rather evident. While there is space for interaction on the platform itself, such as comments under posts, Patreon creators usually also maintain a Discord channel or another chat platform where their followers can communicate. The community also often gets to vote on what they want to see from the creator, allowing them to contribute to the creation process. Patreon supporters share a clear common goal or interest in following and supporting the creator.

On the other hand, Kickstarter is less of a community-oriented channel, otherwise marked by one-off cultural projects that need immediate funding to exist. The platform facilitates communication between backers and project creators, but there is limited interaction among supporters. Yet they share common goals and interests in supporting the project, indicating they are likely part of similar communities and that they use other communication channels, especially since Kickstarter projects often rely on social media and word of mouth to attract supporters. The same is true for podcasts, which also foster a loose community and tend to interact with each other even outside the podcast platform. For example, fans and creators often share notes on the podcast's YouTube channel instead.

Our empirical findings underscore the multitude of digital ecosystems and their role in spreading the word. The platforms examined – Patreon, Kickstarter, and Spotify podcasts – function generally as heterogeneous yet complementary nodes within a broader constellation of digital infrastructure, each affording distinct modalities of content dissemination, audience engagement, and resource mobilization. The predominance of content distribution, co-creation, and social commentary as thematic categories illuminates the dual imperatives driving queer digital production: on the one hand, the pragmatic necessity of securing financial sustainability through creative output; on the other hand, the normative commitment to fostering community cohesion, amplifying marginalized voices, and contesting hegemonic narratives of representation. The relative limitation of political discourse, juxtaposed with the pervasive engagement with intersectional themes such as race, mental health, and disability, reveals a negotiation of visibility and vulnerability in which creators navigate the exigencies of algorithmic governance, platform moderation policies, and audience expectations. Consequently, these digital commons constitute not merely repositories of cultural artifacts but rather dynamic sites of identity formation, collective meaning-making, and practices that likely transcend the instrumental logics of market exchange while remaining inevitably dependent on them.

To clarify our approach, we attempt to visualize the ecosystem and how the different platforms interact and contribute to the flow of information in Figure 7.1.

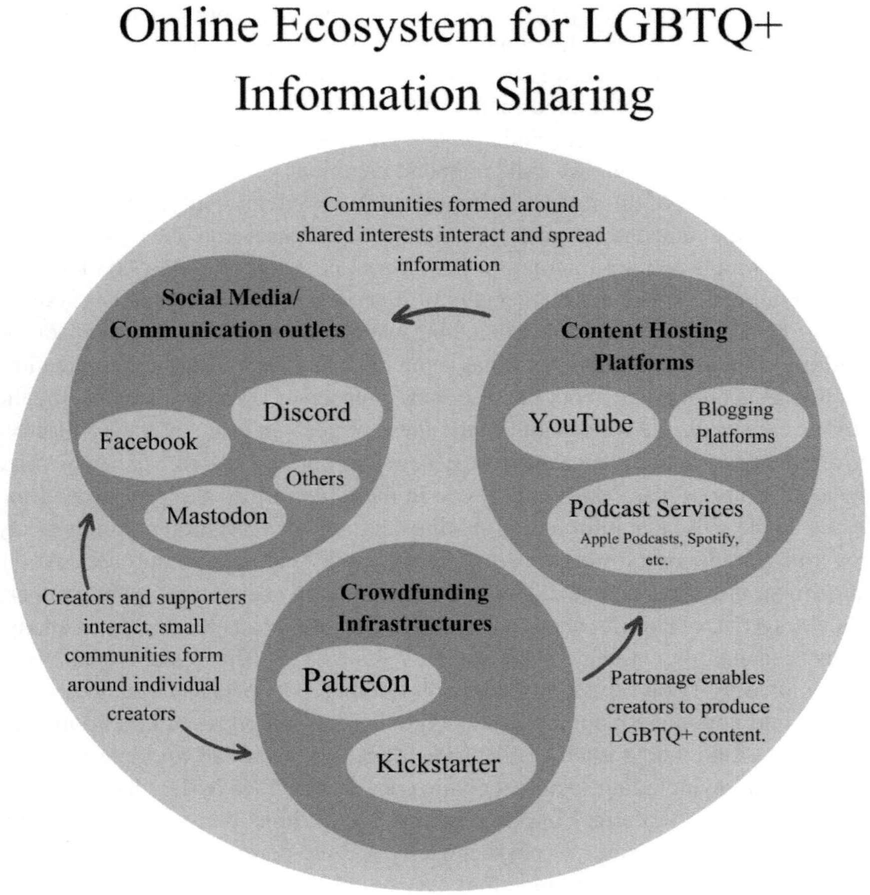

FIGURE 7.1 Online ecosystem based on data

Source: Authors' illustration.

This is a simplified look at the different facets of the online ecosystem, based on our preliminary observations.

Conclusion

At first glance, the core of the content-sharing information we show in this research might seem obvious. Especially in Western Europe, where LGBTQ acceptance is among the highest in the world, and most people have relatively free access to the Internet, it is not surprising that these communities interact online and create/share various kinds of media. The possibility of diversity is crucial for sustaining the different representations and, thus, the acceptance of "the other" in our societies. We argue that it is better for intangibles like culture, knowledge and information to be governed as loosely as possible, enabling various centers of information rather than a few. Furthermore, a polycentric ecosystem of information sharing is better enabled by digitalization's low transaction costs and limited risks to individuals' freedom of expression. Yet, we also discuss in this section, from a critical perspective, the implications of limited socio-political discourses and the absence of narratives of emancipation in our findings. Our conclusions are thus structured in two parts: the benefits of what we call "unbound commons" enabled by digitalization, and the limitations of this relatively "a-political" ecosystem of information sharing.

First, on the unbound commons. Authors have emphasized collective decision-making through bottom-up frameworks (Hess and Ostrom 2007; Mindel et al. 2018; Prainsack 2019) and the benefits of diverse property management systems (Feeny et al. 1990). This is not something we can directly observe in any of the platforms or content. The audience has some input and opportunity for co-creation, but the decision-making about the resources themselves is usually arranged by the project creator. While we cannot discuss these projects in terms of their collective governance per se as the management system was not in question, we can theorize the availability of many diverse projects on these platforms as a form of *polycentricity*, in the sense that information sharing does not obey a central principle, a key governing mode, or a top-down institutionalized decision-making process. At the same time, the dispersion of digital domains can harm accountability. While there is always a risk of harmful anonymous comments, users can also engage in anonymous accountability systems like those on Wikipedia (Shiffman and Gupta 2013). The emphasis on polycentric governance is not merely convenient but an essential insight into how these communities emerge through shared resources, coordinate dispersed action, and sustain resilient identities in the face of multiple forms of marginalization including socio-economic ones as discussed by Drydakis (2024).

As such, the theoretical implications of our findings demand an interrogation through the apparatus of polycentricity and the commons. Whereas classical commons theory, as articulated by Ostrom (1990) and subsequent scholars, presupposes relatively bounded resource pools with discernible boundaries and identifiable user communities, the digital information commons inhabited by queer communities manifests as a fundamentally unbounded, de-territorialized, and generative ecosystem. The online platforms we have examined do not merely facilitate access to pre-existing informational resources but actively constitute new epistemic territories wherein knowledge production, identity articulation, and community formation occur simultaneously and recursively similarly to in-loco art communities (Morea and Dalla Chiesa 2024). This generative capacity reconfigures the commons frameworks: rather than managing scarcity through exclusion mechanisms, these (digital) ecosystems may leverage the non-rivalrous properties of informational goods to proliferate diversity through inclusion. The polycentric architecture thus shows what we might understand as "productive polycentricity" – a mode of governance characterized not by coordination among decision-making centers but by relative semi-autonomous collective creative practices without singular or clear authoritative narratives.

All in all, we argue that by distributing power through various centers of information, polycentricity enables communities to develop context-specific strategies, share knowledge about effective tactics, and coordinate collective responses to repression in alternative media. These are rather optimistic views, however, which are worth contrasted with further critical debate.

Second, on the relatively "a-political" online ecosystem of information sharing, in which any form of emancipation discourse appears to be largely absent. The hybrid models of patronage, crowdfunding, and ad-supported content distribution observed across our sample reveal a fundamental tension between the emancipatory potential of decentralized content production and the constraining needs of financial sustainability. Although our findings do not directly observe the conundrum faced by creators when navigating audiences' expectations and creative freedom, we can infer that these infrastructures may enable access to cultural production (by circumventing traditional gatekeeping) while also instantiating new forms of digital governance, audience capture, and affective labor that subtly discipline creative expression toward platform-compatibility. We see this when it comes to the relative absence of overtly socio-political content – despite LGBTQ communities' historical embeddedness in liberation struggles – which may reflect not simply risk aversion but rather the structural effects of platform affordances that privilege certain cultural genres (entertainment, personal narrative, cultural commentary) over others (collective organizing, direct advocacy, critique and politics). This suggests that the polycentric information commons we observe operates within what Fraser (1990) terms "subaltern counter-publics" – spaces that are simultaneously inside and against hegemonic public spheres, negotiating visibility and vulnerability, commodification and solidarity, individual entrepreneurialism, and collective flourishing.

In sum, the rainbow digital commons inheres not in their independence from market logics but in their capacity to instrumentalize commercial platforms for non-commercial ends, appropriating those infrastructures to produce non-market goods that build community vitality, collective identification, and more equitable informational landscapes.

Finally, we acknowledge that the current research has been limited in scope. Currently, there is limited literature exploring diversity and polycentricity in the context of LGBTQ communities; thus, this exploration has been a first step in examining content-sharing. As stated before, we have only covered a few infrastructures, namely the leading crowdfunding platforms, patronage, and podcast at hand. As such, there are many potential avenues for future research. An interesting continuation of this research might be to examine other parts of the ecosystem, such as the social and communication channels community members use (e.g., Instagram and TikTok), to gauge how tightly knit these communities really are. As the current research has only dealt with static data, delving into communities in real time and interacting with or interviewing providers and supporters may yield insights into the social bonds at play in this ecosystem, participants' motivations, and more. In essence, there is scope to further explore digital polycentric spaces from the standpoints of mainline political economy and queer classical liberalism.

Notes

1 In *commercial* infrastructure used to produce private goods, the infrastructure is the production process or delivery method for manufactured goods. *Public* infrastructure produces public goods that generate positive externalities for non-paying consumers, as public goods are non-excludable: you cannot charge people to benefit from them. *Social* infrastructures produce non-market goods that have value but are not provided through the market mechanism, thus diffusing positive externalities generated with the use of shared resources.

2 The results were, for the most part, in order of number of patrons. However, some pages appeared out of order, such as the ones with more supporters lower on the list. This indicates that there are other filters on Patreon's search function. As such, we could not find information about what the criteria are.

3 This occurs when writers or other media creators hint at queer representation to attract queer audiences but do not provide explicit representation or do it for the sake of attention and money.

4 Transgender topics refer to any issues that are specifically related to the trans community, such as policies related to gender-affirming healthcare.

5 This refers to a series of anti-LGBTQ bills signed by Florida Governor Ron DeSantis in 2022 and 2023, aimed at restricting discussion of LGBTQ topics in education, as well as restricting access to gender-affirming healthcare. These political moves sparked great controversy and were widely discussed in blockbuster media, such as the *Washington Post* ("Florida's Law Limiting LGBTQ Discussion in Schools Explained") and the *New York Times* ("Florida Legislature Passes Bill Banning Gender-Transition Care for Minors").

References

Aligica, Paul D. and Vlad Tarko. 2012. "Polycentricity: From Polanyi to Ostrom, and Beyond." *Governance* 25 (2): 237–262.

Bertacchini, Enrico, Giangiacomo Bravo, Massimo Marrelli, and Walter Santagata. 2012. *Cultural Commons: A New Perspective on the Production and Evolution of Cultures*. Cheltenham, UK: Edward Elgar.

Bollier, David. 2007. "The Growth of the Commons Paradigm." In *Understanding Knowledge as a Commons: From Theory to Practice*, edited by Charlotte Hess and Elinor Ostrom, 27–40. Cambridge, MA: MIT Press.

Bond, Bradley J., and Brandon Miller. 2021. "YouTube as My Space: The Relationships between YouTube, Social Connectedness, and (Collective) Self-Esteem among LGBTQ Individuals." *New Media & Society* 26 (1): 513–533.

Brian & Shay/Queer Theology. n.d. "About." https://www.patreon.com/queertheology/about.

Burns, Katelyn. n.d. "Welcome to My Patreon!" https://www.patreon.com/cw/katelynburns.

Chander, Anupam and Sunder, Madhavi, The Romance of the Public Domain. UC Davis Law, Legal Studies Research Paper No. 13, Available at SSRN: https://ssrn.com/abstract=562301

Charlotte Gaymers Network. 2025. "Charlotte Gaymers Network." Patreon. https://www.patreon.com/CharlotteGN.

Cifor, M., & Rawson, K. J. (2023). Mediating Queer and Trans Pasts: The Homosaurus as Queer Information Activism. Information, *Communication & Society*, 26 (11): 2168–2185. https://doi.org/10.1080/1369118X.2022.2072753

Craig, Shelley L., and Lauren McInroy. 2014. "You Can Form a Part of Yourself Online: The Influence of New Media on Identity Development and Coming Out for LGBTQ Youth." *Journal of Gay & Lesbian Mental Health* 18 (1): 95–109.

Crenshaw, Kimberlé. 1989. "Demarginalizing the Intersection of Race and Sex: A Black Feminist Critique of Antidiscrimination Doctrine, Feminist Theory and Antiracist Politics." *University of Chicago Legal Forum* 1: 139–167.

Dalla Chiesa, Carolina. 2021. "Crowdfunding the Queer Museum: A Polycentric Identity Quarrel." In *Governing Markets as Knowledge Commons*, edited by Erwin Dekker and Pavel Kuchař, 238–255. Cambridge, UK: Cambridge University Press.

Drydakis, Nick. 2024. "The Economics of Being LGBT: A Review: 2015–2020." In *The Routledge Handbook of LGBTQ Identity in Organizations and Society*, edited by Julie A. Gedro and Tonette S. Rocco, 200–213. New York, NY: Routledge.

Feeny, David, Fikret Berkes, Bonnie J. McCay, and James M. Acheson. 1990. "The Tragedy of the Commons: Twenty-Two Years Later." *Human Ecology* 18 (1): 1–19.

Fox, Jesse, and Rachel Ralston. 2016. "Queer Identity Online: Informal Learning and Teaching Experiences of LGBTQ Individuals on Social Media." *Computers in Human Behavior* 65: 635–642.

Fraser, Nancy. 1990. "Rethinking the Public Sphere: A Contribution to the Critique of Actually Existing Democracy." *Social Text* (25/26): 56–80.

Frischmann, Brett M. 2012. *Infrastructure: The Social Value of Shared Resources*. Oxford, UK: Oxford University Press.

Fulk, Janet, Rebecca Heino, Andrew J. Flanagin, Peter R. Monge, and François Bar. 2004. "A Test of the Individual Action Model for Organizational Information Commons." *Organization Science* 15 (5): 569–585.

Ge, Longlong. 2024. "Repression, Permeation, and Circulation: Retracing and Reframing *Danmei* Culture Online in Mainland China." *Feminist Encounters: A Journal of Critical Studies in Culture and Politics* 8 (2): 34.

Gender, Jessie. 2025. "Jessie Gender." *Patreon*. https://www.patreon.com/jessiegender.

Hess, Charlotte, and Elinor Ostrom. 2007. "Introduction: An Overview of the Knowledge Commons." In *Understanding Knowledge as a Commons: From Theory to Practice*, edited by Charlotte Hess and Elinor Ostrom, 3–26. Cambridge, MA: MIT Press.

Ho, Xavier, Remedios Perez Escobar, and Natalie Tran. 2022. "Queer Indie Games on Itch. Io, 2013–2022." *Proceedings of the 17th International Conference on the Foundations of Digital Games*, September 5, 1–10.

House of Glitterific 2022. "LGBT+ films." Kickstarter. https://www.kickstarter.com/projects/glitterrific/lgbt-films?ref=discovery_popular&term=LGBT.

Hsieh, Hsiu-Fang, and Sarah E. Shannon. 2005. "Three Approaches to Qualitative Content Analysis." *Qualitative Health Research* 15 (9): 1277–1288.

ILGA Europe. 2024. "Bulgaria Passes Anti-LGBTI Propaganda Law | ILGA-Europe." ILGA Europe, 7 August. https://www.ilga-europe.org/press-release/bulgaria-passes-anti-lgbti-propaganda-law.

ILGA World. 2025. "Bulgaria." ILGA World Database. https://database.ilga.org/bulgaria-lgbti.

Liao, Sara. 2019. "'#IAmGay# What about You?': Storytelling, Discursive Politics, and the Affective Dimension of Social Media Activism against Censorship in China." *International Journal of Communication* 13: 2314–2333.

Lipscomb, Curtis. 2016. "LGBT Detroit: The Renovation of a Safe, Brave Space." Kickstarter. https://www.kickstarter.com/projects/916953840/lgbt-detroit-the-renovation-of-a-safe-brave-space?ref=discovery_popular&term=LGBT.

Llinares, Dario. 2018. "Podcasting as Liminal Praxis: Aural Mediation, Sound Writing and Identity." In *Podcasting: New Aural Cultures and Digital Media*, edited by Dario Llinares, Neil Fox and Richard Berry, 123–145. Cham, Switzerland: Springer Nature.

Lovelock, M. (2019). 'My coming out story': Lesbian, gay and bisexual youth identities on YouTube. *International Journal of Cultural Studies*, 22 (1), 70–85.

Luhur, Winston, Letlhogonolo Mokgoroane, and Ari Shaw. 2021. "Public Opinion on Transgender Rights in South Africa." UCLA School of Law, Williams Institute. https://williamsinstitute.law.ucla.edu/publications/opinion-trans-rights-south-africa.

James, Onley. 2025. "Onley James." Patreon. https://www.patreon.com/cw/OnleyJames.

Madison, Michael J., Brett M. Frischmann, and Katherine J. Strandburg. 2018. "Knowledge Commons." In *Routledge Handbook of the Study of the Commons*, edited by Blake Hudson, Jonathan Rosenbloom and Dan Cole, 76–90. London, UK: Routledge.

McHugh, Siobhán. 2016. "How Podcasting Is Changing the Audio Storytelling Genre." *Radio Journal: International Studies in Broadcast & Audio Media* 14 (1): 65–82.

Mehra, Bharat, and Donna Braquet. 2011. "Progressive LGBTQ Reference: Coming out in the 21st Century." *Reference Services Review* 39 (3): 401–422.

Miller, Brandon. 2017. "YouTube as Educator: A Content Analysis of Issues, Themes, and the Educational Value of Transgender-Created Online Videos." *Social Media + Society* 3 (2): 1–17.

Mindel, Vitali, Lars Mathiassen, and Arun Rai. 2018. "The Sustainability of Polycentric Information Commons." *MIS Quarterly* 42 (2): 607–631.

Morea, Valeria, and Carolina Dalla Chiesa. 2024. "Scratching the Surface of Urban Change: Art Collectives as Public Entrepreneurs." *International Small Business Journal* 42 (1): 67–89.

Morris, Jeremy Wade. 2020. "Music Platforms and the Optimization of Culture" *Social Media + Society*, 6 (3): 1–10.

Ostrom, Elinor. 2010. "Beyond Markets and States: Polycentric Governance of Complex Economic Systems." *American Economic Review* 100 (3): 641–72.

Ostrom, Elinor. 2000. "Reformulating the Commons." *Swiss Political Science Review* 6 (1): 29–52.

Ostrom, Vincent. 1999. "Polycentricity (Part 1)." In *Polycentricity and Local Public Economies: Readings from the Workshop in Political Theory and Policy Analysis*, edited by Michael Dean McGinnis, 52–74. Ann Arbor, MI: University of Michigan Press.

Ostrom, Elinor. 1990. *Governing the Commons: The Evolution of Institutions for Collective Action*. Cambridge, UK: Cambridge University Press.

Polanyi, Michael. 1951. *The Logic of Liberty: Reflections and Rejoinders*. London, UK: Routledge & Kegan Paul.
Prainsack, Barbara. 2019. "Logged out: Ownership, Exclusion and Public Value in the Digital Data and Information Commons." *Big Data & Society* 6 (1): 1–15.
Prinsloo, Jeanne. 2011. "Negotiating Transgender Identities on the Internet – A South African Study." *Agenda* 25 (4): 30–41.
Queer Sofia. 2023. "Home." https://www.queersofia.org.
Rachel. 2022. "LGBT Flower pins." Kickstarter. https://www.kickstarter.com/projects/billacookie/lgbt-flower-pins?ref=discovery_popular&term=LGBT.
Roxburgh, Cassandra. 2022. "'Queering the Internet': The Importance of Transgender Online Spaces in South Africa–Minority Africa." Minority Africa, August 1. https://minorityafrica.org/queering-the-internet-the-importance-of-transgender-online-spaces-in-south-africa.
Saldaña, Johnny. 2009. *The Coding Manual for Qualitative Researchers*. Los Angeles, CA: SAGE.
Schweik, Charles, and Robert English. 2013. "Preliminary Steps Toward a General Theory of Internet-Based Collective-Action in Digital Information Commons: Findings from a Study of Open-Source Software Projects." *International Journal of the Commons* 7 (2): 234–254.
Seal, Robert. 2005. "The Information Commons: New Pathways to Digital Resources and Knowledge Management." *Proceedings of the 3rd China-U.S. Library Conference*, January 1. https://ecommons.luc.edu/lib_facpubs/13.
Shiffman, Gary, and Ravi Gupta. 2013. "Crowdsourcing Cyber Security: A Property Rights View of Exclusion and Theft on the Information Commons." *International Journal of the Commons* 7 (1): 92–112.
Van Dijck, José, Thomas Poell, and Martijn De Waal. 2018. *The Platform Society: Public Values in a Connective World*. Oxford, UK: Oxford University Press.
Vickery, Savannah. 2016. "Queer Connections: Social Media as a Versatile Tool of the Marginalized Moroccan LGBT." Independent Study Project (ISP) Collection. https://digitalcollections.sit.edu/isp_collection/2522.
Von Hippel, Eric. 2016. *Free Innovation*. Cambridge, MA: MIT Press.
Waggoner, Erin B. 2018. "Bury Your Gays and Social Media Fan Response: Television, LGBTQ Representation, and Communitarian Ethics." *Journal of Homosexuality* 65 (13): 1877–1891.
Waldfogel, Joel. 2017. "How Digitization Has Created a Golden Age of Music, Movies, Books, and Television." *Journal of Economic Perspectives* 31 (3): 195–214.
Wexelbaum, Rachel S. 2017. "Global Promotion of LGBTQ Resources and Services through Social Media" Library Faculty Publications. https://repository.stcloudstate.edu/lrs_facpubs/59.
White, Patricia. 2012. "Teaching Queer Cinema with Independent Media." *Teaching Film* 35: 63–73.
Winkler, Stephen. 2021. "Media's Influence on LGBTQ Support Across Africa." *British Journal of Political Science* 51 (2): 807–826.
Woodford, Michael R., Alex Kulick, Jason C. Garvey, Brandy R. Sinco, and Jun Sung Hong. 2018. "LGBTQ Policies and Resources on Campus and the Experiences and Psychological Well-Being of Sexual Minority College Students: Advancing Research on Structural Inclusion." *Psychology of Sexual Orientation and Gender Diversity* 5 (4): 445–456.
Yang, Ling, and Yanrui Xu. 2017. "Chinese Danmei Fandom and Cultural Globalization from Below." In *Boys' Love, Cosplay, and Androgynous Idols: Queer Fan Cultures in Mainland China, Hong Kong, and Taiwan*, edited by Maud Lavin, Yang Ling and Zhao Jing Jamie, 3–19. Hong Kong: Hong Kong University Press.
Zhang, Yan, and Barbara M. Wildemuth. 2009. "Qualitative Analysis of Content." In *Applications of Social Research Methods to Questions in Information and Library Science*, edited by Barbara M. Wildemuth, 318–329. Westport, CT: Libraries Unlimited.

8

SOCIAL CAPITAL AND RESILIENCE WITHIN THE BLACK TRANSGENDER SEX WORKER COMMUNITY

Malia Dalesandry

I emerged from the Metro in Washington, DC, at the African American Civil War Memorial and walked along Ben's Chili Bowl Way, a block on U Street named for the Black-owned restaurant with historic-landmark designation. Now familiar with slightly-later-than-scheduled start times, and fortified with a bloody mary from the bar across the street—after all, International Day to End Violence Against Sex Workers did fall on a Saturday this year—I walked into the Frank D. Reeves Municipal Center on 14th Street Northwest. It is fitting that the man for whom the building is named helped organize 1963's March on Washington for Jobs and Freedom and 1968's Poor People's Campaign. He also cofounded the National Conference of Black Lawyers, "which promoted racial justice through legal defense" (DC Historic Preservation Office 2024). The Red Umbrella Awards Ceremony is a response to the stigmatization and criminalization of work and bodily autonomy, particularly affecting economically marginalized transgender people of color, and it too promotes addressing these injustices by changing the law.

I was headed to a space where I would be without lived experience—a space where Black people gather safely, the LGBTQ community is home, transgender women are treated like queens, and sex workers are revered. Despite now having more experience in these spaces (and my bloody mary-induced moxie), I still get a bit nervous. It is challenging but rewarding becoming familiar with formerly unfamiliar spaces. Thankfully, Shareese immediately came over to greet me and put me to work stationed at the welcome table with her daughter. While I do not seem representative of HIPS (Honoring Individual Power & Strength), where Shareese Mone is development coordinator, I was happy to oblige. Shareese organized the agenda, procured funding, invited the community, and emceed with gusto. A day of remembrance of sex workers' lives lost in 2022, it was also a celebration and a call to action: to decriminalize sex work.[1]

DOI: 10.4324/9781003615781-8

There was spoken word poetry, a dancer who has choreographed for Janet Jackson, a drag performance (Whitney Houston's "I'm Every Woman"), and a panel with former sex workers from Baltimore Safe Haven, The DC Center for the LGBTQ Community, HIPS, and the Mayor's Office of Lesbian, Gay, Bisexual, Transgender and Questioning Affairs. I won a fundraising raffle for a sixty-five-inch 4K ultra-high-definition television (I donated it back to HIPS but left kicking myself for not giving it directly to Shareese), got my first taste of ball culture, met Shareese's two adult children, and received hugs from her mom. It was a very different experience from when I first encountered Shareese two years earlier to the day. My ability to be in this and other spaces is due in no small part to her effervescence: people gravitate toward her, and she embraces inclusivity. This is how she leverages her social capital and cultivates community resilience. However, she did not always have a sense of empowerment from belonging:

> My stability is what I really wanted, you know, 'cause growing up, I never had my own bedroom. I never had that stable house. I was always brought from grandma's house, aunt's house, uncle's house—everybody else's house but mine—I didn't have one.
>
> So I just wanted stability, which is why I want my home. And, I dunno, I just want to sit in my backyard and turn my little patio lights on and look at my cat and be like, "Alright, you go across that fence, you on your own, girl." [Big laugh].
>
> (Mone, interview by Malia Dalesandry, Zoom, September 9, 2021)

Shareese's cat may be on her own, but these days, Shareese assuredly is not. As evidenced by the above vignette, the Black trans sex worker community in DC, while incredibly stigmatized, is also warm, robust, and resilient. Such stigmatized communities' resilience relies on social capital, broadly conceptualized as "the shared knowledge, understanding, norms, rules, and expectations about patterns of interactions that groups of individuals bring to a recurrent activity" (Ostrom 2000b: 176). Further, it "is a resource that facilitates collective action for mutual benefit" (Chamlee-Wright and Storr 2011: 268). Reciprocally, a shared sense of resilience cultivates social capital. While exploring this relationship from a mainline political economy perspective, this chapter contributes to insights from anthropology, sociology, legal, and policy literatures.

Crenshaw (1989, 2012), who first asked us to consider intersectionality along race and gender lines, has noted the paradox of underprotecting and overpolicing Black women and girls and discusses discrimination, violence, and incarceration, all relevant when considering the experiences of Black trans sex workers. Building on foundational works exploring trans and Black trans history (Stryker 2008; Snorton 2017), as well as contributing to emerging theories on Black trans feminism (e.g., Bey 2022) and resilience, scholars have been adding the additional component of sex work, which has always been a part of these communities to one extent or another. For example, despite decriminalizing in 2003, New Zealand's trans sex workers, especially those of color, still experience a particular brand of "whorephobia" marked by overlapping transmisogyny: "the combination of transphobia and misogyny experienced by trans women" (Easterbrook-Smith 2020: 1014). Among their other case studies of trans and sex worker communities, Easterbrook-Smith (2023: 310) found that sex workers' shared sense of humor contributes to resilience in part by acting as a "mechanism of discussing stigma and discrimination" and "as an agent of activism and social change."

Edelman (2014, 2020), whose research in part consists of ethnographic mapping of trans people, many of whom are Black and do sex work, in Washington, DC, suggests that resiliency frameworks are insufficient to capture agency, structural limitations, and the breadth of experiences and prefers the concept of "trans vitalities" to better understand risk and radical care. Glover (2021) also uses ethnographic methods to engage with Black trans women in the Chicago ballroom scene who often do sex work as primary or supplementary means of income; their "affective labor" demands excellent customer service relying on "embodied knowledge" and "ingenious strategies," rather than institutions.

In Europe and elsewhere, multifaceted identities are recognized for "the resistance and agency that racialised [and trans] sex workers exhibit" via collectives such as Steel Roses, comprised of Chinese migrant sex workers in Paris; Cosmopolitrans based in Hannover; Trans European BPOC [Black People and People of Colour] Network, originating in the Netherlands; and the Black Sex Worker Collective in Berlin (European Sex Workers' Rights Alliance 2022). On the policy side of things in the United States, healthcare and social justice organizations have chronicled the experiences of these identities, notably in a joint report (Bland and Brooks 2020) produced by O'Neill Institute for National and Global Health Law at Georgetown University, Institute for Health Research & Policy at Whitman-Walker, and HIPS, the organization associated with the individuals introduced in this chapter.

When thinking about a mainline political economy approach that would produce a "thick" (Skarbek 2020) description of how the relationship between social capital and resilience manifests among Black trans sex workers, I employed an ethnographic method in part consisting of a lengthy period of community immersion and learning before conducting semi-structured, open-ended interviews. "Ethnographic research is not static or fixed; instead, it is personal, transformational, contingent, and responsive to actually existing and often shifting conditions. It is an open-minded, open-ended collection and celebration of the excess and messiness of human life," and "[it] can be troubled and it requires care and commitment, humility and cooperation, vulnerability and trust, but it is one of the most poignant ways of knowing another and thus, knowing the self" (McGranahan 2014: 24, 33–34).

When analyzing the data—both from recorded, transcribed interviews and from my developing contextual awareness—I continued to consider my positionality by using Braun and Clarke's (2021) guide to thematic analysis.[2] Themes do not "emerge" but rather are developed—an active exercise on the part of the researcher, dependent on multiple points of intimate familiarization with the data, spending time away from them, and reflecting on the researcher's personal relationship with them. As with many types of scholar-activist ethnographic research (e.g., Pacheco-Vega and Parizeau 2018), the researcher's subjectivity and participation are embraced, and being interested in individual experiences and meanings necessitates that knowledge production is not treated as removed from the circumstances in which it was created. This should be viewed as a benefit to the research, not a hindrance. "Rather than defend ourselves against harboring such biases, or make an attempt to minimize the importance of such biases, we think it more productive (and more honest) to admit them freely" (Storr et al. 2015a: 4). In that spirit, I also found that being forthright with trans sex workers was advantageous for the project and so offered a simple but comprehensive phrase when first engaging: "I recognize the inherent dignity of the individual to control their own body and the conditions of their existence."

This chapter contributes to mainline political economy research demonstrating the power of qualitative methods (Ostrom 2005; Chamlee-Wright 2010a, 2010b; Storr et al. 2015b; Skarbek 2020) to better understand emergent orders pertaining to social activity (Chamlee-Wright 2008; Storr 2008) and successful collective action (Ostrom 2000a; Novak 2021) by exploring how trans sex workers endure and overcome hardships within their repressive and extralegal environment. After a discussion of how I engaged with sex workers, the chapter will then describe the formal and informal institutions that bind them, highlighting the relationship between social capital and the mechanisms that promote resilience. Black transgender sex workers, who are especially stigmatized as well as criminalized, demonstrate a remarkable capacity for self-governance. Many members of this community experience family rejection, discrimination, being unhoused, arrest, and violence, and through these experiences, they have forged a collective identity and shared narratives. These shared narratives have facilitated these sex workers to establish institutions for safety and mutual aid. They have also fostered spaces for entertainment, self-expression and selfcare, and community-building. The ability of trans sex workers to create functional, self-governing institutions, even within a hostile social and legal environment, is a testament to their entrepreneurialism and resilience.

Getting to know Black trans sex workers

To better understand this community, I interviewed sex workers in Washington, DC.[3] My empirical strategy was inspired by research that political economists had conducted to examine community resilience in a different context: disaster recovery. Led by coinvestigators Emily Chamlee-Wright and Virgil Henry Storr, with guidance from Peter J. Boettke, a team of researchers from George Mason University conducted hundreds of interviews in the wake of 2005's Hurricane Katrina.

They sought to answer questions about "what affords societies the ability to respond to and recover from catastrophic disaster, and what forces undermine that capacity," as well as "systemic questions of what makes complex societies work and why they sometimes fail to work" (Chamlee-Wright and Storr 2010: 1–2). The project evolved to adopt a broader conceptualization of "crisis," for example, in two edited volumes, *Bottom-up Responses to Crisis* and *Government Responses to Crisis* (Haeffele and Storr 2020a, 2020b). Much of the natural disaster and crisis research is rich with observations and firsthand accounts of staying afloat (sometimes literally) in times of trouble, and it accessibly articulates the details of and justifications for the methodology, which inspired speaking with sex workers about their crises of stigmatization and criminalization. Researchers identified themes such as "norms and narratives," which were secondarily coded as "historical narratives," "stories of identity," and "community practices" (Chamlee-Wright 2010a: 189–190), and they found that communities were most successful dealing with their crisis when they relied on embedded social capital and entrepreneurship. Pertinent when applying this framework to this community, the experiences and stories that unfold suggest that

> communities possess a capacity for resilience that far surpasses what they are usually credited as having. By investigating the socially embedded resources communities have at their disposal, and the creative strategies that employ these resources, perhaps we have an opportunity to remind people struggling to rebound and rebuild that ultimately *they* are the source of community resilience.
> (Chamlee-Wright 2010a: 5)

With the goal of achieving semi-structured, open-ended interviews, I began attending events. The first was the DC Council hearing for Bill 23-0318, the Community Safety and Health Amendment Act of 2019 in October (I stayed for much but not all of the fourteen-hour hearing). This would have decriminalized sex work in the nation's capital. As I listened to testimony and sat among individuals from the seventy-two local and national organizations driving and supporting it, I began to develop my "dream list" of interviewees based on what those who testified spoke about, whether they indicated openness to being contacted, and perceived likelihood of their agreeing to engage in such a personal way.

I was drawn to the earnest and impassioned DC activist population, predominantly consisting of Black trans sex workers, but I needed to learn terminology, norms, faux pas to avoid, etc. before reaching out. This was important because various marginalized communities often rightfully speak about being tired: they are tired of starting from scratch with every new would-be ally; they are tired of redundant questions that can easily be Googled; they are tired of explaining "why this matters." It would not have been welcome to come to the community signaling I was going to be asking the same questions they have answered time and again. To show that I was in touch with the research and had attended community events was imperative and provided much needed context; for example, misgendering someone when their pronouns are right on their organization's website or in a report would not be well received.

Still learning and then pandemically waylaid, I next attended two virtual events on International Day to End Violence Against Sex Workers, December 17, 2020. The first was a panel presenting the report coproduced by HIPS, O'Neill Institute, and Whitman-Walker: "Protecting DC Sex Workers and Promoting Health and Wellbeing"; the second was the "End Violence Against Sex Workers Virtual Vigil." Arranged in honor of Black History Month, February's "Pro-Black, Pro-Hoe: Black Sex Work Activism in 2021" and "Decriminalizing Sex Work in DC is a Racial Justice Issue" further enlightened. In-person events in DC neighborhoods included a drag fundraiser in Dupont in June, a panel on harm reduction in Shaw in September, and the #DecrimPovertyDC campaign launch at Freedom Plaza in October.

By fall of 2021, I mustered the nerve to cold contact someone and simply see what happened; I selected the emcee of the Virtual Vigil. Shareese Mone (she/her/hers) responded promptly, kindly, and affirmatively. She provided much needed wind under sails, a rich interview, and helpful pointers going forward. ("Make it more like it was in the beginning; the flow was natural.") A formerly incarcerated "client"—the term used for people who come to HIPS in need of resources and services—turned development coordinator, Shareese is Black and in her early fifties. With a gift for mobilizing at rallies and other public events, and the lived experience and wisdom of an "auntie" (more on this concept later), she offers clients welcoming hugs, an easy laugh, and a big heart.

Shortly after Shareese's warm reception and robust interview, I approached Alexander/a Bradley (they/them/theirs, she/her/hers, he/him/his), whom I had heard speak at several events and who is described affectionately by Shareese as a "powerhouse." It took several months to coordinate the interview; they are incredibly busy, including managing overnight shifts in "the van," which is a mobile dispensary for hygiene products, cold weather gear, clean needles, candy, condoms, and safety updates. Alexander/a is outreach and community engagement manager at HIPS. The sole participant who cannot be said to have lived experience with sex work, they have other related lived experience and contribute mightily to harm reduction, particularly regarding drug use and healthcare. Alexander/a is white, genderfluid, and in their early thirties. They are especially thanked for their open demeanor, gentle patience, and invaluable education (Bradley, interview by Malia Dalesandry, Zoom, February 11, 2022).

Alexander/a then introduced me to Michaelisa Jones and Michelle Spikes. Michaelisa (she/her/hers) is reentry coordinator at HIPS, where she has also been a client. Kicked out of her family home after coming out at sixteen, she underwent long periods of being unhoused, was arrested fifty-two times, and had just been shot (wrong place, wrong time) a few days before the interview. Now in therapy and a twelve-step program, she is positively poetic, embodies compassion, and is stronger than she perhaps gives herself credit. Michaelisa is Black and in her mid-fifties (Jones, interview by Malia Dalesandry, Zoom, April 10, 2022).

Michelle (she/her/hers) too first came to HIPS as a client, having experienced being unhoused for eleven years as well as drug use and multiple arrests. She began volunteering and is now full-time community health worker at HIPS. Born in California with a childhood spent in Georgia, she moved to DC with her mom in 2000 and was relieved to find the city more LGBTQ-friendly than Atlanta. She is humble when she speaks about how she contributes and sings the praises of her colleagues, in particular Shakita, Alexander/a, Ms. Budd, and Ms. Phyllis. "I really look up to them as leaders of our community. 'Cause they have been doing this work for so long and inspired me to get into it." Michelle is Black, in her late thirties, and a proud dog mom (Spikes, interview by Malia Dalesandry, Zoom, April 14, 2022).

The participants describe the many ways in which HIPS cultivates social capital and fosters community resilience, which can roughly be categorized around a few themes: direct service provision, developing relationships with policymakers and medical research institutions, and liaising with the community at large to promote occupational and reputational legitimacy in order to achieve decriminalization. Foremost, though, and HIPS's raison d'être since its inception in 1993, is locating and building trust with unhoused people, drug users, sex workers, and other marginalized and stigmatized members of the community. First contact is often in the streets, rather than at the brick-and-mortar center in the gentrifying H Street Corridor neighborhood north of Capitol Hill.[4] Shareese lists the myriad services the organization provides:

> We have a mobile unit that goes through the city, a lot of the most popular stroll areas [coordination sites for commercial sex], and passes out condoms, asks everyone if they need any help, [do they] understand what Narcan is, and letting them know about the groups they can attend, training webinars, and things like that.
>
> We have a drop-in center; we provide healthcare, mental care, clothing. You can come in and wash your clothes. You can come in and sit down and have a hot meal. You can register for your birth certificate, Social Security card, housing assessment; you can apply for your insurance, your Medicaid. We have an HPAP [Home Purchase Assistance Program] unit, a MAT [Medication Assisted Treatment for Opioid Use Disorder] clinic. The list keeps going on all the services that we provide.

First contact, whether in the streets or via the drop-in center, is typically at a person's most vulnerable point ("rock bottom," though that point may have persisted for years), so establishing a rapport by repeatedly showing reliability and trustworthiness (Storr and Choi 2019) is crucial in order to help beyond meeting basic needs. Michelle describes her progression.

> I was a client at HIPS before, and I feel like if it wasn't for them, I don't know where I would've ended up at. Because, like, I was on the stroll at one point too, you feel me? … But as I seen them more and more, I was able to say that they're reliable, that I can at least rely on them to come out on the weekends and give us condoms. Then I started going to the office and started accessing their services. And I guess that's how I built my relationship with everybody here.

Before turning to other ways in which this community develops social capital and exercises resilience, such as engaging in adaptability (Boettke 1990) and creativity (Chamlee-Wright 2008), to promote progress in their adverse environment, the following section describes shared narratives of repression, which lead to sense-making within a self-identifiable community.

Stigmatization and criminalization as shared narratives

Black trans sex workers are more prone to being victims of discrimination, violence, and arrest than their white cisgender or cispassing counterparts, not only because of their intersectional identities, but also because they are more likely to participate in street-based survival work (SWOP [Sex Worker Outreach Project] Behind Bars 2021).[5] This is often due to ostracization and banishment by their families at an early age for being queer, which results in lack of educational opportunities, credentials, and the development of professional skillsets; being unhoused and facing food insecurity; chronic unmet healthcare needs including gender-affirming care; general trauma, etc. (Grant et al. 2011; James et al. 2017). Life in the streets is bleak, and many turn to sex work to survive (Homeless Black Trans Women Fund n.d.). While physical and verbal abuse from law enforcement, clients (in this case, the service purchasers), and the general population is certainly traumatic, perhaps equally so is arrest, which may also be thought of as a form of abuse. Trans sex workers often get caught in cycles of arrest, further exacerbating the abovementioned challenges. Michaelisa, who, again, has been arrested fifty-two times, describes this phenomenon:

> I mentioned my record and I got a lot of arrests—it started a vicious cycle. They lock you up, you go to jail, they let you out, you do it again. They lock you back up, you go to jail, they let you out, you do it again. There's no empowerment there, there's no resources there. They make money off of us in the institution, but they don't care. …
>
> And that's what a lot of our decriming [efforts to decriminalize various behaviors] is about. You're punishing us for simply trying to make it through, simply

> trying to make it through *today*, you know, and if it takes a high or a drink or J [marijuana], please understand and let me get that—as long as I'm not hurting anyone—and find my way through. Better yet, why don't you help me find my way through instead of locking me up.

Alexander/a emphatically contends that the targets of enforcement are calculated, stemming from intersectional stigma:

> Gee, I wonder why people are engaged in street-based sex work? Is it possibly anything to do with the fact that, like, I don't know, we have massive discrimination against Black folks and trans folks in the workplace and people can't get jobs and they get kicked outta school and they get kicked out by their family and they're living in the fucking streets and they don't have any other options and it provides flexible hours and lets them make whatever money they wanna make? Is that maybe why? But it's "a problem." Okay, so you've arrested them, now what? Are you gonna give them a job? Now they have a record. Now what are they supposed to do? Now you've ruined their life even more. It's literally a self-perpetuating cycle intentionally. All of this shit is intentional. It's by design.

If criminalization is used to further stigmatize already marginalized populations, Black transgender women who are sex workers therefore necessarily suffer the brunt by virtue of their very being. Michaelisa, who bares all as she bears all, shares vivid descriptions of living in the streets, suffering from the stigma of who she is in addition to what she did to survive. However, she also begins to get at how individuals' mistreatment by and distrust of law enforcement, the criminal justice system, the medical establishment, and the public at large (Goffman 1963; Weitzer 2018; Daniel et al. 2025) coalesce to form shared narratives of repression, which can lead to a certain type of social capital, albeit one that may be considered perverse.[6]

> My sex work started immediately because the girls told me when I came out there, you're gonna have to survive. And it's your responsibility. So they taught me how to trick. They taught me how to boost. They taught me how to pick-pocket. They taught me how to steal. They taught me so many things in the name of survival.

Further, and also seemingly contrary to the notion of contributing to resilience, many trans sex workers feel a sense of isolation and loneliness, and this can be a shared narrative as well.

> It's a very dark and lonely place to be homeless and transgender in the streets. … I remember I've been hurt several times out there for whatever reasons. And when you're simply, "Help me, help me," people just walk past you and look at you like you're an eyesore or you're a disgrace.

Shared narratives of repression, depression, and isolation result in community resilience as trans sex workers use their experiences to mobilize and to help others facing the same challenges.

> So when I have the opportunity to go and advocate for us … I feel like it's only my place to be there, to help support, to help get through. And to try not to have anyone left or lost in the streets like I was. … We embrace our people. We embrace all of the faults, all of the shortcomings, all of the character defects, all of the trauma—we embrace all of it.

"Knowing that I could be used in some way, you know, whether it's volunteering, serving the homeless—if you can use me in some way, that starts making my self-worth grow" (Jones, interview). Not only is reciprocating previously bestowed kindness personally rewarding and affirming, it expands the potential pool of those who will contribute to the community's social capital in the future. Michelle describes her trajectory after experiencing similar cycles as Michaelisa before encountering the community.

> It makes you feel good. It makes *me* feel good to be able to help the next person as I was helped before. I'm a success story, I guess you could say. … In 2014, when I came home from jail for the last time, I just said, "Not no more." And I went to a drug program, and I got my housing, and I stayed on the right track, and I volunteered [at HIPS]. I was working at a restaurant while I was volunteering, but then they actually gave me a job offer after that, so I was just so happy about it.

Shareese, with her characteristic optimism, describes the stigma and obstacles trans women face and speaks not only about entrepreneurship, but also reorienting the downtrodden narrative to one of actualization, empowerment, and beauty.

> I shouldn't have to wear a "T" on my forehead to say that I'm trans, or to say that what's between my legs is something that, you know, is hurting *you* so bad. I'm like, "Well, why? I'm the one walking with it. And *you* mad?! [Laughs] So it's just hard to understand why people do some of the things they do.
>
> I don't treat ourselves as the minorities. Us being "the-LGBTQ-community-that-relates-to-the-LGBTQ-things." … You know, some of us trans women don't even relate to that we're "trans" because we understand that we are women. When do you drop the "trans"? It's time. Let's drop the "trans." … So what I see is just human activities.
>
> Just like prostitution. If you have that ability to get out there and post the ad and service someone and protect yourself all at the same time, you're doing

> entrepreneurship. That means you could get a development job, and you can start building things and posting things [on social media] for your job, and instead of 9:00 at night to 5:00 in the morning, you could do 9:00 a.m. to 5:00 p.m. and make it make sense.
>
> [But] sometimes we can't walk in the daylight. Sometimes we don't have the ability or the courage to stand on a Metro bus and be humiliated before you get to work or to be at work and—you're just trying to do your job comfortably—"Oh, that's the trans woman right there. Oh, but they still beautiful." I mean, "*still* beautiful"?! No babes, I've always been beautiful! [Laughs] I was beautiful *before* I was a trans woman. And now that I *am* a trans woman, you really notice it! [Big grin]

Communal safety and the role of aunties

> They're definitely trying to kill us. And I really only believe in the power of the people. I don't believe our leaders are gonna do shit to save us. It's gonna have to come from the bottom up. It's gonna have to come from what it is coming from, honestly, which is networks within community. Like, you know, people mailing syringes and naloxone to each other. It's a lot of underground machinations and being willing to do shit that might not be totally kosher. Like, a lot of the time.
>
> (Bradley, interview)

As with prison gangs (Skarbek 2014), "[i]n a system that is not governed by a 'rule of law,' there may be central laws and considerable effort made to enforce them, but individuals generally attempt to evade rather than obey the law" (Ostrom 2005: 20). This evasion often results in an alternative "rule of law." Sex work is an extralegal institution, and it follows that mechanisms for exercising resilience within this repressive environment are also often outside the law, if not outright against it. In the absence of access to formal avenues, shared responsibilities for providing communal safety foster resilience in the physical sense.

> We had to do it ourselves. If a girl is being harmed or in danger, if she hollers out, the other girls, more than likely, they'll help because they don't want that person to be able to come back and get them. When I was out there, there were several incidents where I had to be like, "Girls, help! Girls, HELP!" And girls will come running. They know that it's fight or flight—we have to do what we have to do.
>
> We used to have one girl who would be out on the corner—we'd be in the alley asleep—so the guys wouldn't come to the alley and do anything to us. There was a gang called the Gangster Chronicles that used to come through—very abusive—with baseball bats and just beat the girls. And so we had to constantly

> have somebody look out. And a girl might come running down the street, "They here! They're coming!" And everybody, every whore, wigs flying down the street, everybody's just running.
>
> It takes a lot of unity. And if we don't have that unity, then what do we have? There goes the security. There goes somebody to help me if I'm sick and I can't go out to work tonight to eat something. Those kind of things. We build it on our own. We build our own security. We build our own protection. We build our own help.
>
> (Jones, interview)

Further, and contributing to the notion of generalized norms of reciprocity (Chamlee-Wright 2008), sometimes physical help can come from relationships within the geographical, non-sex worker community. When Michaelisa got shot,

> one of the neighbors came out and got right there on the phone, calling the ambulance. And as I was getting in—a couple of neighbors know my name—"Michaelisa, you're gonna be okay. Michaelisa, I'm praying for you." So most times it's each other and/or the community. … [It's] just like when our families discard us and we go out and we make the other girls our families, or the people in the street our families. They also become our security.

Additionally, more formal mechanisms exist that promote safety and general communication.

> We have a thing called 'the bad date sheet.' So that's when the girls report in, like, 'A white car robbed me last week.' We'll put it on our date sheet, and then we'll pass the sheet out to all of the other girls around the stroll. … Or word of mouth, you know, let the girls know when they see the van.
>
> (Mone, interview)

Sex workers themselves can also be bad actors within their community. As Ostrom observed, when a community engages in determining membership and begins to devise rules, which are continually evolving and need not be the result of formal procedures, "the group has made an important first step toward the development of greater trust and reciprocity"; however, this also necessitates "excluding those who do not agree to these rules" (Ostrom 2000a: 149; also Ostrom 2005). Whether prior unmet mental healthcare needs result in turning to sex work to survive, or whether the attendant stigma of sex work leads to mental health issues, some people can face challenges developing their social capital. What do sex workers do when someone violates norms and rules or acts outside of expected behavior? While the community overall is quite tolerant given their similarly shared lived experience, sometimes people who repeatedly do not follow the rules must be sanctioned.

> Basically, it's just the given rule of respect—you gotta give respect to get respect. Just respect each other's boundaries. [If someone is not being respectful], they have to go. You can't have peace if someone's being unpeaceful; you can't have that. If people are around, they have to separate the unpeaceful from the people who just wanna chill out.
>
> (Spikes, interview)

Contributing to the significance of experiential information sharing from one generation to the next, there are often dearly won lessons about squandering social capital. Michaelisa shares a story about a preferred and reliable client.

> And one day I pickpocketed him. I would always depend on him coming. And this particular day, it was so cold, and it was so rainy, and I didn't have an umbrella. And I was just standing on the corner, hoping somebody would pick me up, and he rode past and he looked me right in my face and he kept going, and I knew it was because I had pickpocketed him. So be careful what you do to people along the way.

This type of experiential-based learning is especially relevant as it pertains the role of "aunties" and their relationships with the younger members of the community. Much of the LGBTQ community speaks of chosen family (again, often due to being shunned by their biological families), and though other non-LGBTQ communities and cultures use the term (of endearment, to show deference, etc.), in this context, aunties may be thought of as the matriarchs of the Black trans sex worker family. When reflecting on self-governance,

> I call it [being] an auntie. "C'mon, c'mere, we don't do that, Niecey Pooh, we don't do that, no-no." That's when it takes a village. [Laughs] So that's what you have to do: you have to speak honest, speak about it, like, "Babes, what's going on? 'Cause you're causing harm to yourself."
>
> They are kids. And they are going to do what they want to do. And they are going say, "Oh, you're jealous." Or "You can't take me." Or "You just don't understand." Then you'll be like, "Well, baby, I been there, so I'm just trying to help you." And then when they come back with a busted head from a bottle, you're like, "I told you so. Now, c'mon, let's do it the right way." Because been there, done that, you know. So it's just helping them to see something that they shouldn't have to go through.
>
> I can recall the time when I was looking at *my* auntie and being rebellious, to the point that I turned into the auntie, and now I can look [back] and see why Auntie was saying a lot of those things.
>
> (Mone, interview)

Keeping the youth in check is fraught with anxiety for the aunties and requires boundless patience.

> When I see [misbehavior] with the girls: "What you put out, you'll get back." If you put out deceit and crud and backstabbing and jealousy and hate—if you put all that out, then that's what you're gonna get back. It may not be an easy life, but it can be a lot better than living without the boundaries and without the rules of common courtesy, common respect, and, you know, things of that nature. That's what I try and give the girls.
>
> Now the girls feel like they're young, they're pure, they're beautiful. "Auntie, you can't tell me nothing, girl, I got this." And I'll be like, "Girl, you better listen to an old girl. I may not be right about a lot, but some things I can tell you—don't go down that road right there because this and this is gonna happen." And many of 'em come back and say, "Auntie, I should have listened to you." ... It can be hard sometimes, but you have to just stand still and be there for them. If they're not ready to listen right now, maybe tomorrow they'll listen. Maybe the next day they'll listen.
>
> (Jones, interview)

Ballroom/kiki

A community selfcare institution that aunties have passed down has now come to serve additional purposes coalescing around allyship and activism: ballroom culture. Chronicled by documentarian Jennie Livingston in 1990s *Paris Is Burning*, the same year Madonna brought voguing to mainstream audiences, ball provides an outlet for frustrations and a stage for celebrations. Characterized by luxe drag costumes, makeup, and wigs; dramatic runway walks, dancing, and poses; and astounding contortions and acrobatics, ball often involves mock aggression in the form of challenges as "houses" (chosen families) compete with one another. Further, ball's more economically accessible and less competitive equivalent, kiki, provides a safe space for queer Black and brown youth to express themselves, practice their craft, and showcase their pride.

> [I]t's, I would say, a pageant-slash-competition. You get prizes, and it's underground commentators and has a lot of beauty in it. ... It's showing who's poppin' and, "This ball is your night, but next night's going to be my night," so it's always a good competition. It shows the kids' beauty, their art—'cause there's runway and face and vogue and performance and sex siren and so many categories. ... It's just the community really coming together. And, you know, it's our thing.
>
> (Mone, interview)

DC has a particularly vibrant scene, especially welcoming to trans youth. Moving from Georgia was a godsend for Michelle:

> In Atlanta it was kind of okay, but not as much as it is here; like, they were doing hate crimes when I was still living there, beating up gays and all that, attacking

> them, just walking down the street, stuff like that. So moving here was kind of a blessing, and it made me more comfortable to be able to be who I am.[7]

She was seventeen and quickly heard about SMYAL (Sexual Minority Youth Assistance League).

> I went there, and that's where I got introduced to the gay community here. And from there, I was just astounded. I met a lot of people going to the stroll, going to clubs, just going out to a lot of places. I met a lot of good community. I used to go to the balls a lot when I was younger. I've been going to 'em recently too. I'll go to the one next month for Pride—it's the Unity Ball; it's a free ball.

Novak (this volume) invites us to consider that among the benefits of commercial businesses as social spaces for the LGBTQ community is the opportunity to share these spaces with the non-LGBTQ community. In this way, ball is also used as a tool for demystifying norms and customs for the community at large and for building allyships. Shareese harnesses and grows social capital and political support, in addition to community support, at these events. At the End Violence Kiki Ball 2019,

> I had sponsors and allies and friends all come together to eat, drink, have a little show. A social before the ball. We went downstairs 'cause we at Club Secrets where everybody can go around and look into the pit and see them perform. So I had all the sponsors go around, *and those babies performed.* When I tell you they performed, *they performed.* And it was so amazing.
>
> We even had David Grosso there [the DC councilmember who put forth legislation to decriminalize sex work and arranged for the hearing in 2019] and Mrs. Grosso; they attended; it was so nice. It's just the way you communicate and keep in touch with the community, and this is what they needed to see. And this is the type of community gatherings I want to see.

Work culture

Despite its nonprofit status and primary goal of harm reduction, if we consider HIPS to be in "the marketplace of social change" (or "marketplace of ideas," etc.), Storr's observations are brought into focus pertaining to "the noneconomic sociality that occurs in markets" as members describe their workplace bonds (Storr 2008: 135). How the trans sex worker community treats one another and engages in conflict resolution in its more formal organizational structure is paramount to its success, despite the external climate of repression. Work culture is taken seriously, prioritizing the voices of those with lived experience ("unless it's something truly impossible or something that is unrealistic in the moment or, like, anti-mission-of-the-organization, which is pretty rare" [Bradley, interview]). Alexander/a, for example, was hesitant to take a managerial position at HIPS.

> Nobody wanted it. It had been sitting open for a very long time. I waited very intentionally to see if other people would apply. People with lived experience. But other people like me were applying. And so I was like, well, fuck it.
>
> I sometimes still feel, oh, imposter syndrome. But the fact that I have the relationships with everybody on the team, I feel like they would agree that I've continued to prove myself and bust my ass every day. It was like, alright, I'm not wrong to be here. I'm not taking up space that I shouldn't be. I try to always be mindful of that and know my place and know when to make those decisions.

The overall sex workers' rights movement feels fairly decentralized (with notable exceptions such as organizing for the hearing). This can be good because it allows for more effective bottom-up direct service provision based on the needs of a particular community that has local knowledge. However, it can also pose coordination challenges with other organizations in other jurisdictions and of varied demographics, particularly highlighting distinctions between indoor and street-based sex workers. Additionally, and potentially contributing to tensions within an individual organization, sex workers are like any other civil rights activists—anytime you have a bunch of folks who care deeply, you are going to have strongly held opinions and competing priorities, especially in the face of scarcity and constraints and extralegal institutions. Alexander/a describes how their community navigates these challenges with success. A key point is that rather than putting decisions to a majority vote or strict consensus decision-making (Butler and Rothstein 1987), members deliberate together. They value openness, vulnerability, humility, and trust based on experience and reputation in their negotiations.

> Everybody has a voice, but we didn't just all walk in the door with that trust; that trust-building took a lot of time and energy and consistently—I don't wanna say "proving ourselves" 'cause that's not the right term—but consistently demonstrating that you're a safe person to be around, or a safe-ish person, I mean, nobody is [entirely] safe.
>
> That there is going to be safety in our relationship, that there is going to be accountability, that we are able to talk to each other earnestly and honestly. … [B] eing able to have real conversations about where fuckups came from and what happened, and just open and honest communication about how we operate and how we function. Because all of us bring things to the table that are different, and that's what I love about us.

Finally, when reflecting on the personal stamina required to pursue their community's goals, they identify:

> a core group of people who kind of keep me—I wouldn't say we keep each other "sane" 'cause that's definitely not true—but we take care of each other. And there's a dynamic ebb and flow to who needs help when, and who's falling apart when, and a lot of times we're all falling apart at the same time, which is a nightmare. [Chuckles] But I am surrounded by a very tight-knit community and some very, very deep relationships with people, and I would say that that's really one of the few things that keeps me going.

Partnerships and allies

Hayek (1945) emphasized that market participants have imperfect and dispersed information, but adjust their activities as they glean more knowledge, much of it tacit or inarticulate, which leads to more efficient processes and better resource allocation over time. Likewise, sex workers learn as they go.[8] Based on their experience, they have determined parameters for making rational decisions about when to forgo relationships—not all are necessarily "toxic," but marginal cost exceeds marginal benefit. Like everyone, sex workers face opportunity costs, and some interactions do not result in reciprocation for time and emotional labor rendered, or they result in outright harm. Learning how to make decisions regarding with whom to engage leads to introducing and maintaining relationships with state actors, leveraging associations with academics and medical researchers, and practicing tactfulness with would-be allies.

Black trans sex workers are industrious social entrepreneurs engaging in the discovery process (Chamlee-Wright 2008), and some remarkable success stories have been realized through some seemingly unlikely partnerships, including with policymakers (it is good to have a champion) and healthcare institutions, both of which historically have been among the most egregious. Actors have had to show that they are trustworthy, and sex workers have had to learn how to identify those opportunities least likely to cause harm in order to parse predicted net benefits. They have also developed strategies for engaging diplomatically.[9] Regarding political champions, for example, Shareese found success simply by being her good-natured self.

> I met Grosso in 2016 and we was just organizing SWAC (Sex Worker Advocates Coalition). Not knowing the caliber of people that you're sitting around. I didn't even pay attention that he was a councilman. … I was always sweet, and he was always nice to me, and his wife—I am so in love with—we are, like, the best of buddies. So, you know, it was just like I felt the bond before the bond even was attached to a name.

Other partnerships that contribute to resilience and reinforce social capital are with conscientious medical researchers and providers, particularly those affiliated with universities and training the next generation of healthcare professionals. Prioritizing and determining safety is the crucial component in this calculus.

> I think the main factor, honestly, is our confidence in their capacity to provide services with a harm-reduction approach, their cultural competency. … 'Cause we're not gonna put the people we serve at risk of violence. Now, of course, a lot of that research has strong potential for almost baked-in violence. But the question is whether or not it feels net worth it.
>
> In the context of, for example, this current study, the providers are incredible, like, incredible. They're *so* good. And they are all in with actually listening to people, learning from them. 'Cause these are folks who, definitely compared to other providers, have trans competency, but are still learning from us, constantly asking questions, being sensitive.
>
> (Bradley, interview)

Once expectations of physical and emotional safety are established, studies that are funded well beyond what HIPS could amass result in measurable positive outcomes. The clinic at HIPS has built a reciprocal relationship with the National Institutes of Health (NIH), which, by coming to do studies that are important based on their own calculi, in turn provides HIPS access to general healthcare as well as treatment for specific conditions. Further, by coming to the drop-in center, rather than requiring people without means to have to travel, or attempting to recruit people who would not participate in an unfamiliar clinical setting, NIH increases the likelihood of participation as well as builds trust and social capital for future studies.

> We ended up being *the* research site for the study that proved that you can treat Hep C while people are still actively using [intravenous drugs]. 'Cause prior to that, they literally made it a contraindication for getting treatment for Hep C, which *is* curable, and they would deny treatment to people because they were still injecting.
>
> So when the researchers approached us and were like, "Hey, can we do this study with you?", we were like, "Abso-fuckin'-lutely." And we had one of the best retention rates out of anybody. So, yeah, we changed that rule [intravenous drug use as a contraindication]. Like, our people changed that. And I know a lot of people who got cured at HIPS, and they're like, "My life has changed."
>
> (Bradley, interview)

Another successful relationship, one that has resulted in gender-affirming care for at least a hundred participants, is in conjunction with the University of

Maryland, Baltimore. Transgender and nonbinary participants are prescribed hormones, and after being on hormones for a year, they are eligible for surgery. Access to hormones was previously inconceivable to most people, much less surgery. "So that was a plus for a lot of people. I got, like, maybe fifty-five people enrolled. HIPS is kind of the best place for them to collaborate with because we really serve a lot of the community" (Spikes, interview).

> I'm actually in the study and getting care through HIPS, as well as are several other staff members. So it's a lot of 'We are who we serve,' right? [Giggles] … That's been really cool 'cause we had had a couple of piecemeal relationships in the past, but we have never had such a robust way to get folks access to gender-affirming care.
>
> (Bradley, interview)

Intersectional voluntary associations and mutual aid also foster resilience, and given the dire straits experienced by many Black trans sex workers, if we consider criminalization to be a type of crisis, the movement to decriminalize is potentially a source of social capital for overlapping marginalized communities (Storr et al. 2021). This appeared to be evident at the hearing where contributing organizations included the American Civil Liberties Union of DC, Human Rights Campaign, local Black Lives Matter organizers, and all manner of social justice entities, as well as organizations that provide direct services within countless communities (queer youth, people facing food and housing insecurity, survivors of sexual violence, etc.) (HIPS n.d.). They are incredibly diverse, with varied foci and agendas, but all have "skin in the game" (Taleb 2020) and were united in purpose. When considering engaging with other organizations, in addition to Alexander/a's aforementioned risk assessment, other criteria HIPS considers are "what services they offer, what demographic they usually serve, how they feel about our demographic, and what they can bring to our organization" (Spikes, interview).

Conclusion

"It makes you feel like, 'I am somebody.' I think the whole networking, the whole community involvement—I think that's where I found my freedom" (Jones, interview). Black transgender sex workers face tremendous obstacles within their repressive environment. However, they exercise resilience, and their circumstances improve, as they recognize, rely on, and actively build social bonds. Social capital results from shared narratives of hardship and identity; individuals' roles in contributing to communal safety; experiential, generational information sharing; making spaces for healing and celebration; cocreating rules and work culture; and discerning whom to trust from external institutions. They execute strategic calculations and have learned when to take risks. Further, institutional arrangements change with actors changing; for example, healthcare providers are offering better cultural competency, which leads to trust, which leads to better learning conditions and evaluative criteria for sex workers, and thus better outcomes (Ostrom et al. 1994).

Finally, returning to the discussion of methods, ethnographic qualitative research is a powerful tool within mainline political economy for understanding stigmatized communities:

> [f]or the discipline of paying attention; for learning from others; for becoming more responsibly aware of inequalities; for better understanding the social forces causing suffering and how people might somehow yet find hope; and most generally, for being perpetually pulled beyond the limits of one's own taken-for-granted world.
>
> (Narayan 2014)

These communities have largely not been engaged by mainline political economists (or by economists, in general, for that matter), as well as scholars interested in queer classical liberalism. This chapter proposes to introduce their under-chronicled circumstances to a broader audience. With due regard to intersectionality theory, stigmatization brings about oppressive experiences for Black, transgender, and sex worker communities; these experiences are multifaceted and complex and warrant further research. Also of note, existing insights from mainline political economists and classical liberal thinkers (e.g., Ostrom on social capital, Chamlee-Wright and Storr on resilience, Novak on social movements, etc.) may inform Black trans sex workers and their allies, as well as be useful for expanding and uniting fields of scholarship and researchers and activists.

In sum, to better understand stigmatized communities, identify people with lived experience, do the work and be patient, demonstrate that you are a safe(ish) person, and get to know them. Develop social capital, especially if you wish to contribute to their resilience.[10] They *want* to be known: to destigmatize their identities, and to be at the forefront of discussions that affect them. Encompassing conducting research, developing supportive institutions, and advocating for decriminalization, the motto "nothing about us without us" has come to symbolize how Black transgender sex workers rightfully demand seats at the table, as well as how they value a bottom-up approach informed by their community's social capital, to promote resilience within and flourishing beyond their repressive environment.

Notes

1 Space and topical constraints do not permit engaging with the literature here, but researchers, practitioners, sex trafficking survivors, and human rights organizations worldwide, including leaders in healthcare and justice spaces such as American Civil Liberties Union, Amnesty International, Freedom Network USA (the nation's largest

anti-trafficking coalition), Human Rights Campaign, Human Rights Watch, Joint United Nations Programme on HIV/AIDS, World Health Organization, etc. agree: decriminalizing sex work is the only policy that results in harm reduction across all metrics.

2 Theirs is not the only guide to offer accessible approaches (see, e.g., Morgan and Nica's [2020] iterative thematic inquiry); it is simply the one on which I most relied.

3 These participants are part of a larger research project consisting of sex workers of varied demographics and from diverse geographical locations. All details, e.g., age range and role at HIPS, are accurate as of the time of the interview; participants may or may not have been currently engaged in sex work. Recorded interviews were conducted via Zoom. Quotes are lightly edited for length and clarity. The usual caveats apply.

4 As I wrote this chapter, HIPS launched a massive campaign to raise funds to purchase the building and avoid eviction. It was recently successful.

5 Frankie (they/he), a non-binary trans person I interviewed who primarily works in brothels in New York City but has done survival work, confirms that:

> [t]he majority of people who are street-based workers are Black and brown people. … I have it good for a sex worker, to be quite honest, because I am white and cispassing. … And they [law enforcement] pick and choose who they arrest. And they pick the Black and brown people. Always. Always, always, always. … Even if you're wearing the exact same clothes and you're presenting the same way. And specifically, they'll arrest the trans individuals who are outwardly or openly trans.
>
> (Smith, interview by Malia Dalesandry, Zoom, May 24 and 26, 2022)

6 Ostrom offers examples of the Mafia, gangs, cartels, and authoritarian governments to represent the "dark side to social capital" (2000b: 176–177). Novak discusses emergent social orders "with malign effects" such as patriarchy and rape culture, white supremacy, and transphobia (2021: 171; also this volume).

7 Generations of mettle likely explain this in part:

> I think another reason why DC is amazing is that we don't shut the fuck up if we want something. And the advocacy community is aggressive in a good way. Anytime something has threatened people, people stand up and fight back. There is an ingrained radical streak for a lot of the communities in DC.
>
> (Bradley, interview)

8 With thanks to Savannah Sly, musician, dominatrix, and sex workers' rights advocate, who inspired this theme.

9 Pertaining to people who have a bit more leeway to ruffle feathers, Alexander/a talks about how to be a good ally (they use the term "accomplice") within institutions such as healthcare and the "nonprofit industrial complex."

> [O]ne of the best, most difficult, but most important ways to show up is [to 'try to dismantle the harm in that system from the inside as we're there'] because we [accomplices] have a lot of access. So if we're gonna have access, if we're gonna have privilege? Let's use that privilege to fuck over [change from within by challenging] the system that gave us privilege. Right? Like, fuck it up. Let's go! [Big laugh]

10 Recall Chamlee-Wright's proposal that we take opportunities to remind struggling communities that they are socially resourceful, creative, and resilient (2010a).

References

Bey, Marquis. 2022. *Black Trans Feminism*. Durham, NC: Duke University Press.

Bland, Sean, and Benjamin Brooks. 2020. *Improving Laws and Policies to Protect Sex Workers and Promote Health and Wellbeing: A Report on Criminalization of Sex Work in the District of Columbia*. O'Neill Institute for National and Global Health Law,

Whitman-Walker Institute, HIPS. https://whitmanwalkerimpact.org/wp-content/uploads/2020/12/Sex-Worker-Law-and-Policy-Report-FINAL.pdf.

Boettke, Peter J. 1990. "The Theory of Spontaneous Order and Cultural Evolution in the Social Theory of F.A. Hayek." *Cultural Dynamics* 3 (1): 61–83.

Braun, Virginia, and Victoria Clarke. 2021. *Thematic Analysis: A Practical Guide*. Thousand Oaks, CA: Sage Publishing.

Butler, C. T., and Amy Rothstein. 1987. *On Conflict and Consensus: A Handbook on Formal Consensus Decisionmaking*. Portland, ME: Food Not Bombs Publishing.

Chamlee-Wright, Emily. 2008. "The Structure of Social Capital: An Austrian Perspective on Its Nature and Development." *Review of Political Economy* 20 (1): 41–58.

Chamlee-Wright, Emily. 2010a. *The Cultural and Political Economy of Recovery: Social Learning in a Post-Disaster Environment*. London, UK; New York, NY: Routledge.

Chamlee-Wright, Emily. 2010b. "Qualitative Methods and the Pursuit of Economic Understanding." *The Review of Austrian Economics* 23 (4): 321–331.

Chamlee-Wright, Emily, and Virgil Henry Storr. 2010. *The Political Economy of Hurricane Katrina and Community Rebound*. Cheltenham, UK: Edward Elgar.

Chamlee-Wright, Emily, and Virgil Henry Storr. 2011. "Social Capital as Collective Narratives and Post-Disaster Community Recovery." *The Sociological Review* 59 (2): 266–282.

Crenshaw, Kimberlé. 1989. "Demarginalizing the Intersection of Race and Sex: A Black Feminist Critique of Antidiscrimination Doctrine, Feminist Theory and Antiracist Politics." *University of Chicago Legal Forum* 1: 139–167.

Crenshaw, Kimberlé W. 2012. "From Private Violence to Mass Incarceration: Thinking Intersectionally About Women, Race, and Social Control." *UCLA Law Review* 59 (6): 1418–1472.

Daniel, Toni, Jessica Lamb, and Christine Campbell. 2025. "Avoidance and Empowerment: How Do Sex Workers Navigate Stigma?" *Sexualities* 28 (1–2): 470–491.

DC Historic Preservation Office. 2024. "Civil Rights Tour, Legal Campaigns: Frank D. Reeves, Leveraging the Law." DC Historic Sites. https://historicsites.dcpreservation.org/items/show/964.

Easterbrook-Smith, Gwyn. 2020. "'Not on the Street Where We Live': Walking While Trans under a Model of Sex Work Decriminalisation." *Feminist Media Studies* 20 (7): 1013–1028.

Easterbrook-Smith, Gwyn. 2023. "Sex Workers' Online Humor as Evidence of Resilience." *Sexes* 4 (2): 310–326.

Edelman, Elijah Adiv. 2014. "'Walking While Transgender': Necropolitical Regulations of Trans Feminine Bodies of Color in the US Nation's Capital." In *Queer Necropolitics*, edited by Jin Haritaworn, Adi Kuntsman and Silvia Posocco, 172–190. London, UK: Routledge.

Edelman, Elijah Adiv. 2020. "Beyond Resilience: Trans Coalitional Activism as Radical Self-Care." *Social Text* 38 (1): 109–130.

European Sex Workers' Rights Alliance. 2022. *The Impact of Structural Racism on Racialised Sex Workers in Europe and Central Asia*. https://www.eswalliance.org/sex_work_racism_second_community_report.

Glover, Julian Kevon. 2021. "Customer Service Representatives: Sex Work among Black Transgender Women in Chicago's Ballroom Scene." *The South Atlantic Quarterly* 120 (3): 553–571.

Goffman, Erving. 1963. *Stigma: Notes on the Management of Spoiled Identity*. Englewood Cliffs, NJ: Prentice-Hall.

Grant, Jaime M., Lisa A. Mottet, Justin Tanis, Jack Harrison, Jody L. Herman, and Mara Keisling. 2011. *Injustice at Every Turn: A Report of the National Transgender Discrimination Survey*. Washington, DC: National Center for Transgender Equality and National Gay and Lesbian Task Force. https://www.thetaskforce.org/resources/injustice-every-turn-report-national-transgender-discrimination-survey.

Haeffele, Stefanie, and Virgil Henry Storr. 2020a. *Bottom-up Responses to Crisis*. New York, NY: Palgrave Macmillan.
Haeffele, Stefanie, and Virgil Henry Storr. 2020b. *Government Responses to Crisis*. New York, NY: Palgrave Macmillan.
Hayek, F. A. 1945. "The Use of Knowledge in Society." *American Economic Review* 35 (4): 519–530.
HIPS. n.d. "Harm Reduction Experts Improving Lives Since 1993." https://www.hips.org.
Homeless Black Trans Women Fund. n.d. https://www.homelessblacktranswomenfund.org.
James, Sandy E., Carter Brown, and Isaiah Wilson. 2017. *2015 U.S. Transgender Survey: Report on the Experiences of Black Respondents*. National Center for Transgender Equality, Black Trans Advocacy, and National Black Justice Coalition. https://transequality.org/sites/default/files/docs/usts/USTS-Black-Respondents-Report.pdf.
McGranahan, Carole. 2014. "What Is Ethnography? Teaching Ethnographic Sensibilities without Fieldwork." *Teaching Anthropology* 4: 23–36.
Morgan, David L., and Andreea Nica. 2020. "Iterative Thematic Inquiry: A New Method for Analyzing Qualitative Data." *International Journal of Qualitative Methods* 19: 1–11.
Narayan, Kirin. 2014. "Ethnographic Writing with Kirin Narayan: An Interview." February 3, 2014. https://savageminds.org/2014/02/03/ethnographic-writing-with-kirin-narayan-an-interview.
Novak, Mikayla. 2021. *Freedom in Contention: Social Movements and Liberal Political Economy*. Lanham, MD: Lexington Books.
Ostrom, Elinor. 2000a. "Collective Action and the Evolution of Social Norms." *The Journal of Economic Perspectives* 14 (3): 137–158.
Ostrom, Elinor. 2000b. "Social Capital: A Fad or a Fundamental Concept?" In *Social Capital: A Multifaceted Perspective*, edited by Partha Dasgupta and Ismail Serageldin, 172–214. Washington DC: The World Bank.
Ostrom, Elinor. 2005. *Understanding Institutional Diversity*. Princeton, NJ: Princeton University Press.
Ostrom, Elinor, Roy Gardner, and Jimmy Walker. 1994. *Rules, Games, and Common-Pool Resources*. Ann Arbor, MI: University of Michigan Press.
Pacheco-Vega, Raul, and Kate Parizeau. 2018. "Doubly Engaged Ethnography: Opportunities and Challenges When Working with Vulnerable Communities." *International Journal of Qualitative Methods* 17 (1): 1–13.
Skarbek, David. 2014. *The Social Order of the Underworld: How Prison Gangs Govern the American Penal System*. Oxford, UK: Oxford University Press.
Skarbek, David. 2020. "Qualitative Research Methods for Institutional Analysis." *Journal of Institutional Economics* 16 (4): 409–422.
Snorton, C. Riley. 2017. *Black on Both Sides: A Racial History of Trans Identity*. Minneapolis, MN: University of Minnesota Press.
Storr, Nona Martin, Emily Chamlee-Wright, and Virgil Henry Storr. 2015a. *How We Came Back: Voices from Post-Katrina New Orleans*. Arlington, VA: Mercatus Center at George Mason University.
Storr, Virgil Henry. 2008. "The Market as a Social Space: On the Meaningful Extraeconomic Conversations That Can Occur in Markets." *Review of Austrian Economics* 21 (2–3): 135–150.
Storr, Virgil Henry, and Ginny Seung Choi. 2019. *Do Markets Corrupt Our Morals?* Cham, Switzerland: Palgrave Macmillan.
Storr, Virgil Henry, Stefanie Haeffele, Laura E. Grube, and Jordan K. Lofthouse. 2021. "Crisis as a Source of Social Capital: Adaptation and Formation of Social Capital during the COVID-19 Pandemic." *Cosmos + Taxis* 9 (5+6): 94–108.

Storr, Virgil Henry, Stefanie Haeffele-Balch, and Laura E. Grube. 2015b. *Community Revival in the Wake of Disaster: Lessons in Local Entrepreneurship*. New York, NY: Palgrave Macmillan.
Stryker, Susan. 2008. *Transgender History*. New York, NY: Seal Press.
SWOP (Sex Worker Outreach Project) Behind Bars. 2021. "Top Myths of the Anti-Trafficking/Anti-Sex Work Movement (Part One)." https://www.swopbehindbars.org/post/top-myths-of-the-anti-trafficking-anti-sex-work-movement.
Taleb, Nassim Nicholas. 2020. *Skin in the Game: Hidden Asymmetries in Daily Life*. New York, NY: Random House.
Weitzer, Ronald. 2018. "Resistance to Sex Work Stigma." *Sexualities* 21 (5–6): 717–729.

9

THE TRADEOFFS BETWEEN LIBERALISM AND PUBLIC HEALTH IN QUEER COMMUNITIES

Byron Carson

A critique of market liberalization is that people might fail to improve public health. As people engage in myriad commercial and social activities to make themselves (and others) better off, they might increase infectious behaviors and decrease preventative behaviors. Similarly, as people devise institutions that encourage greater liberalization, intimate relations, and other interactions commensurate with free societies, they might also raise the costs of improving public health. Woerner Troesken develops these ideas in *The Pox of Liberty* wherein he argues that political institutions can exert, at a minimum, dueling effects (Troesken 2015). Institutions like the federalist style of government in the United States, which fostered the protection of property rights, facilitated exchange, and the development of markets, all encouraged rising productivity and the accumulation of wealth. Those same institutions also discouraged the formation of public health services, which made people more susceptible to diseases like smallpox, typhoid, and cholera.

At the same time, however, liberal institutions provide more income and opportunities—via the private sector and organizations in civil society—for people to respond to infectious diseases and improve public health in relatively private ways (Geloso and Bologna Pavlik 2020; Candela and Geloso 2021; Geloso 2021; Geloso et al. 2021, 2023; Furton 2023). Accounting for a broader array of incentives and responses indicates the tradeoffs Troesken points to can be less severe. Institutional diversity involving the income-generating power of markets, the coercive power of the state, and civil society organizations like families and churches seems paramount for responding effectively to epidemics and for learning how to improve those responses (Ogilvie 2025).

One of the main implications of Troesken's work is that with a more severe view of the tradeoffs people face, we might justify greater restrictions on liberty and economic activity so as to strengthen public health bureaus. If we recognize there

DOI: 10.4324/9781003615781-9

are less severe tradeoffs, however, we can try to have our cake and eat it too. People might be better able to improve public health, that is, because of their abilities to engage in commerce, accumulate wealth, and form relationships with others. Both camps are extreme positions, perhaps, but they indicate many opportunities people face to trade between liberty and public health at the margin.

Tradeoffs between liberalism and public health in queer communities provide interesting and underexplored cases to tease out these arguments. In particular, this chapter uses insights from queer classical liberalism and mainline political economy to argue that across easy and hard cases, people in queer communities find the tradeoffs between liberalization and public health to be less severe. Within institutions that encourage economic activity and freedom of association, people within queer communities can acquire income, exchange, associate, and improve private and public health. Forming private health centers and clinics to avoid stigma and cater to members of the queer community provide relatively easy cases, whereas responding to an infectious disease like HIV/AIDS provides a harder case. Both scenarios suggest people in queer communities can find ways to maintain a commitment to liberalism and creatively improve private and public health, especially when economic and political institutions encourage them to do so.

In short, people in and out of queer communities should welcome liberalism and economic freedom as they encourage the accumulation of wealth, individual and community-related goals, and improvements in private and public health outcomes. Formal rules restricting interactions and stigmas, however, discourage the search for marginal improvements and opportunities to learn. At the very least, the analysis highlights novel opportunities to maintain liberal values and improve public health.

Liberalism and health in economics and queer scholarship

Health economists have developed nuanced views toward markets and entrepreneurs. While the field was founded to better understand market failures (Arrow 1963), many scholars recognize that individuals and market-based incentives can influence health in positive and negative ways. One foundational argument, for example, suggests that people tend to allocate resources at their disposal to maximize a bundle of health and consumption goods; relatedly, people tend to improve their health at higher levels of wealth (see, e.g., Grossman 1972; Pritchett and Summers 1996). Pharmaceutical innovation, moreover, depends on some amount of patent protections, as well as other factors like income, human capital, and economic freedom (Mansfield 1986; Qian 2007). Similarly, price controls like through monopsonistic health insurance plans limit drug availability, as well as incentives to provide them in the first place (Atella et al. 2012). Scholars also recognize the potential for more perverse outcomes in healthcare, for example, supplier-induced demand, information asymmetry problems, and externalities.

Outside of economics, many view entrepreneurs, markets, and economics with skepticism, especially when it comes to health, public health, and queer scholarship. Given the goal of public health is to redress perceived inequities and injustices that make some people sick, public health scholars often target markets as a source of injustice (Beauchamp 1976). That is, markets or what Beauchamp refers to as market justice prioritizes the individual, attributes health problems to individual choice, and raises the barriers to governmental forms of public health. Smoking, for example, is often relegated to a problem borne by individuals, with little room for a public response, let alone one for public health. The public health case against markets becomes stronger given actual and perceived market failures, for example, information asymmetry and externality problems (Powers and Faden 2006).

Related to queer scholarship more generally, some scholars write about queer communities and markets with nuance. Specifically, there are at least five effects capitalism has on queer identities (Valocchi 2017: 316–317): capitalism leads to (1) "class-based" inequality that fosters grievances and marginalized identities, (2) differences in people's ability to seek governmental collective action and other political opportunities, (3) the state's ability to define and regulate which people are worthy, fit, and safe citizens, (4) the development of social networks that form collective identities, and (5) ideologies that further influence "freedom, rights, liberty, property" and so on.

While such descriptions of capitalism have definitional problems, the implications for queer communities are noteworthy. We all might recognize the transformative effects of institutions that spurred the industrial revolution, but Valocchi takes this further, however, and suggests the commensurate decline of small-scale manufacturing and family farms and the rise of urbanization (which he calls "monopoly" capitalism) increased anonymity and allowed people to explore their sexual desires and identities. While a seemingly positive development in that it provided an early impetus for queer social and political movements, it also led to anxieties about gender and sexuality, especially because being queer was viewed as choosing the object of one's sexual desires.[1] Moreover, the rise of post-World War II incomes and the growing middle class afforded people in queer communities greater opportunities for businesses, bars, clubs, bookstores, residential properties, and so on. Such developments also indicate tensions between queer communities, like other minorities, and local or "normal" communities during times of sudden economic change, for example, layoffs. In recent decades, finally, a "neoliberal political economy" developed (1) a corporatized queer movement, for example, gay and lesbian advocacy groups, rather than one based on local operations, (2) a more domesticated queer identity one where coupling, marriage, and families are ideal, and (3) a commodifiable queer identity one viewed as niche or merely as a marker of multiculturalism. The connections between capitalism and queer communities, thus, are not necessarily negative, if valid, but they indicate complex links and tensions.

One argument about American family values indicates how "neoliberal" economic theory advances goals that run counter to the goals individuals might have within queer communities. While such arguments are not directly related to health, this chapter suggests they are relevant even if they are deficient in that they ignore the goals individuals might pursue, which can improve private and public health outcomes. Melinda Cooper (2017: 18–24) develops an argument about "neoliberalism" and the effects such a movement (along with "new social conservatism") has had on the family in general and on gay marriage in particular. In their scholarship, their academic institution-building, and in their roles as policy advisors—and spurred by the "panopoly of liberation movements" like queer liberation—neoliberal economists like Gary Becker, Richard Posner, Ronald Coase, and others at places like the University of Chicago, George Mason University, and UCLA worked to rebuff those who desired redistributing wealth and breaking from the "Fordist family wage" via governmental welfare policies.[2]

The neoliberal support of gay marriage provides one extended example of Cooper's argument. Cooper first reviews the argument from Posner and Philipson's 1993 book *Private Choice and Public Health,* which applies rational choice economics to the HIV/AIDS epidemic. Posner and Philipson eventually argue that to help limit the negative external effects of risky sexual activities on other people, for example, a higher prevalence rate of HIV/AIDS, state governments should legalize gay marriage. Such marriages would raise the costs of risky sexual behaviors for men who have sex with men *and for their married partners.* All else equal, such marriages would tend to lower prevalence rates. Cooper indicts the Posner and Philipson argument—and grounds her subsequent arguments in this debate—as it praises older (perhaps antiquated) traditions related to personal and family responsibility and constrains New Deal-like governmental social insurance programs. In this context, men in gay marriages now bear more of the consequences of their potentially risky behavior, which depletes the justification for governmental welfare schemes. Cooper (2017: 174) states that, "… the neoliberal critique of normativity ends up endorsing an alternative form of moral philosophy—one that restores the private family and its legal obligations of care to a foundational role in the free-market order."

Overall, these considerations suggest more explicit economic approaches to improving queer private and public health outcomes might be fraught with atomistic individuals (influenced by neoliberalism and inequality), corporate interests (of private firms and advocacy groups), and market failures related to health, in addition to some of the already pernicious formal and informal rules against queer communities. Rather than view economics as a reaction to the liberation of queer (and other minority) communities (as Cooper does), this chapter argues economics yields insight into how people, especially people in queer communities, can creatively pursue their goals, maintain an appreciation for liberalism, and improve health. People in these communities, moreover, face tradeoffs between liberalism and public health and make choices according to their values, regardless of whether they advance some economic agenda be it neoliberal or otherwise.

The tradeoffs between liberalism and public health

A review of economic principles and institutions suggests the tradeoffs between liberalism and public health—in and out of queer communities—might not be as severe as commonly believed. This is especially the case as we recognize people engage in marginal behaviors within a set of institutions that can incentivize preventative behavior. The next section then applies these insights to the context of queer communities.

Methodological individualism is a foundation of the economic way of thinking that focuses on individuals as the unit of analysis and, importantly, that only they make choices. Individuals, as opposed to groups like families, firms, or nations, make decisions. This approach isn't necessarily atomistic as individuals are influenced by groups and larger communities, but it is an analytical tool to discipline thinking.

Relatedly, the economic way of thinking indicates people are rational; that is, they make choices to pursue their desired ends based on perceived and expected costs and benefits. These ends might include purchasing apples at the grocery store, given a preference for apples over oranges; it might include sleeping with someone of a particular race or sexuality, given one's preferences; and it might include avoiding diseases. Social rules like norms and even temporary fads also influence costs and benefits. This general description of rational behavior indicates people select appropriate means to obtain a desired end, and it does not preclude mistakes or cognitive biases (Becker 1965). Rationality generally suggests people will tend to select cheaper options, given the constraints they face. Just as people select shorter lines at the grocery store and forego items as they become more expensive (Wicksteed 1910), they behave marginally whenever they make choices. People who want apples, for example, will tend to search for and consume apples until the costs of acquiring apples outweigh the benefits.

People even engage in rational and marginal responses to changing prevalence rates of infectious diseases (Philipson 2000). As prevalence (and mortality) rates rise, they tend to engage in more cautious and preventative behaviors; and they tend to engage in riskier behaviors as prevalence (and mortality) rates decline. These *prevalence elastic* responses have been documented for measles, H1N1, and HIV, among other infectious diseases (Ahituv et al. 1996; Dow and Philipson 1996; Goldstein et al. 1996; Agüero and Beleche 2017). With the refinement of the germ theory of disease throughout the 19th century, people also exhibited prevalence elastic responses by cleaning their homes (Mokyr and Stein 1996; Mokyr 2000).

The scope for marginal responses to infectious diseases also applies to sexually transmitted diseases. Even in more intimate situations, people implicitly consider the costs and benefits of risky sexual behavior like unprotected anal intercourse. Despite the benefits of risky sexual behavior, people become wary of such behaviors and more interested in safer sexual practices as prevalence rates rise. That is, they might be more interested in partners they perceive as safer, for example, a partner interested in monogamy, and sexual practices they perceive to be safer like oral sex and wearing prophylactics (McKusick et al. 1985; Philipson and Posner 1993; Francis 2008; Spencer 2024). Note that the preceding statements refer to theories and supporting evidence about marginal behaviors in response to changing prevalence rates. They do not refer to how people should behave based on normative beliefs or values (contrary to Cooper 2017).

Institutions add to the mix of marginal responses people take to improve health. Institutions are humanly devised formal and informal rules that define which behaviors are permissible, encouraged, frowned upon, or forbidden (North 1990; Ostrom 2005). Formal institutions like a government's constitutional rules can encourage property rights, which can expand time horizons and encourage economic calculation and entrepreneurial activity. That is, people might be more interested in advancing long-term productive plans, forming partnerships, entering contracts, and so on, when they have stronger expectations they will retain the rewards of such endeavors.

Informal institutions are also important. These institutions clarify how to behave and can serve as useful coordinating devices, for example, drive on the right side of the road. Informal institutions like customs, traditions, and social norms develop within small and larger groups to pursue community specific normative values via decentralized enforcement; norms against littering provide other examples (Brennan et al. 2013).

Formal and informal institutions, thus, open or foreclose new, additional opportunities for human action. Within a set of institutions, people seek ways to improve their bundle of goods, that is, their well-being. Entrepreneurs, generally, seek additional profit opportunities among a set of permissible behaviors (Kirzner 1978); sometimes institutions encourage entrepreneurs to innovate, while other institutions encourage political entrepreneurship, rent seeking, or more pernicious behaviors (Baumol 1990). People within a family allocate their time and resources to better serve their ends (Becker 1965, 2010). People within a community might also foster strongly held values and social norms defining which behaviors are appropriate; such norms and rules might also conflict with other rules, especially across communities (Boettke et al. 2008).

The responses people take to public health problems, thus, depend on their rational, marginal responses made within a set of institutions that might or might not incentivize subsequent preventative behavior. This allows us to reevaluate the supposed severity of the tradeoffs between liberalism and public health. More severe views imply scenarios wherein (1) individuals mostly engage in infectious behavior (or behaviors generally opposed to public health), (2) institutions allow (or encourage) such behaviors, and (3) it is difficult to change such institutions. Such a view indicates infectious behaviors will persist if we want to maintain commitments to liberalism. Less severe views, alternatively, imply scenarios wherein (1) individuals engage in prevalence elastic responses, (2) institutions can encourage preventative behavior, and (3) people can alter institutions to improve upon existing responses. This view suggests that when outbreaks and other public health problems arise, people can find appropriate responses to overcome them in ways that maintain commitments to liberalism.

Institutions that protect private property, that encourage association, and that facilitate civil society organizations expand how people can respond to public health problems. With greater liberalization, for example, people might be more interested in revamping the production process of private sector firms to produce inputs into prevention (especially if they own the firm and workers are healthier and more productive), they might be interested in changing formal and informal rules (especially if they are members of a community that can easily monitor and enforce rules), and they might be interested in pooling resources with others in civil society (especially with praise for being philanthropic).[3] This feature of institutions, especially of liberal institutions, ultimately indicates a less severe tradeoff.

Liberalism and health in queer communities

The liberal values many people in queer communities maintain, for example, the freedom of association, might counter and limit private and public health. The freedom of association affords many rights to associate, for example, in queer bars, in pride parades, and in other private ways. Rules about economic freedom—a general category of freedom that allows exchange and protects private property rights—encourage people in queer communities to better match with employers, to sell goods, and to earn income. Economic freedom also encourages more competitive housing markets, which enhances mobility and the development of queer-friendly residential communities. Such freedoms, however, are not universal, and they do not preclude restrictions in other areas. People might develop formal and informal rules against freedom of expression, for example, marriage laws that prohibit same-sex marriages; rules against sexual expression, for example, anti-sodomy laws; and rules against associating with queer individuals, for example, stigma.

The cases below on healthcare throughout queer communities and on the HIV/AIDS epidemic explore relatively easy and harder cases about the tensions between liberalism and public health. Overall, these cases indicate that the responses individuals took, while not perfect, enabled them to pursue their goals and to improve public health. Such responses and cases indicate people in these communities face a less severe tradeoff between liberty and public health.

Queer healthcare

Economic freedom and freedoms to associate encourage agglomeration effects and a catering of medical professionals, clinics, and hospitals to individuals within queer communities. Agglomeration effects, broadly defined, arise from a greater concentration of people, homes, and businesses (Glaeser 2010). These effects can refer to new ideas and innovation, a cheaper rate of production, and a greater demand for one's products. Simply, it is much easier and more beneficial to do things in larger urban areas. Just as larger urban areas can develop homogeneous communities based on a nationality or ethnicity, people in queer communities also rely on urban areas to congregate, for example, in San Francisco, in Atlanta, in Chicago, in New York (Knopp, cited in Gluckman and Reed 1997). Agglomeration effects indicate a larger set of opportunities available to queer people. These opportunities include earning (larger) incomes and additional places to receive medical care, to receive charity, and to associate with others.

While the quality and kind of some healthcare services do not depend on sexual behaviors or identities, diagnosis and treatment might (Wiles and Allen, cited in Harvey and Housel 2014). Many people in queer communities express a desire to be seen by medical professionals who are also in a queer community or who are at least allies. Such desires are helpful to reveal one's identity and any relevant medical information. Having doctors and other medical professionals who are welcoming also mitigates potential problems related to indifference, discrimination, harassment, and resistance to having a queer spouse make decisions for an incapacitated patient (Wiles and Allen, cited in Harvey and Housel 2014; Nordmarken and Kelly, cited in Harvey and Housel 2014).

Healthcare and "networks of gay clinics" (Cooper 2017: 183) specifically for members of the queer community are decades old, especially in larger cities. Early examples include the Howard Brown Health Center (which started in 1974 in Chicago), and gay and lesbian health classes at the Fenway community healthcare center (in Boston). The Brown Health Center, for example, developed mobile STD testing, maintained basic healthcare for approximately 2,500 male patients (and approximately 5,600 patient-visits) in one year, and an infectious disease monitoring program (Ostrow and Shaskey 1977).

Clinics that respect and cater to people in queer communities are becoming more prevalent in larger urban areas as a review of the 2022 and 2023 "State of LGBTQ Health National Surveys" indicate. For example, the 2023 survey indicates that while there were respondents (healthcare professionals who serve queer patients) throughout all 50 U.S. states, a larger percentage of respondents came from states with larger population centers: California (9.5 percent), New York (7 percent), Pennsylvania (6.4 percent), Maryland (5.9 percent), and Florida (5.7 percent) (National Coalition for LGBTQ Health 2024). About 40 percent of respondents indicate they provide services mainly to patients in queer communities wherein they most often provide services related to HIV prevention, STI screening, and counseling, but can provide gender affirming care, provide behavioral health services, and social support too. In the same report, 80 percent of respondents indicated confidence in communicating with queer patients in culturally appropriate ways. Most of the respondents indicated they work in non-profit clinics (13.9 percent), local health departments (13.4 percent), federally qualified health centers

(12.4 percent), and AIDS service organizations (12.2 percent). Only three percent and two percent of respondents indicated they worked for private hospitals/clinics and private practices, respectively. These responses are consistent with agglomeration effects, as well as the institutions that encourage entrepreneur-doctors to develop a business and cater to a relatively niche clientele.

Concierge medicine is another area where we should expect commitments to liberalism aid our efforts to improve health. Concierge medicine (or membership medicine, retainer-based medicine, or direct care) is a healthcare model whereby patients pay for services, sometimes in a tiered system, directly to a doctor. When patients in queer communities demand specialized care, doctors interested in profit opportunities and caring for patients are likely to take advantage of such opportunities and provide healthcare. A far from complete sample of convenience indicates concierge models for queer communities exist (Osra Medical and Higher Self Health in San Francisco, CA; Parker Medical in Las Vegas, NV; The Cove in Castle Rock, CO; Elysium in Atlanta, GA; Integra in Jacksonville, FL; PridePoint in Portland, OR), and they provide many of the same services mentioned above through one-on-one relationships between patients and medical professionals.

Telehealth models, for example, through Amazon's One Medical and Mobile Care Health, can also provide services for queer patients. Telehealth is particularly useful for many in queer communities given higher rates of depression and suicidal thoughts, especially queer youth who might be more prone to depression, anxiety, drug use, and engage in riskier sexual behaviors as they realize their sexual identities (Strongin et al., cited in Harvey and Housel 2014; Berry et al. 2023; Goyal et al. 2025). These developing models are also important for providing gender affirming care for transgendered populations who might face greater discrimination and stigma, who have fewer labor market opportunities, and who have lower incomes (Stoehr et al. 2022; Badgett et al. 2024). Concierge medicine and telehealth services might be pricey, but so are all goods in voluntary market settings. Yet, they improve health and create valuable services for customers—especially customers across the range of queer identities in urban and rural areas who might not want alternative forms of healthcare. Greater competition among providers also will lower such costs. Institutions supporting greater liberalization facilitates innovation in these areas and caters to such groups, their values, and improves healthcare.

Responses to HIV/AIDS

Healthcare for queer communities is all well and good, but what about harder cases where individual freedoms infringe upon the goals of others? Negative externalities or costs imposed on others because of your actions indicate a harder case—one where there are likely more severe tradeoffs between liberty and public health. During an epidemic like HIV/AIDS, for example, some people's risky sexual behavior raises the probability of infection, which can make others worse off. We might expect that if institutions encourage greater social interactions, economic development, population growth, and larger queer communities, there are more opportunities for diseases like HIV/AIDS to spread, larger externalities, and more difficulties associated with its prevention.

Largely spread through risky sexual behaviors, aided by newfound freedoms of association, HIV spread among the population of men who have sex with men in the early 1980s. While such freedoms encouraged diseases to spread, they also encouraged additional opportunities for prevention. Consider bathhouses and sex clubs as a case where values for association, sexual freedom, and public health might clash. These spaces were some of the places where risky sexual activity, for example, unprotected anal intercourse, took place and were often closed by public health authorities during the early years of the HIV/AIDS epidemic—at least in areas with large gay populations like in San Francisco. One estimate indicates there were close to 200 baths and clubs in the United States in 1982; about 30 in LA, 15 in NYC, and 13 in San Francisco (Binson and Woods 2012: 83–87).

While closures might have been appropriate to protect public health when the nature of the disease was unknown, the owners and clients of bathhouses both face incentives to keep bathhouses open and to limit the spread of HIV. Owners would like to stay in business and not have their clients die; similarly, clients are self-interested and want to limit their exposure to HIV, as well as the exposure of partners (for more on on-site externalities and how they are easily resolved, see Leeson and Rouanet 2021). While closures temporarily prevented the spread of HIV among bathhouse users who would have engaged in risky sexual behavior, closures also prevented a process of discovering which responses and rules successfully accomplish the combined goals of owners and clients. Once people learned how HIV spread, prevention was much more likely and limited the public health rationale for intervention. The owners and customers of bathhouses and other clubs, for example, could more easily take appropriate precautions, for example, engage in safer sexual practices like wearing prophylaxis, engaging in oral sex, and so on.

Reports and surveys of bathhouses indicate such responses and rules can pursue these combined objectives. At the behest or in conjunction with owners and managers, these programs included the provision of condoms and lubricant at entry points into clubs, educational posters about safer sexual practices, STI tests, monitoring sexual behaviors, and the removal of violators (Woods et al. 2001, 2010, 2013). That bathhouses might serve customers with different preferences also indicates the appropriateness of HIV prevention in some settings but not others. Some evidence indicates they were successful in some Seattle bathhouses, for example, where clients found testing to be convenient, while bathhouses in LA showed mixed results.

HIV transmission also occurs in more disparate and private places where private actors like the owners of bathhouses and formal rules are less effective at enforcing safer sexual practices. Even in more intimate settings, people and their appreciation for liberalism like the freedoms to associate might encourage preventative behavior. Social norms about condom usage were helpful during the HIV epidemic in the United States, for example, the condom code (Carson 2017). These norms clarified the behavior and the goal—wear condoms to lower the prevalence rate of HIV—and they enforced such rules in a decentralized way among individuals in the community. The development and enforcement of these norms occurred across many private and public settings through individual interactions, conversations, and negotiations with partners about the use of condoms; the support of organizations throughout civil society; and through demonstrations, pamphlets, and marketing campaigns that praised the use of condoms. These norms flooded public spaces from queer book shops and bathhouses to billboards. Overall, the tradeoffs between liberalism and public health are not as severe, given the ability to develop social norms.

Income, agglomeration effects, and underlying liberal economic and political institutions commingle to help people throughout civil society learn about the disease and provide care. Throughout the HIV/AIDS epidemic in the United States, while many people who had acquired the disease became unable to work—they lost income, places to live, and access to healthcare too—many were aided by private and public charity. With greater agglomeration effects and income, driven by liberal economic and political institutions, people have more opportunities to help others in need. Organizations like the Gay Men's Health Crisis (GMHC) and Stand Up in New York, became focal points for members of queer communities to pool resources, learn about HIV and medical breakthroughs, and advocate for policy changes (France 2017).

The Brewers bar in Pittsburgh and the GMHC organization provide additional examples of healthcare related philanthropic responses aided by commercial activity and civil society. Brewers was a popular gay bar prior to the epidemic, and it became a convalescent home for HIV/AIDS patients. Freedoms to associate, to secure property, to exchange, and more generally to use property to pursue one's objectives implicitly aided Andy Usner, the owner of Brewers, to turn the bar into a place to care for patients. GMHC sponsored a hotline for patients, home-based care, and other kinds of social services for HIV patients. Similar freedoms facilitated the responses many took to HIV throughout New York.

By the early 2000s, about two decades after the onset of the HIV/AIDS epidemic, websites and smartphone applications for dating and more intimate interactions also indicate examples of less severe tradeoffs between our economic and social interactions and public health. These websites and apps—developed by entrepreneurs and firms under institutions that encourage private property and innovation—pursue several objectives of people within queer communities. They encourage the development of one's social life, they allow for anonymous interactions if desirable, and they can encourage disease prevention (HIV and other STIs). While serosorting—the matching of sexual partners based on the same HIV/AIDS status—technically prevents the spread of HIV there are challenges related to frequent testing and conversations prior to sexual activities that can limit its effectiveness.[4] Dating websites and geosocial-networking smartphone apps facilitate serosorting in several ways. There are websites and apps, for example, that are explicitly for people who have HIV. Other sites and apps also list HIV status as characteristics people can list on their profiles. Evidence on the effectiveness of website and app-based serosorting is limited and mixed, but one study in London indicates that while 62 percent of partnered respondents on a popular smartphone dating/sex application were (positively and negatively) seroconcordant, riskier sexual activities were more frequently reported among these groups, and they were more likely to discuss their seroconcordance (Goedel et al. 2017).

Tradeoffs between liberalism and public health also seem less severe as people learn about the disease and can better allocate their resources and incomes. Even though income might be positively correlated with risky sexual behaviors, for example, going to clubs, additional incomes encourage testing, prevention, and related healthcare, wherein people might be more likely to avoid infection. For example, one survey of patients in federally qualified health centers in New York suggests that people with higher incomes were more likely to be prescribed PrEP (pre-exposure prophylaxis medication) than those at or below the poverty line (Caponi et al. 2019). Similarly, a survey of outpatient clinic patients with HIV in the United Kingdom indicates that lower socio-economic status is associated with non-adherence to an antiretroviral therapy regimen; financial hardship, unemployment, unstable housing, and not having a college degree were also specifically associated with non-adherence (Burch et al. 2016).

Studies on cash transfers and HIV-related health outcomes also indicate a positive relationship between economic development and public health. Cash transfers, for example, tend to improve HIV-related outcomes (Richterman and Thirumurthy 2022). Recently in Brazil, cash transfers are also associated with a lower incidence, mortality, and case fatality rate of AIDS, which suggests cash recipients are more likely to acquire and consistently receive care and medicines that delay the onset of AIDS (Silva et al. 2024). Such determinants also interact with race, wherein Black populations face higher risk at least in the United States (Pellowski et al. 2013).

One of the main implications of this analysis is that people in queer communities often face less severe tradeoffs between liberalism and public health. Liberal institutions that encourage economic development, increasing productivity, innovation, and higher levels of income, as well as additional freedoms, encourage a mix of infectious and preventative behaviors, wherein people typically adjust to limit their exposure to morbidity and mortality (Geloso et al. 2023; Ogilvie 2025). Liberalism doesn't mean every public health problem is magically resolved, but people in queer communities can improve some aspects of their public health via commitments to liberalism.

A more global perspective might reinforce this approach. In Figure 9.1, the horizontal axis shows the 2020 Global Acceptance Index, a measure of social acceptance for LGBTQ communities (with higher values indicating more acceptance) (Flores 2021); the vertical axis shows 2020 ART coverage as a percentage of people living with HIV with data from the World Bank. Countries with higher GAI scores seem to have higher ART coverage and, moreover, a smaller variance in coverage.

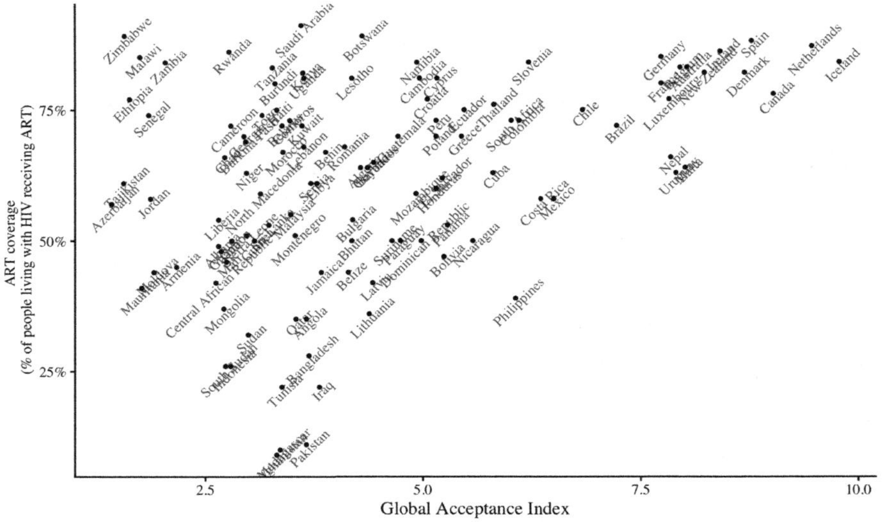

FIGURE 9.1 Social acceptance and HIV/AIDS outcomes

Source: Author's illustration; data sourced from Flores (2021) and World Bank Development Indicators (2026).

Such relationships make sense if we recognize that people with HIV will tend to have more opportunities in areas where people in queer communities are more accepted by others in society. That is, people will have more opportunities to seek medical care and more opportunities to acquire income, employment, and other kinds of relationships that are helpful for managing HIV. There are surely other relevant determinants of ART coverage across the world, for example, income and development assistance for health, and HIV transmission is not exclusive to queer communities, but social acceptance might be relevant. Such factors indicate liberal values related to tolerance might also help develop less severe tradeoffs.

Conclusion

This chapter considers some aspects of queer public health from a mainline political economy analytical perspective and classical liberal normative framework. In addition to the institutional influences upon public health outcomes for LGBTQ people, a related takeaway from this chapter is that private actors might often face incentives to adopt innovative, marginal responses to their public health problems. These responses are tailored to the goals people have given their individual and community values, and they likely include improving public health (see, e.g., LaRose et al. 2025).

Improving public health should account for such responses. Owners of bathhouses are not likely going to be interested in lowering HIV prevalence rates to near zero; but they are interested in ensuring their customers engage in safer sexual practices. Individuals in queer communities might not be interested in developing a clinic for their entire city; but they might be more interested in developing a clinic that caters to the problems queer people face in their community. Moreover, public health officials should then recognize the role institutions—especially liberal institutions that protect property rights and encourage association and tolerance—might play in encouraging these innovative responses.

These insights might also be useful for marginalized populations, for example, younger minority populations. Liberal institutions facilitate, for example, opportunities to use telehealth and, perhaps, concierge medicine in ways they value. Such groups should advocate for greater economic freedom, which tends to alleviate poverty and enhances opportunities people have to creatively respond to public health problems.[5] In lieu of governmental public health responses, which might be lacking or dysfunctional in many areas, liberalism offers a novel pathway to improve both health and flourishing for many people in queer communities.

Finally, the economic way of thinking is a useful lens to view the challenges and tradeoffs between different normative values like liberalism and public health. Alternative views that ignore the goals individuals have, how they might derive marginal, creative responses, and can develop and follow institutions are likely to narrowly constrain the problems people face. As a result, problems might seem more severe. Subsequent studies applying this kind of framework should serve to bolster not only the economic way of thinking but also our understanding of the many tradeoffs people face.

Notes

1 I extend Valocchi's argument beyond gay males, for example, to the larger set of people with queer identities.
2 For full disclosure, I graduated from George Mason University in 2017 with a Ph.D. in economics.
3 Olson (1965) develops a similar argument related to collective action; and for more connections between marginal responses to infectious diseases and collective action problems, see Carson (2022).
4 Assortative matching is common among LGBTQ relationships, especially regarding race and age (Badgett et al. 2024), which indicates additional ways people might limit the spread of HIV (Dow and Philipson 1996).
5 For the effect economic freedom might have on other marginalized groups, for example, women, see Fike (2024) and Grier (2025).

References

Agüero, Jorge M., and Trinidad Beleche. 2017. "Health Shocks and Their Long-Lasting Impact on Health Behaviors: Evidence from the 2009 H1N1 Pandemic in Mexico." *Journal of Health Economics* 54: 40–55.

Ahituv, Avner, V. Joseph Hotz, and Tomas Philipson. 1996. "The Responsiveness of the Demand for Condoms to the Local Prevalence of AIDS." *Journal of Human Resources* 31 (4): 869–897.

Arrow, Kenneth J. 1963. "Uncertainty and the Welfare Economics of Medical Care." *American Economic Review* 53 (5): 941–973.

Atella, Vincenzo, Jay Bhattacharya, and Lorenzo Carbonari. 2012. "Pharmaceutical Price Controls and Minimum Efficacy Regulation: Evidence from the United States and Italy." *Health Services Research* 47 (1): 293–308.

Badgett, M. V. Lee, Christopher S. Carpenter, Maxine J. Lee, and Dario Sansone. 2024. "A Review of the Economics of Sexual Orientation and Gender Identity." *Journal of Economic Literature* 62 (3): 948–994.

Baumol, William J. 1990. "Entrepreneurship: Productive, Unproductive, and Destructive." *Journal of Political Economy* 98 (5): 893–921.

Beauchamp, Dan E. 1976. "Public Health as Social Justice." *Inquiry* 13 (1): 3–14.

Becker, Gary S. 1965. "A Theory of the Allocation of Time." *Economic Journal* 75 (299): 493–517.

Becker, Gary S. 2010. *A Treatise on the Family*. Enlarged edition. Cambridge, MA: Harvard University Press.

Berry, Katie R., Kate Gliske, Clare Schmidt, Ley David Elliette Cray, Michael Killian, and Caroline Fenkel. 2023. "Lesbian, Gay, Bisexual, Transgender, Queer, Intersex, Asexual, and Other Minoritized Gender and Sexual Identities–Adapted Telehealth Intensive Outpatient Program for Youth and Young Adults: Subgroup Analysis of Acuity and Improvement Following Treatment." *JMIR Formative Research* 7 (1): e45796.

Binson, Diane, and William J. Woods. 2012. *Gay Bathhouses and Public Health Policy*. New York, NY: Routledge.

Boettke, Peter J., Christopher J. Coyne, and Peter T. Leeson. 2008. "Institutional Stickiness and the New Development Economics." *American Journal of Economics and Sociology* 67 (2): 331–358.

Brennan, Geoffrey, Lina Eriksson, Robert E. Goodin, and Nicholas Southwood. 2013. *Explaining Norms*. Oxford, UK: Oxford University Press.

Burch, Lisa S, Colette J Smith, Jane Anderson, et al. 2016. "Socioeconomic Status and Treatment Outcomes for Individuals with HIV on Antiretroviral Treatment in the UK: Cross-Sectional and Longitudinal Analyses." *The Lancet. Public Health* 1 (1): e26–36.

Candela, Rosolino A., and Vincent Geloso. 2021. "Economic Freedom, Pandemics, and Robust Political Economy." *Southern Economic Journal* 87 (4): 1250–1266.

Caponi, Mitchell, Carolyne Burgess, Alexandra Leatherwood, and Luis Freddy Molano. 2019. "Demographic Characteristics Associated with the Use of HIV Pre-Exposure Prophylaxis (PrEP) in an Urban, Community Health Center." *Preventive Medicine Reports* 15: 100889.

Carson, Byron. 2017. "The Informal Norms of HIV Prevention: The Emergence and Erosion of the Condom Code." *The Journal of Law, Medicine & Ethics* 45 (4): 518–530.

Carson, Byron. 2022. "Individuals and Externalities in Economic Epidemiology: A Tension and Synthesis." *Journal of Private Enterprise* 37 (3): 1–24.

Cooper, Melinda. 2017. *Family Values: Between Neoliberalism and the New Social Conservatism*. New York, NY: Zone Books.

Dow, William H., and Tomas Philipson. 1996. "An Empirical Examination of the Implications of Assortative Matching on the Incidence of HIV." *Journal of Health Economics* 15 (6): 735–749.

Fike, Rosemarie. 2024. "Economic Freedom and Gender." In *Handbook of Research on Economic Freedom*, edited by Niclas Berggren, 273–296. Cheltenham, UK: Edward Elgar.

Flores, Andrew. 2021. "Social Acceptance of LGBTI People in 175 Countries and Locations, 1981 to 2020." UCLA School of Law, Williams Institute. https://williamsinstitute.law.ucla.edu/projects/gai.

France, David. 2017. *How to Survive a Plague: The Story of How Activists and Scientists Tamed AIDS*. New York, NY: Vintage.

Francis, Andrew M. 2008. "The Economics of Sexuality: The Effect of HIV/AIDS on Homosexual Behavior in the United States." *Journal of Health Economics* 27 (3): 675–689.

Furton, Glenn L. 2023. "The Pox of Politics: Troesken's Tradeoff Reexamined." *Public Choice* 195 (1): 169–191.

Geloso, Vincent. 2021. "Conceptualizing the Cost of COVID Policy: The Role of Institutional Trade-Offs." *The Economists' Voice* 18 (1): 129–136.

Geloso, Vincent, and Jamie Bologna Pavlik. 2020. "Economic Freedom and the Economic Consequences of the 1918 Pandemic." *Contemporary Economic Policy* 39 (2): 255–263.

Geloso, Vincent, Kelly Hyde, and Ilia Murtazashvili. 2021. "Pandemics, Economic Freedom, and Institutional Trade-Offs." *European Journal of Law and Economics* 54 (1): 37–61.

Geloso, Vincent, Kelly Hyde, and Ilia Murtazashvili. 2023. "Disease Mix and How Economic Freedom Matters for Health Outcomes." Cato Institute, Working Paper No. 74. https://www.cato.org/sites/cato.org/files/2023-03/working-paper-74.pdf.

Glaeser, Edward L. 2010. *Agglomeration Economics*. Chicago, IL: University of Chicago Press.

Gluckman, Amy, and Betsy Reed, eds. 1997. *Homo Economics: Capitalism, Community, and Lesbian and Gay Life*. London, UK: Routledge.

Goedel, William C., John A. Schneider, Daniel Hagen, and Dustin T. Duncan. 2017. "Serodiscussion, Perceived Seroconcordance, and Sexual Risk Behaviors Among Dyads of Men Who Have Sex with Men Who Use Geosocial-Networking Smartphone Applications in London." *Journal of the International Association of Providers of AIDS Care (JIAPAC)* 16 (3): 233–238.

Goldstein, K. P., T. J. Philipson, H. Joo, and R. S. Daum. 1996. "The Effect of Epidemic Measles on Immunization Rates." *JAMA* 276 (1): 56–58.

Goyal, Aman, Kamya Thakkar, Haleema Qayyum Abbasi, et al. 2025. "Utilization of Telemedicine in Healthcare Delivery to Lesbian, Gay, Bisexual, Transgender, Queer, Intersex, Asexual, Other Sexual and Gender Minority (LGBTQIA+) Populations: A Scoping Review." *Scientific Reports* 15 (1): 29010.

Grier, Robin. 2025. "The Causal Effect of Economic Freedom on Female Employment & Education." *Contemporary Economic Policy* 43 (4): 698–713.

Grossman, Michael. 1972. "On the Concept of Health Capital and the Demand for Health." *Journal of Political Economy* 80 (2): 223–255.

Harvey, Vickie L., and Teresa Heinz Housel, eds. 2014. *Health Care Disparities and the LGBT Population*. Lanham, MD: Lexington Books.

Kirzner, Israel M. 1978. *Competition and Entrepreneurship*. New edition. Chicago, IL: University of Chicago Press.

LaRose, Rachael Behr, Byron Carson, Anthony M. Carilli, and Justin P. Isaacs. 2025. "Endogenous Public Health Responses in Orthodox Jewish Communities during the COVID-19 Pandemic." *Journal of Institutional Economics* 21: e22.

Leeson, Peter T., and Louis Rouanet. 2021. "Externality and COVID-19." *Southern Economic Journal* 87 (4): 1107–1118.

Mansfield, Edwin. 1986. "Patents and Innovation: An Empirical Study." *Management Science* 32 (2): 173–181.

McKusick, Leon, James A. Wiley, Thomas J. Coates, et al. 1985. "Reported Changes in the Sexual Behavior of Men at Risk for AIDS, San Francisco, 1982–84: The AIDS Behavioral Research Project." *Public Health Reports* 100 (6): 622–629.

Mokyr, Joel. 2000. "Why 'More Work for Mother?' Knowledge and Household Behavior, 1870–1945." *The Journal of Economic History* 60 (1): 1–41.
Mokyr, Joel, and Rebecca Stein. 1996. "Science, Health, and Household Technology: The Effect of the Pasteur Revolution on Consumer Demand." In *The Economics of New Goods*, edited by Timothy F. Bresnahan and Robert J. Gordon, 143–205. Chicago, IL: University of Chicago Press.
National Coalition for LGBTQ Health. 2024. "State of LGBTQ Health™ Second Annual National Survey." https://healthlgbtq.org/stateof/lgbtqhealth-2/
North, Douglass C. 1990. *Institutions, Institutional Change, and Economic Performance*. Cambridge, UK: Cambridge University Press.
Ogilvie, Sheilagh. 2025. *Controlling Contagion: Epidemics and Institutions from the Black Death to Covid*. Princeton, NJ: Princeton University Press.
Olson, Mancur. 1965. *The Logic of Collective Action: Public Goods and the Theory of Groups*. Cambridge, MA: Harvard University Press.
Ostrom, Elinor. 2005. *Understanding Institutional Diversity*. Princeton, NJ: Princeton University Press.
Ostrow, David G., and Dale M. Shaskey. 1977. "The Experience of the Howard Brown Memorial Clinic of Chicago With Sexually Transmitted Diseases." *Sexually Transmitted Diseases* 4 (2): 53–55.
Pellowski, Jennifer A., Seth C. Kalichman, Karen A. Matthews, and Nancy Adler. 2013. "A Pandemic of the Poor: Social Disadvantage and the U.S. HIV Epidemic." *American Psychologist* 68 (4): 197–209.
Philipson, Tomas. 2000. "Chapter 33 Economic Epidemiology and Infectious Diseases." In *Handbook of Health Economics*, edited by A. J. Culyer, Joseph P. Newhouse, Mark V. Pauly, Thomas G. McGuire and Pedro Pita Barros, 1671–1799. Amsterdam, Netherlands: Elsevier.
Philipson, Tomas J., and Richard A. Posner. 1993. *Private Choices and Public Health: The AIDS Epidemic in an Economic Perspective*. Cambridge, MA: Harvard University Press.
Powers, Madison, and Ruth Faden. 2006. *Social Justice: The Moral Foundations of Public Health and Health Policy*. New York, NY: Oxford University Press.
Pritchett, Lant, and Lawrence H. Summers. 1996. "Wealthier Is Healthier." *Journal of Human Resources* 31 (4): 841–868.
Qian, Yi. 2007. "Do National Patent Laws Stimulate Domestic Innovation in a Global Patenting Environment? A Cross-Country Analysis of Pharmaceutical Patent Protection, 1978–2002." *The Review of Economics and Statistics* 89 (3): 436–453.
Richterman, Aaron, and Harsha Thirumurthy. 2022. "The Effects of Cash Transfer Programmes on HIV-Related Outcomes in 42 Countries from 1996 to 2019." *Nature Human Behaviour* 6 (10): 1362–1371.
Silva, Andréa F., Inês Dourado, Iracema Lua, et al. 2024. "Income Determines the Impact of Cash Transfers on HIV/AIDS: Cohort Study of 22.7 Million Brazilians." *Nature Communications* 15 (1): 1307.
Spencer, Melissa K. 2024. "Safer Sex? The Effect of AIDS Risk on Birth Rates." *Journal of Health Economics* 95: 102867.
Stoehr, Jenna Rose, Alireza Hamidian Jahromi, Ezra Leigh Hunter, and Loren S. Schechter. 2022. "Telemedicine for Gender-Affirming Medical and Surgical Care: A Systematic Review and Call-to-Action." *Transgender Health* 7 (2): 117–126.
Troesken, Werner. 2015. *The Pox of Liberty: How the Constitution Left Americans Rich, Free, and Prone to Infection*. Chicago, IL: University of Chicago Press.
Valocchi, Stephen. 2017. "Capitalisms and Gay Identities: Towards a Capitalist Theory of Social Movements." *Social Problems* 64 (2): 315–331.
Wicksteed, Philip H. 1910. *The Commonsense of Political Economy, including a Study of the Human Basis of Economic Law*. London: Macmillan. Accessed

online: Liberty Fund, Online Library of Liberty. https://oll.libertyfund.org/titles/wicksteed-the-commonsense-of-political-economy.
Woods, William J., Diane Binson, Tracy J. Mayne, L. Robert Gore, and Greg M. Rebchook. 2001. "Facilities and HIV Prevention in Bathhouse and Sex Club Environments." *Journal of Sex Research* 38 (1): 68–74.
Woods, William J., Jason Euren, Lance M. Pollack, and Diane Binson. 2010. "HIV Prevention in Gay Bathhouses and Sex Clubs across the United States." *Journal of Acquired Immune Deficiency Syndromes* 55 (Suppl 2): S88–90.
Woods, William J., Nicolas Sheon, Joseph A. Morris, and Diane Binson. 2013. "Gay Bathhouse HIV Prevention: The Use of Staff Monitoring of Patron Sexual Behavior." *Sexuality Research & Social Policy : Journal of NSRC : SR & SP* 10 (2): 77–86.
World Bank. 2026. World Development Indicators. https://databank.worldbank.org/source/world-development-indicators.

10

TRANSPHOBIA AS A PERVERSE EMERGENT PHENOMENON

S. Elliot Bowers and Mikayla Novak

Transgender people are a part of the broader fabric of diverse contemporary societies, and historical accounts of transgender individuals and communities have been the subject of academic research inquiries (e.g., Feinberg 1997; Stryker 2017). Although there is no harmonized definition of transgender status, and public images and stereotypes about transgenderism are themselves non-uniform, the conception of transgender adopted in this chapter is that it denotes, or otherwise relates to, a person whose gender identity does not correspond with the sex registered for them at birth. Although statistical counts of transgender people do vary, it is reasonable to suggest in general that the transgender population share in any given nation is likely to be small.[1]

Difficulties experienced by transgender people throughout the world are often said to stem from societal prejudice. In numerous cases, transgender individuals have suffered from discrimination, harassment, and even violence within various intimate and public settings. These problems not only have adverse cultural and social implications but carry through to poorer economic outcomes relative to the general population. Members of the transgender community have also suffered insufficient access to public sector services, as well as barriers surrounding legal recognition of preferred gender status. The complex and often intersecting array of disadvantages and inequities experienced by transgender and other gender non-conforming individuals are collectively labeled in academic and public policy literature, and throughout public commentaries, as "transphobia."

The key proposition of this chapter is to argue that transphobia is an example of what has been described in recent social theory literatures as "perverse emergent order" (Martin and Storr 2008; Johnson 2010; Harrison 2018; Tuszynski 2021). The concept of emergent (or spontaneous) order is an esteemed one within the social sciences, as it refers to the possibility of generative patterns of order in human

DOI: 10.4324/9781003615781-10

interaction and conduct that do not result from the enunciation and implementation of commands or edicts from a singular authority. As canonically explained by Adam Ferguson ([1767] 2007: 119), emergent orders are "the result of human action, but not the execution of any human design." In other words, "most social outcomes, particularly functional and orderly processes, are more often and better understood as the unplanned by-products of decentralized human interactions" (D'Amico 2015: 118). This understanding of spontaneous order is a cornerstone of the tradition known as "mainline political economy" (MPE) (Boettke 2012; Aligica et al. 2021).

Many identifiable emergent orders – such as language, law, markets, money, and science – are commonly perceived to be benign from the standpoint of human welfare. Our appending of the term "perverse" to "emergent order" is intended to indicate that some kinds of order are, to the contrary, prejudicial to the interests of at least some participants within such evolving interactive situations. Transphobia is one of these. In drawing attention to transphobia as a case of perverse emergent order, this chapter presents an underutilized framing to comprehend the attributes of transphobia, understand the mechanisms that reproduce transphobia in society, and identify the implications of emergent order analysis for redressing transphobic incidence.

The structure of this chapter is as follows. The next section discusses the main features of emergent orders within a classical liberal framework and engages with literature alluding to perverse characteristics and effects of such orders. The status of transphobia as an example of a perverse emergent order is then discussed. This is followed by arguments that the complex and multifaceted attributes of transphobia lend itself to a queer classical liberal (QCL) understanding of the benefits of decentralized, bottom-up approaches to help redress transphobic incidence and effects. This is followed by concluding remarks.

General characteristics of liberal order theory, and the possibility of perversity

General properties of emergent order, and normative implications

The classical liberal intellectual tradition, and the MPE tradition closely associated with it, are arguably at the forefront of intellectual inquiry into the conditions and ramifications of humanly devised orders.[2] In his investigations of the properties of order, Hayek (1973: 36) defines order as

> a state of affairs in which a multiplicity of elements of various kinds are so related to each other that we may learn from our acquaintance with some spatial or temporal part of the whole to form correct expectations concerning the rest, or at least expectations which have a good chance of proving correct.

Orders are understood to be critical to the achievement of not only individual objectives but to the fulfillment of social cooperation. Importantly from the liberal perspective, a functional order can facilitate cooperative outcomes over time, as institutions (and other persistent structures) emerge to both inform expectations as to how to productively and harmoniously act in the world and to incentivize mutually beneficial patterns of human interactivity.

It appears commonplace for scholars and commentators to attribute human order to explicit instances of conscious design by specific agents, or similarly the imposition of esoteric priorities or plans by a given person (or elitist group of persons) upon the remainder of the members of a society. The affairs of government, consisting of its numerous offices and organizations, is regarded as an emblematic contemporary example of a planned order.[3] Firms serve as ubiquitous modes of economic organization in the modern world, which only reinforces widespread impressions to the effect that order must be designed or imposed by planners. What Hayek describes as the "*taxis*" of a planned order is intended to serve a concrete objective, or set of objectives, as specified by those personnel implicated in the design of such order.

What is distinctive about the liberal contribution to order theory is its contrastive explication of a *spontaneous order* idea, or what we synonymously prefer to call *emergent order*. Cases of emergent order were described by Hayek as instances of "*cosmos*," human activities informed by open-ended processes of a nonteleological character and whose outcomes can be imagined, but not preempted or predicted, *ex-ante*. In modern intellectual history the distinctive position of liberal order theory originated with the likes of Adam Smith, David Hume, and other leading figures of the Scottish Enlightenment, through to Austrian economists such as Carl Menger, Ludwig von Mises, and Hayek, and the modern mainline economics of Don Lavoie and Peter Boettke.

Discussions of emergent order are synonymous with analytical and normative depictions of market processes. A good explanatory account of the market as an emergent order, and why the emergently ordered properties of markets are salient to liberals, is represented by the following quote:

> The most significant lesson economics has to offer is that people's activities can be coordinated through the market mechanism to produce a spontaneous order, without anybody planning or designing the outcome. Everybody makes their own individual plans, and the institutions of the market coordinate these individual plans so that, in general, people's plans can be realized, and people can make the best use of the information they possess to produce an outcome that works best for the prosperity of everyone. This insight goes back at least to Adam Smith … who noted that individuals pursuing their own interests are led by an invisible hand to do what provides the greatest benefit for everyone. A comparison of the outcomes of the centrally planned socialist economies of the twentieth century with capitalist economies shows that no central plan is necessary for a desirable outcome, and that, more typically,

the outcome of a spontaneous order is more desirable than the outcome of a top-down plan.

(Holcombe 2020: 6–7)

A non-trivial aspect of the growth and development of modern intellectual thought rests in the expansive identification of human arrangements as examples of emergent order. Michael Polanyi (1962) identified the ideas and similar intellectual schema being generated by the scientific disciplines as another example of spontaneous order. Hayek (1973) and others have suggested that the regularities of the common law emerged as the consequence of legal decisions concerning appropriate adjudicative responses to localized and esoteric disputes, and related conflicts, that have ensued over time.

Other examples of emergent order may be recounted, but it is significant for our purposes that several modern scholars have identified emergent aspects surrounding cultural phenomena.[4] While numerous aspects of human existence are encapsulated in definitions of culture – covering such personal and interpersonal phenomena as cognitive beliefs as well as social customs, practices, and traditions – emergent order theorists generally agree that cultures are generative phenomena arising from shared meanings, senses, and understandings that have persisted (Storr and John 2020). Furthermore, and despite certain attempts throughout human history to ensure otherwise (say, through colonization, the exercise of political totalitarianism, and other efforts to eliminate alternative belief systems and their human carriers), culture is not necessarily centrally directed or planned by any single individual or authority. Hayek (1988) is noted for having advanced a theory of "cultural evolution" suggesting that cultural norms that persist over the long run are those which tend to underpin material prosperity and population growth.

As noted, emergent order theorists recognize that generative patterns of order can assist in the achievement of human purposes. "The patterned nature of the order, in a way, helps the various actors within the system better fulfill their separate goals, because it offers them some reliable predictability from which to inform their plans" (D'Amico 2015: 116). The critical distinction underlying the emergent order notion is that "orderliness was not historically intended or designed by any of the individual actors that nonetheless constitute and contribute to it. Furthermore, no individual could have possibly designed the orderly outcome, neither within the system nor apart from the system" (D'Amico 2015). In other words, "most social outcomes, particularly functional and orderly processes, are more often and better understood as the unplanned by-products of decentralized human interactions" (D'Amico 2015: 118). Individual agents within spontaneously ordered contexts can, and do, use their foresight and ingenuity to effectuate their unique plans under the unique circumstances of time and place they experience. Therefore, the aggregated emanations or outcomes derived from emergent orders, nonetheless, cannot be attributed to the actions of any singular individual or given collective group.[5]

There is no coincidence that emergent orders have proven to be a focal point of conceptualization and analysis in liberal theory, as pointed out earlier. Patterns arising from an emergent process, and which may become institutionally sedimented, cannot possibly be replicated (or otherwise transformed) by aspiring societal planners and reformers. An important reason why is that

> [s]ince a spontaneous order results from the individual elements adapting themselves to circumstances which directly affect only some of them, and which in their totality need not be known to anyone, it may extend to circumstances so complex that no mind can comprehend them all.
>
> (Hayek 1973: 41)

Grasping the intricacies of an emergent order is seen to be beyond the epistemic grasp of any given individual (or any given groups of individuals), and it would be to commit the fallacy of "synoptic delusion" to believe that emergent orders can be reproduced or remodeled through conscious (re)design (Hayek 1973: 14). These insights are pivotal to the contemporary classical liberal critique of governmental intervention toward the market and society.

Perverse emergent orders

A final consideration that warrants attention concerns questions about the effects of emergent orders on human well-being. An impression that may be gleaned from liberal theory is that emergent orders are generally benign in their effects, and that this arguably leads to a certain degree of valorization of emergent order (or *cosmos*) vis-à-vis planned order (or *taxis*). Recent scholarship has sought to rectify this impression by chronicling that certain emergently developed orders exist which may promote an array of social harms, or at least bring forth arrangements that are deemed as unsatisfactory for at least some individuals.

The possibility that the operation or effects of certain emergent orders may be less than ideal from a welfare standpoint was recognized in Hayek's own works in political philosophy. Certainly, an emergent order has the potential to service "the multiplicity of separate and incommensurable ends of all of its separate members" (Hayek 1976: 108). But it is also the case that the "character of the resulting order" would be "very indeterminate and by itself certainly would not be sufficient to give it a beneficial character" (Hayek 1973: 45). Consider, for example, that "[t]he fact that law that has evolved ... has certain desirable properties does not prove that it will always be good law or even that some of its rules may not be very bad" (Hayek 1973: 88).

Others have sensed that Hayek's emergent order account does not preclude unsatisfactory outcomes. Whitman (1998), Caldwell (2000), and Angner (2004) have estimated that Hayek's theory of cultural evolution does countenance, at least implicitly, the prospect of undesirable cultural configurations arising as the by-product of interactions between people. Indeed, certain cultures that are prone to inhibit the realization of certain important normative values that people may ordinarily aspire to – such as production, saving, respect for property, etc. – may persist, therefore limiting the capacity of certain cultures to achieve material prosperity (and values associated with this, such as peace, prosperity, and happiness). This may occur through a diffuse process of meaning construction and sense-making among individuals which ingrains norms *qua* expectations about how one should behave and conduct themselves in the world, with gradated penalties such as social sanctions applicable to those who deviate from the norms.

Acknowledgement of the existence of perverse emergent orders can be found elsewhere. A description of certain orders with malign societal effects is given by Robert Nozick (1974) in his seminal tract, *Anarchy, State, and Utopia*. Examples cited include the patterns of spatial segregation consistent with Thomas Schelling's (1971) famous agent-based model, patterns of class stratification, the effects of government intervention on markets and macroeconomic stability, and the failure of collective action episodes owing to free-riding behaviors by non-paying, non-participant individuals. Economist Israel Kirzner (1982: 8) similarly recognized that theorists have "claimed, correctly or otherwise, to perceive theory as showing the systematic emergence of social *im*moralities or social *in*efficiencies." He elsewhere describes how phenomena as diverse as urban congestion and arms races suggest that "whether benign or otherwise, these spontaneous processes proceed as they do because each step taken systematically renders it more rational for other similar steps to be taken by others. This results in the familiar snowballing effect" (Kirzner 1990: 44).[6]

Scholarly interest in perverse emergent orders reawakened with a 2008 contribution by Nona Martin and Virgil Storr. It was here that they identified that

> [l]ike language, the common law, society itself and other positive spontaneous orders, perverse emergent orders are the result of human action but not human design. But, unlike positive spontaneous orders, perverse emergent orders cannot be said to be socially beneficial.
>
> (Martin et al. 2008: 74)

Given that "the spontaneous character of a social order does not, by itself, guarantee that the order will be beneficial" (Martin et al. 2008: 75), Martin and Storr suppose that "judgments regarding the nature of spontaneous orders (i.e., is it socially harmful or socially beneficial?) cannot be decided by pointing to the fact that a particular order emerged spontaneously" (Martin et al. 2008: 86).

The perpetuation of "negative belief systems" features prominently in Martin and Storr's work. Negative belief systems are "a range of beliefs and cultural attitudes that might hamper individual and social progress" (Martin et al. 2008: 74), and may be modeled as an example of arrangements which emerge as a by-product of human interaction but which, nevertheless, render harms at least to certain sub-groups within society. Discrimination may be classed as a form of negative belief system, with the effect that "[w]hen members of the discriminated group are less successful than members of other groups who are not similarly constrained or locked out of opportunities to better themselves, the system of prejudice is reinforced" (Martin et al. 2008). Again, the enforcement of a perverse order such as this can arise as multiple (if not large) numbers of people form coherent expectations, and can effectively punish deviation from adherence to those expectations. Negative belief systems are said to emerge without any central direction by any given person (or identifiable sub-group) but, nevertheless, can be self-reinforcing because, *inter alia*, of a degree of mutual recognition and acceptance of "rules concerning who to target" (Martin et al. 2008).[7]

Tuszyniski (2021) built upon Martin and Storr's formative approach to further explore perverse emergent orders as an attribute of relational entanglements between political and commercial organizations within the social environment. This "entangled" approach to political economy leads to an appreciation of the fact that "[f]ew orders emerge within a pure market context, and few political actions are able to be fully centrally planned" (Tuszyniski 2021: 87). Combining this situational reality with the observation that "people are alert to opportunities to better their circumstances in all environments" suggests that "some emergent orders might evolve which are considered perverse from the standpoint of those participating in those orders" (Tuszyniski 2021). A corollary of the entangled and emergent contexts in which individuals and groups interact is that

> it is not always clear whether systemic failures are due to a failure of the marketplace or a failure of the political system. This makes perverse emergent orders all the more pernicious; it is often unclear whether further political actions or a movement back toward a market order would remedy the situation.
>
> (Tuszyniski 2021: 88)

From these theoretical investigations have come a variety of papers focusing upon specific cases of perverse emergent orders. Charles Johnson draws upon feminist theory of "rape culture" to describe patriarchal systems of gender relations as an example, in which "women's social being – how women appear and act, as women in public – will be *systematically* and *profoundly* circumscribed by a diffuse, decentralized threat of violence" (Johnson 2010: 13). Johnson illustrates the constraining effects of threats (and practices) of sexual violence against women upon the exercise of female individual agency:

> restrictions on women's everyday lives, their use and exploration of public space, what they feel they can safely do or say, especially in the presence of men, simply mean that women's freedom is systematically constrained by the

> fear of men, as a ripple-effect of the danger of widespread, intense, random male violence, and the practical need to solicit the aid of some seemingly safe man for protection against the threat other men create. ... while some of the "intimidation" ... [as perceived by women] ... is expressed in self-conscious adjustment to felt dangers and explicit warnings, a lot of it is tacitly inscribed in everyday relationships, or simply incorporated into an intensification of the sort of small-scale, subconscious acts of vigilance and self-protection that we all carry out, as a daily routine, or as an expression of felt anxiety.
>
> (Johnson 2010: 12)

Johnson generalizes his case study to make the broader point that "nothing *conceptually* requires that emergent orders need be *benign* orders" (Johnson 2010: 11). Furthermore,

> [i]f widely distributed forms of intelligence, knowledge, virtue, or prudence can add up, through many individual self-interested actions, into a benign undesigned orders [*sic.*], there's no reason why widely distributed forms of ignorance, prejudice, folly or vice might not add up into unintended, malign orders.
>
> (Johnson 2010)

Another useful contribution to literature is presented by Caleb Harrison (2018), who argues that the socio-cultural phenomenon of white supremacy is a perverse emergent order. White supremacy is defined by Harrison as a societal configuration wherein "whites dominate over non-whites, whether that be through judicial or non-juridicial means" (Harrison 2018: 241). White supremacy is classified as a perverse emergent order because the unequal patterning of societal benefits favoring whites results from environments in which individuals are "responding to local knowledge of the environment from a potentially wide variety of motives within the limits defined by the system of rules in force in the group" (Harrison 2018: 242). This local knowledge is inclusive of scenarios in which the expectation is accepted that whites would be advantaged, and non-whites not, in widespread social scenarios. As Harrison states, "[w]idespread ideas of white entitlement and superiority in America, whether they are consciously endorsed or unconsciously acted on, dispose Americans to respond in a patterned way" (Harrison 2018: 243) reinforcing relational dominance of whites over blacks (and other racial minorities).

Applying perverse emergent order theory to the case of transphobia

Manifestations of transphobia

The challenging conditions and outcomes experienced by transgender individuals and communities have been regarded as symptoms of a broader phenomenon known as "transphobia." One study refers to transphobia as "the disgust toward individuals not conforming to society's gender expectations" (Bandini and Maggi 2014: 49). Another study notes that

> [s]imilar to homophobia, the fear or aversion to homosexuals, transphobia involves the feeling of revulsion to masculine women, feminine men, cross-dressers, transgenderists, and/or transsexuals. … transphobia manifests itself in the fear that personal acquaintances may be trans or disgust upon encountering a trans person.
>
> (Hill and Willoughby 2005: 533–534)

U.K. advocacy group TransActual acknowledges the complexities of transphobia but ultimately argues that "[t]he core value underlying all transphobia is a rejection of trans identity and a refusal to acknowledge that it could possibly be real or valid" (TransActual 2024). Explanations for transphobic conduct typically refer to cognitive and psychological perspectives surrounding individual antipathy toward perceived non-conforming behaviors along gendered criteria, which is reflected in socio-cultural and institutional biases against those identifying as transgender or gender non-conforming.

Transphobia is an important problem from the perspective of personal autonomy and freedom of expression with respect to gender. Manifestations of transphobia are numerous and complex, ranging from stigmatic verbal expressions of disgust or ridicule through to physical acts of violence against those who do not conform to conventional gendered expectations. The effects of transphobia are economically significant, with studies showing that transgender people suffering relatively higher unemployment, lower wages, and higher poverty rates when compared against the general population (e.g., Leppel 2016; Badgett et al. 2019; Ciprikis et al. 2020; Shannon 2022). Critics of transphobia also refer to it as imparting adverse socio-cultural effects, including limitations of movement, social isolation, delays or self-refusals to engage in self-expression, reduced personal self-esteem, and suicide and suicidal ideation (Novak 2016: 38–39).

Generic properties of transphobia as a perverse emergent order

In this section, we indicate that transphobia qualifies as another case of a perverse emergent order. But to do this, we must first understand the socio-cultural dimensions attributable to gender expression and identity. In this regard, it is said that many human societies sustain beliefs according valuational esteem toward seeing gender as discrete and polar categories, that are reproduced over time (Butler 1988). In contemporary Western societies, if not elsewhere, priority is given to the fixity of binarized categories of male and female both as a naturalized and normative preference and which, furthermore, correspond with male-female biological sex distinctions (c.f., Fausto-Sterling 2020). As identified by feminists and critical social theorists, this gendered convention also elevates behavioral distinctions and stereotypical variations between men and women.[8]

The underlying basis of transphobia, and the acts, expressions, and sentiments associated with it, is that fixed and binary gender precepts are prioritized as rules that ought to be followed by members of society. In other words, transphobia arises from the social expectation that one's gender is fixed and limited to binary categorizations of male and female. Fluid expressions of gender – or, otherwise, gendered expressions and identities deviating from fixed and binary expectations – are to be repressed, and as indicated this can take the form of discrimination, prejudice, ostracism, or victimization of transgender (and other gender non-conforming) people. Transphobia is perverse because it harms those whose gender identity or expression is stigmatized. But what makes transphobia an *emergent order*? To answer this, we are going to draw from Harrison's (2018) analysis of white supremacy as an emergent order, transposing the logic of racialized orders to the case of the gender order.

Transphobia emerges from the actions, and interactions, of large numbers of people in an environment that allows them to draw satisfactory expectations about appropriate (and inappropriate) modes of conduct. Craig and Goodman (2023) indicate that gender is one of the more fundamental-yet-pervasive socio-cultural categories about which individuals can learn and emulate to help coordinate our plans with others. It is true that individuals act based on their knowledge of the idiosyncratic spatial, temporal, and socio-cultural environments in which they live, and they additionally respond to their environment in ways that are informed by a potentially wide variety of motives (Harrison 2018), but gender is often seen as important in imparting a semblance of structure to, and stable expectations in, an otherwise chaotic world. The predominance of fixed, binary gendered conceptions reflects upon its normalization and sustainability over generations and so, given that adherence to such conceptions of gender is what people are commonly expected to conform to, gender may be aptly represented as an institution (Craig and Goodman 2023).

Complementing its function in undergirding socio-cultural expectations the "cis-normative" gender standard applies as a practical heuristic appraising the appropriateness of gendered modes of expression and identity. Gender attributes effectively provide a set of instructional "dispositions to respond – to see, feel, or possibly judge something – in a patterned way" (Harrison 2018: 243). If most people adhere to beliefs and practices to the effect that gender is (and ought to be) fixed and binary, and they do, it is then likely that transgender and other gender non-conformists will endure majoritarian disapproval as well as galvanize mistrust toward those transgressing the gender norms (Harrison 2018: 238–241; Jones et al. 2018). As the following quotation indicates, a lack of trust toward those who transgress gender conventions has tended in modern societies to assume a pathological dimension:

> those who dispute gender fluidity and trans identities do so both in dismissing their existence, by re-asserting gender as a biological binary, but also through

> the implication that gender fluidity is a form of social perversion. They seek to rhetorically dismiss that gender identity is a form of identity that morally requires respect, by categorizing it as delusional or at least, a mistaken view about gender.
>
> (Malamet 2018: 19)

The longevity of institutional rules is grounded in the sense of legitimation conferred to them. If we assume that cisnormativity is expected, and therefore widely held as a *desideratum*, it follows that fluid expressions of gender (or, otherwise, gendered expressions and identities that deviate from the fixed and binary constructions) are to be repressed. The most extreme case of gender-based rule enforcement is that attempted through violence waged against transgender individuals. As Martin and Storr (2008: 78) described it, "violence … rarely involves indiscriminate violence; it is usually aimed at the persons or property of members of particular groups. Stated another way, social violence is rule-governed." A key issue for transgender communities is that violent modalities of gender norm enforcement, and transphobic actions more generally, tend to be diffuse and stochastic by nature.[9] A lack of predictability surrounding when, and under what circumstances, a transgender (or other gender non-conforming) person might be confronted by violence is posited to constrain, to some extent, a preparedness to display, express, or otherwise reveal diverse gender expression and identity that transgress conventional attitudes and practices.

Actions within orders: Reconciling transphobia as an emergent order with deliberate acts of transphobia

The rule-following aspects of gender as an institution impart an impression that individuals are passively adhering to the gender arrangements that have prevailed in society, and have no grounds to challenge or question them. The existence of gender non-conformity rebuts this impression. But it is also true that the gender conventions that give rise to transphobia do not literally materialize out of thin air. Recall that decentralized kinds of agency and intentionality are not ruled out by emergent order theorists, but that any single individual or specific group is not complicit in the formation and persistence of a given emergent order (beneficial or perverse) in its totality.

Even a casual inspection of contemporary social and political developments suggests that there are conscious efforts throughout the polycentric ramparts of society to reinforce the fixed, binary gender norm. Gender is an active process of social construction, with transphobia creating a set of regular expectations about how people will behave and what type of stigma and coercion people might face if they deviate from those expectations (specifically, that gender will be manifested in fixed, binary ways). From the standpoint of an order theory grounded in the need to establish common expectations about how to act and interact in the world, transphobic activities may be interpreted as reinforcement of cultural, social, and political contexts affirming the primacy of fixed, binary gender behaviors, roles, and understandings.[10]

Certain activists and organizations – such as conservative lawmakers, theologians, moral campaigners, social media influencers, and the like – have communicated transphobic sentiments as a way of framing their concerns to preserve conventional meanings and understandings surrounding gender issues. During the 2020s, there has been a noticeable increase in contentious political activity surrounding transgender and other gender non-conforming individuals, on issues as diverse as bathroom access, sports participation, incarceration, and the medical treatment of minors. Governments in the United States, Britain, and elsewhere have introduced legislation in response to these issues,[11] and have foreshadowed additional restrictions of rights and liberties including an inability to change gender status on official documentations. Anti-trans activists have also targeted several corporations and civil societal organizations which have been seen to be supportive of transgender issues and concerns.[12]

Transphobia does not require centralized planning or coordination for it to manifest itself in the world. Nonetheless, it is the case that well organized, and intentional, activities are being carried out to bolster conventional gender institutions and, as a part of that, to denigrate perceived acts and beliefs regarding gender non-conformity. These activities may be interpreted as adding to the complexities and subtleties of transphobia as a perverse emergent order, with significant implications for the well-being of those who wish to articulate, express, or identify with gendered arrangements falling outside the scope of the fixed, binary gender understandings and sensibilities.

Addressing the perverse emergent order of transphobia: Combining polycentric awareness with non-statist forms of redress

Against state-centric approaches to resolving all aspects of transphobia

As we have described thus far, transphobia is a perverse emergent order. The belief that gender identity is both fixed and binary becomes – either through gendered rule-following behavior in everyday life or values-oriented activism surrounding the propriety of gender institutions – an aspect of "conventional wisdom," and transphobic acts and sentiments attach to the emergent beliefs about gender that have come to assume socio-cultural dominance. Innumerable individuals, organizations, and groups are implicated in the development and persistence of gender conventions in complex ways. Gender certainly conveys a set of expectations about how to behave and to identify, but there exists no centralized "Department for the Suppression of Gender Vices and Promotion of Gender Virtues" that designs, propagates, and institutionalizes gender norms.[13] The emergent character of transphobia goes some way toward explaining the largely, though not exclusively, non-state complexion of distaste and hostility toward gender fluidity and dynamism.

The experience of transphobia – and the losses of economic, financial, and social opportunities associated with abuse, discrimination, and violence against gender diverse forms of being, knowing, and doing – have led to calls by transgender people and their allies for negation of these systems of belief and practices. However, the emergent character and complex manifestations of transphobia, and not to mention the deep-seated expectations surrounding conformity with fixed, binary gender norms, suggest that it is difficult to apprehend all aspects of the problem straightforwardly. Also, "a people's cultural system can be quite resistant to change. Cultural habits tend to endure and are actually quite difficult to alter" (Martin and Storr 2008: 85). This is not to suggest, however, that transphobia *qua* emergent order cannot be redressed. Indeed, such a desire for reform rests upon a general proposition that we "may be in a position to alter *at least some* of the rules of conduct which the elements obey, [and] we shall thereby be able to influence … the general character … of the resulting order" (Hayek, cited in Harrison 2018: 249).

There may be an instinctual temptation to repel transphobic norms through legal, regulatory, and other statist means. This reflects the dominance of political action in contemporary human affairs and the concomitant presentation of modern politics as a comprehensive "corrective" for social ills. Our position is that some care needs to be taken when subscribing to a state-centric response to any perverse emergent orders, including transphobia. Not all forms of harm experienced by transgender people come as a direct result of governmental activities, but the modern state itself does have a checkered record on the question of protecting gender non-conformists. Indeed, state repression of deviations from cis-normative expression and identity has been (and continues to be) the empirical reality in many parts of the world. Examples include police harassment and violence (e.g., Stenerson et al. 2022; Stenerson et al. 2024); repression of assembly through prostitution, temperance, vagrancy, and other laws (e.g., Spade 2015; Bolivar 2017); regulatory allowance of conversion therapies and other forms of pathologization (e.g., Inch 2016; Campbell and Rodgers 2023); refusal to accept changes to gender identity markers on official documents (e.g., Maier 2020; Obasi and Nick 2023; U.S. Department of State 2025), and so on.

Due to its touted capacities to enforce changes within the broader society, activists may express a willingness to privilege governmental solutions as the means to combat transphobia and the cis-normative sentiments which arguably underpin it. We do not question the significance of legal and regulatory reforms easing the barriers imposed upon the ability of individuals self-identifying their preferred gender status,[14] and to have that preferred status recognized in identity documents and in the context of public services access (Novak 2016). Reformist projects in relation to the treatment of transgender people in criminal justice contexts, education, and health and aged care will necessarily involve interactions with legislators and other public officials, given the dominant role of government in these activities.

Skepticism of solely political measures to redress transphobia not only rests upon observation of the decidedly patchy relationships between the state and transgender citizen-voters. Drawing upon order theory, we sketch out in this chapter certain dimensions of transphobia may originate from beyond the political realm, and may well remain non-political in their character. As has been stated elsewhere on a similar subject, but which has applicability to the transphobia problem, "[a]ggression towards women and sexual minorities is often diffuse and unplanned. Part of the response to it has to be similarly grounded in everyday practices rather than state policies" (Cowen 2013: 29). The significance of understanding transphobia as a perverse emergent order is that it widens our analytical and investigatory lenses to better understand the contexts contributing to it. This understanding should then help ensure that any interventions (driven politically or not) can appropriately alter those contexts, hopefully improving the lived experiences of people and communities affected by transphobia.

Roles and contributions of transgender grassroots organizations to redress transphobia

Consistent with the rise of sexual and gender politics in Western countries over the past few decades there has been a notable increase in the number of transgender advocacy and support organizations. In the U.S. context, Nownes (2019) has noted the presence of transgender rights interest groups both at national and state levels, as well as efforts by other queer advocacy bodies to include transgender and other gender-diverse constituencies. From a handful of entities aiming to represent the interests of transgender people in the early 1960s, Nownes counted over 80 U.S. transgender organizations that existed in 2016. While political lobbying is a feature of transgender organizations such as the Advocates for Trans Equality, Transgender Law Center, and other bodies, efforts at political representation by no means represent the sum of activities undertaken by members of the transgender community. It appears that numerous bodies which organize political advocacy on behalf of transgender people also provide a host of social and support services that may assist in overcoming transphobia (including by building greater self-acceptance regarding gender nonconformity).[15]

Numerous transgender organizations seek to provide opportunities for transgender, non-binary, and other gender non-conforming individuals to strengthen resilience by building peer social networks. In Los Angeles, for example, Gender Justice LA (https://gjla.nationbuilder.com) is a grassroots organization that "organizes, holds space, provides resources, and collaborates with others so that our communities can: resist oppression, develop community responses to violence, heal from present and historical trauma, and come together in ways that feel brave and affirming." On the East Coast, bodies such as the New York Transgender Advocacy Group (NYTAG) (https://www.nytag.org), TransNewYork (https://transnewyork.org), and Translatinx Network (https://translatinxnetwork.org) provide a range of peer support services for individuals and groups, educational services for corporations and service practitioners, and building community leadership.

Similar activities by transgender advocacy and support organizations are outside of the United States. In the United Kingdom, TransActual (https://transactual.org.uk) provides networking opportunities for transgender and other gender diverse people, as well as workshops, information, and advisory services for health sector workers and other professionals that engage with community members. The Trans Programme provided by the Manchester-based LGBT Foundation (https://lgbt.foundation/trans-programme) offers workshops, events, and community groups that, *inter alia*, aim to build community resilience and reduce isolation. Efforts by these and other transgender community groups have been described by writer Shon Faye (2021) as key lines of activity within a broader polycentric tapestry of trans activism in the United Kingdom, which is not limited to political lobbying efforts. In addition to the activities described here, "trans people have adopted tactics including charity and community organizing, mutual aid groups, solidarity funds, demonstrations, protest marches, and coordinated social media campaigns" (Sharp 2024).

Numerous associations exist throughout continental Europe to help strengthen social ties among transgender people, and to counter transphobia within society. A German association for trans men, TransMann eV (https://transmann.de), provides a range of opportunities for interaction such as "group meetings, online information, peer-to-peer advice, information materials, events, training courses, public appearances, as well as a leisure platform and sponsorship project." Meanwhile, an umbrella organization in Germany known as Bundesverband Trans (BVT) (https://www.bundesverband-trans.de), aims for a "reduction of (psycho-) pathologization and stigmatization" of gender diverse communities including through "the elimination of discrimination against multiply marginalized people such as refugees, trans* people, sex workers or people with disabilities." Many transgender advocacy groups have developed mature networks not only nationally but across the European Union area.

Looking wider afield geographically, we also see efforts in the Asia-Pacific region, the Gender Centre based in Sydney, Australia, provides a range of support groups facilitating social connections and providing support for gender transitioning (https://gendercentre.org.au/support-groups). The Centre also provides counselling and professional advice to support transgender individuals transitioning in the workplace. Transgender Victoria (https://www.tgv.org.au) is another Australian group providing an array of services to promote community resilience, including an "Affirmation Station" initiative hosting gender-affirming activities, workshops, and services. In New Zealand, Gender Minorities Aotearoa (https://genderminorities.com) provides an array of activities including advocacy work to address transphobic sentiments within the community. Efforts to "de-pathologize trans people" is identified as a priority, as well as "campaigning or working with media to improve public perception of trans people." Complementing such initiatives are a host of activities aiming to connect transgender and other gender diverse communities, including peer support services and physical and online social events.

Numerous transgender collectives perform crucial socio-cultural work aimed at ameliorating the causes and effects of transphobia. These include collaborative efforts to eliminate negative internalized feelings resulting from repeated exposure to transphobic norms, as well as seeking to normalize transgender lives in public perceptions by, in part, working with coalitions to counter transphobic stereotypes of deviancy surrounding gender non-conformity. Other strategies, such as the development of the internationally recognized Transgender Day of Remembrance, have emerged as a symbolic "oppositional mirror" to a society modeled on adherence to cis-normativity by questioning, if not resisting, the bases of transphobic violence (Ryan 2008). What seems common to these examples is the underlying motivation of transgender people, in conjunction with their allies, in cultivating a collective self-identity as well as curating collective knowledge (and sensibility) against prevailing gender expectations and stereotypes that are seen to galvanize transphobic behavior and conduct.

Implications of interpersonal transactions for transphobic prevalence

In addition to voluntaristic collective actions by transgender advocates to address the symptoms and effects of transphobia, another potential avenue for a non-state-centric response is to foster the building of interpersonal relationships. Whereas the previous sub-section recalls several efforts around the world by organizations to build and strengthen "bonding" social capital within transgender and other gender diverse communities, we also have in mind activities that could further develop "bridging" social capital between societal groups irrespective of their gender perceptions and behaviors (Ostrom and Ahn 2009). Psychologist Gordon Allport (1954) explicated a "contact hypothesis" that repeated interactions between the members of different social groups would tend to lessen discriminatory attitudes and feelings of prejudice toward individuals otherwise identified as being affiliated with the "out-group" category.

An immense social scientific literature has been generated to test the plausibility of the contact hypothesis. Several key studies have concluded that, under certain conditions, intergroup contacts may be successful in quelling intergroup animosity as well as promoting feelings of empathy if not solidarity between groups (e.g., Tropp and Pettigrew 2005; Pettigrew and Tropp 2006; Dovidio et al. 2011; Imperato et al. 2021). An emerging sub-strand of studies on the contact hypothesis investigates whether contacts between transgender and other groups have stymied transphobia dispositions. Research indicates that contact tends to improve attitudes toward transgender people, although the strength of contact-induced prejudice reduction varies across settings (e.g., King et al. 2009; Barbir et al. 2017; Tadlock et al. 2017; Michelson and Harrison 2023). To what extent online contact diminishes transphobia is another research subject (e.g., Boccanfuso et al. 2021).

Key activities undertaken by transgender organizations imply an understanding on their part of the potentially anti-prejudicial effects of contact promotion between transgender and other people. As noted, a significant component of modern trans activism is political lobbying to improve conditions facing transgender and other gender non-conforming individuals, with the target of political engagement by transgender groups presumably targeting largely non-transgender legislators and other public officials. Certain organizations, such as the U.K.-based Trans+ Solidarity Alliance (https://www.transsolidarityalliance.com), are constituted to solidify (in this case, political) networks between transgender individuals and cisgender allies.

In addition to political activities, we see examples in both physical and online spaces of efforts to enhance public awareness of transgender people as well as major gender identity issues. In 2023, groups around the world coalesced around a social media #TransPeopleAreLoved hashtag campaign to promote public solidarity and allyship with transgender communities. On March 31 of each year, a "Transgender Day of Visibility" is celebrated to showcase the lives of transgender people and the positive contributions they make to society, together with promoting awareness about the discrimination still being faced by those expressing and identifying gender diversity.[16] Outreach efforts between the transgender and wider communities also take place in more localized settings in Western countries and elsewhere around the world.[17]

Conclusion

We agree with Martin and Storr that the possibilities of perverse emergent orders existing "are arguably quite common," although "spontaneous order theorists have not paid much attention to them" (Martin and Storr 2008: 74). In this chapter, we contend that emergent order theory, a key element of the MPE toolkit, offers descriptive frameworks that capture major elements of transphobia. The emergent order perspective also provides a set of interpretations about how best to redress the antipathy, hatred, ridicule, and violence expressed against those who behave or otherwise express a gender identity adjudged to abridge societal norms. Addressing these harms requires a wide range of voluntary association and non-state actions. This decentralized, bottom-up approach to LGBTQ activism is consistent with QCL's recognition of the validity of voluntaristic modes of collective action.

Transphobia assumes a character that transcends formal public sector restrictions upon gender expression and identity, as important as they are, to recognize the coercive effects of societal attitudes, beliefs, expectations, norms, and practices. All in all, the operationalization of transphobia is seen to circumscribe "freedom of expression, identity, movement, and speech for people in diverse gender communities, and places severe constraints upon people's freedom to accumulate incomes and properties and to build social networks" (Novak 2016: 33). Responding to the diffuse nature of transphobia as a perverse emergent order necessitates decentralized, community-centered approaches that raising awareness about the complex and evolving dimensions of transphobia, and partaking in painstaking efforts to promote mutual acceptance, respect, and tolerance wherever transphobia is experienced. The opportunity to significantly improve the quality of life as experienced by members of the transgender community, and other gender diverse communities, demands nothing less than a key role for non-state-centric responses to what is the perversely emergent phenomenon of transphobia.

Notes

1 For example, data indicate that up to one percent of the U.S. national population identifies as transgender (Herman et al. 2022).
2 Emphasis upon humanly devised orders contrasts notions of order identified in biological, chemical, and other physical realms.
3 The distinction originally made by Carl Menger that government is an *organization*, but that the state (in the abstract sense) represents an *order* that possesses emergent properties resulting from interactions among people over questions of governance (Becchio 2014). Gus diZerega (1989) advanced the claim that political democracy may be considered an example of an emergent order. Long (2010) refers to statism itself as an emergent order possessed with perverse qualities.
4 Examples include language (Hayek 1973, [1960] 2011) and the arts (Camplin 2010).
5 This is an important point to bear in mind with respect to our later discussion about the organizational activities of pro-trans and anti-trans groups within society. Emergent order theory implies that any given group is *not uniquely responsible* for the generation and propagation of transphobic (or, for that matter, anti-transphobic) attitudes, sentiments, and practices.
6 We thank Nathan Goodman for referring this quote to us.
7 Martin and Storr also nominated "mob group" activity, such as rioting, as an example of a perverse emergent order.
8 According to these accounts, men are to desirably demonstrate masculine virtues, such as bravery, strength, and emotional detachment, whereas women should exhibit feminine virtues of compassion, physical vulnerability, and emotional attachment.
9 However, certain aspects of transphobic expression may reflect a degree of herd behavior, either in physical or non-physical (e.g., digital) spaces. The social media backlash against the appearance of trans influencer Dylan Mulvaney in Bud Light commercials in the United States in April 2023 may be seen as one example of the herd aspect of transphobic activity.
10 As has been noted in this chapter, the nature of reinforcement of conventional gender stereotypes can range from mild criticism of perceived gender nonconformity through to outright violence against people expressing diverse gender identities.
11 The Translegislation Tracker website (https://translegislation.com) provides information on the number of legislative bills specifically aimed at transgender individuals in areas such as education, health care, sports, performance (including gender non-conforming events), and bathroom access. In 2021, there were a total of 153 bills specifically aimed at transgender individuals (18 of which were enacted), increasing to 701 bills in 2024 (51 of which were enacted). As of November 2025, there were 1,012 anti-trans bills under consideration during 2025 (124 of them have been enacted).
12 An example that points to tensions between the broad (albeit loose) coalition of interests on sexual orientation and gender identity issues is the LGB Alliance, a U.K. outfit established in opposition to transgender issues pursued by other LGBTQ groups such as Stonewall.

13 Again, this kind of statement is not contravened by the recognition that maintaining cis-normative socio-cultural environments does involve some conscious measure of promotion throughout various reaches of society – whether these are attributable to public adherence to government regulations and statutes over identity matters, through cultural exhortations of the virtues of fixed, binary gender identities by moralizing agents, or through similar phenomena.
14 Which may be inclusive of genderqueer or non-binary identifications.
15 It is notable that interviewees for a study by Jauk (2013) testified to the frustration of experiencing or witnessing systemic discrimination, prejudice, and ill-treatment of gender diverse minorities as a motivating factor informing transgender activism.
16 See https://www.hrc.org/campaigns/international-transgender-day-of-visibility (accessed January 14, 2025).
17 A notable example is that of Christian religious denominations accepting transgender worshippers (Beardsley and Dowd 2020).

References

Aligica, Paul Dragos, Ginny Seung Choi, and Virgil Henry Storr. 2021. *Culture, Sociality, and Morality: New Applications of Mainline Political Economy*. Lanham, MD: Rowman & Littlefield.

Allport, G. W. 1954. *The Nature of Prejudice*. Cambridge, MA: Addison-Wesley Publishing.

Angner, Erik. 2004. "Did Hayek Commit the Naturalistic Fallacy?" *Journal of the History of Economic Thought* 26 (3): 349–361.

Badgett, M. V. Lee, Soon Kyu Choi, and Bianca D. Wilson. 2019. "LGBT Poverty in the United States: A study of differences between sexual orientation and gender identity groups." UCLA School of Law. Williams Institute. https://williamsinstitute.law.ucla.edu/wp-content/uploads/National-LGBT-Poverty-Oct-2019.pdf.

Bandini, Elisa, and Mario Maggi. 2014. "Transphobia." In *Emotional, Physical and Sexual Abuse: Impact in Children and Social Minorities*, edited by Giovanni Corona, Emmanuele A. Jannini and Mario Maggi, 49–59. Cham, Switzerland: Springer.

Barbir, Lara A., Anna W. Vandevender, and Tracy J. Cohn. 2017. "Friendship, Attitudes, and Behavioral Intentions of Cisgender Heterosexuals Toward Transgender Individuals." *Journal of Gay & Lesbian Mental Health* 21 (2): 154–170.

Beardsley, Christina, and Chris Dowd. 2020. *Trans Affirming Churches: How to Celebrate Gender-Variant People and Their Loved Ones*. London, UK: Jessica Kinglsey Publishers.

Becchio, Giandomenica. 2014. "Carl Menger on States as Orders, not Organizations: Entangled Economy into a Neo-Mengerian Approach." *Advances in Austrian Economics* 18: 55–66.

Boccanfuso, Emery, Fiona A. White, and Rachel D. Maunder. 2021. "Reducing Transgender Stigma via an E-contact Intervention." *Sex Roles* 84 (5–6): 326–336.

Boettke, Peter J. 2012. *Living Economics: Yesterday, Today, and Tomorrow*. Oakland, CA: Independent Institute.

Bolivar, Andrea. 2017. "For Chicago's Trans Latina Sex Workers, A Cycle of Fear, Violence, and Brutality." *NACLA Report on the Americas* 49 (3): 323–327.

Butler, Judith. 1988. "Performative Acts and Gender Constitution: An Essay in Phenomenology and Feminist Theory." *Theatre Journal* 40 (4): 519–531.

Caldwell, Bruce. 2000. "The Emergence of Hayek's Ideas on Cultural Evolution." *Review of Austrian Economics* 13 (1): 5–22.

Campbell, Travis, and Yana van der Meulen Rodgers. 2023. "Conversion Therapy, Suicidality, and Running Away: An Analysis of Transgender Youth in the U.S." *Journal of Health Economics* 89 (2): 102750.

Camplin, Troy Earl. 2010. "The Spontaneous Orders of the Arts." *Studies in Emergent Order* 3: 195–211.

Cowen, Nick. 2013. "What Would Hayek Say About Gendered Violence?" In *What Would Hayek Say Today (Really)?*, edited by Legatum Institute, 27–29. London, UK: Legatum Institute.

D'Amico, Daniel J. 2015. "Spontaneous Order." In *The Oxford Handbook of Austrian Economics*, edited by Peter J. Boettke and Christopher J. Coyne, 115–142. New York, NY: Oxford University Press.

diZerega, Gus. 1989. "Democracy as a Spontaneous Order." *Critical Review* 3 (2): 206–240.

Dovidio, John F., Anja Eller, and Miles Hewstone. 2011. "Improving Intergroup Relations through Direct, Extended and Other Forms of Indirect Contact." *Group Processes & Intergroup Relations* 14 (2): 147–160.

Faye, Shon. 2021. *The Transgender Issue: Trans Justice Is Justice for All*. London, UK: Verso Books.

Feinberg, Leslie. 1997. *Gender Warriors: Making History from Joan of Arc to Dennis Rodman*. Boston, MA: Beacon Press.

Ferguson, Adam. [1767] 2007. *An Essay on the History of Civil Society*. Cambridge Texts in the History of Political Thought. Cambridge, UK: Cambridge University Press.

Ciprikis, Klavs, Damien Cassells, and Jenny Berrill. 2020. "Transgender Labour Market Outcomes: Evidence from the United States." *Gender, Work & Organization* 27 (6): 1378–1401.

Craig, Alexander, and Nathan P. Goodman. 2023. "Gender as an Institution: LGBT Identities and Economic Coordination." https://papers.ssrn.com/sol3/papers.cfm?abstract_id=4616300.

Fausto-Sterling, Anne. 2020. *Sexing the Body: Gender Politics and the Construction of Sexuality*. New York, NY: Basic Books.

Harrison, Caleb. 2018. "Bad Spontaneous Orders: Trust, Ignorance, and White Supremacy." In *Exploring the Political Economy and Social Philosophy of F. A. Hayek*, edited by Peter J. Boettke, Jayme S. Lemke and Virgil Henry Storr, 233–258. New York, NY: Rowman & Littlefield.

Hayek, Friedrich A. 1973. *Law, Legislation and Liberty. Volume 1: Rule and Order*. London, UK: Routledge & Kegan Paul.

Hayek, Friedrich A. 1976. *Law, Legislation and Liberty, Volume 2: The Mirage of Social Justice*. London, UK: Routledge and Kegan Paul.

Hayek, Friedrich A. 1988. "The Fatal Conceit: The Errors of Socialism." In *The Collected Works of F. A. Hayek, Volume 1*, edited by W. W. Bartley III. London, UK: Routledge.

Hayek, Friedrich A. [1960] 2011. "The Constitution of Liberty: The Definitive Edition." In *The Collected Works of F. A. Hayek, Volume 17*, edited by Ronald Hamowy. Chicago, IL: University of Chicago Press.

Herman, Jody L., Andrew R. Flores, and Kathryn K. O'Neill. 2022. "How Many Adults and Youth Identify as Transgender in the United States?" UCLA School of Law. Williams Institute. https://williamsinstitute.law.ucla.edu/publications/trans-adults-united-states.

Hill, Darryl B., and Brian L. B. Willoughby. 2005. "The Development and Validation of the Genderism and Transphobia Scale." *Sex Roles* 53 (7/8): 531–544.

Holcombe, Randall G. 2020. *Advanced Introduction to The Austrian School of Economics*. Second edition. Cheltenham, UK: Edward Elgar.

Imperato, Chiara, Barry H. Schneider, Luca Caricati, Yair Amichai-Hamburger, and Tiziana Mancini. 2021. "Allport Meets Internet: A Meta-analytical Investigation of Online Intergroup Contact and Prejudice Reduction." *International Journal of Intercultural Relations* 81 (7): 131–141.

Inch, Emma. 2016. "Changing Minds: The Psycho-Pathologization of Trans People." *International Journal of Mental Health* 45 (3): 193–204.

Jauk, Daniela. 2013. "Gender Violence Revisited: Lessons from Violent Victimization of Transgender Identified Individuals." *Sexualities* 16 (7): 807–825.

Johnson, Charles. 2010. “Women and the Invisible Fist: How Violence Against Women Enforces the Unwritten Law of Patriarchy.” https://charleswjohnson.name/essays/women-and-the-invisible-fist/rpa-2010.
Jones, Philip Edward, Paul R. Brewer, Danngal G. Young, Jennifer L. Lambe, Lindsay H. Hoffman. 2018. “Explaining Public Opinion toward Transgender People, Rights, and Candidates.” *Public Opinion Quarterly* 82 (2): 252–278.
King, Mark E., Sam Winter, and Beverley Webster. 2009. “Contact Reduces Transprejudice: A Study on Attitudes towards Transgenderism and Transgender Civil Rights in Hong Kong.” *International Journal of Sexual Health* 21 (1): 17–34.
Kirzner, Israel M. 1982. ““Spontaneous Order” – A Complex Idea.” *Literature of Liberty* 5 (4): 7–8.
Kirzner, Israel M. 1990. “Knowledge Problems and Their Solutions: Some Relevant Distinctions.” *Cultural Dynamics* 3 (1): 32–48.
Leppel, Karen. 2016. “The Labor Force Status of Transgender Men and Women.” *International Journal of Transgenderism* 17 (3–4): 155–164.
Long, Roderick T. 2010. “Invisible Hands and Incantations: The Mystification of State Power.” Presentation to Molinari Symposium on Spontaneous Order, Boston.
Maier, Megan Brodie. 2020. “Altering Gender Markers on Government Identity Documents: Unpredictable, Burdensome, and Oppressive.” *University of Pennsylvania Journal of Law and Social Change* 23 (3): 203–250.
Malamet, Akiva. 2018. “Spontaneous Order as Social Construction: A Social Analysis of Emergent Institutions.” Unpublished manuscript.
Martin, Nona P. and Virgil H. Storr. 2008. “On Perverse Emergent Orders.” *Studies in Emergent Order* 1: 73–91.
Michelson, Melissa R., and Brian F. Harrison. 2023. “Ties That Bind: The Effects of Transgender Contact on Transphobia.” *Journal of Homosexuality* 70 (12): 2848–2900.
Novak, Mikayla. 2016. *Gender Identity and Libertarianism*. Center for a Stateless Society. https://c4ss.org/wp-content/uploads/2015/06/GIandLib.pdf.
Nownes, Anthony J. 2019. *Organizing for Transgender Rights: Collective Action, Group Development, and the Rise of a New Social Movement*. Albany, NY: SUNY Press.
Nozick, Robert. 1974. *Anarchy, State, and Utopia*. New York, NY: Basic Books.
Obasi, Sharon N., and I. M. Nick. 2023. “Laws and Policies Regulating Personal Names and Transgender and Gender Diverse Identities in the US and Canada.” In *Names, Naming, and the Law: Onomastics, Identity, Power, and Policy*, edited by I. M. Nick, 51–68. New York, NY: Routledge.
Ostrom, Elinor, and T. K. Ahn. 2009. “The Meaning of Social Capital and Its Link to Collective Action.” In *Handbook of Social Capital: The Troika of Sociology, Political Science and Economics*, edited by Gert Tinggaard Svendsen and Gunnar Lind Haase Svendsen, 17–35. Cheltenham, UK: Edward Elgar.
Pettigrew, Thomas F., and Linda R. Tropp. 2006. “A Meta-Analytic Test of Intergroup Contact Theory.” *Journal of Personality and Social Psychology* 90 (5): 751–783.
Polanyi, Michael. 1962. “The Republic of Science: Its Political and Economic Theory.” *Minerva* 1 (1): 54–73.
Ryan, Joelle Ruby. 2008. “Death By Transphobia: Increasing Gender Awareness through Teaching the Day of Remembrance.” *Transformations: The Journal of Inclusive Scholarship and Pedagogy* 19 (2): 81–91.
Schelling, Thomas C. 1971. “Dynamic Models of Segregation.” *Journal of Mathematical Sociology* 1 (2): 143–186.
Shannon, Matthew. 2022. “The Labour Market Outcomes of Transgender Individuals.” *Labour Economics* 77: 102006.
Sharp, Sabine. 2024. “A Brief History of Trans Activism in the UK.” https://blogs.manchester.ac.uk/edi/2024/01/23/dr-sabine-sharp-a-brief-history-of-trans-activism-in-the-uk.
Spade, Dean. 2015. *Normal Life: Administrative Violence, Critical Trans Politics, & The Limits of Law*. Durham, NC: Duke University Press.

Stenerson, Madeline R., Kathryn Thomas and Sherry McKee. 2022. "Police and Transgender and Gender Diverse People in the United States: A Brief Note on Interaction, Harassment, and Violence." *Journal of Interpersonal Violence* 37 (23–24): NP23281–NP23305.

Stenerson, Madeline R., Kathryn Thomas and Sherry McKee. 2024. "Police Harassment and Violence Against Transgender & Gender Diverse Sex Workers in the United States." *Journal of Homosexuality* 71 (3): 828–840.

Storr, Virgil Henry, and Arielle John. 2020. *Cultural Considerations within Austrian Economics*. Cambridge, UK: Cambridge University Press.

Stryker, Susan. 2017. *Transgender History: The Roots of Today's Revolution.* New York, NY: Seal Press.

Tadlock, Barry R., Andrew R. Flores, Donald P. Haider-Markel, Daniel C. Lewis, Patrick R. Miller, and Jami K. Taylor. 2017. "Testing Contact Theory and Attitudes on Transgender Rights." *Public Opinion Quarterly* 81 (4): 956–972.

TransActual. 2024. "Transphobia." Accessed August 1, 2024. https://transactual.org.uk/transphobia.

Tropp, Linda R., and Thomas F. Pettigrew. 2005. "Relationships Between Intergroup Contact and Prejudice Among Minority and Majority Status Groups." *Psychological Science* 16 (12): 951–957.

Tuszynski, Meg Patrick. 2021. "Entanglement and Perverse Spontaneous Orders." In *Emergence, Entanglement, and Political Economy*, edited by David J. Hebert and Diana W. Thomas, 87–102. Cham, Switzerland: Palgrave Macmillan.

United States Department of State. 2025. "Sex Marker in Passports." https://travel.state.gov/content/travel/en/passports/passport-help/sex-marker.html.

Whitman, Douglas Glen. 1998. "Hayek Contra Pangloss on Evolutionary Systems." *Constitutional Political Economy* 9 (1): 45–66.

11

LGBTQ RIGHTS AND THE TYRANNY OF ASIAN COMMUNITARIANISM

Bryan Cheang

On March 25th, 2025, the Osaka High Court became the fifth high court in Japan to rule that the country's current gay marriage ban is unconstitutional, finding that it violated the principle of equality under the law enshrined in the Japanese Constitution. However, in response, a conservative member of the Liberal Democratic Party (LDP) commented to The Asahi Shimbun that the ruling was "insane," asserting that "the 'order' of society should be protected rather than the rights of individuals" (Nikaido 2025). This discourse of personal rights violating social harmony is also reflected in the introduction to the 2022 Indonesian Criminal Code, which grants the state the power to prosecute same-sex relationships on morality grounds. The new code, it states, is intended to "regulate the balance between … written law and the law that lives in the community … and between human rights and human obligations" (Law of the Republic of Indonesia 2023). Public protests against the bill occurred both in 2019, when it was first considered and again in 2022, when it was ultimately passed (Reza 2022). These developments are reflective of what we identify as the broader persistence of communitarianism in Asia, where individual rights are framed as being in tension with, or to be subordinated to, the perceived "social good."

In this chapter, we analyse the tyranny of Asian communitarianism, using its impact on LGBT rights as a case study. Despite notable breakthroughs in formal legal rights for sexual minorities, genuine social acceptance remains elusive, constrained by deeply entrenched communitarian governance. Communitarianism here refers to a political philosophy granting state elites legitimate authority to prioritise the perceived "social good," defined by prevailing national, social, or political norms, over individual liberties. Asian communitarianism specifically denotes governance grounded in the belief systems and cultural traditions indigenous to Asia, particularly in Southeast and East Asia where Buddhism, Islam, and Confucianism

DOI: 10.4324/9781003615781-11

predominate. Some of these traditions are more social-philosophical than strictly religious, as Buddhism and Confucianism notably do not involve worship of a deity but emphasise social roles and collective harmony.

Indeed, the discourse prioritising communal welfare is not unique to Asia. The U.S. Supreme Court's 2015 Obergefell decision legalising gay marriage represented a liberal triumph over previous decisions that upheld restrictions on "deviant sexual conduct" for "social stability" (Saunders 2017). Dissenting justices framed Obergefell as an unwarranted "transformation" disrupting an "unvarying social institution" (Roberts 2015: 22; Scalia 2015: 6). Such "stability-oriented" discourses, which frame cultural dynamism as a threat to social cohesion, are commonplace. However, East Asia is fundamentally different from the West in historical development and political culture, lacking the same robust inheritance of liberal individualism. Arguably, its adherence to harmonious social order was so entrenched that it contributed to the lack of capitalist wealth transformation in East Asia as compared to the West (see Weber [1915] 1968).

Admittedly, significant progress has been made globally and within Asia on the formal legislative level. Many countries have democratised, criminal restrictions on consensual homosexual acts have been abolished in some cases, and there are instances of official recognition of same-sex marriage. However, if we are genuinely concerned with liberty and dignity for cultural minorities, specifically queer people, formal legal recognition alone is insufficient. Liberty simply means the negative freedoms of individuals to act and live as they choose, requiring the abolition or circumscription of state restrictions on personal lifestyles. The problem is that even hard-won progress in the law remains tenuous if there is a persistence of communitarian norms in society. These achievements become dependent on the lukewarm benevolence of a prevailing majority, as their continued existence relies on a fragile "communitarian equilibrium" of what the majority deems the common good. If these elites perceive their cultural comfort being upset by the spontaneous unfolding of individual liberties, the hard-won rights of minorities can easily be revoked. Even when formal equality is granted, it is on the terms of the cultural majority, rather than on individual rights as an independent value. This communitarian mindset, which prizes stability and cohesion, sets the boundaries within which the cultural minority must navigate. For this chapter, it is not only *liberty* that matters, but also *dignity*, where minorities are not classified as deviant in the social realm for their personal choices. Liberty without dignity is hollow and entails deleterious consequences for authentic living and self-esteem.

Communitarianism in Asia is an affront to the liberty and dignity so described, due to the confluence of state interference in cultural matters and how this interference is legitimised by the language of stability and cohesion found within these belief systems. While all belief systems could potentially be co-opted or "hijacked" by elites to violate individualism, some are more susceptible to this than others. For instance, Hinduism tends to be more socially permissive than the traditions explored here. Confucianism often favours stability and social cohesion, while specific interpretations of Islam (and monotheistic faiths like Christianity) tend to be rigidly focused on divine command with less scope for deviation.

Historical developments in Asia illustrate communitarian resistance to social progress. During China's early 20th-century New Culture Movement, intellectuals such as Chen Duxiu criticised Confucianism's family-centred morality as a repressive force that obstructed individual liberty and democracy (Levenson 1958). Similarly, in contemporary Singapore, communitarian governance legitimised by a language of social cohesion has stalled democratic progress and acts as a disciplinary device that punishes dissent (Rajah 2012; Cheang and Choy 2024). In Southeast Asia, Buddhist traditions similarly emphasise "social harmony" and gradual "moral improvement," historically reinforcing existing hierarchies and discouraging collective rebellion or disruptive social activism (Tambiah 1992). Moreover, Southeast Asian instantiations of Islam have integrated communal morality directly into national identities, particularly in countries like Malaysia and Indonesia, where Islam is closely tied to ethnic identity and social order. Political leaders frequently invoke Islamic communal values to justify policies restricting gender and sexual freedoms, asserting communal harmony as paramount over individual rights (Inglehart and Norris 2003; Yuniar 2022). Thus, even as formal democratisation and reforms occur, deeply embedded communitarian norms can swiftly undermine or reverse progress should majority sensibilities feel threatened by individual liberties.

The structure of this chapter is as follows. The first section will further elaborate on the concept of a dynamic liberal social order based on cultural creative destruction. I argue that a genuinely progressive society that dignifies queer people allows all minorities not only to enjoy formal equal rights but also to create and recreate their identities experimentally. Importantly, this is distinct from the "politics of recognition" perspective which prizes democratic public reason. We stress that queer dignity does not and should not require the social permission of the majority – let alone having to negotiate a cultural consensus with it – but rather in *trailblazing* alternative lifestyles which may be in contradistinction to prevailing cultural sensibilities. This combined legal and cultural environment of liberation is normatively endorsed by proponents of queer classical liberalism (QCL). Unfortunately, such liberation is found wanting in much of Asia, as the following sections will explore, using Confucianism and Islam as case studies, focusing on Japan and Indonesia. This selection is deliberate, given that available surveys on Asia show that Japan appears to have the most favourable views on same-sex marriage, while Indonesia has the least (Gubbala and Miner 2023). Despite these results, we show that genuine progress remains stifled due to the persistence of communitarian discourse that prizes "harmony," the "common good," and "stability." In such environments, even formal legislative wins are precarious, and minorities face a double burden: they must not only overcome illiberal barriers but also contort their public reasoning to conform to the demands of the majority. They are denied the freedom to exist or express themselves *on their own terms*.

Political communitarianism and the dynamic liberal response

Discussions on LGBT rights often focus on achieving legal equality. On this metric, the decriminalisation of private sexual activity and the recognition of same-sex unions are welcome. The consistent application of the liberal ideal of equal rights for all, encompassing ethnic, gender, and now sexual minorities, should be regarded as a significant achievement. However, liberty is distinct from the notion of dignity. Queer individuals may be legally free yet be oppressed due to the broader social environment they inhabit. Accordingly, this section argues that the persistence of political communitarianism in East Asia, which prioritises cohesion, harmony, and social stability, is violative of the liberty and dignity of cultural minorities, even as formal democratic practices gain traction. In contrast, I argue for a liberal conception of society grounded in dynamic transformations of rules and culture.

Communitarianism, as a political philosophy, asserts the legitimate authority of the state to prioritise the common good, as defined by the prevailing national or cultural community, over individual preferences (see Kymlicka 2001: 208–282 for an analysis). There are often two claims made. First, individuals are not "unencumbered" but deeply embedded in communal attachments. Second, legitimate political action derives not from abstract rights but from a shared way of life. These arguments naturally appeal to Asian sensibilities.

In response to the first claim, there is no reason to insist on an atomistic individualism. The perspective presented here fully recognises that individuals are embedded within a web of social attachments. A gay teenager growing up in a conservative Asian family will necessarily take certain cultural realities as a starting point and may even wish to retain some of them. His parents may never fully grasp his plight, and a lifetime of complicated family dynamics will likely ensue. The liberal insists, however, that this individual possesses, and should be granted, the space to rationally revise his future, incrementally, according to his conscience. While the range of cultural choices may not be unlimited, the crucial point is that one's inheritance should not be a prison from which escape is impossible. The cultural fabric in which an individual is embedded, then, should dynamically evolve as he interacts with it.

The danger of believing that political rights stem primarily from a shared history, language, or way of life is that it can easily slide into cultural policing, where dissenters from tradition are viewed not merely as minorities, but as *deviants* to the social order. The communitarian valorisation of tradition risks becoming a license for exclusion. Any formal rights won in the legislative sphere can become flimsy, a shaky achievement that may be revoked by elites who hold the power to speak on behalf of the collective. Perhaps the chief threat to queer dignity in Asia is the requirement, whether real or perceived, to conform to a "shared way of life" that minorities had no part in creating. Even if non-discrimination laws or equal rights provisions are passed, communitarian norms mean that queer people, or indeed any minority, still need to contend with social resistance if their choices are deemed transgressive or offensive.

Such resistance is all too likely, given that every positive step forward in the history of civil rights movements has *involved some transgression on mainstream cultural sensibilities*. Consider the audacity of Rosa Parks to offend her racist oppressors, and today the daring of queers to overturn dress codes and behavioural norms. How could Black individuals sit in the same café as whites, how could women enjoy the right to vote in elections, and how could two men kiss in public? Some degree of cultural "offence," or an "assault" on the shared way of life, is often necessary for minority lifestyles to break the cultural hegemony that once policed them.

The problem with pervasive communitarian norms, particularly if they cut across various social domains, is that individuals may be pressured and politically disciplined into conforming, leading to the suppression of their authentic selves. The world they inhabit is never truly theirs and remains perpetually alien. As the liberal scholar John Stuart Mill wrote, individuality is "one of the principal ingredients of human happiness, and quite the chief ingredient of individual and social progress" (Mill [1859] 2003: 122). Allowing individuals to develop their distinct characters is vital for societal advancement. Mill lamented how "society has now fairly got the better of individuality" through the formidable forces of public opinion and conventional sentiment, which tend to "make all persons assume a similar character" (Mill [1859] 2003: 126). He warned against a societal environment where the individual slavishly conforms to "custom as custom" or the opinion of the world. For Mill, individualism is crucial because it is the exercise of agency that is the "distinctive endowment of a human being" (Mill [1859] 2003: 123). The communitarian emphasis on cohesion is what can strangulate this very agency that Mill saw as essential for both individual flourishing and a vibrant society.

Some classical liberals, such as those in the Hayekian tradition, might find the position put forth so far to be too radical regarding traditions. They stress that traditions embody accumulated wisdom and the folly of rationalistically sweeping them away. There is much value in this position. However, this perspective is inappropriate when analysing Asia, which is fundamentally different from the West, where mainline political economist F. A. Hayek, for instance, wrote. In societies like England or the United States, a preexisting cultural inheritance of individual liberty emerged and consolidated over centuries, especially since the Enlightenment, which conservative-liberals in those contexts might rightly conserve. Asia, by contrast, does not share this liberal heritage, making the application of this traditional analysis inappropriate (Cheang 2025). Instead, its traditions have historically been intertwined with cultural elitism and authoritarian power, lacking a broad-based social appreciation of individualism.

Social traditions in such authoritarian environments are artificially shaped by political and clerical elites and have historically operated as instruments of social control. They reflect not spontaneous order but entrenched hierarchy. Indeed,

Hayek himself cautioned that respect for tradition must depend "on the direction of existing tendencies." In cases where inherited values are manifestly hostile to liberty, they must be challenged. As he wrote, "what is most urgently needed in most parts of the world is a thorough sweeping away of the obstacles to free growth" (Hayek 1960: 399). The communitarian traditions of Asia, I argue, are precisely the obstacles that a Hayekian liberalism ought to confront. Religion, tradition, and "Asian values" have been repurposed as tools of ideological conformity and moral policing (Sen 1997; Kirsch and Welzel 2018; Siegle 2024; Cheang 2026). The problem is that these traditions, shielded by the rhetoric of "cohesion," act as a primary moral justification for repressing dissent and diversity.

My position distinguishes itself from theories advocating a "politics of recognition." While sharing the belief that formal liberty alone is insufficient, the mainstream view remedies social injustice through the public validation and democratic acceptance of group identities. It posits that misrecognition, that is, the denial of recognition or the imposition of a demeaning image, inflicts deep psychological wounds on one's identity (Taylor 1995). To address this, it aims to revalue unjustly devalued identities and affirm the worth of a group's unique culture, treating this not just as a courtesy but as a vital human need. This supposedly needs to be achieved through the vehicle of democratic public reason, a deliberative process where all citizens engage in open discussion to articulate their needs and perspectives (Young 1990: 91–95). These "democratic processes of public justification" are seen as central to achieving a just society where all individuals and groups are recognised as "full partners" in social interaction (Fraser 2000: 119).

The view just described seeks dignity through democratic public reason, with several problems. First, it presupposes the existence of social knowledge that is epistemologically impossible to centralise, much less adjudicate, since much of it is tacitly held in culturally specific practices that cannot be easily articulated in explicit political debate (Pennington 2003). Democratic deliberation becomes an impoverished forum to negotiate the complexities and richness of cultural identity. Second, while its philosophical foundation posits that group identities are anti-essentialist (meaning they are not fixed categories with rigid boundaries), its political solution of group recognition ironically requires that these fluid boundaries be institutionally "closed off" to be politically effective (Tebble 2003). Some specific representative gets to "speak" on behalf of the entire "group" being "recognised," foreclosing the fluidity and dynamism of the community in question. Last and most seriously, it is deeply insulting to suggest that the political legitimacy of a minority's existence depends on the discursive approval of a majority that may never be genuinely interested in or even comprehend the traditions it seeks to regulate.

The dynamic liberalism championed in this chapter finds dignity through cultural entrepreneurship. Here, minorities actively *trailblaze* new ways of life, much like an entrepreneur disrupting an industry. Dignity and authenticity are found not in the seeking of permission from the majority, but in the freedom to live independently and on one's terms, allowing people to carve out their own "small worlds" aligned with their deeply held norms (Cheang and Ho 2026). Consider, for example, lesbian bars and clubs that offer a space free from the male gaze and the heteronormative expectations of mainstream nightlife, or queer communes and co-housing arrangements that create alternative family structures and living environments outside of traditional norms. These are cases of LGBTQ people carving their own "small worlds," where they do not seek or even need a consensus from the majority, where they do not see themselves as dependents seeking a handout of acceptance. These spaces stand as a testament to the ongoing *defiance* of cultural rebels against an intolerant world. They are cultural heroes, forging alternative narratives and *refusing* to be confined by a script written by others. Liberty meets dignity in the ongoing process of cultural creative destruction. This suggests that QCL and emancipatory social change are built not merely through centralized democratic deliberation, but through entrepreneurial processes. As has already been noted throughout this volume, analysis of such processes is a cornerstone of mainline political economy (Aligica et al. 2021).

Confucianism and the politics of cohesion

The liberal ideal presented in this chapter views institutional rules of governance, social practices, and indeed the individual self as subject to ongoing transformation. Yet, the prevailing belief systems in East Asia are antithetical to such fluidity. The discourse of flux is subordinated to that of stability. We begin the analysis here with Confucianism, followed by Islam in the following section.

The Confucian philosophical system rests on the moral cultivation of individuals within ordered relationships, a vision central to which is the value of harmony (和, he). In Confucian thought, harmony is deemed a "most precious" value, and to be made the "top priority" in the execution of rites (Confucius 2002: 1.12; Key Concepts in Chinese Thought and Culture, n.d.). Harmony serves as a regulative principle that shapes ethical conduct, governance, and interpersonal life. Within this worldview, societal order is secured not through individual rights or expressive freedom, but through mutual role fulfilment within hierarchical relationships, most notably those between ruler and subject, parent and child, and husband and wife.

Confucianism, as a perfectionist theory, is inclined to view ethical disagreements as regrettable and resulting from human error that can be overcome through proper moral training. It aims for a high degree of ethical uniformity, believing that "failing to rectify names, and failing to set up clearly a set of ethical standards about roles and responsibilities for people to follow, would result in mistaken judgments and wrongful actions, leading ultimately to nothing but moral and social disorder" (Chan 2008: 119). The core substance of rites, which defines appropriate duties and norms of conduct, is considered unchanging, as it is based on the "Way or the Principle of Heaven and Earth" (Chan 2008: 120). Therefore, any view or action that fundamentally rejects these basic principles of human relationship would be regarded as "fundamentally wrong" and "unreasonable" by Confucians. This strong emphasis on uniformity means that social disruption and disequilibrium are resisted because the Confucian ideal "can at once solve problems of individual morality, social harmony, and political stability" (Chan 2008: 123). This aversion to societal upheaval is encapsulated in the belief that "when the people keep their several places, there will be no poverty; when harmony prevails, there will be no scarcity of people; and when there is such a contented repose, there will be no rebellious upsettings" (Confucius 2002: ch 16).

This desire for harmony and cohesion penetrates the realm of personal relationships. The family is a fundamental institution shaping all social and political relationships. Indeed, "in traditional China, the purpose of the individual was to nurture the family," contrasting with a Western perspective where "the purpose of the family was to nurture the individual" (Wood 2023: 383). This highlights a difference in societal orientation, where the collective familial unit takes precedence, leading to political authority in East Asia being seen as an extension of paternalistic family authority.

Accordingly, the Confucian tradition emphasises five key relationships: ruler-subject, parent-child, husband-wife, elder sibling-younger sibling, and friend-friend. Notably, four of these five relationships are explicitly hierarchical, with the person in the superior position expected to provide instruction, guidance, and protection, and those in inferior positions expected to be obedient and supportive (Moore 2023: 367). When individuals behave appropriately according to their social position, harmony is expected to prevail. The parent-child relationship is governed by the precept of filial piety (xiao 孝), which expects children to be deferential, obedient, and devoted to their parents and other elders, including ancestors. This injunction extends to public behaviour, as a filial child should act in a way that sustains the good reputation of the family. The continuity of the family line, often through the birth of sons, was seen as a "virtual manifestation of immortality," and the failure to produce a son was traditionally regarded as a "serious offense, a betrayal of one's family line" (Moore 2023: 373). This emphasis on procreation echoes the traditional view of sexuality not as a personal domain, but as instrumental for reproduction and family continuity. Same-sex relationships, by not involving biological reproduction, are easily perceived as transgressing this entrenched norm.

Importantly, in these social relationships, there is a premium placed on differentiation and distinction (*bie*) between roles, reflecting a well-ordered cosmic ideal. Traditional texts describe the role of the wife as one of obedience, childbearing, and support for the husband, mainly focusing on domestic affairs. Men and women play gendered roles in sex, family, and social relationships. Closely related is the concept of "yin-yang," which, while representing complementary forces, was historically interpreted by cultural elites to establish a hierarchical, male-dominant order (Wang 2012; Pang-White 2016: 9; Chan 2023: 410–411). For centuries, patriarchal and patrilineal family structures persisted. Overall, the implication is that homosexuality could subvert long-held views about the proper roles of male-female, husband-wife, the ideal family, and sexual dynamics.

Crucially, we stress that it is not necessary for Confucianism to explicitly condemn homosexuality (or to call for coercion) for it to be problematic for queer dignity. Sin Yee Chan (2016) demonstrates that nothing in Confucianism inherently condemns homosexuality. She shows, through impressive intellectual somersaults, how homosexual lifestyles may still be compatible with Confucian values. However, that is beside the point. What matters for us is that it is wedded to a political ideal that defines moral worth through conformity to normative familial roles, rituals, and harmony-preserving behaviour. The degree of ethical pluralism that Confucianism permits is severely circumscribed by an underlying obeisance to proper rituals and ren (Chan 2008). Confucian ethics prioritises social order and stability, which subordinates the free exercise of individual agency, which, if given weight, can easily subvert the social fabric. Indeed, early Japanese Confucian texts declare that "harmony is to be valued, and contentiousness avoided" (Shōtoku 1975). Unsurprisingly, "respect for authority, and for hierarchy, was also built into every aspect of Chinese society from early times down to the present" (Wood 2023: 388).

LGBT identities, particularly in their public expression and their deviation from long-established sexual mores, would inevitably disrupt such cherished social expectations, which can be seen as undermining "social harmony." Even when individual sentiment may lean towards "non-discrimination," the underlying fear of causing "disharmony" or cultural opprobrium limits genuine acceptance. Remember that the very birth of the queer liberation movement, like other civil rights initiatives, was rooted in some degree in cultural defiance of the prevailing sensibilities of the day. For instance, the value of queer pride parades lies precisely in challenging the heteronormativity of everyday life. The inbuilt penchant towards *stability* in Confucian thought resists the *dynamism* that cultural pluralism requires.

Japan

In Japan, Confucian values have long influenced social norms. Although Japan is a parliamentary democracy with a liberal constitution, the electoral dominance of the conservative LDP, a party rooted in "family values," dictates the pace of policy change on LGBT rights despite significant public support for the legalisation of gay marriage (The Mainichi 2024). This emphasis on traditional values was notably reflected in the LDP's proposed 2012 revision to the 1948 constitution, which stressed the "family" as the "natural and foundational unit of society" and deemphasised human rights in favour of social harmony (Matsui 2018). The influence of Confucian values in Japan is also evident in historical texts, such as Prince Shotoku's Seventeen Article Constitution from the 6th century CE, which is considered one of the most referenced treatises in Japanese political history and directly quotes from Confucian texts (Paramore 2023). Accordingly, the *koseki* (family registry) system, a powerful legal framework, normalises heterosexual nuclear families, implicitly excluding identities that do not conform to this structure (Dale 2020).

Japan's domestic gay marriage politics are at odds with its international profile as a liberal democracy and free-trade leader; it remains the only G7 nation that bans same-sex marriage. This situation has led to complex global and domestic pressures, especially as an increasing number of high courts rule that current laws are unconstitutional. For instance, in the context of the Tokyo Games and international pressure from other G7 nations, there was increased pressure on the LDP to pass an equality act, but an ambitious anti-discrimination bill was abandoned due to conservative opposition within the ruling party (Yamaguchi 2022).

When its professed liberal outlook sits in tension with its communitarian history, strange contortions are conducted to balance rival ideals. The 2023 Act on the Promotion of Public Understanding of the Diversity of Sexual Orientation and Gender Identity, passed by Prime Minister Kishida's government, aimed to promote "understanding" rather than explicitly protect against discrimination (Gallagher 2024). The bill's language, though condemning "unfair discrimination," was watered down and emphasised "peace and security," prioritising social harmony and majority viewpoints (Gallagher 2024). The LDP consistently blends liberal human rights language with "traditional Japanese values," as seen in Article 3, where "unfair discrimination" is condemned based on "respecting each other's personality and individuality," but this tolerance is justified on the grounds of "contributing to the realization of society" (Matsui 2018). Directives to schools, employers, and the government to foster "understanding" of sexual orientation and gender identity diversity are repeatedly framed with communitarian language, emphasising duties to society and ensuring all citizens can live in "peace." It is almost as if communitarian sensibilities cannot be provoked.

Even Prime Minister (at the time of writing) Shigeru Ishiba, though more outspoken than his predecessors, frames LGBT freedom within a discourse that "balances" progressive goals with communitarian considerations. In a Budget Committee meeting, he suggested that legalising gay marriage would make the nation happier and have a "positive and beneficial impact on the overall well-being of Japan" (Kuniyoshi 2024). This framing casts queer freedom as a pragmatic social benefit for national welfare, rather than an independent value in its own right. Admittedly, there are positive developments, like the recognition of equal legal rights for gay couples. At the local level, many municipalities have issued "partnership certificates" recognising same-sex unions, covering an estimated 65 per cent of the Japanese population (SBS News 2023). While these advancements indicate progress in Japan, they primarily occur outside the legislative and koseki systems, suggesting that socially liberal values are often resisted by illiberal institutions, which are reinforced by the LDP's dominance. Overall, whatever progress that has been achieved remains framed within existing discourses of stability and harmony. Free agency is marginalised on the communitarian stage.[1]

Political Islam and LGBTQ

Political communitarianism has shaped not only Confucian governance but also Islamic practice. In its dominant historical forms, Islam is often lived as a comprehensive, totalising doctrine that extends beyond personal piety to encompass governance, economics, and social life. For many Muslims, Islam is not merely a faith but "the whole of life, and its rules include civil, criminal, and even what we would call constitutional law" (Lewis 1994: 4). In early Islamic history, "religious truth and political power were indissolubly associated: the first sanctified the second, the second sustained the first" (Lewis 2003: 6). This broad scope often subordinates individual agency to religious texts or clerical authority, as "the concepts of authority and duty overshadow those of freedom and the rights of the individual" (Watt [1968] 2003: 96–98; Bowering 2015: 4). The concept of *din wa dawla* (religion and state) underscores the unity of spiritual and temporal authority in Islam (Voll 2013: 61–63). Reflecting a *communitarian emphasis on stability*, there is "less distinction between the religious and the secular" in Islamic thought (Watt [1968] 2003: 29). As a result, secularism, which entails separating religion from state power, has faced resistance across many Muslim societies, often viewed as an alien imposition rather than an organic development (Lewis 2002; Pipes [1983] 2017).

It is essential to clarify that this tendency is not *intrinsic* to Islam. Many religions can develop and manifest themselves in illiberal ways. Islamic history includes periods of remarkable intellectual and social openness that fostered reason, freedom, and tolerance. Early Islamic civilisation, for example, promoted a "self-made" individual who could pursue knowledge independently of societal or traditional constraints, and the Mu'tazila rationalist school emphasised free will and reason as sources of moral knowledge alongside revelation (Akyol 2011, 2021). Yet, Islamic societies eventually diverged from the Western development trajectory, especially after the Enlightenment. In the Muslim world, political culture and social norms were shaped by the close entanglement of religious authority and political rule, producing systems where conformity to orthodoxy and cultural policing often superseded individual freedoms. The critique here is not of Islam *per se*, but of its historical and sociological development into a communitarian system that limits personal liberty and facilitates cultural control.

In many Muslim-majority societies, a thoroughly liberal and individualistic governance model remains elusive, even when democratic elements are nominally adopted. The spirit of individual liberty is often resisted, as evidenced by the challenges faced by pro-democracy movements. A 1991 Cairo poll showed that while 56 per cent supported Western-style democracy, 52.3 per cent also favoured implementing sharia, suggesting "deep confusion in the Arab public mind" and that the "idea of democracy is quite alien to the mindset of Islam" (Kedourie 2013: 1). The Arab Spring, once seen as a gateway to liberal reform, proved a false dawn. As Watt ([1968] 2003: 121) explains, "Islam does not normally think of the rights of man because it is more conscious of the commands of God." As a result, obedience, rather than liberal norms of dissension, disagreement, or divergence, becomes the guiding principle of this worldview (Lewis 1994: 45–46; Lewis 2011, ch. 24; Bowering 2015: 193; Pipes [1983] 2017, ch. 3).

Islamic communitarianism also impacts women's rights. One striking example is veiling, which Marnia Lazreg, in her groundbreaking work, argues is not merely attire but a symbolic "fixture of the Muslim landscape," reflecting a conservative social mood and intensifying male surveillance of women's appearance (Lazreg 2009: 2, 7). This pressure, reinforced by the "power of socialization," often leads women to *self-police*, feeling compelled to conform (Lazreg 2009: 4, 29). A tragic example is the Mecca fire, where schoolgirls were prevented from fleeing a blaze because they were improperly veiled, a fatal consequence of communitarian enforcement (Lazreg 2009: 5). While "modesty" is often invoked, in such frameworks it quickly collapses into rigid behavioural codes, making women's lifestyle experimentation subject to disciplinary control.

Historically, Islam advanced women's rights in areas like property and marital consent, though patriarchal interpretations and customary practices later undermined these gains. Margot Badran (2013: 112) admits that "patriarchal ideology has been at the center of political Islam." Many regimes in the Middle East have subordinated women's liberty. Religious texts, such as Hadiths proclaiming "a people who entrust their affairs to a woman will never know prosperity," were used to justify narrowing women's public participation (Mernissi 1991, ch. 3). Importantly, such repression is not intrinsic to Islam, as its texts can support both egalitarian and regressive interpretations (Badran 2013; Chaudhry 2015). The key issue is that in societies lacking a strong liberal tradition and valuing individualism, religious concepts can be readily weaponised by conservative elites to oppress women and minorities.

In *actual practice* therefore, Islamic societies often resist queer lifestyles and sexual permissiveness, due to widely held interpretations of religious texts and the emphasis on traditional structures. Mainstream Muslim scholars commonly portray same-sex acts as forbidden, often citing the story of *Lut* (Lot). Neo-orthodox interpretations frame homosexuality as a "perversion of the natural order" and a misuse of sexual organs, linking sexuality to heterosexual reproduction (Zollner 2010). These scholars also reject queer identity, denying innate sexual preference and portraying homosexuality as a lifestyle choice, with individuals described as "slaves to their lusts" (Zollner 2010: 200). Marriage and family, considered "half of the religion" in normative Islam, are sacralised, and non-reproductive lifestyles are resisted as threats to traditional norms (Babayan and Najmabadi 2008: 311; Beckers 2010: 62). Again, Islam does not *inherently* forbid liberal, feminist, or egalitarian practices. Yet, in political and social *reality*, Muslim-majority countries often sustain illiberal attitudes and policies towards queer communities (see Adamczyk and Pitt 2009; Wormald 2013; Jäckle and Wenzelburger 2014 for systematic cross-national analyses of social attitudes).[2]

Disapproval of queer lifestyles is also reinforced by historical, cultural, and political forces, though the actual historical record is more nuanced. While religious condemnation of homosexuality has long existed, it grew stricter over time, partly shaped by dubious hadiths and "exogenous effects of European colonialism," which introduced Western notions of homosexuality as "perversion" (Abukhalil 1997). This contributed to a "Puritanical Islam" that reinforced moral superiority in contrast to Western decadence. Despite official prohibitions, male same-sex contact historically persisted in private or semi-private contexts under a tacit "will not to know" policy, as long as it didn't endanger lineage or public morality (Murray 1997). However, the modern rise of queer visibility, emphasising exclusive gay identity, has intensified homophobic rhetoric in the Arab-Muslim mainstream. Such visibility provokes the sense of LGBT identities being a foreign threat to local norms, though sexual fluidity was always historically more common than portrayed. Political leaders in some Muslim-majority countries have naturally exploited these fears to bolster conservative religious identity, their support base, and justify harsh legal penalties against LGBT people.[3]

Indonesia

In Indonesia, there is a recurring pattern of using law to enforce morality, a trend that intensified after independence, gained momentum post-New Order in 1998, and reached new heights following the 2008 Pornography Law. Islamic values frequently serve as moral justification for policing private lives. This aligns with a communitarian tendency, where anti-gay sentiment is most effectively activated when homosexuality is framed as a threat to traditional Islamic values and family structures.

Since 2004, the MUI (Indonesian Ulema Council) has served as the government-endorsed issuer of *fatwas*, issuing legal opinions condemning secularism, liberalism, religious minorities, and the LGBT community. The government has codified some of these into regional or national law; by 2019, there were an estimated 770 local Islamic regulations based on the MUI's interpretation of sharia (Hodge 2019). Conservative Muslim readings of sacred texts often produce "intolerant, homophobic attitudes" in implementing shari'a (Polymenopoulou 2020). Scholars cite the Lot parable as a prohibition on homosexuality, and numerous hadith (of varying authenticity) reportedly depict the Prophet condemning *liwat*, or sodomy (Jahangir and Abdul-latif 2015). Other discourses frame homosexuality as a "sin" akin to adultery, or as a disease linked to social decay (Siraj 2012; Kutty 2015). Because marriage, sex, and family are deeply gendered in conservative Muslim societies, LGBT people are seen as threats on multiple fronts.

This moralising has translated into legal policing. From the early 2000s, anti-LGBT regional laws emerged, with many explicitly framing LGBT activity as immoral, sinful, adulterous, akin to prostitution, antithetical to public order and for "violating religious norms" (Katjasungkana and Wieringa 2016). The 2008 Pornography Law was a significant escalation. It includes lesbian and gay sexual activity in its definition of deviant sexual intercourse in Article 4, alongside necrophilia, bestiality, and oral or anal sex. The use of vague and sweeping language not only allows for the criminalisation of LGBT activities, which has occurred, but has encouraged society to "become voyeuristic peeping Toms monitoring cultural performance" (Bellows 2011; Renaldi 2017).

These laws operate within a conservative Islamic culture. A 2023 Pew survey found that only 4 per cent of Muslim Indonesians support gay marriage, compared to 5 per cent of the general population (Gubbala and Miner 2023; see also Equaldex 2025), the lowest among 12 Asian publics surveyed. "LGBT" entered public discourse in 2014, shortly after the MUI's "Fatwa 57" condemned homosexuality. Since 2016, LGBT rights have increasingly been framed as a national threat, with the discourse focusing on acts rather than identity, with same-sex acts portrayed as moral deviance (Kholid 2024).

After this turning point, there has been growing anti-LGBT violence involving vigilante groups, radical Islamists, and state officials, often in mutual collaboration. Political and religious elites have denounced LGBT individuals, fuelling a moral panic. In 2017 alone, over 300 arrests were recorded, the highest on record (Knight 2018). Police, often tipped off by neighbours, raided private homes and evicted occupants. Local bylaws targeted non-normative sexualities. In September 2017, in Tugu Jaya, police and community leaders forced some women from their homes after Islamic groups and clerics alleged their cohabitation was "against the teachings of Islam" (Pausacker 2020: 450). They were suspected of being lesbians based on appearance: one leader remarked, "Some have short hair, acting as the males. Some have long hair, acting as the females. It's against Islamic law. It's obscene" (Pausacker 2020: 450).

The most extreme example of this moral puritanism is Aceh, where suspected gay men have been publicly flogged under its Islamic Criminal Code (*Qanun Jinayat*). In 2017, two men caught in bed by vigilantes were sentenced to 83 cane strokes, the first such caning since the implementation of the *Qanun* began in 2015. The flogging, conducted in a public square before a jeering crowd shouting "Do it harder!," was filmed by onlookers (BBC 2017). President Joko Widodo reportedly instructed the Governor to conduct canings privately to protect foreign investment. A 2018 Governor's Regulation mandated that they occur inside prison facilities, but local officials have largely ignored this, and public canings continue (see Mann and Afrianty 2020 for an analysis of Aceh).

The *Qanun Jinayat* criminalises *liwat* (penetrative anal sex between men) and *musahaqah* (female same-sex acts involving genital rubbing), punishable by up to 100 lashes, a fine of 1,000 grams of gold, or up to 100 months in prison. This represents an attempt to override Indonesia's national Criminal Code, which only criminalises same-sex acts with minors (Butt 2020). Of the *Qanun*'s ten offences, eight regulate consensual or non-consensual sexual activity, revealing a broader "social engineering" attempt to reshape Acehnese society according to Islamic norms (Cammack 2015). Even minor infractions are targeted: in 2015, two suspected lesbians were detained for public cuddling and sent for "rehabilitation," despite the *Qanun* not yet being in effect. Many cases are handled informally by the *Wilayatul Hisbah* (Shari'a Police), who offer "moral instruction" or refer offenders to community leaders, highlighting the pervasive enforcement of Islamic morality (see Feener 2013; Yulius 2018 for similar analyses).

The latest expression of this communitarianism, often legitimised by Islamic values and upheld by religious-state elites, is the new Criminal Code passed in 2022. During its years of drafting, explicit criminalisation of homosexuality was proposed; for example, the March 2015 academic draft (*Naskah Akademik*) recommended outlawing "indecent acts with an adult of the same sex" and "sodomy" as new moral crimes (Naskah Akademik RUU KUHP 2015: 240). Although later drafts, such as July 2018, removed explicit references to same-sex relations, vague definitions of "indecent acts" as "all acts which violate moral feelings (*rasa kesusilaan*) and other despicable (*keji*) acts ... related to sexual desire (*nafsu birahi*)" leave room for discriminatory interpretation (Pausacker 2020: 433).

The final version, passed in 2022 and set to take effect in 2026, omits explicit LGBT references but continues moral policing. Its general explanation cites Pancasila's principle of "Belief in One God" as a legal foundation, reinforcing collective norms over individual rights (Ariffin et al. 2023: 609). Articles 411 and 412 outlaw adultery (sex outside marriage) and cohabitation, respectively, and enforcement depends on complaints from family members, enabling communal moral policing (Human Rights Watch 2022). Since same-sex relationships are neither recognised nor protected under law, these provisions directly endanger LGBT people. Public expressions of same-sex intimacy are also criminalised through bans on "obscene acts toward others of the same or different sex ... in public," which has been criticised for its vagueness and thus scope for arbitrary application (Butt 2023).

Most alarmingly, the Code institutionalises unwritten norms grounded in sharia, stating that crimes may be defined by "the sense of justice that lives in the community" (Law of the Republic of Indonesia 2023, Article 153). In sharia-governed provinces like Aceh, this has enabled criminalisation of *liwat*, *musahaqah*, *khalwat* (unmarried dating), and *zina* (adultery), with punishments including lashes, imprisonment, or fines (Mann and Afrianty 2020: 515–522). If legal interpretation rests on officials' moral views, personal freedoms are left with limited protection. Officials have framed the Code as aligning the justice system with "Indonesian values" (Lamb and Teresia 2022). Yet, this moralistic enforcement has ironically not prevented the legal inaction surrounding widespread sexual abuse in unregistered religious boarding schools, which are often overlooked or even protected by state authorities (Arnez and Nisa 2024).

Conclusion

Despite praiseworthy legislative wins for LGBT people in Asia, genuine progress remains limited by the persistence of political communitarianism. The concern is not with individuals choosing to live in tightly knit communities governed by shared norms. Rather, the critique is directed against *political* communitarianism, where centralised political authority becomes implicated in perfecting moral behaviour across multiple domains, typically at the level of the nation-state. The threat to individual liberty arises because it often incorporates a perfectionist component that legitimises, and in some cases even necessitates, the involvement of state elites to preserve the "social good" against undesired change. While such illiberalism can and has arisen in various cultural contexts, the problem in Asia is that it lacks a historical appreciation of individualism. In fact, in medieval Islamic societies and ancient China, their high degree of cohesion reduced the need to develop theories of liberty, diversity, and pluralism like that which grew out of social conflict in 16th–17th century Europe; since "for over a millennium, religion often played a constructive role as an agent of stability and predictability" (Crone 2005; Hashemi 2013: 81). Therefore, while there is nothing inherent in Confucianism or Islam, for instance, that *inexorably* leads to tyranny, the actual political practice and development of this region have often manifested in governance that prizes stability and cohesion, motivating the totalising use of state power to "defend" the dominant culture.

Queer dignity calls for a political philosophy that champions the revisability of norms and identities. Dignity, in this context, is not found in seeking permission or consensus in the collective democratic arena, but in the freedom of *individuals to exercise artistic license over their personhood and, in doing so, customise their own worlds*. The expectation that queer lives justify themselves through procreation, lineage, or cultural fit denies the legitimacy, validity, and joy of lives lived differently. Just as the Great Enrichment was fuelled by dignity for commercial entrepreneurship so too will queer progress require similar dignity for those who dare to engage in permissionless cultural innovation. This dynamic liberalism views social order as subject to ongoing transformation, allowing for the spontaneous exercise of individualism under a limited state that political communitarianism tends to suppress.

Acknowledgements

I wish to acknowledge that the framing of a "dynamic liberalism" is obtained from Alexander Schaefer, University of Buffalo. I also thank Thomas Jamie P-H of Bolzano, who helped me realise the high and personal stakes of queer dignity.

Notes

1 Similar dynamics may also be found in South Korea, where communitarian Confucian norms are arguably more intensive, and where LGBTQ acceptance is much lower.
2 An interesting poll also found in 2016 that over half of British Muslims think homosexuality should be illegal (Zorthian 2016).
3 See, for instance, Sharia laws against homosexuality in Malaysia (Human Rights Watch 2021). Even a forum was recently castigated as promotions of a "deviant culture" (Saieed 2025).

References

Abukhalil, As'ad. 1997. "Gender Boundaries and Sexual Categories in the Arab World." *Feminist Issues* 15 (1–2): 91–104.

Adamczyk, Amy, and Cassady Pitt. 2009. "Shaping Attitudes about Homosexuality: The Role of Religion and Cultural Context." *Social Science Research* 38 (2): 338–351.

Akyol, Mustafa. 2011. *Islam without Extremes: A Muslim Case for Liberty*. New York, NY: W. W. Norton & Company.

Akyol, Mustafa. 2021. *Reopening Muslim Minds*. New York, NY: St. Martin's Essentials.

Aligica, Paul Dragos, Ginny Seung Choi, and Virgil Henry Storr. 2021. *Culture, Sociality, and Morality: New Applications of Mainline Political Economy*. Lanham, MD: Rowman & Littlefield.

Ariffin, Ridwan, Nadiyah Meyliana Putri, Mutia Azizah Aksan, Radhitya Pratama, and Angel Maris Linda. 2023. "Pancasila Values in the New Indonesian Criminal Code: Does the Code More Humanist?" *Journal of Law and Legal Reform* 4 (4): 597–618.

Arnez, Monika, and Eva Nisa. 2024. "Advocating for Change: Cultural and Institutional Factors of Sexual Violence in Indonesia." In *Gender, Islam and Sexuality in Contemporary Indonesia*, edited by Monika Arnez and Melani Budianta, 21–44. Singapore: Springer.

Babayan, Kathryn, and Afsaneh Najmabadi. 2008. *Islamic Sexualities*. Cambridge, MA: Harvard University Press.

Badran, Margot. 2013. "Political Islam and Gender." In *Oxford Handbook of Islam and Politics*, edited by John L. Esposito and Emad El-Din Shahin, 112–128. New York, NY: Oxford University Press.

BBC. 2017. "Indonesian Men Caned for Gay Sex in Aceh." BBC, May 23. https://www.bbc.com/news/world-asia-39996224.

Beckers, Tilo. 2010. "Islam and the Acceptance of Homosexuality: The Shortage of Socio-Economic Wellbeing and Responsive Democracy." In *Islam and Homosexuality*, edited by Samar Habib, 57–98. Westport, CT: Praeger.

Bellows, Laura L. 2011. "The Aroused Public in Search of the Pornographic in Indonesia." *Ethnos* 76 (2): 209–232.

Bowering, Gerhard. 2015. *Islamic Political Thought: An Introduction*. Princeton, NJ: Princeton University Press.

Butt, Simon. 2020. "Aceh and Islamic Criminal Law in the Courts." In *Crime and Punishment in Indonesia*, edited by Tim Lindsey and Helen Pausacker, 535–558. London, UK: Routledge.

Butt, Simon. 2023. "Indonesia's New Criminal Code: Indigenising and Democratising Indonesian Criminal Law?" *Griffith Law Review* 32 (2): 190–214.

Cammack, Mark. 2015. "The Punishment of Islamic Sex Crimes in a Modern Legal System: The Islamic Qanun of Aceh, Indonesia." *Southwestern Law Review* 45: 595–630.

Chan, Joseph. 2008. "Confucian Attitudes Toward Ethical Pluralism." In *Confucian Political Ethics*, edited by Daniel Bell, 113–138. Princeton, NJ: Princeton University Press.

Chan, Sin Yee. 2016. "Would Confucianism Allow Two Men to Share a Peach? Compatibility between Ancient Confucianism and Homosexuality." In *Bloomsbury Research Handbook of Chinese Philosophy and Gender*, edited by Ann A. Pang-White, 173–202. London, UK: Bloomsbury Academic.

Chan, Sin Yee. 2023. "Confucianism and Gender." In *Oxford Handbook of Confucianism*, edited by Jennifer Oldstone-Moore, 408–422. New York, NY: Oxford University Press.

Chaudhry, Ayesha S. 2015. "Women." In *Islamic Political Thought: An Introduction*, edited by Gerhard Bowering, 263–272. Princeton, NJ: Princeton University Press.

Cheang, Bryan. 2025. "Liberal Democracy, Non-Western Governance, and the Bloomington School." In *Governing Differences: Social Diversity, Polycentric Political Economy and*

Modus Vivendi, edited by Paul Aligica and Jennifer Murtazashvili, 135–152. Cheltenham, UK: Edward Elgar.

Cheang, Bryan. 2026. *Southeast Asia's Development: Toward Liberal Individualism and Inclusive Institutions*. New York, NY: Oxford University Press.

Cheang, Bryan, and Donovan Choy. 2024. "Culture of Meritocracy, Political Hegemony, and Singapore's Development." *International Journal of Politics, Culture, and Society* 37 (2): 265–290.

Cheang, Bryan, and Daniel Ho. 2026. "Beyond Confucian Meritocracy and Democracy: The Cultural Knowledge Problem and Liberal Polycentrism in East Asia." *Review of Politics*, https://doi.org/10.1017/S0034670525100351.

Confucius. 2002. *The Analects of Confucius*. Project Gutenberg. https://www.gutenberg.org/cache/epub/3330/pg3330.txt.

Crone, Patricia. 2005. *God's Rule: Government and Islam*. New York, NY: Columbia University Press.

Dale, Sonja Pei-fen. 2020. "Same-Sex Marriage and the Question of Queerness – Institutional Performativity and Marriage in Japan." *Asian Anthropology* 19 (2): 143–159.

Equaldex. 2025. "LGBT Rights in Indonesia." March 5. https://www.equaldex.com/region/indonesia.

Feener, R. Michael. 2013. *Shari'a and Social Engineering: The Implementation of Islamic Law in Contemporary Aceh, Indonesia*. Oxford, UK: Oxford University Press.

Fraser, Nancy. 2000. "Rethinking Recognition." *New Left Review* 3 (3): 107–118.

Gallagher, Erin. 2024. "Japan's Debate over LGBTQ+ Rights: The Diet." Council on Foreign Relations. https://www.cfr.org/blog/japans-debate-over-lgbtq-rights-diet.

Gubbala, Sneha, and William Miner. 2023. "Across Asia, Views of Same-Sex Marriage Vary Widely." Pew Research Center. November 27. https://www.pewresearch.org/short-reads/2023/11/27/across-asia-views-of-same-sex-marriage-vary-widely.

Hashemi, Nader. 2013. "Islam and Democracy." In *Oxford Handbook of Islam and Politics*, edited by John L. Esposito and Emad El-Din Shahin, 68–88. New York, NY: Oxford University Press.

Hayek, F. A. 1960. *The Constitution of Liberty*. London, UK: Routledge.

Hodge, Amanda. 2019. "Sharia Spread by Stealth." Australian. October 9. https://www.theaustralian.com.au/inquirer/sharia-spread-by-stealth-across-indonesia/news-story/72d67b018ae846bbe0aaedd6b7c31499.

Human Rights Watch. 2021. "Malaysia: Government Steps up Attacks on LGBT People." Human Rights Watch. January 25. https://www.hrw.org/news/2021/01/25/malaysia-government-steps-attacks-lgbt-people.

Human Rights Watch. 2022. "Indonesia: New Criminal Code Disastrous for Rights." Human Rights Watch. December 8, 2022. https://www.hrw.org/news/2022/12/08/indonesia-new-criminal-code-disastrous-rights.

Inglehart, Ronald, and Pippa Norris. 2003. "The True Clash of Civilizations." *Foreign Policy* 135: 62–70.

Jäckle, Sebastian, and Georg Wenzelburger. 2014. "Religion, Religiosity, and the Attitudes Toward Homosexuality – A Multilevel Analysis of 79 Countries." *Journal of Homosexuality* 62 (2): 207–241.

Jahangir, Junaid B., and Hussein Abdul-latif. 2015. "Investigating the Islamic Perspective on Homosexuality." *Journal of Homosexuality* 63 (7): 925–954.

Katjasungkana, Nursyahbani, and Saskia Wieringa. 2016. "Creeping Criminalisation: Mapping of Indonesia's National Laws and Regional Regulations That Violate Human Rights of Women and LGBTIQ People." OutRight Action International. https://outrightinternational.org/sites/default/files/2022-10/CreepingCriminalisation-eng.pdf.

Kedourie, Elie. 2013. *Democracy and Arab Political Culture*. London, UK: Routledge.

Key Concepts in Chinese Thought and Culture. n.d. "Harmony Is Most Precious." https://www.chinesethought.cn/EN/shuyu_show.aspx?shuyu_id=3972.

Kholid, Anwar. 2024. "Criminalisation and Care: Indonesian Muslim Mass Organisation's Perspectives on LGBT People." In *Gender, Islam and Sexuality in Contemporary Indonesia*, edited by M. Arnez and M. Buditanta, 45–64. Springer Singapore.

Kirsch, Helen, and Christian Welzel. 2018. "Democracy Misunderstood: Authoritarian Notions of Democracy around the Globe." Social Forces 98 (1): 59–92.

Knight, Kyle. 2018. "Fresh Wave of Anti-LGBT+ Moral Panic Hits Indonesia." Human Rights Watch, November 6. https://www.hrw.org/news/2018/11/06/fresh-wave-anti-lgbt-moral-panic-hits-indonesia.

Kuniyoshi, Mika. 2024. "Ishiba Expresses Sympathy for Same-Sex Couples but No Legal Step." The Asahi Shimbun, December 17. https://www.asahi.com/ajw/articles/15553727.

Kutty, A. 2015. "How to Give up Homosexuality." Onislam. 2015. https://web.archive.org/web/20130412083804/http://www.onislam.net/english/ask-the-scholar/morals-and-manners/morals-and-values/169454.html.

Kymlicka, Will. 2001. *Contemporary Political Philosophy: An Introduction*. Second edition. New York, NY: Oxford University Press.

Lamb, Kate, and Ananda Teresia. 2022. "Explainer: Why Is Indonesia's New Criminal Code so Controversial?" Reuters, December 6. https://www.reuters.com/world/asia-pacific/why-is-indonesias-new-criminal-code-so-controversial-2022-12-06/.

Law of the Republic of Indonesia. 2023. "NUMBER 1 of 2023." https://the-world-is-watching.org/wp-content/uploads/2023/02/2023-Indonesia-Penal-Code.pdf.

Lazreg, Marnia. 2009. *Questioning the Veil: Open Letters to Muslim Women*. Princeton, NJ: Princeton University Press.

Levenson, Joseph. 1958. *Confucian China and Its Modern Fate*. Oakland, CA: University of California Press.

Lewis, Bernard. 1994. *Islam and the West*. New York, NY: Oxford University Press.

Lewis, Bernard. 2002. *What Went Wrong? The Clash between Islam and Modernity in the Middle East*. New York, NY: Harper Perennial.

Lewis, Bernard. 2003. *The Crisis of Islam*. New York, NY: Modern Library.

Lewis, Bernard. 2011. *Islam in History*. Chicago, IL: Open Court.

Mann, Tim, and Dina Afrianty. 2020. "Aceh's Islamic Criminal Code." In *Crime and Punishment in Indonesia*, edited by Tim Lindsey and Helen Pausacker, 507–534. London, UK: Routledge.

Matsui, Shigenori. 2018. "Fundamental Human Rights and 'Traditional Japanese Values': Constitutional Amendment and Vision of the Japanese Society." *Asian Journal of Comparative Law* 13 (1): 59–86.

Mernissi, Fatima. 1991. *The Veil and the Male Elite: A Feminist Interpretation of Women's Rights in Islam*. New York, NY: Basic Books.

Mill, John Stuart. [1859] 2003. *On Liberty*. Edited by David Bromwich and George Kateb. New Haven, CT: Yale University Press.

Moore, R. L. 2023. "Confucianism and the Family." In *Oxford Handbook of Confucianism*, edited by Jennifer Oldstone-Moore, 365–381. New York, NY: Oxford University Press.

Murray, Stephen O. 1997. "The Will Not to Know: Islamic Accommodations of Homosexuality." In *Islamic Homosexualities: Culture, History, and Literature*, edited by Will Roscoe and Stephen O. Murray, 14–54. New York, NY: NYU Press.

Naskah Akademik RUU KUHP. 2015. https://bphn.go.id/data/documents/naskah_akademik_tentang_kuhp_dengan_lampiran.pdf.

Nikaido, Yuki. 2025. "LDP Keeps Same-Sex Marriage Discussion on the Back-Burner." Asahi Shimbun, April 3. https://www.asahi.com/ajw/articles/15695728.

Pang-White, Ann A. 2016. *The Bloomsbury Research Handbook of Chinese Philosophy and Gender*. London, UK: Bloomsbury Academic.

Paramore, K. 2023. "Confucianism in Japan." In *Oxford Handbook of Confucianism*, edited by J. Oldstone-Moore, 270–283. New York, NY: Oxford University Press.

Pausacker, Helen. 2020. "Homosexuality and the Law in Indonesia." In *Crime and Punishment in Indonesia*, edited by Tim Lindsey and Helen Pausacker, 430–462. London, UK: Routledge.

Pennington, Mark. 2003. "Hayekian Political Economy and the Limits of Deliberative Democracy." *Political Studies* 51 (4): 722–739.

Pipes, Daniel. [1983] 2017. *In the Path of God: Islam and Political Power*. London, UK: Routledge.

Polymenopoulou, Eleni. 2020. "Same-Sex Narratives and LGBTI Activism in the Muslim World." Georgetown Journal of International Affairs, May 18. https://gjia.georgetown.edu/2020/05/18/same-sex-narratives-and-lgbti-activism-in-muslim-world/.

Rajah, Jothie. 2012. *Authoritarian Rule of Law*. New York, NY: Cambridge University Press.

Renaldi, Adi. 2017. "Queer Indonesians Are Being Arrested under a Vague Anti-Porn Law." VICE, May 31. https://www.vice.com/en/article/queer-indonesians-are-being-arrested-under-a-vague-anti-porn-law/.

Reza, Agustian. 2022. "Mahasiswa Demo Di DPR, Tolak KUHP Dan Kenang 1.000 Hari Korban Tewas #ReformasiDiKorupsi." Kompas.com., December 15. https://megapolitan.kompas.com/read/2022/12/15/16400131/mahasiswa-demo-di-dpr-tolak-kuhp-dan-kenang-1000-hari-korban-tewas?page=all.

Roberts, John. 2015. "Dissenting Opinion." *Obergefell v. Hodges*.

Saieed, Zunaira. 2025. "Gay-Themed Forum Is Canceled in Malaysia." New York Times, May 31. https://www.nytimes.com/2025/05/31/world/asia/malaysia-lgbt-forum.html.

Saunders, Dylan. 2017. "From Griswold to Obergefell: Tracing the Evolution of the Gay Marriage Discourse in the United States Supreme Court." PhD diss., Northern Arizona University.

SBS News. 2023. "Why Is Japan the Only G7 Country That Does Not Recognise Same-Sex Marriage?" SBS News, April 24. https://www.sbs.com.au/news/article/japanese-fete-lgbtq-progress-demand-marriage-rights-as-g7-summit-looms/yj8l56ktj.

Scalia, Antonin. 2015. "Dissenting Opinion." *Obergefell v. Hodges*.

Sen, Amartya. 1997. "Human Rights and Asian Values." In *Sixteenth Morgenthau Memorial Lecture on Ethics & Foreign Policy*. New York, NY: Carnegie Council on Ethics and International Affairs.

Shōtoku, Taishi. 1975. "Shōtoku Taishi Shū." In *Nihon Shisō Taikei 2*, edited by Saburō Ienaga, 12–13. Tokyo: Iwanami Shoton.

Siegle, Joseph. 2024. "Winning the Battle of Ideas: Exposing Global Authoritarian Narratives and Revitalizing Democratic Principles." National Endowment for Democracy, February 5. https://www.ned.org/wp-content/uploads/2024/02/NED_FORUM-Authoritarianism-Narratives.pdf.

Siraj, Asifa. 2012. "'I Don't Want to Taint the Name of Islam': The Influence of Religion on the Lives of Muslim Lesbians." *Journal of Lesbian Studies* 16 (4): 449–467.

Tambiah, Stanley Jeyaraja. 1992. *Buddhism Betrayed? Religion, Politics, and Violence in Sri Lanka*. Chicago, IL: University of Chicago Press.

Taylor, Charles. 1995. "The Politics of Recognition." In *Campus Wars: Multiculturalism and the Politics of Difference*, edited by John Arthur and Amy Shapiro, 25–73. London, UK: Routledge.

Tebble, Adam. 2003. "Does Inclusion Require Democracy?" *Political Studies* 51 (1): 197–214.

The Mainichi. 2024. "Japan's Ban on Recognizing Same-Sex Unions Is Unconstitutional, a Court Finds. Here's What to Know." The Mainichi, December 14. https://mainichi.jp/english/articles/20241214/p2g/00m/0na/017000c.

Voll, John. 2013. "Political Islam and the State." In *Oxford Handbook of Islam and Politics*, edited by John L. Esposito and Emad El-Din Shahin, 56–67. New York, NY: Oxford University Press.

Wang, Robin. 2012. *Yinyang: The Way of Heaven and Earth in Chinese Thought and Culture*. Cambridge, UK: Cambridge University Press.
Watt, W Montgomery. [1968] 2003. *Islamic Political Thought*. Edinburgh, UK: Edinburgh University Press.
Weber, Max. [1915] 1968. *The Religion of China: Confucianism and Taoism*. New York, NY: Free Press.
Wood, Alan T. 2023. "Confucianism and Social Structure." In *Oxford Handbook of Confucianism*, edited by Jennifer Oldstone-Moore, 382–394. New York, NY: Oxford University Press.
Wormald, Benjamin. 2013. "The World's Muslims: Religion, Politics and Society." Pew Research Center's Religion & Public Life Project. Pew Research Center, April 30. https://www.pewresearch.org/religion/2013/04/30/the-worlds-muslims-religion-politics-society-overview/.
Yamaguchi, Mari. 2022. "Japan Sole G7 Country to Ban Same-Sex Marriage." National Post. National Post,. June 21. https://nationalpost.com/news/japan-sole-g7-country-to-ban-same-sex-marriage.
Young, Iris Marion. 1990. *Justice and the Politics of Difference*. Princeton, NJ: Princeton University Press.
Yulius, Hendri. 2018. "Rethinking the Mobility (and Immobility) of Queer Rights in Southeast Asia: A Provocation." Heinrich Böll Foundation. https://th.boell.org/en/2018/12/26/rethinking-mobility-and-immobility-queer-rights-southeast-asia-provocation.
Yuniar, Resty. 2022. "Indonesia Urged to Look the Other Way as Singapore, Vietnam Ease Anti-Gay Laws." South China Morning Post, August 24. https://www.scmp.com/week-asia/people/article/3189935/muslim-scholars-urge-indonesia-look-other-way-singapore-vietnam.
Zollner, Barbara. 2010. "Mithliyyun or Lutiyyun? Neo-Orthodoxy and the Debate on the Unlawfulness of Same-Sex Relations in Islam." In *Islam and Homosexuality*, edited by Samar Habib, 193–222. Westport, CT: Praeger.
Zorthian, Julia. 2016. "Over Half of British Muslims Think Homosexuality Should Be Illegal: Poll." TIME, April 11. https://time.com/4288592/british-muslims-survey-homosexuality.

12

CONCLUSION

Nathan P. Goodman, Jordan K. Lofthouse, and Mikayla Novak

Historically, LGBTQ individuals have faced profound personal discrimination as well as exclusion from economic, political, and social life. The marginalization and oppression of the queer community has receded in a meaningful way in recent decades and across numerous countries, such that LGBTQ people have become freer, more prosperous, and better able to participate in civic life. Although difficult problems persist, there has been undeniable progress for queer people across the West and beyond. Queer emancipation has been an important feature of the modern achievement of liberalization across many domains of human affairs.

Understanding the causes and consequences of improving life circumstances of LGBTQ people, and comprehending the challenges that remain for them, is an important academic pursuit. One of the core contributions of this volume has been the appraisal of queer experience using the framework of queer classical liberalism (QCL), which integrates normative classical liberal commitments with the analytical tools of mainline political economy (MPE) as they relate to queer issues.

Classical liberalism has had a centuries-long history of examining institutions that lead to emancipation. At its core, the liberal tradition is concerned with safeguarding individual freedom, especially for people pushed to the margins by legal and policy exclusions and by cultural and social repressiveness. Although the classical liberal perspective of LGBTQ progress has been relatively scarce in scholarly literature, we consider this approach to be especially well-equipped to help examine *how* and *why* LGBTQ circumstances have improved over time.

QCL is posed as an alternative to non-liberal methodologies and perspectives that have long dominated queer scholarship. Queer theories built upon non-liberal postulates have been associated with an intellectual wariness of markets, and, to a lesser extent, are dubious of the utility of social openness and restraints upon governmental power as mechanisms to help undermine the oppression of

DOI: 10.4324/9781003615781-12

LGBTQ individuals and communities. We view QCL as an academically fruitful way to study a wide variety of LGBTQ issues. As the contributions to this volume demonstrate, governance and institutional postures – such as receptivity toward freer markets, restraining public authorities, and encouraging toleration of alternative ways of living – are seen as *facilitating, and not hindering*, queer flourishing.

The development of the QCL framework in this volume is built upon the use of MPE as the primary toolkit of social-scientific concepts and methodologies to understand social phenomena. As the contributors have shown, there are numerous aspects to MPE, but we think there are three core ideas that have proven to be useful to studying queer contributions and experiences. First, individuals are fallible but capable, meaning they navigate the world with limited benevolence and knowledge. Second, humans create both formal and informal rules to channel behavior in the face of those limits. Third, certain institutional arrangements can make broad patterns of cooperation possible without centralized control.

There are several key implications of MPE which stand out for queer scholars. There are no philosopher-kings to whom we can turn (or even necessarily trust) to dispel animosity and hate toward LGBTQ people. Instead, we must rely on the community's own ingenuity and grounded insights and perspectives to make life better and expand freedom for expressing gender identity and sexual orientation. While LGBTQ people have often been born and raised into repressive institutional structures, the reality is that individuals still have a capacity for creativity and imagination. This allows even people affected by harsh laws and social constrictions, such as queer community members, to adapt to and alter their worlds by acting entrepreneurially. Through this entrepreneurship, they forge their own future (both individually and collectively) to some degree. Institutions structure and constrain, but in an open, democratic liberal society they are not totalizing therefore giving LGBTQ people opportunities for self-expression, communal experimentalism, and opportunities necessary for self-actualization. The MPE approach shows how complex social orders can emerge and why liberal institutions can sustain peaceful, prosperous coexistence among diverse individuals, including members of queer communities.

This volume brings together contributions showing how QCL and MPE can be applied to real-world issues affecting LGBTQ individuals and the communities in which they live. Markets have both historically and in contemporary settings offered queer people vital opportunities and resources that have facilitating their flourishing. As Alexander Craig (Chapter 2) explained, the opportunities markets provide to fulfill plans, including to lead a life contrary to gender and sexuality conventions, are superior to that offered by socialist or traditional (customary) systems. Jordan Lofthouse and Zane Willard (Chapter 3) have indicated that the benefits provided by markets are supported by a combination of liberal institutions and entrepreneurial activity, propelling queer emancipation forward by expanding visibility and altering public attitudes.

Decentralized patterns of self-governance within a polycentric social order can empower LGBTQ individuals to build healthier, happier, and more connected lives. As shown in Chapters 4 (Novak) and 6 (Goodman and Lofthouse), these emergent processes of queer community building are applicable even when dominant cultural, legal, and social norms are not especially hospitable to queerness. As shown in Chapter 7 (Dalla Chiesa and Zaharieva), LGBTQ people have demonstrated remarkable ingenuity to develop online "queer commons" that mobilize and consolidate peer support and other crucial resources for resilience.

Markets and civil society can contribute to a blossoming of queer life and help LGBTQ people gain broader public acceptance. But these statements do not dismiss the realities that life continues to remain difficult for many people within queer communities, even within affluent Western countries. As Elliot Bowers and Mikayla Novak (Chapter 10) have stated, transphobia is one example of a "perverse" emergent order in which the discrimination and prejudice experienced by transgender, nonbinary, and other gender non-conforming individuals is attributed to economic, political, and socio-cultural factors that are not necessarily attributable to the transphobic actions or beliefs held by any given individual. Malia Dalesandry (Chapter 8) provides a qualitative account of the marginalized experiences of black trans sex workers in the Washington, D.C., area. In both these chapters, it is shown that in response to systemic hardships, trans and gender-nonconforming communities have developed a range of cultural, organizational, and other strategies to reduce harm and cultivate more inclusive environments.

Governments have occasionally been implicated in legal and other changes that have helped promote autonomy and freedom for queer people. But as classical liberals have long acknowledged, governments can also suffer from the paradox of power – an entity powerful enough to effectively protect life, liberty, and property is also powerful enough to become predatory. In Chapter 5, Nathan Goodman states that for much of modern history LGBTQ communities have had to defend themselves against the very law-enforcement institutions charged with their protection. Goodman shows that non-state protections are vital components in securing dignity and security for LGBTQ individuals and communities, especially when the state is unreliable.

In the modern age, governments are also presumed to be necessary to uphold public health standards, protecting people from the ravages of illness and disease. But as the HIV-AIDS crisis of the late twentieth century has attested, governments have a patchy record in ensuring the health of stigmatized communities, such as gay men. Trey Carson (Chapter 9) provides insight on the public health aspects of queer life by illustrating that economic and social liberties generally strengthen queer public health rather than weaken it. Liberty allows people to organize, exchange information, and support one another in responding to emerging health risks with community-specific solutions. Restrictive public health regimes can sometimes produce unintended harms, worsening health outcomes for queer people.

Queer liberation is not only a Western phenomenon. LGBTQ communities in non-Western countries. As Bryan Cheang (Chapter 11) has shown, in regions such as East and Southeast Asia queer people have pressed for legal recognition, built up cultural acceptance, and forged networks of solidarity. Other chapters have discussed a range of case examples beyond North America and Europe illustrating how markets, civil associations, and political engagement have contributed toward freeing up gender identity and sexual orientation.

In this volume, we wish to convey the idea that QCL conveys a hopeful orientation concerning the possibilities of queer emancipation and progress throughout the world. All human beings, irrespective of their gender identity and sexual orientation, ought to be free. Individuals have the right to self-determination – to be, act, and know; use their bodies and labor; and to identify and express themselves – without being inordinately constrained in coercive fashion by others or the state. People should enjoy civil liberties to be able to exercise their freedoms meaningfully in association with others, inclusive of the rights to expression, assembly, and privacy. Markets are conducive to material flourishing, enabling entrepreneurs to be alert to (and discover) opportunities to provide others with goods and services they desire. Finally, governments should provide essential public goods and uphold the rule of law to prevent abuse and discrimination at the hands of public authorities.

QCL is the radical aspect of classical liberal philosophy applicable to the lives and circumstances of queer people. But scholars using this approach are keenly aware that for most of human history in most places, domination and privilege have been the norm. Indeed, gender and sexuality have been used as criteria to harass and stigmatize queer people, discriminate against them, and, worse still, mete out violence against those who digress from gender and sexuality conventions. QCL is not merely capable of problematizing the illiberal, anti-queer past. We argue that QCL is necessary to address some of the more urgent challenges facing LGBTQ people throughout the world today.

Queer people have achieved some important liberatory milestones, especially over recent decades. But many of these achievements appear precarious in the face of the backsliding of liberties and rights, even in certain Western countries where queer freedoms have felt most assured of being entrenched. In the United States, transgender rights in relation to issues such as education, healthcare, legal recognition, sports participation, and bathroom access, have generated intense public controversy over recent years. A result of these discussions have been legislative initiatives, and executive actions at the federal level, aimed at restricting the capacity of transgender people to express themselves, receive healthcare, and engage in certain associational activities along various margins.[1] While much of the LGBTQ rights backsliding appears to pertain to transgender people, it is notable that opposition to queer liberties may be extending to sexual orientation. In 2025, a petition was received by the U.S. Supreme Court to overturn the *Obergefell v. Hodges* decision ratifying same-sex marriage (Marimow 2025). While the Court declined to hear the case, this example is arguably one instance of a range of mobilizations and pressure acts by anti-LGBTQ groups to reverse key advances for queer people.

Over the past decade, there have been developments around the world reversing improvements in the legal status of LGBTQ individuals. Notable examples have included the "anti-gay" laws of Russia and Uganda (Human Rights Watch 2022; Madowo and Feleke 2023), whereas international LGBTQ organizations have pointed to broader signs of backtracking in Africa, the Middle East, and East Asia (Mendos and Rohaizad 2024). Shaw (2025) has suggested that LGBTQ rights tend to correlate with democratic freedoms more generally, and that the erosion of queer freedoms has corresponded with measures that have compromised constitutional integrity, judicial independence, and the weakening of civil societal organizations.

It is in this context of threats to queer freedoms and rights that the presentation of the QCL framework in this volume is showcased with some urgency. This urgency could translate into a wave of new, and vigorous, research efforts to understand both the opportunities and challenges that queer people face in liberal (and non-liberal) societies in leading happy, connected, and prosperous lives. Central to these research efforts would be investigations explaining the extent of fragility of freedoms enjoyed by LGBTQ individuals, and what kinds of governance, institutional, policy, and other measures might be necessary to ensure resilience of freedoms that have been hard won. Despite criticisms directed toward it by non-liberal queer theorists, we suggest that in exploring these questions the QCL research agenda would fully countenance the realities of individuals being embedded in webs of emotion, judgments, cooperation, and power.

In addition to the issue of redressing backsliding proclivities, the QCL framework opens many additional potential research questions. One such area of potential research is queerness in the Global South. Most contributions in this volume draw from Western liberal democracies, but queer life in the Global South has very different institutional and cultural dimensions and contexts. A QCL lens could examine how queer communities pursue autonomy and build protective institutions in places where the rule of law is weak and market access is uneven. Comparative research efforts could show how queer people navigate life under legal and cultural repression.

This volume has focused relatively narrowly on LGBTQ people, but the spectrum of queerness is much broader. The queer spectrum includes individuals who are intersex, nonbinary, pansexual, asexual, and aromantic. Additionally, there is a wide variety of polyamorous or "kink" communities who could reasonably be considered as queer. Each of these categories of people faces unique challenges. QCL scholarship could examine such issues as how market provide tailored goods and services for these groups, or how civil society creates spaces for belonging and self-expression. Another research question surrounds issues relating to legal recognition of queerness beyond the confines of LGBTQ identities.

Future work should also grapple with tensions within liberal orders. Although markets play a beneficial social role, they also produce inequalities on some margins. Civil society can facilitate mutual aid, but it can also be exclusionary. Public power exuded by governmental authorities could be a tool of social progress, but it can also destroy queer relationships, depending upon how institutions are designed and implemented. Scholars interested in the QCL framework should not shy away from any of these tensions, using intellectual investigations to engage with non-liberal approaches such as critical theory, feminism, and (non-liberal strands of) queer theory.

Classical liberalism and MPE are not staid, overly abstract accounts of humanity divorced from the lives experiences of people interacting beyond the Ivory Towers of academia. To be free is an essence of rich, flourishing life that affords dignity, and is respectful, of the rich heterogeneity of real, flesh-and-blood human beings. These propositions are well and truly inclusive of queer people who identify with, and express, their gender identities and sexualities in diverse ways in personal and collective capacities. Therefore, we argue that it is feasible and appropriate to inject classical liberal insights into the scholarly body of queer literature. QCL offers the vehicle to study a wide variety of LGBTQ issues in fresh and captivating ways. We believe that the normative foundation of classical liberalism, and theories, methodologies, and analytical tools available under the rubric of MPE, allows us to better appreciate the diverse rainbow of queer life.

Note

1 As indicated by the "Trans Legislation Tracker" website (https://translegislation.com).

References

Human Rights Watch. 2022. "Russia: Expanded 'Gay Propaganda' Ban Progresses Toward Law." November 25. https://www.hrw.org/news/2022/11/25/russia-expanded-gay-propaganda-ban-progresses-toward-law.

Madowo, Larry, and Bethlehem Feleke. 2023. "Uganda Passed One of the World's Harshest Anti-gay Laws. LGBTQ People Describe Living There as 'Hell'." CNN, June 29. https://www.cnn.com/2023/06/29/africa/uganda-life-for-lgbt-community-intl-cmd.

Marimow, Ann E. 2025. "Supreme Court Denies Request to Revisit Same-Sex Marriage Decision." New York Times, November 10. https://www.nytimes.com/2025/11/10/us/politics/supreme-court-same-sex-marriage.html.

Mendos, Lucas Ramon, and Dhia Rezki Rohaizad. 2024. *Laws on Us: A Global Overview of Legal Progress and Backtracking on Sexual Orientation, Gender Identity, Gender Expression, and Sex Characteristics*. Geneva, Switzerland: ILGA World.

Shaw, Avi. 2025. "The Global Threat to LGBTQ Rights." UCLA Williams Institute, July. https://williamsinstitute.law.ucla.edu/publications/the-global-threat-to-lgbtq-rights.

INDEX

For Product Safety Concerns and Information please contact our EU representative GPSR@taylorandfrancis.com Taylor & Francis Verlag GmbH, Kaufingerstraße 24, 80331 München, Germany

Batch number: 10747622

Printed by Printforce, the Netherlands